Grassroots housing models in Europe

Manchester University Press

Grassroots housing models in Europe

Translocal networks, innovations, community

Edited by

Corinna Hölzl

Manchester University Press

Published by Manchester University Press
Oxford Road, Manchester, M13 9PL

www.manchesteruniversitypress.co.uk

British Library Cataloguing-in-Publication Data
A catalogue record for this book is available from the British Library

ISBN 978 1 5261 9037 6 hardback
ISBN 978 1 5261 9038 3 ebook

DOI: https://doi.org/10.7765/9781526190390

First published 2026

EU authorised representative for GPSR:
Easy Access System Europe, Mustamäe tee 50, 10621 Tallinn, Estonia
gpsr.requests@easproject.com

Typeset by Newgen Publishing UK

Acknowledgement

The publication of this work was supported by the Open Access Publication Fund of Humboldt-Universität zu Berlin.

The research was supported by the Deutsche Forschungsgemeinschaft (DFG, German Research Foundation) – [391047069].

HUMBOLDT-UNIVERSITÄT · ZU BERLIN ·

Funded by

DFG Deutsche Forschungsgemeinschaft
German Research Foundation

To Selma and Helen

Contents

Part II: Translocal networks, institutions and solidarity

Part III: Conversations with and about translocal grassroots networks

List of Figures and Tables

Figures

Tables

List of Contributors

Nele Aernouts

Nele Aernouts is Assistant Professor of Housing and Urbanism at the Cosmopolis Centre for Urban Research. Her research centres on housing initiatives and planning processes aimed at tackling housing insecurity and social-spatial exclusion. In one of her current projects, she reconceptualises the right to housing from a personal and neighbourhood perspective.

Tom Archer

Tom Archer is a Senior Research Fellow at the Centre for Regional Economic and Social Research. His research is focusing on housing affordability, supply and alternative forms of provision and management, as well as community-led housing solutions and community ownership structures.

Pierre Arnold

Pierre Arnold is a community-led housing specialist and co-founder of UrbaMonde – France. Between 2020 and 2025 he served the organisation as Project Manager in charge of partnerships including the CoHabitat network and academic partners.

Bettina Barthel

Bettina Barthel holds a PhD in economics and social sciences from the University of Kassel. She has been researching and teaching for several years on urban commons, solidarity economies, sociology of law, and collective subjectivities at the Center for Interdisciplinary Women's and Gender Studies at TU Berlin. She is an active member of the Mietshäuser Syndikat and currently works for an auditing organisation for cooperatives.

Jan Malý Blažek

Jan Malý Blažek is an economist and social geographer. He holds a PhD degree in Environmental Studies from the Department of Environmental Studies, Faculty of Social Studies, Masaryk University Brno, Czech

Republic. His doctoral thesis focused on economic aspects of European eco-communities. His professional interests include studying and 'co-producing' mobility innovation of CH in the Czech and European context and implementation of participatory processes in the governance of social and ecological transformation of human settlements.

Silvia Cafora

Silvia Cafora is a Research Fellow at the Department of Architecture and Urban Studies of the Polytechnic of Turin. She is currently researching community-led and alternative housing developments and their role in an affordable housing transition. She is also a housing policy analyst and scientific member of Legacoop Abitanti, Fondazione Gian Giacomo Feltrinelli.

Ana Džokić

Ana Džokić is an architect, co-Founder of STEALTH.unlimited, an internationally active spatial practice connecting cultural production, research and teaching on issues including housing alternatives and commons. Through her work with MOBA Housing SCE and the cooperative housing ecosystem in Belgrade, Serbia, she has spent the past 15 years advancing community-led, non-speculative housing models in Central and South Eastern Europe. Ana's dedication to sustainable and citizen-led solutions through cooperatives extends in the field of energy.

Ana Margarida Esteves

Ana Margarida Esteves is the coordinator of the Sustainable Societies Research Group of the Center for International Studies of the University Institute of Lisbon, ISCTE-IUL and Guest Assistant Professor of the Department of Political Economy of the same institution. Her research and teaching focuses on sustainability transitions and regenerative development, including issues of social justice, inclusion and democratic participation, synergies between nature, culture and technology and the role of critical pedagogy and the arts in these fields.

Rossella Ferro

Rossella Ferro is a Research Fellow at the Department of Architecture and Urban Studies. With a background of activism in social movements and housing struggles, she carries out social research and public policy design on housing and housing issues in marginal contexts.

André Girardi

André de Freitas Girardi is a Doctoral Researcher at the School of Sociology and Public Policy. His current research focuses on sustainable transitions, specifically grassroots movements efforts in (re)scaling policies and disclosing alternative pathways for development.

Anna Heilgemeir

Anna Heilgemeir is part of Coopdisco, an urban design and architecture cooperative working on non-profit, community-led projects, often in collaboration with groups organised within the Mietshäuser Syndikat. She is currently doing her PhD at the Chair of Urban Design at TU Berlin, where her research focuses on spatial commons and ownership models between public institutions and bottom-up governance. Anna has also been active in Berlin's urban policy and tenants' movement, including the initiative kommunal & selbstverwaltet Wohnen.

Gabu Heindl

Gabu Heindl is Professor for Building Economy and Project Development and Head of the ACE – Architecture Cities Economies | Department for Building Economy and Project Development at the University of Kassel. Her research is centred around affordable housing, climate action in housing and radical democratic project development. Gabu Heindl also works as an architect and urban planner in Vienna, where her office GABU Heindl Architecture is located and where she plans collaborative not-for-profit housing projects. She has published extensively – with the most recent book (with Drehli Robnik) being 'Nonsolution'.

Johanna Hoerning

Johanna Hoerning is Professor for Sociology at TU Berlin. Her core research interest is in how inequalities and social conflicts are (re)produced and mediated through spaces, looking at a range of empirical phenomena from migration and territorial conflicts to conflicts over access to land, soil and housing.

Knut Höller

Knut Höller holds a degree in economics and an MBA and has in-depth knowledge of housing policy in Germany, Eastern Europe and Central Asia. Mr Höller is also a founding member of the first European housing cooperative LiM Living in Metropolises SCE, based in Berlin, and has been a member of the LiM Executive Board since 2019.

Corinna Hölzl

Dr. Corinna Hölzl is Senior Researcher at the Department of Geography, Humboldt-Universität zu Berlin. With a background in human geography, sociology, and business studies, her core research interest lies in socio-ecological alternatives and their spatial entanglements. Within this framework, her work focuses on urban commoning – particularly community-led housing – and grassroots movements toward de-financialised spatial futures, as well as the associated political framework conditions and power relations. Over the past decade, she has studied the translocal mobilisation of housing commons and the role of grassroots housing networks in the context of global financialisation processes, ultimately leading to this edited volume.

Tomáš Hoření Samec

Tomáš Hoření Samec holds a PhD in Sociology and is an Assistant Professor at the Faculty of Architecture, Czech Technical University in Prague and a Researcher at the Institute of Sociology of the Czech Academy of Sciences and the Faculty of Architecture, Brno University of Technology. He has completed various international research visits and training such as at University of Vienna. He focuses on analysis of housing discourses and power relations in the housing context, and on exploration of opportunities and limits of introduction of participative forms of housing provision in the Czech Republic and relies on qualitative methods of data analysis. He has led a research project dealing with power hierarchies related to the experience of overindebtedness.

Sabine Horlitz

Sabine Horlitz is an architect and urban researcher with a focus on housing and non-profit ownership models. She is a co-founder of the Berlin-based Stadtbodenstiftung, the first Community Land Trust in German-speaking countries, and serves on its Executive Board. Together with Oliver Clemens, she founded the architecture practice Studio CHplus, which works exclusively for non-profit clients, tenant-led projects, and organisations dedicated to the common good.

Scott Jennings

Dr Scott Jennings is an active figure in the student cooperative sector. He set up the Nottingham Student Housing Co-op, and has been an active member supporting the cooperative to this day. He project managed the creation of Student Co-op Homes. He is a director of the Confederation of Co-operative Housing (CCH). His involvement in cooperative housing organisations, at a local level and in national federations, has taught him a range of governance skills as well as stakeholder engagement and communication strategy across a breadth of contexts.

Goran Jeras

Goran Jeras is an expert on sustainable finance, circular economy, cooperatives and development of local communities. He is currently the CEO at Echoes – a European Fairshares company behind setting up the first digital European Ethical Bank, licensed in Lithuania with the ambition to manage a 100% sustainable impact-oriented portfolio and to provide a full range of banking services to social and solidarity economy organisations across Europe. Echoes believes that a community-owned, efficient, scalable and replicable ethical bank is essential for the scale-up and development of alternative economic.

Peter Kämmerling

Since 2014, Peter Kämmerling has been an active member of the Mietshäuser Syndikat's International Working Group. In 2023, he co-founded the Commoning Spaces Network, a European network of community-led houses. He has voluntarily provided consulting services to emerging community-led housing (CLH) projects and networks across Germany and Europe. Peter advocates for community-led housing and intentional communities as a sustainable solution to the European housing crisis.

He holds degrees in computer science, economics, and business administration. He is a researcher at a German research center, and has also been an active member of the Eine Welt Forum Aachen e.V. for 30 years.

Florin Keuneke

Florin Keuneke is an Urban Geographer from Humboldt University Berlin, who was involved at TU Berlin with the Collaborative Research Center 1265 "Refiguration of Spaces" as a student assistant. In his research, he focuses on the spatialities of digital infrastructures.

Jens-Uwe Köhler

Jens-Uwe Köhler is the CFO of the Studentendorf Adleshof. There he has been part of the management team since the foundation of the cooperation in 2002 and is responsible for Finance and Operations. Prior to this Jens-Uwe Köhler was involved in the student self-administration and management of the club A 18.

Petr Kodenko Kubala

Petr Kodenko Kubala holds a PhD in sociology. He is currently working at the Department of Socio-Economics of Housing at the Czech Academy of

Sciences. His focus is on housing studies, particularly CH models and smart homes. In the past, he has also explored the housing paths of young adults, and the housing of homeless families using the Housing First approach. His research and thinking are influenced by actor-network theory, especially its application in urban studies, known as the 'urban assemblages' approach. Methodologically, he primarily leans towards qualitative methods, including interviews, focus groups, media discourse analysis and ethnography. Petr studied sociology at Masaryk University's Faculty of Social Studies in Brno and in Freiburg, Germany, and Vienna, Austria.
models.

Michael LaFond
Michael LaFond is the Founder and Director of id22: institute for creative sustainability. As a Community and Project Developer and Consultant, one focus is on international, community-oriented, self-organised, communal, sustainable forms of living. He has been personally involved with housing projects, cooperatives and building communities for decades.

Julie LaPalme
Julie LaPalme is expert in cooperative housing and former Secretary General for Cooperative Housing International – CHI, responsible for developing partnership initiatives, managing the communications programme and promoting cooperative housing globally. To further environmental sustainability in housing coops, she founded the Greener Co-op Microgrants programme which she manages for the Cooperative Housing Federation of Canada.

Verena Lenna
Verena Lenna is a transdisciplinary Postdoctoral Researcher at the Cosmopolis Centre for Urban Research. Her research generally explores the impact of rights on urban developments. She currently investigates emerging forms of welfare at the crossroads of social and ecological justice.

Iva Marčetić
Iva Marčetić is a Researcher at the ACE – Architecture Cities Economies | Department for Building Economy and Project Development at the University of Kassel. Her overall research interest is the interconnection between architecture, planning and housing policies. Concurrently, as a founding member of the European Cooperative Society MOBA, she is working on the democratisation of urban planning mechanisms and improving housing rights in Croatia and the region.

Tom Moore
Tom Moore is Senior Lecturer in the Department of Geography and Planning at the University of Liverpool. His research interests include community-led housing, affordable housing policy and citizen participation in urban and rural planning processes.

David Mullins
David Mullins is Emeritus Professor of Housing Policy at the School of Social Policy. His research focuses on housing need, regulation and governance, while promoting community-led housing solutions and reforms to private renting and social housing, most prominently in the UK.

Rolf Novy-Huy
Rolf Novy-Huy is trained as a banker and worked for the GLS-Bank for over a decade. He is a founding member and former managing director of the Foundation trias as well as a member of the board of directors of the Ko-Operativ eG NRW. His expertise lies in the financing of self-organised, communal housing projects.

Václav Orcígr
Václav Orcígr is a doctoral student of sociology at the Faculty of Social Sciences, Charles University in Prague, where he is also active as a lecturer, and he is the head of the Prague – City for Life campaign at Arnika, an ecological NGO. His professional interests include neoliberal urban development, gentrification, housing and the right to the city. During the years 2022–23 he was a Fulbright fellow at the George Mason University and took part in joint research on corporate development in Washington, DC and surrounding areas.

Léa Oswald
Léa Oswald is Project Coordinator and Administrative Manager at UrbaMonde. She is responsible for international cooperation projects in Latin America and Asia on the social production and management of participatory housing. She coordinates the CoHabitat Network and facilitates experience exchanges internationally.

Sascha Rentzsch
Sascha Rentzsch is a research associate at the Department of Regional Planning at Brandenburg University of Technology Cottbus-Senftenberg. His research focuses on the socio-spatial impacts of transformation processes,

particularly in the context of structural change in the coal-mining regions of Eastern Germany. Additionally, his work explores the evolving relationships between urban and rural areas, aiming to better understand how these dynamics influence regional development in times of socio-ecological transitions.

Guido Schwarzendahl

Guido Schwarzendahl is Vice-President of Cooperative Housing International – CHI and Managing Director of Bauverein Halle & Leuna eG. His primary interest, focus and drive has always been social housing and specifically cooperative housing.

Anke Schwittay

Anke Schwittay is Professor in Anthropology and Global Development at the School of Global Studies. Her overall research interest is in emerging actors and practices in global development and her current research focuses on the student housing cooperative movement in the UK and globally.

Preface

Julie LaPalme and Guido Schwarzendahl,
Cooperative Housing International

As housing challenges grow more acute across Europe, grassroots movements are leading the way with innovative, community-led housing solutions that challenge the traditional market-driven approach. This book delves deeply into a variety of grassroots models, from community land trusts (CLTs) and tenement syndicates to student cooperatives and self-managed projects, that have emerged as responses to skyrocketing housing costs, gentrification and the commodification of living spaces. These models offer a refreshing perspective: housing as a right and a communal resource, rather than simply a market commodity.

Through detailed case studies, the book illuminates how people across Europe are reclaiming the notion of home, prioritising affordability, sustainability and community resilience over profit. Cooperative Housing International (CHI) has long championed grassroots housing models as a vital approach to addressing housing challenges around the globe. Through its work, CHI highlights the power of collective action and community-driven solutions, showcasing how cooperative housing empowers individuals and strengthens social cohesion. This collection of essays on grassroots housing models in Europe resonates deeply with CHI's mission.

The book provides an in-depth examination of the legal frameworks, regional variations and key players involved in grassroots housing movements. It delves into the political, financial, cultural and historical contexts that shape these movements while showcasing diverse approaches to creating transformative and accessible housing solutions. By focusing on multiple dimensions – ranging from public and grassroots perspectives to small-scale best practices, large housing estates, and transnational as well as local negotiations on housing policies – it offers a comprehensive understanding of the subject.

Initiatives like Germany's Mietshäuser Syndikat, Austria's habiTAT, and the Netherlands' Vrijcoop highlight the power of community-driven models that resist market pressures through self-organisation and solidarity. These efforts are further strengthened by international collaboration, such as the European Commoning Spaces Network. Among the standout examples is the CLT movement, which aims to decommodify housing and protect communities from displacement and financial speculation. Similarly, the rise of student housing cooperatives in the UK demonstrates the growing agency of younger generations in addressing the housing crisis. By reclaiming control over governance and management, these students are creating secure, affordable housing alternatives that reflect the value of collective ownership.

The book traces traditions of housing cooperatives, which have advanced housing rights and affordability since the late nineteenth century in some European countries. After aligning more with the market in the 1980s–2000s, in Italy these cooperatives are now seeing renewed interest as public agencies and non-profits embrace their potential in an ownership-driven market. What stands out in Central and Eastern Europe, is that new cooperative housing initiatives have emerged in response to the lack of affordable rental housing and high homeownership rates. Combining historical insights, interviews and European case studies, the book highlights cooperatives' evolving role in addressing today's demand for affordable, sustainable housing.

Through transnational networks, such as MOBA and the development of a 'European Ethical Bank', these efforts are expanding cooperative housing options and creating sustainable, community-driven financing solutions across Europe. These grassroots movements innovate within local contexts and actively engage in international networks like the CoHabitat Network and the Global Ecovillage Network. Such networks underscore the significance of solidarity and shared knowledge in advancing alternative housing solutions.

In an era where housing has become increasingly financialised, the book reminds readers that these grassroots housing models are part of a broader effort to 'reclaim the commons'. Whether experimenting with novel financing or pioneering democratic decision-making, these movements exemplify a rejection of housing as merely an investment and a commitment to creating living spaces that reflect collective needs and values. By focusing on 'scaling up' and 'scaling out' alternative housing visions, this book addresses the potential and challenges of expanding these models and underlying societal perspectives while also identifying barriers such as restrictive political and financial environments.

Beyond documenting existing models, *Grassroots housing models in Europe* takes an interdisciplinary approach, drawing on contributions from both scholars and activists to advance a broader conversation about housing as a common good. The insights gathered here make a compelling case for grassroots models as viable alternatives to the conventional housing market, one that too often fails to meet the needs of residents. By blending theory and practical case studies, the book emphasises the innovative potential of these models to shape new approaches to urban living, solidarity and socio-ecological transition.

This volume is essential for anyone interested in understanding the future of housing. It offers policymakers, scholars, activists and community organisers a vision of housing rooted in values of equality, cooperation and sustainability. As the chapters explore the successes and the challenges facing these movements, they provide valuable lessons for those working to create housing that serves the common good rather than private interests. By bridging local initiatives with transnational networks, *Grassroots housing models in Europe* demonstrates the capacity of these models to inspire and influence housing policy across Europe and beyond.

As we witness the rise of these community-led movements, we are reminded of the transformative potential of solidarity, collective ownership and sustainable living in addressing housing needs. The book invites readers to imagine a future where housing is not simply a commodity but a resource shaped by collaboration, innovation and shared responsibility. Through its rich exploration of grassroots housing models, this work offers critical reflections on current challenges and a hopeful vision for a housing future grounded in social justice and community resilience.

Grassroots housing models in Europe – debates and the potential of translocal networks. An introduction

Corinna Hölzl

In the face of various social transformations, a multitude of new grassroots housing initiatives have emerged throughout Europe over the past two decades. First and foremost, these transformations include the increasing shortage of housing, rising housing costs and the need to reconceptualise housing in an ecologically sustainable way. They equally contain demographic changes, health factors, changing working conditions, etc., as well as the associated new housing needs. Grassroots housing initiatives develop long-term affordable, participatory, ecologically sustainable and/or communal housing alternatives with different focuses. In doing so, they use new operator models in terms of housing and land ownership and financing formats. They experiment with sustainable housing use and grassroots democratic decision-making formats while entering into partnerships with municipal actors. Among the latter, housing cooperatives in various legal forms – such as limited or zero-equity, tenant or right-to-use cooperatives, community land trusts (CLTs), tenement syndicates, and other local types of community-led housing such as self-help housing – are particularly noteworthy (Huron, 2015; Engelsman, Rowe and Southern, 2016; Hölzl, 2022; Ferreri and Vidal, 2022). Thus, an innovative housing policy player has emerged in many European countries, attempting to assert itself alongside traditional non-profit housing enterprises.

In the English-speaking world, these models are usually subsumed under the terms community-led housing or collaborative housing. Collaborative housing, introduced by Czischke, Carriou and Lang (2020) and meanwhile most commonly used in Continental Europe, emphasises the meaning of resident control over production, conception and management of housing and of collaborative network relations among housing stakeholders. Moreover, it emphasises the role of architecture and design for sharing facilities. In turn, community-led housing pronounces the key principles of community orientation, long-term affordability and self-governance (Heywood, 2016). It has its roots in UK housing research and appears to be most frequently used among the many international grassroots housing initiatives and

NGOs (to whom we basically owe the essays in this book). The understandings largely overlap and deviations might also relate to different disciplinary interests.

The growing number of grassroots housing models has led to a rise of many more terms that address a variation of models on the one hand, and national differences in terminology and academic debates on the other. Most of the terms bring specific aspects to the centre. While cohousing, for instance, emphasises aspects of communal living such as sharing space and time and barely engages with tenure (Jarvis, 2015), literature that relates to housing commons argues for shifting the attention to the 'thorny issue of permanent decommodification' (Ferreri and Vidal, 2022: 149). The latter focuses on specific institutionalised forms of collective appropriation such as non-speculative and self-managed cooperatives instead of all-embracing umbrella terms. Correspondingly, housing commons comprise long-term affordable, participatory and collective housing located on/in decommodified land and real estate, that is created, used, organised and reproduced in solidarity by (ideally) heterogeneous communities. In addition to housing, social, cultural and small business uses are often part of housing commons. The practices of commoning, which are particularly emphasised in the commons literature, include institutional aspects, such as specific rights of use and property rights, decision-making structures and policies (Stavrides, 2015; Arbell, 2023). Another body of recent housing literature on grassroots housing models has aimed to bring order to this fuzzy terminological field with partly overlapping definitions and allocations of legal forms on the basis of typologies and glossaries (e.g., Crabtree-Hayes, 2023; Guisan, Liu and Gerber, 2025). Griffith, Jepma and Savini (2022), for instance, allow for new insights into collaborative housing by differentiating key features along three dimensions: architecture of the estate, institutional set-up of property rights and underlying values of collective living and management. And Bossuyt (2022) unpacks the broad variety of tenure structures within collaborative housing, which is a crucial category for assessing and evaluating collaborative housing forms along the commons-oriented debate. All debates in the field point out the risks related to collaborative or community-led housing, particularly insularity and nepotism (Tummers, 2015; Ferreri and Vidal, 2022).

Since this book pronounces the role that communities fill, community-led housing, ideally *non-speculative* community-led housing, is the favoured umbrella term for the conceptual and empirical analyses in this anthology. Communities are, as our empirical analyses show, repeatedly the protagonists who moderate, summarise and express common objectives, who start organising, who insist, who implement, who coordinate and who convince other social groups and policymakers through their outputs. This is the starting point for actual, continuous and specific forms of collaboration with other local stakeholder groups. The term 'grassroots housing models' in the book title indicates the meaning of local communities and places, of self-governance and participation and bottom-up innovations, and wishes to provide an umbrella for both contributors who identify with collaborative or community-led housing as well as to link to an audience beyond housing studies, to those generally interested in transnational and translocal networks of grassroots movements and to activist readers who are not familiar with established academic terms.

A broader academic debate has now developed around the topic of grassroots housing. After a series of initial studies were devoted to the characteristics and challenges associated with individual case studies, several centres of focus have recently emerged that are addressed in this volume: the implementation, design and challenges of grassroots housing models with a view to internal governance arrangements, often in the context of the debate on housing commons and commoning (Huron, 2018; Durose et al., 2021; Hölzl, Hölzl, and Amacher, 2021; Leyva del Río, 2022; Arbell, 2023); and the discussion of community-led housing models as a possible response to current social challenges and transformative conflicts of objectives. In particular, these include: a) health, ageing and general well-being, empowerment, changes in work, ecologically and socially sustainable renewal and the development of urban districts (with simultaneous scarcity and housing financialisation) (Hudson et al., 2021; McClatchey et al., 2023; van den Berg et al., 2023; Czischke, Peute, and Brysch, 2023); b) the conditions for implementing the models, particularly with regard to (housing) policies and other actions to support this form of housing provision and increase its acceptance (Aernouts and Ryckewaert, 2018; Bunce et al., 2020; Lang, Chatterton and Mullins, 2020; Hölzl and Hölzl, 2022; Ferreri and Vidal, 2022); and c) scaling up and wider transformative impact of grassroots housing models, for example in the context of debates on degrowth and at the interface with other materialisations of community innovations, such as in the areas of food, energy and mobility (Chatterton, 2016; Köhler et al., 2019).

Grassroots housing models are by now seen to expand dynamically and internationally and to show mutual connections (Moore and McKee, 2012; Moore and Mullins, 2013). As already indicated, this trend strongly interrelates with political framework conditions and organising capacities of housing initiatives, so that currently emerging, new community-led housing in Europe varies immensely between and within countries. While housing initiatives in Central and Eastern Europe are confronted with the strongest challenges (Vilenica et al., 2021), new community-led housing is constantly growing in other parts of Europe; for instance, in German-speaking countries, Belgium, the Netherlands – countries that in part already cherish a long tradition of non-profit and participatory housing schemes – or Catalonia and parts of England and Wales where, due to the recent housing crisis, new funding programmes have been developed. In fact, the quantitatively respectable stocks of some housing cooperatives in German-speaking countries can be attributed to a history of different forms of public support in the sense of a 'public-cooperative nexus' (Ferreri and Vidal 2022).

Tenant, right-to-use and limited-equity housing cooperatives, as the prevailing forms of housing cooperatives that are currently (newly) discovered, are primarily based on shared ownership and limited equity, and are funded by membership fees, rents and one-time refundable deposits (Balmer and Gerber, 2018; Leyva del Río, 2022). Contrary to tenant cooperatives, members of ownership cooperatives have the right to sell their flats under certain conditions (Sørvoll and Bengtsson, 2018). While some tenant cooperatives with large housing stocks of several thousand units partly date back to the end of the nineteenth century, workers' movements or post-World War II foundations (Barenstein et al., 2021), a young cooperative scene has been established since the 1980s and more recently the 2010s after the global financial crisis. The cooperative sector in Europe thus often resembles a clash of large, sluggish but experienced mature formations and innovative (but solitary) new experiments that often stand out, for example, in terms of diversity, participation and mutual aid (Hölzl et al., 2023).

Within the growing field of non-speculative community-led housing, CLTs appear to be amongst the internationally most visible types of housing lately (Davis, Algoed and Hernández-Torrales, 2020). On the basis of a shared ownership structure between land and property, CLTs largely elude the market-oriented exploitation logic and provide democratically organised affordable housing. Moreover, community organising and capacity building play an important role. Nonetheless, the specific design of individual CLT projects varies greatly (Baldwin, 2016). In some cases, CLTs cover large areas in rural regions or are concentrated in individual districts, and the trust is sometimes in municipal or private ownership and co-determination rights, the organisation of housing (rental, cooperative, ownership) and financing instruments vary. Most CLTs are located in the US (almost 300 CLTs and 15,000 apartments) and in England and Wales there are a total of 350 active CLTs with 1,700 apartments (5,400 apartments planned) (2025). Presently, however, there are also examples in Australia, Puerto Rico, Brazil and Kenya. And as the first CLT on the European mainland, CLT Brussels meanwhile completed five projects with 100 housing units (four more projects are in construction). Ghent, Leuven and other cities that are largely located in Western Europe have started following the example.

The tenement syndicates form another prominent grassroots housing model, which is largely comparable to tenant cooperatives. However, the legal form differs and it strongly pronounces self-organisation, decommodification, and solidarity as key principles, while relying heavily on the use of private microcredits to enhance housing affordability. The Mietshäuser Syndikat in Germany consists of almost 200 housing projects with approximately 5,000 residents. In Austria, around ten projects and several other initiatives, in addition to farm collectives (rural housing and agricultural projects) are part of the habiTAT umbrella organisation founded in 2016. The Vrijcoop ('buy free' association) was founded in the Netherlands in 2018, which currently includes five housing projects and other initiatives. Le Clip, the French umbrella organisation, currently manages six projects. Three projects form part of Sdílené domy (shared houses), the Czech sister umbrella. Furthermore, there are close contacts with young, independent coalitions and related housing projects, for example, in Spain, Portugal, France or Central and (South-)East Europe. These and more European initiatives recently formalised their exchange network and founded the European Commoning Spaces Network.

The key theme and unique contribution of the book to the literature are the translocal networks and interlinkages of grassroots housing models (rather than their more frequently discussed institutional and policy contexts). Network strategies are an important, broadly discussed social-movement repertoire and key to maintain urban commoning (Andretta et al., 2006; Helfrich and Bollier, 2019). Drawing on the understanding that space is socially produced (Harvey 2006), we view networks as a collection of meeting places, where open interaction processes between actors, events and actions generate new relationships, spatial identities, and effects at different scales (Massey 1991). Networks are never single closed entities. Instead, human geographers like Cumbers, Routledge and Nativel (2008) propose to consider a network as a federation of cells which are (re-)produced through interactions between actors, events and materialities. Following global activism scholars, speaking of translocal (instead of transnational) networks, we refer to the nuanced interplay of interconnections at multiple scales, as well as the significance of interrelated spatialities such as places and networks (Escobar, 2008; McFarlane, 2011).

Isolated studies from various disciplines have taken up the international spatial mobilisation, networking and innovative appeal of grassroots housing models. For example, more than a decade ago, Mayer (2013) noted that the political practices of place-based social movements are becoming increasingly multiscalar. This can also be observed for different forms of community-led housing, where specific but increasingly multiscalar mobilisation strategies are used. And Moore and Mullins (2013) investigated applied forms of support to facilitate the diffusion of CLTs and self-help housing in the UK, while Moore and McKee (2012) compared variants of the CLT model in various countries. Thompson (2018) explored the historical development of CLTs in Liverpool through mobile urbanism, amongst others. Raynor (2018) investigated the process of assembling an innovative social housing project, and how such innovations may be scaled up or scaled out. Herrle et al. (2015) addressed the role and complex global networks of community-based organisations in processes of housing for the urban poor. And McFarlane (2011) analysed the translocal assemblages of housing movements. Finally, Hölzl (2022) studied how grassroots housing movements circulate translocally and what role spatial learning processes and network dynamics play in that regard.

So far, however, the discussion about translocal mobilisation, scaling possibilities and the transformative impact of grassroots housing innovations appears to be a diffuse and incomplete field (Lang et al., 2018: 20; Thompson, 2018: 85), which also often remains anchored in different disciplines. One of the main aims of this book is to bring together the different approaches and their specific findings in an edited collection. The volume considers the mobilisation of innovative community-led housing – in terms of housing production and even more as a voice to stimulate and support the fight for alternative visions of owning and organising housing – as a potential transformation pathway to sustainable housing provision and thus follows a twofold purpose. First, it aims to contribute to the research on the scope of grassroots housing production and to demonstrate under which circumstances translocal grassroots housing networks are able to create genuine alternative models against predominantly commodified housing markets. Second, the book aims to contribute to European solidarity in terms of community-led housing provision and to actively support transition processes by presenting innovative practices and by including the voices of committed protagonists. The corresponding key intervention of this book in the field is to identify translocal innovative approaches to often shared bottlenecks across countries that question existing housing systems from inside and outside to bring forward new logics of housing production and organisation, and to scale up and scale out forms and framings of decapitalised and collectively owned community-driven housing, as frequently claimed in the debate on urban commons and transition studies (Harvey, 2012; Chatterton, 2016). This way the book tries to answer to an urgent political necessity. Ultimately, this is about creating alliances among diverse forms of community-led housing and across varying social and spatial characteristics to renew the logics of organising and producing housing according to the necessities of a just socio-ecological transformation.

To this end, scholars from the fields of human geography, housing studies, urban studies, sociology, economics, political science, architecture and anthropology, practitioners from the NGO sector and charities, and grassroots activists were invited to contribute to this collection and will centre around this matter. Their work is based on various concepts and methodological approaches or specific objectives and principles. What they all have in common is a translocal comparative and unifying perspective on the phenomenon of grassroots housing production and thus the quest to explore the following questions. Which translocal learning and networking processes can be identified between organisations, and why? How are these spatial networks organised and what opportunities do they offer? What characterises the innovators and what potential do the developed forms of housing hold? How do they reply to challenging regulatory frameworks and other bottlenecks at legal, financial and public level? What differences and similarities can be identified on the national and international levels?

Such a collaborative approach for an edited volume might sound easier in theory than it actually is in practice. What articles are actually of interest for academics, practitioners, and the many positions in between? How to implement smooth academic-civic knowledge and text production without overstraining time capacities? How to tackle power imbalances between the groups? We have taken these and other challenges seriously and are sure that the contributions close different knowledge gaps around community-led housing.

Structure of the book

The book is organised around two thematic sections and a conversations section reflecting important facets of community-led housing: 1) national and local similarities and differences of grassroots housing production in Europe, 2) the role of translocal (solidarity) networks and institutions, and 3) conversations with and about translocal grassroots networks. The analyses in sections 1 and 2 are predominantly based on qualitative methods. They build on interviews, action research and evaluations (e.g., of local housing programmes), and include direct insights of activists, engaged entrepreneurs and NGO representatives, among others.

The chapters give insights into different legal housing models, target groups, geographical spreading, networks, and actor constellations. They examine varying spatial contexts shaped by political, financial, cultural and historical conditions, as well as strategies and opportunities in terms of long-term affordability, sustainability, empowerment, and innovation etc. Furthermore, they address challenges related to finance, conflicts, time pressure, resources, technical and legal expertise, and finally, discuss influences (e.g., of philanthropic institutions etc.) and controversies (e.g., the dilemma between activism and professionalisation). They consider different conceptual approaches, such as housing commons, policy mobility, social movement studies, production of space, property rights and centre-periphery. They put the focus on bridging differences: between initiatives in central and peripheral European regions, between emerging and established housing cooperatives, and between community-led housing and traditional social housing providers. And they build on knowledge from different stakeholder groups across Europe to strengthen the European movement of community-led housing.

The book's first section – 'Grassroots housing production in Europe: National and local similarities and differences' – starts with the contribution 'Zagreb and Vienna: 7,681 affordable housing units', in which Iva Marčetić and Gabu Heindl explore the concept of 'community-led housing' beyond a small-scale perspective, delving into a comparative analysis of Vienna and Zagreb's housing systems during a period when both cities aimed to address housing issues as a part of broader societal transformations. Focusing on the Alt Erlaa estate in Vienna and the Dugave estate in Zagreb, the analysis considers similarities and differences in housing architecture, standards and urban planning, challenging the simplistic East v. West housing production narrative of the twentieth century. The chapter investigates the communal aspects of housing development, emphasising that, despite ideological differences, European states during the examined period shared a commitment to providing affordable and healthy housing. Ultimately, the authors suggest that historical lessons can be drawn from these communal, large-scale housing experiments with respect to contemporary challenges in terms of going beyond small-scale housing provision.

In Chapter 2, 'Community-led housing in England: Emergence, growth and prospects', David Mullins, Tom Archer and Tom Moore discuss the possibility of developing a more substantial community-led sector within the English housing system. They particularly draw on a three-year evaluation of a funding programme, Homes in Community Hands (HCH), which, alongside a larger state programme (the Community Housing Fund), has supported community-led housing in five urban areas. The evidence from the HCH programme, including qualitative interviews, case studies, surveys and monitoring data, highlights key success conditions for community-led housing as a space for alternative solutions to housing challenges: the alignment between policy, investment, infrastructure and technical support, self-organisation and values-based collaboration; factors that are similarly emphasised by other contributors to this volume.

Correspondingly, in Chapter 3 – 'The transformative role of institutional capabilities: The diffusion of the community land trust model in Belgium between community agency and political will' – Verena Lenna and Nele Aernouts identify institutional support, strategic advocacy, partnerships, trust-building and aligning interests with social organisations as key factors that influence CLT development in Belgium. In response to the housing crisis, some European cities, with Brussels, Ghent and Leuven leading the way, are increasingly attempting to implement CLTs. While the present literature focuses on the positive aspects of CLTs, this contribution examines the obstacles encountered during their formation. The study explores the interplay between public institutions, civil society organisations and the structure of Belgian CLTs through a combination of literature review and interviews with key stakeholders.

In Chapter 4 – 'Between provision and self-determination: New forms of self-governance in public and collectively owned housing in Germany' – Bettina Barthel and Anna Heilgemeir discuss the forms and ambivalences of self-governance as necessary but also excluding precondition of community-led housing on the basis of two examples: the Mietshäuser Syndikat, a nationwide association of collective and decommodified housing projects developed in the 1990s, and an initiative claiming self-governance in municipal housing in Berlin called kusWo (*Kommunal & Selbstverwaltet Wohnen*).

In Chapter 5 – 'Housing cooperatives in Italy: A discontinuous tradition amid crisis and re-emerging public-cooperative synergies' – Silvia Cafora and Rossella Ferro explore Italy's extensive history of housing cooperatives, which is rooted in traditions of mutual aid traditions going back to the late nineteenth century. These played a key role in increasing housing rights and affordability, introducing innovative economic models such as undivided co-ownership housing cooperatives. After a phase of institutionalisation and convergence with the private market in the 1980s–2000s, renewed interest has evolved in housing cooperatives today. Public housing agencies view their heritage as a model for large public housing districts, while the non-profit sector sees their traditional tenure forms as a means to create affordability in a predominantly homeownership-oriented market. The chapter focuses on Milan, describing the history of housing cooperatives and examining their response to the growing demand for affordable, liveable and sustainable housing alternatives. Qualitative interviews with housing cooperatives and leagues inform the research, addressing issues related to innovation in mutualistic culture and the cooperative housing model. The study draws insights from European case studies, policies and the legacy of 140 years of history. Unlike other European countries, a detailed historical reconstruction of cooperative housing in Italy has so far been missing in international research.

In Chapter 6 – 'Collaborative housing in the Czech Republic: Focusing on the layers of obduracy' – Tomáš Hoření Samec, Petr Kodenko Kubala, Václav Orcígr and Jan Malý Blažek present their findings from recent empirical research in collaboration with six municipalities that aimed to uncover whether and in what form an innovative wave of novel collaborative housing could be expected in the Czech Republic, similar to various Western European countries, in response to the housing crisis. In that country, cooperative housing has a long tradition dating back to the nineteenth century. Nevertheless, the authors reveal that the recent wave of collaborative housing innovation has bypassed the Czech Republic due to severe societal obstacles, such as profound distrust and social inertia, which appear to be closely related to the overall super-homeownership arrangement of the housing sector in Central and Eastern Europe.

While housing is a local practice, which is deeply connected to national legal frameworks, translocal and transnational links and solidarity networks have become apparent, particularly in research on housing financialisation, housing systems and social movements. The first chapter of the book's second section, 'Advocating housing politics transnationally and translocally' by Johanna Hoerning and Florin Keuneke (Chapter 7), deals with the production and strategic use of scalar references in housing politics. Both the local and the national account for a multitude of different sets of meaning that are taken up by state, non-state, economic and political actors alike when negotiating housing politics. The study explores how both local and national dimensions contribute to the complex meanings negotiated by state, non-state, economic and political actors in housing politics. Based on the analysis of non-governmental organisations, the research compares multiple scales ranging from Berlin and Germany to the EU and global organisations. It aims to uncover how these actors shape and define the boundaries of local and national aspects in housing politics, illustrating how scalar references are framed, contested, valued, capitalised, politicised and transcended in the realm of housing policy.

In Chapter 8 – 'The emergence of student housing cooperatives in the UK: Grassroots activism, translocal networks and situational challenges' – Anke Schwittay discusses the financialisation of student housing in various countries, leading to unaffordability and inadequate living conditions for students. The chapter focuses on the rise of student housing cooperatives in the UK as a form of student activism, where students establish housing alternatives to take control of governance and management, aiming to create affordable, decent and secure housing. Drawing on interviews with key participants involved in setting up cooperatives in Edinburgh, Birmingham, Sheffield and Brighton, the analysis explores how students navigate challenges related to their youth and transience by forming alliances with secondary organisations. The chapter highlights students' agency, networking skills, and political awareness. It also addresses the challenges of scaling student housing cooperatives, raising questions about cooperative labour, beneficiaries and community relations. The research situates student housing cooperatives within a broader historical and institutional context, utilising literature on urban commoning and alliance building to map this emerging movement.

In Chapter 9 – 'The NETCO Collaborative Housing Network – European Cities: Practising, cooperating and recommending' – Michael LaFond delivers practical insight into a transnational city network of fifteen European cities that aims to promote different forms of collaborative housing. The author summarises recommendations resulting from conferences held in Bologna, Barcelona, Berlin and Brussels (2022–23), made with respect to housing and urban development policy and programmes at the local level. Finally, based on (critical) reflections of the network establishment process by the municipal NETCO members, proposals are outlined regarding the further development of this European network.

In Chapter 10 – 'Community-led housing as an opportunity for development and growing together in Europe. A call for civil society financing instruments and more public support' – Rolf Novy Huy emphasises that public support structures reaching from subsidies to special banks could help to overcome the obstacles for the many promising, emerging community-led housing initiatives in Europe. Drawing from his professional experience in the community-led housing sector, he reveals that in spite of enormous economic differences between Eastern and Western Europe, the initiatives share many needs in terms of political contacts, finding the suitable legal form, sufficient equity and financing of community-led housing forms. He observes critically that politicians tend to consider civil society to be irritating if not hostile, instead of seeing the chances for social innovations and the willingness to invest personal resources in the future of cities.

The Global Ecovillage Network Europe (GEN Europe) is an international housing organisation that promotes a multi-dimensional regenerative future in accordance with the UN Sustainable Development Goals (SDGs), which results in consistent EU funding for educational projects disseminating ecovillage innovations. In Chapter 11 – 'Engaging with EU funding: How the Global Ecovillage Network leverages projects in Europe' – André de Freitas Girardi and Ana Margarida Esteves critically examine the tension between participating in EU-funded projects and the overarching goal of generating systemic societal change. Using grassroots innovation movements as a framework, the chapter analyses various dimensions, including context, spaces, strategies and pathways. The projectification of GEN Europe is scrutinised, considering the impact of aligning with mainstream incentives on internal structures and goals. Employing a mixed-method approach, including participatory action, participant observation, in-depth interviews and document analysis, the findings emphasise the importance of knowledge dissemination through EU-funded projects. The paper critically evaluates the implications of a workforce primarily driven by short-term grants, highlighting potential misalignments in the core goals of non-profit organisations and emphasising the need for strategic coherence in pursuing alternative and regenerative futures.

In Chapter 12 – 'Transnational pathways: Taking the CLT framework from place to place to transform structures and debates on land ownership' – Sabine Horlitz and Corinna Hölzl discuss the different ways of transferring the CLT model from place to place. In this context they reflect on the so-called European CLT Network, which was launched in 2023, and discuss the importance of spatial networks for CLT pioneers (especially in Europe). The article is based on Sabine's personal experiences as co-founder of Berlin's Stadtbodenstiftung, which is one of the founding members of ECLTN, and a series of qualitative interviews with most of the members of the European CLT Network Corinna conducted from 2022 to 2023.

The third section of the book contains three conversations with grassroots initiatives from all over Europe. It starts with Chapter 13, titled 'The CoHabitat Network: Connecting civil society around community-led housing across the globe – in conversation with UrbaMonde'. Founded in 2014, the CoHabitat Network is a joint initiative that includes international grassroots federations from all over the world, as well as non-profit organisations and academic institutions working in the field of community-led housing. The chapter is based on a conversation between Corinna Hölzl and Sascha Rentzsch with Pierre Arnold (project manager at UrbaMonde-France). The interview partner discussed the need for data production and practice systematisation with regard to community-led housing and how an international network platform is able to serve the interests of housing federations that are embedded into highly varying national and local contexts.

In response to the shortage of affordable rental housing and extent of super-homeownership in Central and Eastern Europe, new cooperative housing initiatives that have been emerging over the past decade soon started to join forces translocally to implement new housing cooperatives with increased agency. They have been founding European Cooperatives (Societas Cooperativa Europaea – SCE), are developing transnational financing instruments and creating new banks. Examples include a) MOBA, so far active in Central and South-Eastern Europe, b) LiM Living in Metropolises that, among others, engages in the Baltic countries, c) the European-wide Commoning Spaces Network, and d) the 'European Ethical Bank', which is under development. In Chapter 14 – '"We need to mainstream the alternatives": In conversation about transnational financial instruments and legal forms to allow for new housing cooperatives in Europe' – Corinna Hölzl and Sascha Rentzsch talk with Ana Džokić, Peter Kämmerling, Goran Jeras and Knut Höller, representatives of the four organisations, about financial social innovations and the ways in which existing bottlenecks could be tackled.

In a final interview, Anke Schwittay addresses 'The European Student Cooperative Housing Alliance: A conversation about growing student housing cooperatives' (Chapter 15). The model of student housing coops has enabled student coop organisations to acquire more properties and to maintain housing affordability for generations to come. In this conversation, initiators and experienced leaders from Switzerland, Germany and England – Léa Oswald, coordinator at La Ciguë, Geneva, Jens-Uwe Köhler, CFO at Studentendorf Schlachtensee, Berlin, and Scott Jennings, Director of Student Co-op Homes, UK – share their experiences with respect to creating new housing solutions and community environments while elaborating on the activities, objectives and limits of creating a European student cooperative housing network.

In 'Conclusion: Contemporary character of community-led housing and the capacities of translocal networks', the editor of the book takes up the key intention of the book, that is, contributing answers to the global housing crisis, and summarises the key findings of the chapters in this edited collection along two dimensions: the transformative potentials and contradictions of community-led housing and the role translocal networks play in that context. In this vein, the chapter illustrates the harmonious research perspective on community-led housing that prevails today and reveals how far translocal networks are able to support alternative non-speculative imaginaries of housing and more generally public wealth, thus providing the grounds for extensively establishing non-profit- and community-oriented forms of housing.

References

Aernouts, N., and M. Ryckewaert (2018), 'Reproducing housing commons. Government involvement and differential commoning in a housing cooperative', *Housing Studies*, 34:1, 1–19, https://doi.org/10.1080/02673037.2018.1432756

Andretta, M., D. Della Porta, L. Mosca, and H. Reiter (2006), 'Globalization from below: Transnational activists and protest networks', Minneapolis, MN.

Arbell, Y. (2023), 'The Circle of Commoning: Conceptualising Commoning through the Case of Community-Led Housing', *International Journal of the Commons*, 17:1, 228–42, https://doi.org/10.5334/ijc.1210

Baldwin, B. (2016), 'Networked Community Land Trusts: An Analysis of Existing Models and Needs Assessment for the Greater Boston Community Land Trust Network'.

Balmer, I., and J.-D. Gerber (2018), 'Why are housing cooperatives successful? Insights from Swiss affordable housing policy', *Housing Studies*, 33:3, 361–85, https://doi.org/10.1080/02673037.2017.1344958

Barenstein, J. D., P. Koch, D. Sanjines, C. Assandri, C. Matonte, D. Osorio, et al. (2021), 'Struggles for the decommodification of housing: the politics of housing cooperatives in Uruguay and Switzerland', *Housing Studies*, 37:6, 955–74, https://doi.org/10.1080/02673037.2021.1966392

van den Berg, P., J. Sanders, S. Maussen, and A. Kemperman (2023), 'Collective self-build for senior friendly communities. Studying the effects on social cohesion, social satisfaction and loneliness', *Housing Studies*, 38:7, 1323–41, https://doi.org/10.1080/02673037.2021.1941793

Bossuyt, D. (2022), 'Who Owns Collaborative Housing? A Conceptual Typology of Property Regimes', *Housing, Theory and Society*, 39:2, 200–16, https://doi.org/10.1080/14036096.2021.1888788

Bunce, S., N. Livingstone, L. March, S. Moore, and A. Walks (2020), *Critical Dialogues of Urban Governance, Development and Activism London* (London: UCL Press), https://doi.org/10.14324/111.9781787356795(accessed 8 April 2026).

Chatterton, P. (2016), 'Building transitions to post-capitalist urban commons', *Transactions of the Institute of British Geographers*, 41:4, 403–15, https://doi.org/10.1111/tran.12139

Crabtree-Hayes, L. (2023), 'Establishing a glossary of community-led housing', *International Journal of Housing Policy*, 24:1, 1–28, https://doi.org/10.1080/19491247.2022.2155339

Cumbers, A., P. Routledge, and C. Nativel (2008), 'The entangled geographies of global justice networks', *Progress in Human Geography*, 32:2, 183–201, https://doi.org/10.1177/0309132507084818

Czischke, D., C. Carriou, and R. Lang (2020), 'Collaborative Housing in Europe: Conceptualizing the Field', *Housing, Theory and Society*, 37:1, 1–9, https://doi.org/10.1080/14036096.2020.1703611

Czischke, D., M. Peute, and S. Brysch (eds) (2023), *Together: Towards Collaborative Living* (TU Delft OPEN Publishing), https://doi.org/10.59490/mg.80

Davis, J. E., L. Algoed, and M. E. Hernández-Torrales (eds) (2020), *On Common Ground* (Madison, Wisconsin: Terra Nostra Press).

Durose, C., L. Richardson, M. Rozenburg, M. Ryan, and O. Escobar (2021), 'Community Control in the Housing Commons: A Conceptual Typology', *International Journal of the Commons*, 15:1, 291–304, https://doi.org/10.5334/ijc.1093

Engelsman, U., M. Rowe, and A. Southern (2016), 'Community Land Trusts, affordable housing and community organising in low-income neighbourhoods', *International Journal of Housing Policy*, 18:1, 1–21, https://doi.org/10.1080/14616718.2016.1198082

Escobar, A. (2008), *Territories of Difference: Place, Movements, Life, Redes* (Durham, NC: Duke University Press), https://doi.org/10.2307/j.ctv1198wg2

Ferreri, M., and L. Vidal (2022), 'Public-cooperative policy mechanisms for housing commons', *International Journal of Housing Policy*, 22:2, 149–73, https://doi.org/10.1080/19491247.2021.1877888

Griffith, E. J., M. Jepma, and F. Savini (2022), 'Beyond collective property: a typology of collaborative housing in Europe', *International Journal of Housing Policy*, 24:1, 1–21, https://doi.org/10.1080/19491247.2022.2123272

Guisan, A. O. T., T. Liu, and J.-D. Gerber (2025), 'Housing Commons? A Scoping Review', *International Journal of the Commons*, 19:1, 158–72, https://doi.org/10.5334/ijc.1490

Harvey, D. (2006), *The Limits to Capital* (London: Verso).

Harvey, D. (2012), *Rebel Cities* (New York: Verso).

Helfrich, S., and D. Bollier (2019), *Free, Fair, and Alive: The Insurgent Power of the Commons* (Gabriola, BC: New Society Publishers).

Heywood, A. (2016), *Local Housing, Community Living: Prospects for Scaling Up and Scaling Out Community-Led Housing* (London: Smith-Institute).

Hölzl, C. (2022), 'Translocal Mobilization of Housing Commons. The Example of the German Mietshäuser Syndikat', *Frontiers in Sustainable Cities*, 4, www.frontiersin.org/articles/10.3389/frsc.2022.759332 (accessed 19 March 2026).

Hölzl, C., and D. Hölzl (2022), 'Establishing new housing commons in Vienna in the context of translocal networks', *Housing Studies*, 39:5, 1–24, https://doi.org/10.1080/02673037.2022.2104820

Hölzl, C., D. Hölzl, and D. Amacher (2021), 'Netzwerkstrategien von „Housing Commons" in der Gründungsphase – Das Beispiel der „habiTAT"-Hausprojekte „SchloR" und „Bikes and Rails" in Wien', *Mitteilungen der Österreichischen Geographischen Gesellschaft*, 163, 171–98, https://doi.org/10.1553/moegg163s171

Hölzl, C., H. Nuissl, F. Beran, and T. Kormeyer (2023), 'Nonprofit Landlord Types on the Housing Market – A Key to Rising Displacement in Berlin?', *Housing Policy Debate*, 35:2, 1–21, https://doi.org/10.1080/10511482.2023.2271898

Hudson, J., K. Scanlon, C. Udagawa, M. F. Arrigoitia, M. Ferreri, and K. West (2021), '"A Slow Build-Up of a History of Kindness": Exploring the Potential of Community-Led Housing in Alleviating Loneliness', *Sustainability (Switzerland)*, 13:20, 11323, https://doi.org/10.3390/su132011323

Huron, A. (2015), 'Working with Strangers in Saturated Space: Reclaiming and Maintaining the Urban Commons', *Antipode*, 47:4, 963–79, https://doi.org/10.1111/anti.12141

Huron, A. (2018), *Carving out the Commons: Tenant Organizing and Housing Cooperatives in Washington, DC* (Minneapolis: University of Minnesota Press).

Jarvis, H. (2015), 'Towards a deeper understanding of the social architecture of co-housing: evidence from the UK, USA and Australia', *Urban Research & Practice*, 8:1, 93–105, https://doi.org/10.1080/17535069.2015.1011429

Köhler, J., F. W. Geels, F. Kern, J. Markard, E. Onsongo, A. Wieczorek, et al. (2019), 'An agenda for sustainability transitions research: State of the art and future directions', *Environmental Innovation and Societal Transitions*, 31, 1–32, https://doi.org/10.1016/j.eist.2019.01.004

Lang, R., C. Carriou, and D. Czischke (2018), 'Collaborative Housing Research (1990–2017): A Systematic Review and Thematic Analysis of the Field', *Housing, Theory and Society*, 0:0, 1–30, https://doi.org/10.1080/14036096.2018.1536077

Lang, R., P. Chatterton, and D. Mullins (2020), 'Grassroots innovations in community-led housing in England: the role and evolution of intermediaries', *International Journal of Urban Sustainable Development*, 12:1, 52–72, https://doi.org/10.1080/19463138.2019.1663525

Leyva del Río, S. (2022), 'Conceptualising the commons as a relational triad: Lessons from the grant of use cooperative housing model in Barcelona', *Geoforum*, 136, 112–21, https://doi.org/10.1016/j.geoforum.2022.09.007

Massey, D. (1991), 'A global sense of place', *Marxism Today*, 38, 24–29.

Mayer, M. (2013), 'Multiscalar mobilization for a just city: New Spatial Politics of Urban Movements', in W. Nicholls, B. Miller, and J. Beaumont (eds), *Spaces of Contention. Spatialities and Social Movements* (Farnham: Ashgate), pp. 163–96.

McClatchey, R., K. McClymont, E. Griffin, and L. Carmichael (2023), 'Community led housing, health and wellbeing: a comprehensive literature review', *International Journal of Housing Policy*, 25:1, 18–55, https://doi.org/10.1080/19491247.2023.2232200

McFarlane, C. (2011), *Learning the City: Knowledge and Translocal Assemblage* (Malden: Wiley-Blackwell).

Moore, T., and K. McKee (2012), 'Empowering Local Communities? An International Review of Community Land Trusts', *Housing Studies*, 27:2, 280–90, https://doi.org/10.1080/02673037.2012.647306

Moore, T., and D. Mullins (2013), 'Scaling-up or going viral? Comparing self-help housing and community land trust facilitation', *Voluntary Sector Review*, 4:3, 333–53, https://doi.org/10.1332/204080513X671931

Raynor, K. (2018), 'Assembling an innovative social housing project in Melbourne: mapping the potential for social innovation', *Housing Studies*, 34:8, 1263–85, https://doi.org/10.1080/02673037.2018.1535054

Sørvoll, J., and B. Bengtsson (2018), 'The Pyrrhic victory of civil society housing? Co-operative housing in Sweden and Norway', *International Journal of Housing Policy*, 18:1, 124–42, https://doi.org/10.1080/14616718.2016.1162078

Stavrides, S. (2015), 'Common Space as Threshold Space: Urban Commoning in Struggles to Re-Appropriate Public Space', *Footprint*, 9:1, 9–19, https://doi.org/10.7480/FOOTPRINT.9.1

Thompson, M. (2018), 'From Co-Ops to Community Land Trusts: Tracing the Historical Evolution and Policy Mobilities of Collaborative Housing Movements', *Housing, Theory and Society*, 37:1, 1–19, https://doi.org/10.1080/14036096.2018.1517822

Tummers, L. (2015), 'The re-emergence of self-managed co-housing in Europe: A critical review of co-housing research', *Urban Studies*, 1–18, 2023–40, https://doi.org/10.1177/0042098015586696

Vilenica, A., I. Florea, V. Popovici, and Z. Pósfai (2021), 'Urban Struggles and Theorising from Eastern European Cities', in C. McFarlane and M. Lancione (eds), *Global Urbanism: Knowledge, Power and the City*, 1st edn (London: Routledge), https://doi.org/10.4324/9780429259593

Part I

Grassroots housing production in Europe: National and local similarities and differences

1

Zagreb and Vienna – 7,681 affordable housing units: Revisiting large-scale, not-for-profit housing provision

Iva Marčetić, Gabu Heindl

What does it mean to have collaboration in housing?

Grassroots housing initiatives that have, over the last decades, sprung up in (primarily Western) Europe are difficult to systematise and, perhaps even more importantly, reproduce outside of their place of inception. However, there are attempts to make its specific models of housing provision more accessible to both scientific inquiries and practical application. Projects such as Housing 2030[1] or networking efforts of various NGOs and municipalities promoting (mostly) cooperative housing have been useful tools for comprehending the particularities of the trend. But it has seen its application mostly within EU-15 countries (including the UK) and, for the most part, speaks to the projects that are singular in their characteristics, rather than what perhaps could be called a systematic, or universal housing policy. In regards to naming the trend, we find that collaborative housing has so far been the most successful umbrella term for the field. Czischke, Carriou and Lang even offer something close to a definition by claiming that collaborative housing 'can be understood as an umbrella term that encompasses a variety of housing forms with different degrees of collective self-organisation' (2020). The authors go on to state that the main characteristics of such a type of housing provision are 'the presence of a significant level of collaboration amongst (future) residents, and between them and external actors and/or stakeholders, with a view to realising the housing project', adding that 'the term collaboration stands for coordinated action towards a common purpose' (Czischke et al. 2020). More importantly for our paper, the same authors also ask what are the boundaries of this field and what is the relation between the development of such models to the changes in the welfare state. Hence, we would like to focus on Aernouts and Ryckewaert's (2015) concept of 'publicness' and critically assess the term collaborative housing as housing provision that is no longer provided by the state, but performs the tasks the state (or other public entity) was historically mandated to do.

We would also like to acknowledge that it has been a longstanding critique of collaborative housing models in Europe that many of them have an 'inward-looking nature' (Thompson, 2018) and are expressing what is called an 'internal solidarity' (Sørvoll and Bengtsson, 2018). As many of the projects in the field are associated with housing production that caters to the needs of a specific and well-organised social group, that by definition does not include those without flexibility of time, appropriate social relations or who may have limited access to information when it comes to organising around their housing (Hölzl et al., 2021), we question the scope of participation that is purported as one of the main features of collaborative housing projects. We do not deny that most of these projects are considered a welcome variation to the current housing market and that there are, of course, exceptions to the level of homogeneity of socio-economic make-up of tenants in such projects, or, to stay within the terminology, when it comes to the 'publicness' or 'internality' of these models. For example, in the case of Zurich's new generation of cooperatives, some housing units can be set aside for government or city assistance programmes, while the CLT Brussels that serves almost exclusively the low-earning population in need of safe housing, has not much capacity for upward residential heterogeneity.

It would be dishonest to dismiss a multitude of initiatives that are simply working on making some people's homes more secure and affordable. So, in an earnest effort to bypass the obvious critique, we would like to expand the concepts of collaboration, community and participation by challenging their scale and their replicability, both geographically and along class lines. We feel that in understanding participatory housing and architecture, there is too sharp a break between comprehensive municipal programmes of housing production and the current trend of Europe's collaborative housing models. Therefore, we reach for an umbrella concept that goes beyond understanding housing as a field, but as a litmus test for what Piketty (2022) dubs an economy that builds on public wealth and not on private wealth accumulation.

Two examples of public housing projects and their collaborative values

In this text, we will try to broaden the meaning of collaborative housing by extending our timeline and analysing examples of public housing built en masse in the 1970s in two European cities, Vienna and Zagreb, based on their characteristics compared to the contemporary definitions of

Figure 1.1 Alt Erlaa towers, 2016. Photo © David Evers, all rights reserved.

collaborative housing, participation, and the extent of a housing community. We analyse two iconic examples of housing estates, Dugave in Zagreb and Alt-Erlaa in Vienna, both built from the mid-1970s until early to the mid-1980s for a similar number of residents, and both still very high-quality and sought-after places to live.

We chose these cities in part because each author comes from one of them, but apart from the personal connection, these cities, whose histories converge in multiple ways, do speak to the differences within the current issue of financing housing in Europe. For example, Zagreb does not feature any contemporary collaborative housing programme, and one of the reasons for this is the lack of commercial financial institutions that would be willing to offer credit for a non-profit civic investment into housing. With more than 90% of the Croatian banking sector privatised and in the hands

Figure 1.2 Dugave housing estate, Zagreb, 2024. Photo © Antun Sevšek, all rights reserved.

of mostly Austrian or Italian banks (Croatian National Bank, 2007), the only financial products on the housing supply side are short-term loans with high equity specifically designed for building and selling housing units for profit, even though the same banks operating in Vienna do offer more financial variations. On the other hand, public financial institutions such as the European Investment Bank (EIB) have not been able to invest in the sector due to the scale of the loan that would need to be absorbed based on the EIB's own lending rules and practices.

This means that, on the civic side, there were no established networks or actors capable of managing a loan of the minimum threshold set by the EIB. In contrast, within EU-15, such investments have been more feasible for collaborative housing models supported by municipal and state actors, as well as housing providers equipped to absorb these types of investments (Eurocities, 2025). This speaks to the very clear demarcation between the intent of such a supranational financial structure and the possibility of its application. Moreover, it presents a clear centre/periphery relation when it comes to the housing question (Bródy and Pósfai, 2020) (see Chapter 14). This is not a particularly new dynamic, and therefore the relation between the two cities we use as examples can be standalone cases that present a materialisation of such uneven development dynamics.

The history of the interconnectedness of Zagreb and Vienna reaches into the times of the empire, with Vienna as metropolis and Zagreb as its periphery, whose urban parameters were set up by the imperial economic and transportation needs. Even though today both Zagreb and Vienna are equal members of the EU (albeit with Vienna again in the centre and Zagreb on the periphery of the Union), the differences between them in terms of existing housing provision models are bigger than in the time of the twentieth century (Kazepov and Verwiebe, 2022). This is in no way unusual and speaks to the timeline that Piketty names 'A brief history of equality' (2022), positioning the years of the mid-twentieth century as years of public wealth production.

Yet, unlike today's trend of collaborative housing investments, this kind of public housing production was present in all of Europe almost equally. Back in the 1970s, which is the main focus of our exploration, Zagreb was a city within a multi-ethnic socialist Yugoslavia whose economy, governance and urban development were organised as a system of socialist self-management. Hence, the city of Zagreb, rather than being subjugated to Vienna or some other outside centre of power, was part of the global opposition to the capitalist states, thus triggering the thriving of the Western welfare state as an answer to that opposition. By analysing and comparing elements such as the level of democratic decision-making, and tenants' participation in the financing, managing, ownership and architecture of mass public housing projects from these two cities, we are focusing on the scale of the housing need in relation to the ability of the non-profit housing models to satisfy it. We ask what are the similarities between the ideas that were conveyed through housing projects of the 1970s that produced housing for the many and how those ideas help with scaling up horizons for thinking about collaborative housing today.

Housing as a theory of change

Harry Glück, the principal architect of the Wohnpark Alt-Erlaa is often attributed as having said that social housing projects should be about building a good life for the many. Ivan Čižmek, one of the lead architects of the Dugave estate, believed that it is a 'housing estate that is being built for the present', adding that 'the present is our future' (Čižmek, 1979). These statements speak to the broader social and political climate within which an architect's imagination can work 'towards a common purpose', where what is common is universal and reflected in the scale of the projects. Since the production of housing is a long-term process of building but a much longer process of developing a home, family and communal life, to think about housing models is to think about the future, to relate it to the current (willingly or not) politics of home and aspirations of the society within which that home is created. In her writings about Red Vienna, Eve Blau (1999) claims that the famed Viennese housing model of the interwar era was not conceived as one more *housing reform* but rather as *a path towards socialism*. Blau's methodology in analysing the housing model overlaps both 'the operation of ideology and the instrumentality of a form of knowledge particular to architecture' (Blau, 1999: 3). Following Blau's method, to examine housing models would be to simultaneously analyse the theory of social change they create through their development and subsequent use but also to see their architecture as an ideological symbol of the materialised level of equality and quality of life.

The development of Dugave housing estate started in 1975 with the architectural and urbanistic competition held only one year after the new Yugoslav Constitution came into effect. The Constitution set in place the possibility for more autonomy of self-managing collectives, or as Flaherty (1992) puts it, it was 'to design a system of central guidance of the economy consistent with self-management' (Flaherty, 1992: 103). The competition prescribed that only architects and planners working in self-managed organisations in the Zagreb region can apply to the competition. This aspect of insisting on local design production is hailed by architects both then and now, but in the overall history of the development of the Yugoslav experiment, it can also be understood as increasing territorial insularity which can hinder the idea of solidarity between regions (Suvin, 2014). The housing estate was planned for 13,000 people or 4,550 housing units, and it was the first of its kind to be completely designed, organised and built through the housing model of the so-called Društveno Usmjerena Stambena Izgradnja (Socially Directed Housing Construction, DUSI). In line with the new Constitution and reformed economy, DUSI multiplied the agency of both professional planning and architecture organisations, as well as the participation of those who financed, organised, inhabited and managed housing production. Even though the system of housing production became exponentially more complex compared with the two previous decades, it almost tripled the number of housing units produced in the coming one (Korlaet, 2015). Bjažić and Korlaet (2020) claim that both the planning and architecture of Dugave were greatly influenced by the French concept of *ville nouvelle* that departs from CIAM (Congrès Internationaux d'Architecture Moderne) in the way that it purposefully incorporates the existing built environment into its design and communal life. This formal relation was not coincidental and had much to do with some of the lead architects and planners previously working within the French context and establishing networks within the field.

In a similar timeline, the construction of the Viennese Alt-Erlaa housing estate started only two years after its initial conception, in 1973. Alt-Erlaa is a large housing estate with 3,181 apartments set on the southwestern edge of the city and, like Dugave, a part of the urban plan of the city expansion at the time. It was conceived as a housing estate that aims to deliver so-called 'happy living' for around 10,000 of its future inhabitants. The idea was to introduce not only quality housing units, but also luxuries such as various rooftop pools and community spaces that featured prominently in the housing programme of 1920s Red Vienna. Within the deep plinths of the buildings, Alt-Erlaa incorporated many spaces for free communal organising as well as for greater participation by tenants in decision-making about the management of the estate – which until today is given in the possibility to join, for instance, the tenants' council; however, few people actually see a need to do so. Nevertheless, residents mobilize when major decisions arise – for example, they voted against privatizing block maintenance.

Renter decision-making in Alt-Erlaa makes for a substantial leap in the standard of non-profit housing, especially when compared to the historic top-down provision-of-services-attitude of Red Vienna (Heindl, 2020). It also stands out against contemporary collaborative projects, which often focus on complementing private living spaces with shared areas for recreation, community organising and leisure, encouraging a more collective use of free time. Providing community spaces is something that has continued in Vienna's contemporary social housing projects as part of a competitive bid for communal land through property developer competitions. It has also featured prominently in the projects of new cooperatives such as Kalkbreite in Zurich as a model that creates spaces for family life, not just inside the housing unit, but within the housing complex. It is also interesting to note that the enclosed community spaces are mainly focused on communalising the leisure time, rather than household work of cooking and washing as was the case of the early twentieth-century communal housing projects.

Universal distributive policies of housing

Land

Urban land, as a scarce and non-replicable resource, can make for the single biggest expense in housing development. In the current housing production climate, securing the appropriate urban land to build affordable housing is almost impossible without a strong public land policy that in one way or another subsidises the land price. If land politics does not serve as an equalising factor of distribution, then land price is predominantly determined by the structure of market players and available credit lines for (mostly housing) developers, hence its value is non-intrinsic to its nature, but rather speculative.

Therefore, if we know that the cost of housing is foremost determined by the price of (mostly urban) land, then we should be able to accept that the absence (or presence) of strong anti-speculative policies is a determining factor of the distributive level of urban and housing development. To illustrate this, we can use Arnstein's ladder of participation and position the amount of political inclusion via distributive land policy high up on the ladder, signalling a genuine citizen control over the process of urbanisation (Arnstein, 1969). We purposely make this analogy in order to challenge the constraints of citizen participation in urban planning. Treatment of land policy as a tool of distribution of resources through a political process goes a long way towards achieving the aforementioned 'presence of a significant level of collaboration amongst (future) residents, and between them and external actors and/or stakeholders as an element of collaboration between different stakeholders' (Czischke, Carriou and Lang, 2020). Therefore, we position the model of land policy present on the level of the cities and catering to the projects we analyse here, as a level of participation that allows for collaboration between future and current residents that is inclusive and replicable.

Alt-Erlaa was developed on municipal land in a city whose land policies from the 1920s onward worked toward lowering the price of land and making it available for city purchase. Unlike socialist Zagreb, throughout its twentieth-century history Vienna purchased its land strictly on the open market. But the city indirectly manipulated that market through, for example, the 1922 Rent Control Law. This law made it impossible to make extra profit from rental housing, thus making building land unattractive as a speculative asset (Heindl, 2019). Coupled with a policy of land banking, we can say that Vienna innovated land reforms within the capitalist system in order to make it possible to distribute land in order to build affordable communal housing and support limited-profit cooperative housing.

In the case of the socialist period in Zagreb, all inner urban rental housing was nationalised from 1959 until 1990. Once an apartment building was nationalised in the inner city, the owner was paid 10% of the total yearly rent as compensation (the price was set in 1959). It is important to note that not all urban housing was subject to expropriation, but only those buildings that consisted of more than four apartments. Buildings with fewer than four apartments and family houses were never subject to expropriation. The Law on Expropriation that specifically regulated the unbuilt building land came into effect two years earlier, in 1957. It is perhaps interesting as a token in the debates around socialising the assets of big housing companies in Germany today that, according to Yugoslavian law back then, housing was legally categorised as vital infrastructure, thus enabling the prerequisites for legal expropriation. This meant that when an urban plan for the housing estate came into effect, the process of expropriation could be triggered. In the case of Dugave, once the urban plan was voted in, the 78 hectares of land for the future housing estate, then mostly swamp and small agricultural land, became subject to expropriation. The law stipulated that compensation for the land would not be determined by the market prices, but by other determining factors that were deliberated in the negotiating process between the private owner and the city. In case the owner was a private person, the living and economic circumstances of their family were the main factors taken into account. The payment could be monetary or in kind, such as land or housing, depending on the decision of the private owner.

Financing construction

The investor into Alt-Erlaa housing estate was the non-profit housing stock AEAG – Gemeinnützige Wohnungsaktiengesellschaft Wohnpark Alt-Erlaa. It was founded for the project in 1973 as a subsidiary of the Gemeinnützige Siedlungs- und Bauaktiengesellschaft (Non-profit Settlement and Construction Company – GESIBA). GESIBA is incorporated into the city-owned Wien Holding (Vienna Holding). Its origins trace back to 1921 when it was founded by the Republic of Austria and the City of Vienna, tasking it with providing affordable materials for cooperatives that were building detached and terraced houses, a socio-economic programme complementary to municipal building efforts of so-called Red Vienna. From 1950 onwards, at the behest of the city, the company started developing large rental housing estates, and Alt-Erlaa is one of them. In 1993, GESIBA transformed its legal form from a limited company to a limited-profit public joint stock company, signalling a more neoliberal departure from its initial form, in line with the broader city transformations.

The housing development of Alt-Erlaa was co-funded by social housing funds, based on an income tax and on exemption from corporate tax for limited-profit housing associations, both of which are earmarked for housing and directed toward either municipal housing development or into subsidies for non-profit housing construction. GESIBA's rent revenues, as well as its assets, certainly play an important role in securing investment through favourable loans and considering the management capabilities that were developed over decades. There was no direct engagement from tenants during the building process in terms of direct participation at either time, or direct decisions regarding architecture, but there could be an argument made that there was significant inclusion in the political process that ensured sufficient distribution of wealth both through taxes and through aforementioned distributive land policy. This model of housing provision ensured that all apartments built in this project remain rental apartments and are subject to the protections of the Austrian Limited-Profit Housing Act (Wohnungsgemeinnützigkeitsgesetz – WGG) that allows for a significant amount of tenant security. The apartments are all owned by the non-profit housing stock company AEAG, but each tenant is also a shareholder for the duration of their tenancy, guaranteeing them voting privileges when it comes to managing the estate. AEAG, as a subsidiary of a hundred-year-old company established by the city and the state, should be the real focal point for discussions on participation, where inclusion is measured by the degree of citizen oversight and control over its development. This is particularly relevant if we envision scaling-up efforts, where the goal of achieving more affordable and high-quality housing extends beyond the interests of a specific social group to benefit the broader community. We are not claiming that AEAG is a perfect form of participatory housing, but wish to point out that the scope of participation should turn to creating (and re-creating) institutions that are universal mechanisms of solidarity and public, rather than private, wealth accumulation (see Piketty, 2022).

The longevity of GESIBA and the stability of Vienna's institutions allow us to use contemporary language when analysing the financial inputs into constructing Alt-Erlaa. When it comes to understanding the financing scheme for constructing Dugave estate in Zagreb, we have to reach for the language of the Yugoslavian experiment of self-management, an institutional framework that no longer exists and can be challenging to comprehend. The investor and main organising body of the process of funding of Dugave housing estate was the Udružena Samoupravna Interesna Zajednica za Stanovanje i Komunalne poslove (United Self-managed Community of Interest for Housing and Communal Infrastructure Zagreb – USIZ). Self-managed Communities of Interest (SIZ) functioned like 'some kind of a mutual fund formed based on the self-managing agreement to collect percentages from personal incomes and funds from the Organizacija Udruženog Rada (Organisations of United Labour – OUR)' (Duda 2023: 23) in order to organise and align development of either housing, culture, communal infrastructure, education or other elements of reproduction. They could be formed on the level of OUR, or on the level of associations of citizens through their local community of neighbourhoods. In the case of large cities such as Zagreb, they helped to form a Union of self-managed communities of interest (USIZ) in order to collect funds efficiently and plan for larger housing developments within a unified General Urban Plan. The funds for Dugave came from the amalgam of cooperative funds, a percentage of each gross salary of the citizens employed on the territory of Zagreb and funds earmarked by the OURs. Flaherty's (1992) explanation of the reforms of the 1970s in Yugoslavia as central guidance of self-management can best describe the coordination of funding and urban planning of housing. Decisions about the level of funding for housing were made on the level of individual workers' councils, cooperatives or other low-level organising entities, yet for example, the law stipulated that a minimum of 4% of each salary needed to be collected for a solidarity housing fund. Each company or organisation could, however, opt for a higher percentage and the final percentage was negotiated on the level of the municipality. This meant that there had to be at least 50% of the workers' councils agreeing with the final decision. In the period in question, workers in Zagreb allocated 6–8% of gross salary to the housing fund (Korlaet, 2015).

It is important to note that from 1974 onwards (development of Dugave started in 1975), the funds for housing were more and more organised through local, municipal self-managed agreements between economic producers, rather than through the municipal budget. This reform was often dubbed the market reform. It could be paralleled with outsourcing the organising of housing in the case of Vienna to limited-profit housing companies instead of opting for municipal housing production. We can interpret it both as a possibility of allowing more participation and decision-making on the lower level of social organisation in the case of Yugoslavia, or the efficacy of outsourcing housing production away from the burdens of too much administration in the case of Vienna. However, it can also be assessed as leaning towards the insularity of interests which became evident in the 1990s (Suvin, 2014). This, of course, makes for a much wider discussion that is outside of the scope of this chapter. Nevertheless, we can state that non-profit collective housing production, including large-scale systems such as Alt-Erlaa and Dugave, always entail a promise of democratisation and a trap of insularity, depending on how the scale of solidarity mechanisms and institutions is organised.

Local community and participatory architecture

Community construction

Both of the housing estates were planned and built at a time when social housing architecture was slightly diverging from the idea of *Existenzminimum* and into experimenting with design that could offer more quality of both private and communal life. They are equally developed as part of the urban plans to extend their respective cities and as such fit into the ideas that emerged in the 1960s and 1970s. The planning team of Alt-Erlaa was influenced by terrace housing concepts, especially the idea of the 'stapled detached house' (Glück, 1979). The planners and architects of Dugave were greatly influenced by the formal aspects of French *villeneuve* projects, but they were equally influenced by the plan for expansion of the coastal city of Split that reintroduced a Mediterranean street into the modernist social housing plan (Bjažić, Klarin and Korlaet, 2020). Thus, the plan for Dugave is non-schematic and non-orthogonal, consisting of semi-opened housing blocks that make space differentiations between public outside and semi-public inside. The plan incorporates the old riverbed as part of its connection to the existing elements, clearly breaking with the modernist overpowering of nature. South-east edges of the estate are planned as parcels for single family housing, thus gradually incorporating the estate with the morphology of the surroundings rather than ignoring it, as was the case in previous phases of mass housing development. Both housing estates were complemented with additional community functions such as schools, kindergartens and commercial centres as well as multifunctional halls.

The housing estate Dugave functioned as both a unit of an urban plan, as well as an administrative territorial unit, the Neighbourhood Community (Mjesna zajednica MZ). Edvard Kardelj defined first 'a unit of the city plan', second 'a unit and form of self-government in the commune', and third 'a carrier of the widening material-technical base for the everyday life of the family and the individual' (Kardelj as cited in Fisher, 1965: 63). The main idea behind the MZ was that it was organised on the principle of voluntarism and that it functions as a mirror organisation to the workers' council. However, instead of a company, MZ was a territorial unit. It was a place where the workers organised in the community and simultaneously a space for creating community. This was especially important in new urban developments with a large influx of new residents who needed to establish what was then deemed a *practice of creating an extended family* (see Duda, 2023). MZ functioned as one side of the aforementioned self-management triangle as an active participant in establishing agreements between the OUR and SIZ that operated on its territory in order to provide for social and cultural life of the neighbourhood (Duda, 2023). It was also incorporated into the organisation of the development of the Dugave estate under the auspices of the DUSI model of housing production as a connection between the future tenants and the technical aspects of housing production (Bjažić, Klarin and Korlaet, 2020). Once built, each of the dwellings, or several of them together, were organised into housing councils that were tasked with building management, as well as choosing their delegates for the local neighbourhood community and SIZ.

Unlike the Dugave project, the architects Harry Glück, Kurt Hlaweniczka, Thomas Reinthaller and Franz Requat did not challenge the orthogonal

CIAM-like floor plan, but they significantly departed from its orthogonality by controlled vertical shapeshifting of the towers. Their central idea consisted of stapling units with as much green space as possible to provide an urban alternative to the ideology of detached houses – a typology which until today is the reason for long waiting lists of future tenants. In 1995, the extension of the subway to Alt-Erlaa provided an important infrastructural quality boost. Alt-Erlaa has six longitudinal housing towers positioned parallel to each other and connected with the lower perpendicular structure that contains administration, commercial, educational, cultural and other amenities. Interior plinth spaces are still used for maintenance of the building, but also as spaces for self-organised tenant clubs. In her documentary '27 Storeys – Alt-Erlaa forever' (AT/DE 2023), director Bianca Gleissinger depicts, albeit in a very picturesque way, the longevity of this kind of communal life. At the same time, Gleissinger questions the future purpose of such club spaces that feature an increasingly ageing membership. The section of the large-scale buildings is a double concave curve whose facade for the first twelve floors is adorned by lush green terrace-gardens that create a soft contact of the tower base with the ground. This was enabled by prefabricated support structures for the large, semi-barrel soil pots, which form the nonlinear green border between the building and its surrounding. This feature is one of the most prominent aspects of the towers which visually connects the towers with the carefully landscaped, open communal space. The soft landing of the towers is made possible by the connection between the design of the architect and the maintenance of private balconies by the tenants, whose labour of creating gardens in the facades' structural elements in turn creates the architecture of the facade itself. The wide trunk of the base provides space for communal amenities that do not need direct sunlight such as a pool, sauna and meeting and workshop spaces. The typical floor plan features an inner hall with entrances to the apartments on both sides of the hall, except the end of the hallway apartment that takes advantage of two-corner side direction. The housing complex consists of thirty-five different housing unit floor plans. The average unit size is a three-room apartment ($74m^2$) and each of them is extended with either a large terrace or a loggia on higher floors which features a slight rotation of the part of the facade. Even though the higher floors do not have as much outdoor space as the lower ones, the apartment is extended with a wide view of the city which then becomes an added feature of the apartment.

Decentralised participation

The land of Alt-Erlaa was bought by GESIBA in 1968 before developing the scheme of the Wohnpark. The cooperative ownership structure of

Wohnpark Alt-Erlaa is an important factor in the sectional concept of the towers with the deep plinth and its extra functions. Becoming a tenant in Alt-Erlaa today also means becoming a partial owner of the AEAG by purchasing a prescribed amount of company shares. The shares do not change in value and are given back at the moment of moving out of the estate. In a sense, this can be understood as a tenant's financial contribution in exchange for ownership and decision-making rights without the possibility of speculating with that ownership, but also as an impediment to certain social groups who are not able to afford to buy the said shares.

Dugave was built on what was then legally deemed *socially owned land*. Upon completion of the estate, the land remained in social ownership regardless of the ownership structure of the individual apartments, but the majority of them were socially rather than privately owned, like the land beneath them. Division of ownership of land and private housing units was an important legal tool in Yugoslavia that was in place to ensure the improbability of land and housing speculation. Social ownership was a Yugoslavian *sui generis* legal form of ownership that was neither public nor private.

One of the definitions of such a form of ownership is given by the lead theorist of the economy of self-management, Branko Horvat, who explains that social ownership 'implies the negation of the very essence of property in pre-socialist societies – the appropriation of income from property' (Horvat, 1983). Each tenant in such a socially owned apartment had a tenancy right that most resembles the rights of ownership in liberal economies, except the right to freely trade this housing unit in an open market. Also, the right was only available as long as that was the only liveable housing that the tenant and their family had. The umbrella rules of housing distribution, rights and obligations were defined by the State Law on Housing Relations, whose mandate was to ensure universality of rights and resource distribution, but the priority lists were defined on the level of the specific economic unit and/or self-managed community of interest and/or municipality. But there was no authority or managing body of the apartments that were an outside authority to the collective tenant bodies. This means that the buildings were governed by their tenants, or aforementioned housing councils that consisted of leaseholders, owners or tenants, each apartment having one voice in the council, or in the case of the larger buildings, a delegate system was organised. Rent was usually a single-digit percentage of the tenant's salary and collected by the self-managed communities of interest. The revenue from the rent was divided between the fund and the housing council. The housing council was tasked with maintenance and enabled to open credit lines in the name of the building in the case of bigger maintenance expenses. The land that served the building was also managed by the council.

Here we can evoke Branko Horvat again to contextualise such distribution of powers and governance. Horvat claimed that 'Socialist ideology eliminates' the division between rulers and ruled and 'replaces it with participation' (Horvat, 1983: 231). He relates the multiplicity of groups that are tasked with making collective decisions as the only way of 'effective decentralisation of power' (Horvat, 1983: 322), a claim we consider key to the question of participation.

We propose to extend the idea of effective decentralisation to the question of participation in architecture. Participation in housing architecture has been a prominent avenue of exploration and an award-winning tool in the last couple of decades. For instance, the principal of the architecture group Elemental, Alejandro Aravena, won the Pritzker prize in 2016 for, among other things, his innovative approach to the participatory architecture exemplified in publicly subsidised housing developments in Chile, for example, Quinta Monroy (Aravena et al., 2004). Another proof of the growing impact of participation is the newly established European Collective Housing Award (since 2024) that aims at recognising 'the most significant contributions in the field of collective housing'. Even though these efforts contain interesting approaches to the relation between architects and the users of architecture, their effectiveness can be challenged by their scope, by the lack of imagining structural anti-speculative and collective governing tools (as in the Chile example), but maybe most importantly their small scale of operation and, in the end, in some cases also the quality of built space. We think that architectural autonomy to a certain degree needs to be accepted in order to socialise the know-how of architects that is challenged by the design task, which can be inclusive and participatory. Hence, we would like to read some of the elements of our two examples through the lens of their effectiveness in their speed of delivery and flexibility and quality of housing produced.

The architectural competition for the Dugave project specified that one of the main tasks was the flexibility of the apartment and the possibility of fast and efficient construction. Similar to the Alt-Erlaa example, the standard of living was, at the time, departing from the two-room housing units that made for the majority of newly built structures in Zagreb. Therefore, the average size of the apartment in the estate is 84.6m^2, featuring a scale from 1.5 to 5 rooms apartments, including duplexes. Efficacy and speed of building were achieved by using sliding formworks to build transversal reinforced concrete walls spanning 5.4 metres and attaching prefabricated facade elements to them. One housing unit was simultaneously one structural unit with load-bearing structural walls on each side of the apartment, sanitary facilities in the middle and partition walls that were easy to dismantle. This flexibility provides that each apartment can be redesigned according to the tenant's changing needs (Bjažić, Klarin and Korlaet, 2020). However, the project did not just achieve the flexibility of the apartments but also varied ways of entering them, making variations within the repetition one of the main characteristics of mass housing production. The ground floor apartments can be entered directly through the garden in the inner block, others from the gallery, or an inner corridor on every third floor. Positioning inner corridors and galleries on every third floor made for maximum use of living space, but also created a section that allows for the apartments to be connected along vertical and horizontal axes without structural change and with minimal building intervention. In their analysis of Dugave, Bjažić Klarin and Korlaet (2020) claim that the design of galleries intentionally evokes Team 10's 'street in the air', a space of meeting and the community, signalling a departure from the strictly modernist schematic organising of space. In the end, the design provided for quality housing of a higher standard by carefully variegating standardised elements in such a way that the tenant becomes a participant in the design by allowing for transformations of the apartment.

Conclusion

Both projects exemplify how building *en masse* can also satisfy the attention to detail and variation within quite limited versions of construction elements, hence, more efficient building. At the time of conception of these projects, participation in design as we have come to understand it today was not considered. However, one of the main features of architectural know-how is building for non-familiar users and we would like to claim that the architectural task that comes before the design can hold within itself a higher level of political, economic and social inclusion. When it comes to the final architectural expression, we find that the architects of both estates were anticipating not just the needs of future tenants, but incorporating the possibility of the co-creation of architecture by future users. This is perhaps most exemplified within the facade of Alt-Erlaa. The architect's treatment of the design of the terraces and their openness for individual use and planting schemes incorporates the possibility of changes in the life of the tenant, while the series of community spaces allows for collective sharing of interests – all of which is quite reminiscent of the current day's calls for participatory design. Understanding participation and bottom-up agency as a direct involvement in the project of non-profit collaborative housing can hinder the possibility of designing for an unknown tenant, which is a prerequisite of universalist policies and transformation towards political and socio-economic equity that we understand as crucial for the process of real participation. Although we do not claim that more communication and understanding between architects and users of architecture are not needed – quite the contrary – we warn of a simplified version of participation in architecture. With this text we also caution against understanding participation solely as direct involvement of tenants, since this not only determines the scale of a project, but also raises the question of developing housing architecture as an expression of collective rather than just individual rights.

If there is a position that cannot be refuted, it is the one that we need more housing that delivers security of tenure for many, which, in the nature of things, means that our cities cannot sustain the dominance of market relations in housing. Therefore, we view the scale of intervention in the field as one of the most critical aspects – one that must strike a careful balance between specific technical expertise and the pursuit of social equity, which inherently demands active participation. The two examples we examined speak to this combination in a way that, as the Dugave estate architects claimed, standardisation is the only way to deliver housing for the many, but it is also an opportunity to experiment with variations (Bjažić, Klarin and Korlaet, 2020). Harry Glück (whose family name translates into English as 'happiness') often spoke of relating his large-scale housing estate to the utilitarianist concept of providing 'the greatest happiness of the greatest number'.

Our aim was to position the question of collaborative housing and the broader question of participation in urban planning within the history of equality and universal application of housing as public wealth and a collective right, rather than within a very recent trend of innovative but specific small-scale projects. We would like to conclude with the claim that participation is a question of political equity that is, according to Horvat (1983: 231), 'a precondition for genuine equity in the field of production and consumption', with housing combining both fields. The two case studies contain a high level of political equity through distributive policies. In the Zagreb case, the project concept also includes a broader level of autonomy. Yet this autonomy was negated through the process of privatisation and political transformation in the 1990s. The fact that the Vienna example still represents public wealth and a non-speculative asset, even though it was conceived in a system that was much unlike the self-governing one of Yugoslavia, warrants a further comparative exploration of the possible longevity of participation and equity in housing.

Note

1 www.housing2030.org (accessed 19 March 2026).

References

Aernouts, N., and M. Ryckewaert (2015), 'Reconceptualizing the "Publicness" of Public Housing: The Case of Brussels', *Social Inclusion*, 3:2, 17, https://doi.org/10.17645/si.v3i2.63

Aravena, A., A. Montero, T. Cortese, E. De La Cerda, and A. Iacobelli (2004), 'Quinta Monroy', *ARQ (Santiago)*, 57, https://doi.org/10.4067/S0717-69962004005700007

Arnstein, S. (1969), 'A Ladder of Citizen Participation', *Journal of the American Planning Association*, 35:4, 216–24.

Bjažić Klarin, T., and L. Korlaet (2020), 'The Housing Development of Dugave in New Zagreb: A New Model for Creating a Housing Community', *Život umjetnosti,* 107:2, 94–119.

Blau, E. (1999), *The Architecture of Red Vienna, 1919–1934* (Cambridge, MA: MIT Press).

Bródy, L. S., and Zs. Pósfai (2020), *Household Debt on the Peripheries of Europe: New Constellations Since 2008* (Budapest: Periféria Policy and Research Center).

Čižmek, I. (1979), 'Sadašnjost je naša budućnost', *Čovjek i Prostor*, 5, 314.

Croatian National Bank (2007), *Annual Report 2006* (Zagreb).

Czischke, D., C. Carriou, and R. Lang (2020), 'Collaborative Housing in Europe: Conceptualizing the Field', *Housing, Theory and Society*, 37:1, 1–9, https://doi.org/10.1080/14036096.2020.1703611

Duda, I. (2023), *Socijalizam na Kućnom Pragu: Mjesna Zajednica i Svakodnevica Društvenog Samoupravljanja u Jugoslaviji* (Srednja Europa: Sveučilište Jurja Dobrile u Puli).

Eurocities (2025), *Improving Cities Access to EU Funding for Housing* (Brussels), https://eurocities.eu/wp-content/uploads/2025/03/Improving-cities-access-to-EU-funding-for-housing.pdf (accessed 23 July 2025).

Fisher, J. C. (1965), 'City Planning and Housing Administration in Yugoslavia', *Urban Affairs Quarterly*, 1:2, 59–71.

Flaherty, D. (1992), 'Self-management and the future of socialism: Lessons from Yugoslavia', *Science and Society*, 56:1, 92–108.

Glück, H., and K. Freisitzer (1979), *Sozialer Wohnbau. Entstehung, Zustand, Alternativen* (Wien, München, Zürich, Innsbruck: Molden).

Heindl, G. (2019), 'Towards a Radical Democratic Politics of Urban Land: The Case of (Red) Vienna', in *Critical Care: Architecture and Urbanism for a Broken Planet* (Cambridge, MA: MIT Press).

Heindl, G. (2020), *Stadtkonflikte: Radikale Demokratie in Architektur und Stadtplanung* (Wien: Mandelbaum).

Hölzl, C., D. Hölzl, and D. Amacher (2021), 'Netzwerkstrategien von "Housing Commons" in der Gründungsphase – Das Beispiel der "habiTAT"-Hausprojekte "SchloR" und "Bikes and Rails" in Wien', *Mitteilungen der Österreichischen Geographischen Gesellschaft*, 163, 171–98, https://doi.org/10.1553/moegg163s171

Horvat, B. (1983), *The Political Economy of Socialism: A Marxist Social Theory* (Armonk, NY: Sharpe).

Kazepov, Y., and R. Verwiebe (eds) (2022), *Vienna: Still a Just City?* (New York, NY: Routledge).

Korlaet, L. (2015), *Prostorni Razvoj Stana u Zagrebu 1975–2005. U Okvirima Programa Društveno Poticane Stanogradnje*, Doctoral thesis (University of Zagreb Faculty of Architecture).
Piketty, T. (2022), *A Brief History of Equality*, translated from French by Steven Rendall (Cambridge, MA: The Belknap Press of Harvard University Press).
Sørvoll, J., and B. Bengtsson (2018), 'The Pyrrhic victory of civil society housing? Co-operative housing in Sweden and Norway', *International Journal of Housing Policy*, 18:1, 124–42, https://doi.org/10.1080/14616718.2016.1162078
Suvin, D. (2014), *Samo Jednom se Ljubi. Radiografija SFR Jugoslavije 1945.-72., uz hipoteze o početku, kraju i suštini* (Beograd: Rosa Luxemburg Stiftung).
Thompson, M. (2018), 'From Co-Ops to Community Land Trusts: Tracing the Historical Evolution and Policy Mobilities of Collaborative Housing Movements', *Housing, Theory and Society*, 37:1, 1–19.

2

Community-led housing in England: Emergence, growth and prospects

David Mullins, Tom Moore, Tom Archer

Introduction

Community-led housing is 'a grassroots-based housing niche in England' (Lang et al., 2020: 52) with similar characteristics to collaborative housing (Czischke, Carriou and Lang, 2020). It usually involves a mix of self-organisation and partnership with key actors such as municipalities and non-profit housing associations to secure support, resources and expertise. Community-led housing is comprised of several niche forms of housing provision (described as sub-niches in this chapter), such as housing cooperatives, community land trusts, cohousing and self-help housing, which have all grown in recent years (Heywood, 2016).

This chapter has a particular focus on the role of the state and the potential of intermediary organisations to facilitate sector growth. It builds on earlier work by the authors analysing the growth of community-led housing in England between 2000 and 2016. Moore and Mullins (2013) outlined some strategies and dilemmas involved in early attempts to expand grassroots activity into more mainstream housing options to provide alternatives to a broken housing system. Lang et al. (2020) applied a multi-level perspective and strategic niche management to assess the potential for niche actors to engage with and influence regime actors and the wider landscape. This chapter takes the analysis forward to consider the impact of significant government funding, the Community Housing Fund and associated system changes between 2016 and 2024. It will be of interest to scholars working in different contexts. Whilst it provides a detailed account of the development of community-led housing in England, there are critical lessons here which transcend place, government legislation and national housing markets, notably concerning the structures of public funding for non-state/non-market housing provision, as well as the critical infrastructure that makes this possible. Those working in other countries can learn from the shortcomings and successes in the English context.

The Community Housing Fund was seen as the largest injection of funding for community-led housing by the UK government for several decades, with the potential to radically grow the sector. But what have been the main strategic changes as a result of this funding? The Fund itself included several components to assist projects at distinct stages of the journey from pre-development to planning and construction. The Fund provided access to government capital grants for affordable housing (allocated by a public body called Homes England) and helped leverage funding from other partners (from charitable foundations and social investors to commercial lenders). To support these project-level investments there was further 'infrastructure funding' for the national bodies who represent the sub-niches of community-led housing.[1] A key aim of the Community Housing Fund was to build a national network of regional/sub-regional hubs through which groups could secure advice on all forms of community-led housing. There was also investment in training and accreditation of project advisers, who were expected to work with hubs where feasible.

There has not been a full evaluation of the Community Housing Fund itself, though we outline the key components and developments of this. A recent Community Housing Fund Delivery Review also provides valuable evidence (CLTN, 2024) and several sources provide more specific insights into the role of enabler hubs (Duncan and Lavis, 2018; Moore, 2018; Ward, 2024; Hughes, 2024). The main evidence source for this chapter is an evaluation of the Homes in Community Hands programme led by the authors (Arbell et al., 2022). This programme was a national lottery-funded initiative run by Power to Change, which ran parallel to the Community Housing Fund and sought to promote the growth of community-led housing in five predominantly urban areas. This chapter draws on learning from this evaluation in relation to the roles played by these five enabler hubs in meeting specific challenges of urban areas which had hitherto been seen by many as less fruitful locations for community-led housing compared to rural areas. The evaluation was composed of eighty-two qualitative interviews, two in-depth case studies, a survey and monitoring data to develop a contribution story for the programme. The evaluation followed the five hubs over three years.

The chapter begins by reviewing the emergence of community-led housing in England, drawing on the strategic niche management framework (Lang et al., 2020). It moves on to review developments in the period between the establishment of the Community Housing Fund in 2016 and 2024, drawing on our Homes in Community Hands evaluation (Arbell et al., 2022) to assess the extent and nature of community-led housing growth and the strategic approach followed through the operation and impact of the five hubs.

We conclude by taking stock of the progress made in embedding community-led housing before the 2024 General Election and the prospects for further growth and potential for system change in the next period.

We discuss the extent of influence over the regime and landscape at national and sub-regional levels and identify some potential directions for future change. While the Labour Government elected in 2024 is committed to building 1.5 million homes in five years, there is little sign yet that it will diversify who builds them, and there is no policy commitment to renew the Community Housing Fund. In the absence of such a commitment, we put forward the potential role of regional strategic alliances and consider the possibility of unanticipated policy triggers for community-led housing growth (as in earlier periods).

Strategic pathways and institutional challenges in community-led housing

Origins and emergence: Community-led housing in England

Community-led housing stands at the intersection between self-organisation and state support. This has long been a space in which alternative solutions to housing challenges can emerge. For example, to provide opportunities for resident control of the building and management of their homes (including self-build and self-management), provide social bonds and inclusive communities, helping to tackle loneliness, stabilise communities in new settlements and support residents in areas of decline to take back control. It has provided a test bed for environmentally sustainable modes of construction and living and pioneered new methods of construction (McClatchey et al., 2023). Community-led housing projects often provide a higher proportion of social rented housing and more affordable homes than equivalent housing association projects (Arbell et al., 2022), and in many cases have protected this affordability in perpetuity through exemption from the Right to Buy and restrictions on the resale prices of homes. The strategic roles of community-led housing are to diversify the housing market so as to create more homes at prices people can afford and where they are needed (Nationwide Foundation, 2024). Whilst community-led housing as a concept seeks to generalise across sub-niches, we acknowledge that this variation has an important bearing on development and liveability. Sub-niches of community-led housing may express different dimensions in relation to the role of individuals and collectives, and variance in ownership and management through land acquisition, commissioning, design, construction and habitation (Parvin et al., 2011).

Yet for this potential to be realised, alignment is required between a sustained policy and investment framework, infrastructure and technical support and successful self-organisation. There have been a few periods in England when these conditions have aligned, notably with the Cooperative

Housing Agency in the 1970s, the Housing Corporation's Community Housing programme in 2010, the Empty Homes Community Grants Programme 2012–15 and the Community Housing Fund 2016–21. But these programmes have all been short-lived, with limited ability to generate lasting change in the housing system. Moreover, taking advantage of such opportunities depends on the capacity of grassroots organisations to form, organise and link with state-level actors and comply with ever-changing eligibility and access requirements, such as the requirement to be a registered provider of social housing in order to receive capital subsidy.[2]

While the development of many individual community-led housing projects was driven and partly defined by the terms of these funding programmes, the community-led housing heritage in England can be primarily understood as 'grassroots social innovations with groups forming to respond to the local situation and the values of the communities involved' (Seyfang and Smith, 2007: 585, cited by Lang et al., 2020). Although initiatives were local, they were often inspired by international models, with CLT concepts imported and adapted from the US (United States), cohousing from Scandinavia and cooperative models originating in Rochdale but recycled and refined in the housing context to 'bring democracy home' (CCH, 2009) (see also Chapter 8).

Lang et al. (2020) provided a theoretically informed analysis of the origins and emergence of community-led housing in England. Drawing on a multi-level framework and concepts of strategic niche management and regime transition (Geels, 2002) and social capital (Agger and Jensen, 2015), they traced the path taken by these grassroots social innovations towards influencing regime level actors (see Figure 2.1).

The starting point for applying niche management to community-led housing was a series of sub-niches (Level 1). Early innovations had been locally based, involved different models and organisational forms (coops, CLTs, tenant management organisations, cohousing, community anchors, wider based social enterprises etc.), different driving forces (from 'housing ourselves' to 'revitalising our neighbourhood' to 'meeting local housing need' to 'bringing empty homes into use') and resource bases (ability to harness public, collective, individual or charitable funding).

In the next stage, sub-niches began to develop new 'peak bodies' (Level 2). Variously known as 'secondaries', 'intermediaries' and 'enabling hubs', these bodies provided a range of peer exchange, coordination and promotional roles for these sub-niches. A first wave of these bodies arrived between 1975 and 1979 in the form of secondary cooperatives in Liverpool, London and Birmingham, which were formed to enable and support local/sub-regional groups of housing cooperatives to receive grants from the Cooperative Housing Agency. In 1993 the Confederation of Cooperative

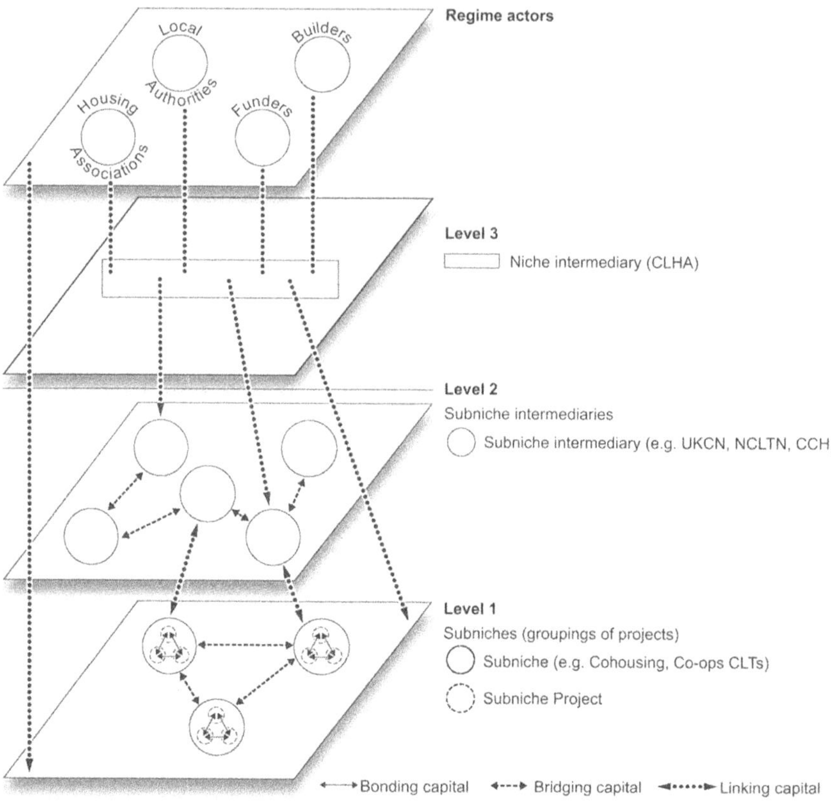

Figure 2.1 Multi-level map of community-led housing enabling in England, 2020. Graph © Lang et al., all rights reserved.

Housing was formed as the first (community-led housing) national intermediary. Later, similar developments occurred in the other sub-niches with the Community Land Trust Network formed in 2010 following a CLT Demonstration Programme 2006–08 and several earlier regionally based umbrella CLTs. The Cohousing Network (from 2007) and Self-Help Housing (from 2009) took on similar roles for these sub-niches.

Lang et al. (2020) described the characteristics of five forms of community-led housing in terms of driving force, organisational form and resource base. Drawing on Heywood (2016) they estimated numbers of projects by sub-niche. Coops were the largest sub-niche (836 coops with 169,000 homes) reflecting the longest history, the stimulus provided by the Cooperative Housing Agency in the 1970s and other public funding such as the urban renewal programme in Birmingham in the late 1970s and 1980s. CLTs were starting to grow rapidly, particularly in rural locations, and had reached

160 projects, 532 homes and a development pipeline of over 700 homes, again supported by intermediaries known as umbrella CLTs. Meanwhile, there were twenty cohousing groups with 266 homes and a pipeline of 291 homes, supported nationally by the Cohousing Network. Thanks to the Empty Homes Community Grants Programme 2012–15 and the umbrella body Self Help Housing.org, self-help housing now had 170 projects with a total of 2,750 bedrooms in use. So, before the injection of funding from Community Housing Fund in 2016 there were already well over 170,000 community-led housing homes in England and 2,200 community-led housing groups, mostly cooperatives of quite long standing. It is against this baseline that the contribution of the Community Housing Fund and related programmes such as Homes in Community Hands can be understood.

The development of sub-niche intermediaries performed three principal functions: connecting individual projects (bonding), strengthening the sense of common purpose, and making links with external actors (bridging) to secure resources and support (linking). However, to establish and sustain vertical links with regime actors required a new project to build a strategic unity between the sub-niches. Several forms of collaborations developed between sub-niche intermediaries including the Mutual Housing Group (2010–14), a group formed to extend influence and lobby for resources, and 'Getting it Built' roadshows sharing dissemination activities by the Community Land Trust Network and Cohousing Network in 2012. In the next period there was a stronger drive towards strategic unity between sub-niches (see next section).

Moore and Mullins (2013) provided an early consideration of the dilemmas of scaling up what had been defined as a small-scale locally based field. Their work highlighted how those strategies of scaling up – which could be implied to mean an increase in the size of organisations and/or in terms of professionalised partnerships and operations – could threaten grassroots community leadership that typified the resurgence of community-led housing activity in the early 2000s and 2010s. This was contrasted with more viral forms of horizontal peer-to-peer sharing and learning. Recent developments in some sub-niches imply a parallel approach of attempting to embed grassroots community-led activity into professional frameworks of planning and development.

Strategic unity and influencing regime actors?

Returning to Figure 2.1, the period that led to the 2016 Community Housing Fund saw significant mobilisation between the sub-niches and connections made with charitable foundations, politicians, mainstream housing providers and local activists (links between Level 3 intermediaries and regime actors). This created the conditions required for a historic public funding commitment. However, a more immediate political trigger was the worsening housing affordability position in Conservative-held rural constituencies with large numbers of second homes and holiday homes, leading to the lobbying of constituency Members of Parliament. Thus, the first round of the Community Housing Fund, allocated through local authorities, was targeted towards such constituencies, adding to prevalent assumptions that community-led housing was primarily relevant for rural communities. Very few urban areas were in receipt of round 1 funding through the Community Housing Fund (see next section).

A key direction in this period was an increasingly unified niche approach, symbolised by the dual leadership of the community-led housing alliance taken on by the then directors of the Community Land Trust Network and the Cohousing Network and a commitment of other key partners, i.e., the Confederation of Cooperative Housing, Self-Help Housing and Locality, to work collectively. Between 2014 and 2016, a range of partners contributed to a shared alliance building project.

Once the Community Housing Fund was established, this strategic unity was institutionalised by the formation of Community Led Homes as a partnership project between the sub-niche bodies (Level 3 in Figure 2.1). Alongside the partnership's aims to work more collectively at the national level was the decision to undertake enabling and support work for projects through geographically dispersed regional hubs which would have expertise across the sub-niches.

Extent and nature of community-led housing growth 2016–24

In 2016, discussions with the UK Government were underway concerning the types and quantum of funding required by the community-led housing sector. Reports were produced setting out how capital and revenue funding could strengthen the support infrastructure and ensure community-led housing groups transitioned through development stages (Archer, Harrington and Kear, 2018). These ideas informed the design of the Community Housing Fund, Homes in Community Hands and several other support programmes.

The Community Housing Fund consisted of a series of three short-lived tranches, allocated in a variety of ways and for three main purposes; revenue support for community-led housing groups, capital grants for the construction of their projects, and revenue funding for enabling hubs. Phase 1 began in 2016 with a proposed allocation of £60 million to local authorities. Phase 2 followed between 2018 and 2020 and was intended to combine revenue grants and capital funding through Homes England to a total of £163 million, including £38 million capital funding allocated through the Greater London Authority. In 2021–22 a much smaller allocation of £4 million was administered by Locality (an independent national membership body supporting the community sector) for revenue support only, while capital funding would now need to be secured from the mainstream Approved Development Programme.

While in theory £227 million was made available for community-led housing across the different phases of the Fund, against an original proposal for £60 million a year for five years (£300 million), there were several factors which meant that the funding to groups was significantly less than this quantum. There has been no formal evaluation of the Community Housing Fund, and the impact of the initial phase of funding for local authorities is largely unknown. This £60 million in funding was 'unrestricted' and there is no publicly available evidence of how much was drawn down and for what purposes. Qualifying authorities had little prior notice of this funding but were encouraged to work with community-led housing groups and to contact Community Led Homes. However, there was no requirement to do so. Initially they received 50% of their allocation and would get the remainder if they could demonstrate that they were spending it in support of community-led housing.

The delivery of phases 2 and 3 was hampered by several factors, not least the emergence of Covid-19, which impacted on group formation, provision of advice and support and project development. The Community Housing Fund started and stopped periodically, with short application windows and tight deadlines for drawing down grants to build and complete homes. To apply for this funding, groups needed to have either already succeeded in becoming a registered provider (usually a very lengthy process) or have a partnership with an existing registered provider who would bid on their behalf. These factors led to significant underspend on the capital element in phase 2. After phase 2, Homes England disbanded regional community-led housing teams and dedicated revenue grant funding was passed over to Locality to administer. In this phase capital funding had to be secured through generic affordable homes programmes. This was difficult for some community-led housing groups to access and did not always allow them to progress models that met their aspirations.

Despite these limitations, the Community Housing Fund demonstrated that there was increasing interest in community-led housing, with projects pipelines growing significantly. In 2021 a rigorous attempt was made to estimate the number of homes being planned by the sector (Archer and Harrington, 2021). Using data from national community-led housing bodies and enabler hubs, the authors identified 650 active community-led housing projects, planning an estimated 12,000 homes. Most homes planned (82%) were for the main government-funded affordable tenures (i.e., affordable rent, social rent or shared ownership). These projects would require £45m in revenue funding to get their schemes to the build phase, and for those at the stage of securing planning permission, an estimated £64m in capital funding would be required.

Table 2.1 draws on the Community Housing Fund Delivery Review (CLTN, 2024). This identified a pipeline of over 4,200 homes in active projects supported by the Community Housing Fund (913 were either completed or under construction). The completion of 492 homes since the Community Housing Fund began is broadly in line with standard development timescales (Archer and McCarthy, 2021).

The 2024 Delivery Review revealed that there was a strong demand for tenures not generally funded through national affordable homes programmes, and that these restrictions were suppressing delivery of the community-led homes people wanted. This problem was exemplified in our Homes in Community Hands evaluation case studies, where a group wished to replicate a successful mutual ownership tenure model but found that this could no longer be grant-funded by Homes England after phase 2 of the Community Housing Fund ended. The alternative tenure of shared ownership was described by a group interviewee as 'complicated, market based and assumes houses will be sold at market value and enable members to buy up to 100% of the home negating the aim of the CLT' (Arbell et al., 2022: 26). Furthermore, a range of cost pressures and reductions in revenue funding from non-governmental resources hampered the development of schemes.

The Community Housing Fund review revealed pent-up demand for community-led housing, signalled by revenue funding bids of £27m for a

Table 2.1 Stages of community-led housing projects supported by the Community Housing Fund

Current stage	Active projects	Affordable homes	Market homes	Unknown homes	Total homes
Concept	1	0	0	20	20
Site	56	1,228	215	173	1,616
Plan	80	1,482	104	87	1,673
Build	18	278	23	120	421
Live	36	410	15	67	492
All stages	**191**	**3,398**	357	**467**	**4,222**

Source: Community Housing Fund Delivery Review (CLTN, 2024).

£16m available in revenue funding between 2018 and 2020. Affordable housing accounted for 90% of all homes being planned, with half of the supported projects being developed on public land. The review also noted the very low failure rate (5%) among the schemes studied. It also stressed the critical role played by enabler hubs in fostering this development pipeline:

> The engagement of the community-led housing enabler hubs and advisers (the body of expertise funded under Community Housing Fund) appears to be a factor in the success of projects … We can say that, of the projects currently at the 'site' or 'plan' stages, those supported by a hub are much more likely to have submitted a planning application (41%) than those not supported (8%). (CLTN, 2024b: 1–15)

Homes in Community Hands

The Homes in Community Hands programme was created by a foundation called Power to Change, with funding from the UK National Lottery. Homes in Community Hands was developed in consultation with the sector bodies, already collaborating as Community Led Homes, and with other active funders (including the UK government) with the aim to boost the development of community-led housing with a primary focus on five urban areas. Sixty grants totalling £5 million were awarded to forty-four different organisations, including grants to five urban enabler hubs. This programme partly supported the planned development of between 4,000 and 5,000 homes (often through co-funding with the Community Housing Fund). Homes in Community Hands had in the view of stakeholder interviewees 'augmented the significant support that Community Housing Fund gave to the community-led housing partnership'; 'the national infrastructure is stronger than it has ever been' (Arbell et al., 2022: 9).

Enabler hubs – changing the multi-level map

The decision to fund five new urban hubs reflected emerging thinking in the sector that community-led groups are best supported by locally rooted organisations, who can foster and utilise relationships with partners such as local authorities, housing associations, developers, builders and landowners. These hubs would also need strong leadership as well as skills and knowledge concerning development, in addition to the ability to nurture community organisations (CLTN, 2022). This would enable the support to be well-informed about local contexts and be accessible to the grassroots.

Power to Change wanted to invest in enabling capacity in urban areas, but before doing so it commissioned research to understand what support already exists for community-led housing groups, and what is working/not working in current practice (Duncan and Lavis, 2018). Two 'vanguard projects' were established in Bristol and Leeds building on existing local partnerships between sub-niches in those cities. Further hubs were supported in the West Midlands, Liverpool and the Tees Valley. Duncan and Lavis drew on earlier experiences of secondary housing cooperatives and rural CLT umbrellas to advise on the template for the Homes in Community Hands hubs. Some key learning points were that hubs would require a stable source of grants for at least four years to gain momentum; this would be front-loaded and phased out after year four to be replaced by a mix of development fee income (based on a unit fee from projects progressing to development stage), other sources of fee income including community shares and asset ownership generating rental income. It was recognised that reliance on development fee income would require higher levels of grant funding, and it was critically stated that 'in areas of low market values it is not possible to charge high development fees without compromising the financial viability of schemes' (Duncan and Lavis, 2018: 39).

Following the niche management strategy, most of this activity was seen as generic across sub-niches; local groups in the process of forming would be able to access advice on a wide range of organisational options. This would be informed by a specialist knowledge base at national level on each of the community-led housing niches. Further national infrastructure was developed to support enabling activity at the sub-regional level; this included an accreditation scheme for project advisers, alongside a national website and training and knowledge-sharing activities.

Funding opportunities dictated the emergent geographies of sub-regional hubs with a total of twenty-six developed at the peak. The five new Homes in Community Hands hubs were located to fill perceived gaps in the national network, particularly in urban areas and areas of high deprivation.

Quantitative impact of urban enabler hubs on sector growth

One key insight from the various funding programmes for community-led housing is that investment in enabling support affects the number of community-led housing projects planned in an area. Our Homes in Community Hands evaluation used a difference-in-difference test to explore the effect of enabler hub activity on community-led housing development pipelines (Arbell et al., 2022: 45–47). This revealed that hubs funded through the Homes in Community Hands programme were, on average, supporting the development of 160 more homes than the authors would otherwise have expected. Across the five areas funded through the programme, a pipeline for over 3,216 homes was identified.

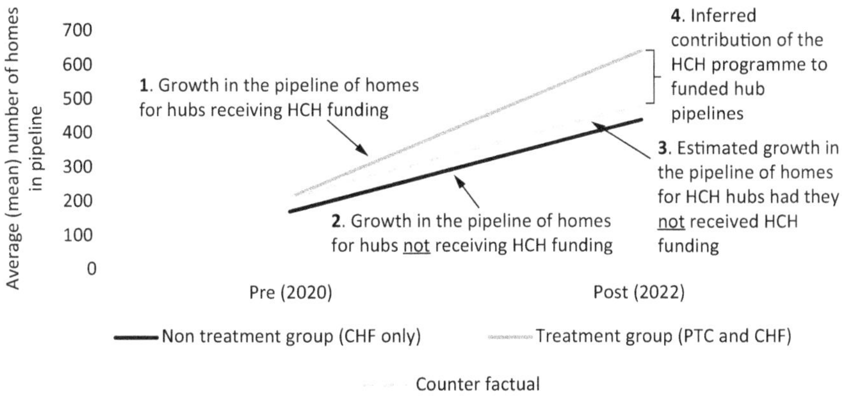

Figure 2.2 Additional homes resulting from Homes in Community Hands Hubs, 2022. Graph © Arbell et al., all rights reserved.

As Figure 2.2 shows, the combined pipelines of the funded hubs (the light grey line) were considerably higher in 2022 than the counter-factual scenario (the grey dotted line). The gap between these two lines in 2022 represents the estimated contribution of the funding to hub pipeline development (Arbell et al., 2022: 45–47).

Creating urban ecosystems of support

The focus of Homes in Community Hands on urban contexts reflected an enthusiasm to diversify the adoption and diffusion of community-led housing activity to communities of different geography, socio-economic status and identity. While community-led housing has long featured in urban development, including sub-niches such as cooperatives, self-help-housing and tenant management organisations, contemporary growth of community-led housing in the 2000s was strongly associated with rural housing delivery, reflected in significant allocations to hotbeds of rural community-led housing groups in the first tranche of the 2016 Community Housing Fund. In urban areas, longstanding cooperatives continued to operate, often managing significant portfolios of housing, while self-help housing was strengthened by dedicated government grants to support community-led purchase and leasing of empty homes.

The Homes in Community Hands programme was conceived as a way of growing community-led housing in urban areas by building on the historic success and legacy of these sub-niches. The formation of hubs, including their founding organisations or members and the partnerships they built, reflected local histories of sub-niche development, with different starting points for formation and development, including some forming from existing housing projects (Moore, 2018). In the Tees Valley, in the North East of England, the hub was hosted by an existing longstanding project in the self-help housing sub-niche, facilitating the input of stakeholders involved in the broader local self-help housing network, while others were formed as new entities within or attached to organisations involved in regeneration (as in the Liverpool City Region), from the cooperative housing sector (as was the case in the West Midlands), from the CLT movement (as in Bristol) and from an existing cross-niche partnership (Leeds Community Homes).

The Homes in Community Hands hubs were formed to help community-led housing projects respond to problems encountered in the planning and development process. Such barriers include awareness of community-led housing among communities, local policymakers and potential professional partners; access to specialist technical support and guidance for community-led groups; the need to curate relationships with professionals to facilitate new projects; and access to capital funding and important resources such as land and/or assets. Over the course of the Homes in Community Hands programme, enabling hubs achieved significant impacts, ranging from tangible policy developments to assist resource acquisition in some areas, to more qualitative perceptions of the growth in awareness of and opportunity for community-led housing. As well as influencing policy at local authority and combined authority levels, hubs also attracted powerful local actors into their membership, governance and sphere of influence, creating openings for new joint activities. In Bristol and Liverpool, lobbying by hubs helped to develop Council policies for dedicated community-led housing land release policies.

Hubs were tasked with delivering enabling support to projects as locally as possible. This support was generic across sub-niches until groups had made choices regarding specific models they wished to develop. This approach helped projects to explore unfamiliar options in preliminary stages, typically followed by more dedicated technical support from hubs bespoke to a project's local circumstances and needs. Many hubs acted as an additional resource for community-led housing groups, helping to provide advice and expertise to progress projects, drawing upon a pool of expert advisors with expertise and experience in a range of specialised skills and a range of community-led housing sub-niches. While hubs often worked on a responsive basis, supporting groups who approached them with enquiries, their organisational models also involved developing collaborative structures of governance and outreach to under-represented diverse communities (Hendrickson et al., 2024).

Hubs also sought to develop professional relationships with regime-level actors to enhance conditions for community-led housing growth. This included stakeholder mapping and targeted engagement to align community-led housing with statutory priorities. However, some hubs encountered difficulties in embedding community-led housing within local strategy and policy, and relationships were often dependent upon the enthusiasm of key personnel rather than permanent, institutionalised structures and long-term support.

Discussion and conclusions

Whilst centred on community-led housing in England, these findings highlight important learning points for the development of collaborative housing internationally. Government policy and funding was welcome and important in facilitating initial growth of community-led housing in England, but such initiatives needed to be longer-term and more consistent and reliable to achieve successful institutionalisation. Similarly, the infrastructure changes stimulated by funding programmes represented a positive shift in the growth and recognition of community-led housing solutions, but the expiry of funding before enabler hubs were fully established limited the establishment of community-led housing as a niche innovation.

As a consequence, wider landscape change has been very limited and new community-led housing projects encounter similar challenges to those experienced by innovators prior to the establishment of the funding and policy interventions discussed in this chapter. In this sense, one may reflect that little has changed. However, the development of urban ecosystems of support and linkages with devolved policy and funding to forms of sub-regional governance in England offer opportunities to build on the important contribution made by hubs and projects in recent years. We encourage readers to reflect on the differences in funding programmes, enabling infrastructure and broad policymaking on housing and planning in their places and – with the lessons outlined below – whether they can pre-empt the mistakes made in England, or refine the more successful processes adopted here.

Growing the sector

As expected, community-led housing has grown, albeit modestly, from the 2016 baseline. Table 2.1 identifies a pipeline of over 4,000 Community Housing Fund-funded homes, with nearly 400 at the live stage by 2024 (CLTN, 2024b). Enabling infrastructure established in association with the Community Housing Fund helped facilitate this growth. Social media posts celebrate the progress of innovative projects, including two case studies tracked in our Homes in Community Hands evaluation report at Lowfield Green and Stirchley (Arbell et al., 2022: 21–39). Latent demand for community-led housing opportunities was evidenced by revenue grant applications, and urban hubs have helped to realise this demand. Figure 2.2 estimates additional community-led housing homes being delivered through these hubs. Such evidence has supported optimism on the wider role that community-led housing might play in the future, with CLTs alone said to be capable of adding up to 278,000 community-led homes through a mix of housing association and developer partnerships, small parts of large mixed tenure new communities and regeneration, suburban infill and CLT solo projects (CLTN, 2023). A sign that community-led housing could break through from niche roles came from the national homeless charity, Shelter (2024), whose call to 'create new ways of delivering' social rent homes to tackle homelessness included 7,600 CLT homes and bringing 7,100 empty homes into use each year.

Beyond Community Housing Fund-funded projects, broader measures of sector growth include an increase in active CLTs in England and Wales from 20 in 2008 to over 350 in 2023 (CLTN, 2023; 2024), while cohousing has also expanded since 2016, with eleven new-build and fifteen retro-fit completions and a pipeline of sixty projects (UKCN, 2024). New housing coops are emerging alongside other forms of self-help housing. This sustained interest in community-led housing reflects broader housing market problems and inadequacies of mainstream housing.

Changing sector architecture

In addition to numerical growth, our findings highlight the limitations of the niche management growth of community-led housing. Niches are where learning and innovation occur at localised levels and in experimental ways. The Community Housing Fund and related investments after 2016 represented opportunities to develop strategic unity between the sub-niches of community-led housing and to combine action to influence policy regimes and the wider landscape.

The second section of this chapter provided an analysis of the mobilisation across the sub-niches and engagement with key actors at regime level that led to the 2016 Community Housing Fund. Strategic unity was symbolised by the establishment of Community Led Homes as a cross-niche vehicle to take forward the project. Community Led Homes initiated key system changes including a national website and accredited advisers, joining up funding programmes to support projects at each stage of their development.

One positive but short-lived change early in the Community Housing Fund was the designation of community-led housing advisers in each of the regional offices of Homes England to process revenue and capital funding applications. These posts gave direct access to a key regime actor at regional level but were discontinued after phase 2 of the Fund. Thereafter, capital grant funding had to be applied for through generic affordable housing programmes and these programmes did not support some tenure models favoured by community-led housing groups.

The most significant change to system architecture was the emergence of up to twenty-six hubs operating mainly at sub-regional levels. These hubs operated across sub-niches and enabled more direct contact with regime level actors. While enabler hubs have a strong record of facilitating community-led housing in rural areas such as the south-west (Ward, 2024), Homes in Community Hands marked the emergence of similar models more relevant to urban contexts. As demonstrated in the third section of this chapter, hubs had a significant impact in building local ecosystems of support for community-led housing in the five urban areas, with connections made between actors across the wider subregion. While resources were quite limited and diminished as grants expired, and relationships were often informal and based on individuals, these connections provided the opportunity for ongoing collaborations after the Homes in Community Hands funding ended (e.g., for land assembly, community asset transfers and peer learning).

By 2021, the new community-led housing infrastructure map had expanded, but its full institutionalisation was stalled by the premature closure of the Community Housing Fund in 2022 and the gradual phasing out of Homes in Community Hands' investment in hubs from 2021. As in previous periods, state support for community-led housing had been short-lived and pipelines of projects assembled by the hubs proved difficult to progress. Research at the end of the Homes in Community Hands project charted the disappointments entailed in scaling back activity that had only recently been established. Hub funding models premised on grant being replaced by development fees and other earned income (Duncan and Lavis, 2018) proved to be over-optimistic in urban areas. In the view of some interviewees, these models were less applicable there because of longer timelines for complex regeneration projects, greater social capital barriers to community empowerment and less straightforward financial models for development partners. The loss of grant funding for early-stage work with groups, and later the loss of core funding for hub staff, further contributed to stalling pipelines. Nationally more than half of the hubs funded from all sources had effectively folded, while others offered a reduced service (CLTN, 2024).

Despite these challenges, the legacy of Homes in Community Hands, through its investments in the hubs, is seen in the lasting impacts on sub-regional landscapes. By 2024, one Homes in Community Hands hub was becoming an asset-holding registered provider with a continued enabling programme, while two were continuing to operate as unfunded partnerships, one with short-term support from three housing association partners, the other having moved to a new community sector host. Two hubs had dissolved, but community-led housing work continues to benefit from the collaborative partnerships, land disposal policies, that had been brokered by hubs.

With the continued devolution of functions to elected mayors under the 2024 Labour Government there is potential for support ecosystems to become more formally embedded. Earlier devolution of capital funding for affordable housing to the Greater London Authority had allowed the Community Led Housing London hub to work more closely with a dedicated £38 million community-led housing fund over five years, partially accounting for the higher level of output there than in most urban areas. Recently the Greater London Authority Housing Committee launched an inquiry into the future of community-led housing to understand how communities have benefitted and the net gain for housing delivery from the fund. Results will be important for wider urban community-led housing strategies. In London, projects required a connection to the hub in order to secure GLA capital funding; this is a feature that CLTN has subsequently recommended for all hubs (CLTN, 2024).

Changing the landscape?

Despite this growth, there are limits in the extent to which community-led housing has taken on a more mainstream role in the English housing system and there remain significant barriers to moving in this direction. A leading activist sums up the limited extent to which the achievement of more 'homes in community hands' have been matched by wider systems change:

> The wider community-led sector in the UK is stuck on the fringes of additionality and exceptionalism, frustrated by being frozen out of mainstream policy and access to funding and finance ... What if power and resources to build our neighbourhoods were in community hands. (Mean, 2024).

Community-led housing remains a niche, or indeed a series of loosely connected sub-niches. These niches have limited ability to influence the national landscape in terms of policy, finance and land allocation systems. This relative powerlessness to catalyse community activism into radical social change is a product of deep-seated forces structuring our economy and society. The most potent force is the financialisation of housing and the view of houses as assets to generate a return rather than homes to be lived in to provide a stable base for a healthy society. Community-led housing interventions seeking to take housing out of the market to protect affordability and control rents and prices in perpetuity swim against a powerful neoliberal tide and require buy-in from many potential allies. More specific barriers include the requirement for involvement of registered providers in securing capital funding from Homes England and in aspects of planning. Securing partnerships with mainstream registered providers has often been problematic due to differing logics and values, while forming new registered providers is a difficult and time-consuming process. The earlier experience of the Empty Homes Grant Programme, which was specifically designed to enable non-registered providers to become involved in housing refurbishment and management, highlighted a significant limitation of the Community Housing Fund in enabling greater community involvement in housing.

These limitations are not surprising, as a key tenet of niche management theory is that landscapes are highly institutionalised and slow to change (see Chapter 7). Generally, niche actors can have little direct influence on landscape change; niches are where learning and innovation occur often at very localised and experimental level. Community-led housing actors continue to talk about the need to 'rewire the system', reflecting the barriers such as inflexible planning decisions that even successful projects have faced, and which continue to limit replication and constrain the extent to which project learning can be passed on to system change.

Influencing the regime?

In the lead-up to the 2024 UK general election, the main political parties outlined their visions for housing, acknowledging the current state of crisis. Manifestos centred on increasing housing supply, with the Conservatives committing to changes in environmental planning, brownfield land, densification and urban regeneration, and changes to planning rules. Labour favoured changes to land compensation and compulsory purchase rules to bring forward land for development, mandatory local housebuilding targets and to add 1.5 million additional homes within the next parliament. Neither Labour nor the Conservatives committed to increased funding for social or affordable homes. The Liberal Democrats promised more new affordable homes and made specific commitments to community-led development in towns and cities (Liberal Democrats, 2024). However, few details were given as to how this would be enacted.

While the Conservatives had enacted some policies favourable to community-led housing whilst in government, and the Liberal Democrats' commitments reported above followed their earlier lead on the Empty Homes Community Grants Programme from within the 2010 Coalition

Government, Labour may be the party least supportive of community-led housing despite historic links with the cooperative movement. Labour's determination to 'back the builders' (Labour, 2024) to meet the ambitious 1.5 million homes target via planning reforms has been read as implicit support for the dominant market actors, who develop most new homes in the UK (Archer, 2024). There is little sign yet that in trying to rapidly increase housing supply, Labour will diversify who builds those homes. Without specific community-led housing policy commitments, government support for community-led housing still seems uncertain, but there is no lack of creative thinking within the sector.

Hughes (2024) reviews the potential contribution that community-led housing could make to the Government's housebuilding targets, particularly in mobilising trust to overcome local opposition to new homes and in providing additional affordable homes with wider social benefits. She highlights the importance of enabling hubs in facilitating scaling up and professionalisation while maintaining independence and grassroot links. Ward (2024) reviews the 'tailored technical support' and 'strategic scaling' deployed by rural enabler hubs and housing association partnerships to achieve significant CLT expansion in the south-west. Proposals from national infrastructure bodies for 'growth labs' focus on diffusing and replicating delivery models that assume an element of standardisation and may appeal to funders and professional partners (CLTN, 2024a).

Thinking beyond this strategic sector agenda, it is worth remembering that previous opportunities for community-led housing often came from the periphery of the policy agenda. In 2012, £50 million of funding for the Empty Homes Community Grants Programme was triggered by the need to give substance to a rhetorical policy agenda of Big Society and Localism. Similarly, the immediate trigger to the Community Housing Fund was the rural second homes and holiday homes impact on Conservative constituencies. So, what are the possible triggers for community-led housing support associated with Labour's growth agenda?

Some possibilities include the need to secure a higher proportion of 'affordable homes' in new developments, difficulties faced by registered providers in taking these homes forward and the potential to partner with community-led housing groups to generate greater diversity in supply and housing/community management. Larger-scale new settlements provide another potential opportunity for community-led housing organisations to offer community governance and public realm solutions to stabilise new communities through social infrastructure; a new wave of garden cities closer to Ebenezer Howard's heritage (Howard, 1902). Recent Homes England (2024) support for a private development with a significant cohousing component may signal wider acceptance of this 'community stabiliser' role in new settlements.

The Independent Commission on Neighbourhoods was launched at the Labour Party Conference (Local Trust, 2024), expressing commitment to community-led approaches to regeneration and potentially aligning with the self-help housing sector's ambition to support regeneration and retrofit of empty properties. This work could be accelerated by supplementing current commercial borrowing with low-interest loans from the Public Works Loans Board and by restoring a dedicated funding stream like the 2012 EHCGP (Northern Tribes, 2024).

All the above could be taken up by urban community-led housing hubs by forging partnerships with combined authorities, local authorities and housing associations. It remains to be seen to what extent the continued neoliberal regime influences will drive Labour's new housing growth agenda away from these collaborative possibilities. Our optimistic conclusion is that urban hubs have provided platforms to negotiate strategic alliances with regional and local government. Future devolved funding to Combined Authorities could accelerate the role of community-led housing in sub-regional landscape change. Such partnerships have much to learn from other cities with more comprehensive public policy and community alliances for community-led housing such as Vienna (Lang and Stoeger, 2018) and Barcelona (Larsen, 2020).

Acknowledgements

Thank you to the five Homes in Community Hands hubs for their contribution to the underlying research that informs this chapter, based in Tees Valley, the Liverpool City Region, West of England, Leeds and West Midlands City Region. Thanks are also due to Jon Fitzmaurice for valuable insights and commentary, the Community Land Trust Network for sharing data and ideas, and Power to Change for funding the authors to conduct the Homes in Community Hands evaluation.

Notes

1 These national bodies include the Confederation of Cooperative Housing, the National CLT Network, Self-Help Housing and the UK Cohousing Network.
2 Registered providers are landlords registered with the Regulator of Social Housing, a statutory body established by Parliament. Registration is required to secure financial support from Homes England. There is a rigorous application

process and ongoing regulatory compliance system. Community-led housing groups face a key strategic choice between a lengthy registration process or partnering with an existing RP who may not share community-led housing values (see discussion section later in this chapter).

References

Agger, A., and J. O. Jensen (2015), 'Area-based initiatives – and their role in bonding, bridging and linking social capital', *European Planning Studies*, 25:10, 2045–61.

Arbell, Y., T. Archer, T. Moore, D. Mullins, and M. Rafalowicz-Campbell (2022), *Homes in Community Hands: Year Three Evaluation* (Power to Change). Available at www.shu.ac.uk/centre-regional-economic-social-research/projects/all-projects/homes-in-community-hands-evaluation (accessed 9 March 2026).

Archer, T. (2024), 'Delivering 1.5m homes: Why we need a diverse and competitive housebuilding industry'. Available at https://redbrickblog.co.uk/2024/05/diverse-competitive-housebuilding/ (accessed 9 March 2026).

Archer, T., C. Harrington, and A. Kear (2018), 'Targeting funding to support community-led housing'. Available at www.powertochange.org.uk/wp-content/uploads/2018/08/TargetingFunding-_final.pdf (accessed 9 March 2026).

Archer, T., and C. Harrington (2021), 'Delivering the Community Led Housing Pipeline in England'. Available at https://nationwidefoundation.org.uk/wp-content/uploads/2021/09/Delivering-the-Communtiy-Led-Housing-Pipeline-in-England-FINAL.pdf (accessed 9 March 2026).

Archer, T., and A. McCarthy (2021), 'Community-led Housing and Speed of Development'. Available at https://nationwidefoundation.org.uk/wp-content/uploads/2021/10/Speed-of-Development-Briefing-Note-Final.pdf (accessed 9 March 2026).

CCH (2009), *Bringing Democracy Home* (Commission on Cooperative and Mutual Housing). Available at www.cch.coop/wp-content/uploads/2015/07/bdh-commission-report.pdf (accessed 9 March 2026).

CLTN (2022), 'Enabling Community Land Trusts'. Available at www.communitylandtrusts.org.uk/working-together/enabling-clts/ (accessed 9 March 2026).

CLTN (2023), 'State of the Community Land Trust Sector 2023'. Available at www.communitylandtrusts.org.uk/wp-content/uploads/2023/03/State-of-the-Sector-2023-PRESS-1.pdf (accessed 9 March 2026).

CLTN (2024a), 'Unveiling the Community Led Housing Growth Lab'. Available at www.communitylandtrusts.org.uk/news-and-events/unveiling-the-community-led-housing-growth-lab/ (accessed 9 March 2026).

CLTN (2024b), 'Community Housing Fund Delivery Review'. Available at www.communitylandtrusts.org.uk/wp-content/uploads/2024/09/CHF-Delivery-Review-2024.pdf (accessed 9 March 2026).

Czischke, D., C. Carriou, and R. Lang (2020), 'Collaborative Housing in Europe: Conceptualising the Field', *Housing Theory and Society*, 37:1, 1–9.

Duncan, P., and J. Lavis (2018), 'Delivering a community-led housing enabling hub service: experience and lessons from existing practice'. Power to Change Research Institute. Available at https://eprints.icstudies.org.uk/id/eprint/76/1/WP-2018-06-Delivering%20a%20community-led%20housing%20enabling%20hub%20service.pdf (accessed 9 March 2026).

Geels, F. W. (2002), 'Technological Transitions as evolutionary reconfiguration processes: A multi-level perspective and case study', *Research Policy*, 31:8–9, 1257–74.
Hendrickson, C., H. Baptiste, T. Moore, and Y. Arbell (2024), 'Community-led housing for all'. Available at https://nationwidefoundation.org.uk/wp-content/uploads/2024/10/Community-led-housing-for-all_FINAL.pdf (accessed 9 March 2026).
Heywood, A. (2016), *Local Housing, Community Living: Prospects for Scaling Up and Scaling Out Community-led Housing* (London: Smith Institute).
Homes England (2024), 'Homes England goes to TOWN for Northstowe co-housing project'. Available at www.gov.uk/government/news/homes-england-goes-to-town-for-northstowe-co-housing-project (accessed 9 March 2026).
Howard, E. (1902), *Garden Cities of Tomorrow* (London: Swann Sonnenschein & Co).
Hughes, P. (2024), 'Enabling Community-led Housing in England', *Heseltine Institute for Public Policy, Series 3 Briefing*, 16. Available at www.liverpool.ac.uk/media/livacuk/publicpolicyamppractice/pbseries3/PB16,combined,final.pdf (accessed 9 March 2026).
Labour Party (2024), Change: Labour Party Manifesto 2024. Available at https://labour.org.uk/wp-content/uploads/2024/06/Labour-Party-manifesto-2024.pdf
Lang, R., P. Chatterton, and D. Mullins (2020), 'Grassroots Innovations in Community-led Housing in England: the Role and Evolution of Intermediaries', *International Journal of Urban Sustainable Development*, 12:1, 52–72.
Lang, R., and H. Stoeger (2018), 'The role of local institutional context in understanding collaborative housing models: Empirical evidence from Austria', *International Journal of Housing Policy*, 18:1, 35–54.
Larsen, H. G. (2020), 'Barcelona: Housing Crisis and Urban Activism', in P. Hagbert, H. G. Larsen, H. Thorn, and C. Wasshede (eds), *Contemporary Co-housing in Europe: Towards Sustainable Cities?* (London: Routledge), pp. 74–93.
Liberal Democrats (2024), 'For a Fair Deal: Manifesto 2024'. Available at www.libdems.org.uk/manifesto (accessed 9 March 2026).
Local Trust (2024), 'Independent Commission on Neighbourhoods'. Available at https://localtrust.org.uk/news-and-stories/news/press-release-independent-commission-on-neighbourhoods-launches/ (accessed 9 March 2026).
McClatchley, R., E. McClymont, L. Griffin, and L. Carmichael (2023), 'Community-led housing, health and wellbeing: A comprehensive literature review', *International Journal of Housing Policy*, 25:1, 1–38, https://doi.org/10.1080/19491247.2023.2232200
Mean, M. (2024), 'Towards the people-powered housing manifesto we need', *We Can Make*. Available at https://medium.com/@wecanmake/towards-the-people-powered-housing-manifesto-we-actually-need-100adbf941d2 (accessed 9 March 2026).
Moore, T. (2018), 'Replication through partnership: the evolution of partnerships between community land trusts and housing associations in England', *International Journal of Housing Policy*, 18:1, 82–102.
Moore, T., and D. Mullins (2013), 'Scaling up or going viral? Comparing self-help housing and community land trust facilitation', *Voluntary Sector Review*, 4:3, 333–53.
Mullins, D. (2018), 'Achieving policy recognition for community-based housing solutions: the case of self-help housing in England', *International Journal of Housing Policy*, 18:1, 143–45.

Nationwide Foundation (2024), 'Decent and Affordable Homes for All: Five Proposals for a Fairer Housing System'. Available at https://nationwidefoundation.org.uk/our-programmes/decent-and-affordable-homes-for-all-five-proposals-for-a-fairer-housing-system/ (accessed 9 March 2026).

Northern Tribes (2024), *Community Housing – The Northern Way: Regenerating Neighbourhoods* (Hull: Giroscope).

Parvin, A., A. Saxby, C. Cerulli, and T. Schneider (2011), 'A Right to Build: The Next Mass-housebuilding Industry'. Available at https://static1.squarespace.com/static/5a9837aa8f513076715a4606/t/5eac3dafcdbffc0abd29ce95/1588346311289/RIGHT+TO+BUILD_LR.pdf (accessed 9 March 2026).

Seyfang, G., and A. Smith (2007), 'Grassroots innovations for sustainable development: towards a new research and policy agenda', *Environmental Politics*, 16:4, 584–603.

Shelter (2024), 'Brick by Brick: A Plan to Deliver the Social Homes We Need'. Available at https://england.shelter.org.uk/professional_resources/policy_and_research/policy_library/brick_by_brick (accessed 9 March 2026).

UKCN (2024), 'UKCN Co-Design and Cohousing Summit, October 2024'. Available at https://cohousing.org.uk/news/report-uk-cohousing-summit-2024/ (accessed 8 April 2026).

Ward, A. (2024), 'The impact of technical support for Community Land Trusts'. MBA Dissertation, Cardiff University.

3

The transformative role of institutional capabilities: The diffusion of the community land trust model in Belgium between community agency and political will

Verena Lenna, Nele Aernouts

Introduction

In a relatively short time, community land trusts (CLTs) have become known in various parts of the world for their anti-speculative approach. CLTs consist mostly of housing and other built units owned by individual entities – households or organisations – and land owned by an association or foundation. Since the land is never sold, this approach ensures the affordability of built units in perpetuity for current and future generations. The mechanism that ultimately retains the ownership of the land in the hands of the CLT, away from the speculative dynamics of the market, is a tripartite governance structure that equally distributes decisional power across the public, private and civil society actors involved. This avoids arbitrary decisions on the assets owned by the CLT. Additionally, this governance system empowers individuals and communities by involving future residents, local authorities and the surrounding neighbourhood in the site's development through inclusive, participatory activities and organisation.

Literature on CLTs – scientific and for practitioners – covers a variety of aspects. A significant body of research has examined the viability of CLTs as a potential solution to the current housing crisis. CLT advocates have shared key methods and best practices to support their broader adoption. They have provided an overview of how the CLT model can be adapted to various contexts, ranging from Europe to Latin America and North America to Africa, addressing issues such as racism, discrimination, gentrification and displacement while promoting ownership, community and empowerment (Davis, 2010; Davis, Algoed and Hernández-Torrales, 2020) (see Chapter 12). Research has also explored their common ideological foundation, the realisation of specific CLT projects, the challenges and demands to accelerate their development, their applicability in different contexts and the success factors. Regarding the Community Land Trust Brussels (CLTB), over thirty publications, comprising books, articles, studies and dissertations, have been written, in addition to extensive annual reports since 2012. These studies cover topics similar to the international CLT literature, such as architectural innovations, development processes, the communal and empowering nature of CLTs, legal aspects and the reconceptualisation of property rights (Aernouts and Ryckewaert, 2018; Lenna, 2019b; 2019a; Vercellone, 2020). In addition, the Ghent CLT has been the focus of detailed analyses of its development and challenges, aimed at facilitating future renovation projects for low-income households.[1] Furthermore, feasibility studies of the three existing CLTs in Belgium are publicly available, providing a comprehensive understanding of their emergence, the political views on their effectiveness and their initial approaches (Petry, 2023).

While much of the current research is limited to the technical or social aspects of CLTs, less research has focused on their political impact. Here, 'political' refers to the processes of dialogue, negotiation, and collective decision-making among actors with differing interests and perspectives (Healey, 2005). This is despite CLTs' *raison d'être*: addressing the housing question as an inherently political matter; a matter of power relations and collective negotiation. The existing literature mainly highlights the role of political parties in supporting CLTs' development and the role of communities and local organisations as catalysts. However, to our knowledge, little research has explored the political impact of CLTs, particularly as societal and institutional transformation.

In this contribution, we will address the political impact by looking at the establishment of three CLTs in Belgium. We conceptualise their development as a process of expanding community agency while continuously navigating the challenges and favourable conditions of their operational environment. In this view, the angle of the capabilities approach (Nussbaum, 1988; 1992; Sen, 1993) seems particularly adequate as, according to this framework, the effectiveness of a given action is not a matter of the exclusive responsibility of a single individual or entity, CLTs, in this case. In contrast, the capabilities approach foregrounds operational conditions, questioning how responsibilities are distributed and how other actors involved normatively contribute to individual capabilities. Adopting the theoretical framework of the capabilities approach enables an understanding of CLTs' mission and purpose to realise the right to housing from a larger ecosystemic point of view. As such, the approach shifts the focus from what is framed as an abstract and individual right to examining the societal conditions contributing to its fulfilment, thereby highlighting the need and potential for a broader political transformation. This seems particularly relevant for CLTs, as their tripartite governance structure, including public, collective and private actors, is *de facto* meant to fuel such a transformation. As we shall explain, the deployed collective capabilities of CLTs are not only about the resilience of the organisation or the fulfilment of the needs of its individual members and actors (as defined in the literature) but are – at a more fundamental level – about the transformation of the culture and institutions of homeownership and land tenure (Lenna, 2024).

On these grounds, we will first describe the geneses and development processes of the three CLTs in Belgium.[2] Their establishment is conceptualised as a result of community agency seeking to provide perpetually affordable housing, on the one hand, and political will and partnerships as the environmental or operational conditions of these organisations, on the other.[3] Next, we will introduce the concept of collective capabilities, developed to respond simultaneously to collective agency and environmental conditions. Building on the existing literature, we recognise three forms of collective capabilities; in particular, we introduce a new category named 'institutional capabilities', i.e., capabilities aiming at a societal institutional[4] transformation, ultimately resulting in political impact. From this perspective, political will is not simply passively accepted or reacted to but is shaped at a cultural level. A brief conclusion summarises the collective capabilities of the studied CLTs, particularly in terms of institutional transformation.

Variations on a theme: Community land trusts in Belgium

Belgium offers a valuable case for studying the political implications of CLTs' development, given the country's relatively long history with CLTs, starting with CLTB in 2012. This provides a temporal perspective necessary for understanding the political impact of CLTs. Additionally, the different levels of progress of CLTs in Brussels, Ghent and Leuven highlight the role of political support and other factors, such as regional differences between Flanders and Brussels and the varying involvement of actors in each city.

Housing activism and the variable of government support: Community Land Trust Brussels

The emergence of CLTB was closely tied to the significant rise in housing prices between 2000 and 2010 as well as the shortage of social housing, which spurred the creation of local activist groups and non-profit organisations focused on affordable housing solutions.[5] Le CIRÉ, one of the participating associations involved from the start, established a solidarity savings group in 2004, enabling low-income families to accumulate the capital needed to enter the housing market. Beyond financial support, the association emphasised participation, training and empowerment of its members.

In 2007, Bonnevie, a community centre in Molenbeek, one of Brussels' most socio-economically disadvantaged areas, initiated the L'Espoir project, which provided affordable and passive housing units. By 2009, fourteen families had become official owners of these homes. While this project demonstrated the feasibility of creating affordable, energy-efficient housing for economically disadvantaged groups, it also highlighted the necessity of government subsidies to scale such efforts and the need for new models to make affordable housing more widely accessible. This led to the exploration of the CLT model as a potential solution.

After visiting the CLT Champlain Housing Trust in Burlington, Vermont, in early 2011, fifteen associations, including the associations and community centre mentioned above, formed a platform to promote CLTB and convinced the Minister of Housing of the Brussels Capital Region, Christos Doulkeridis of Green political party Ecolo, to commission a feasibility study. Completed in June 2012, the study provided a comprehensive overview of the CLT model, analysed the housing situation in Brussels and outlined how a CLT could address specific local issues. It included recommendations for target groups, operational structures, sale and resale prices, contractual agreements, organisational structure and a detailed proposal for two sites in Molenbeek and Anderlecht.

The positive results of the study, coupled with the Green Party's interest in alternative social housing models, led the minister to allocate a budget of €200,000 to develop CLTB's legal structures, communicate about the project, recruit potential residents and plan the proposed sites. A team of four employees established a Foundation of Public Utility (Fondation d'Utilité Publique) that would own the land and a non-profit organisation to manage daily operations. By December 2012, the platform had been rebranded as CLTB, and the non-profit board – comprising equal representation of future residents and involving non-profits and regional authorities – was officially installed. In 2013, CLTB purchased its first building, Le Nid in Anderlecht, inaugurating the first CLT on the European mainland (Lenna, 2019b; 2019a) (see Figure 3.1). The renovation project focused on a blend of housing affordability, high energy efficiency and accessibility for people with reduced mobility, with a semi-public interior courtyard and communal spaces for residents and neighbours. The inhabitants moved in in 2020, after a long and complicated renovation process which taught CLTB important lessons about participatory dynamics, as a key aspect of CLTB's approach to the realisation of the projects. Arc-en-Ciel in Molenbeek was the first newly built project, with thirty-two housing units, an interior garden and a community space. L'Écluse, on the other hand, has been the first inhabited CLTB project, inaugurated in 2015 by adopting CLTB property and governance models for a previously realised housing building. As of

Figure 3.1 The project Le Nid (CLTB), 2024. Photo © Verena Lenna, all rights reserved.

now, six projects have been completed, with six more in progress. CLTB aims to provide twenty to thirty new homes annually, with a goal of 1,000 housing units by 2030.

CLTB quickly established itself as a leading CLT in Belgium, outpacing other initiatives, such as CLT Ghent. However, its development was not without challenges. The adaptation of the Anglo-Saxon CLT model to the Belgian context faced scepticism from politicians, necessitating complex legal adjustments to enable the separation of land and building ownership and secure political support for the model's implementation (Lenna, 2019b; De Pauw and Aernouts, 2022).

After the 2014 elections, Green Party Ecolo was no longer part of the Brussels governing coalition, and the new administration's stance on CLTB shifted. The new Minister of Housing, Céline Fremault of the Christian Democratic Party (CDH), along with the coalition consisting of the Socialist Party (PS) and the Liberal Party (DéFI), showed less interest in alternative social housing models. The regional policy statement of October 2018 indicated that the CLT mechanism would be reassessed and potentially transferred to public service institutions such as the autonomous urban development company Citydev or the cooperative company Fonds du Logement (Housing

Fund), with alternative property acquisition methods being explored as well, potentially jeopardising CLTB's existence. With its first pilot project Le Nid yet to be inhabited, the policy shift felt like a threat to the community-based governance model, potentially reverting to traditional public processes. Additionally, despite the previous government's assurance of funding until 2018, CLTB faced challenges due to the lack of a long-term financial perspective. The loss of collaboration with Fonds du Logement, which had supported CLTB's intensive architectural and construction needs, compounded these difficulties. As CLTB scaled up its projects, it was compelled to seek new financing and partners, including European support options.

At that moment, two things occurred that changed the course of events for CLTB. In 2017, Sustainable Housing for Inclusive and Cohesive Cities (SHICC), an EU-funded research programme on the viability, support and promotion of the CLT model, was established. SHICC boosted the reputation of CLTB on a European level, thus strengthening its position in its negotiations with the government of the Brussels Capital Region.[6] Not long after, the European Union programme UIA[7] provided a €1.5 million subsidy to develop a CLT project in Brussels, based on a collaboration with various Brussels associations, whose construction would be financed by a cooperative investment scheme (Smetcoren et al., 2022). With the support of EU funding and a growing international interest in the project, CLTB not only continued innovating its model but also engaged in new partnerships in the Brussels context,[8] thus increasing political pressure.

CLTB's efforts and achievements were finally acknowledged with several prizes.[9] In 2019, new elections resulted in a government consisting of a coalition between the PS, Ecolo and DéFI. This provided the final push to further integrate CLTB into the official functioning of the housing market. Through increased funding, the full integration of CLTB in the housing code and its recognition as a social housing actor, the coalition decreased taxes on the cost of construction from 21% to 6% and established challenging goals to be achieved as part of the agreement with the government.

A pioneering initiative in Flanders: Community Land Trust Ghent

Ghent explored the CLT model around the same time as CLTB in Brussels. The community building association Saamo Ghent spearheaded this effort by drafting a memorandum on CLTs in April 2010, which garnered positive feedback from housing stakeholders, civil society and politicians. By 2011, the Flemish Ministry of Housing and Social Economy commissioned a feasibility study for a CLT in Ghent, led by Saamo and potential long-term partners. Published in October 2012, the study outlined the CLT model and its applicability to Ghent, including a proposed mission, vision and operational plan. The study emphasised the importance of involving future residents and civil society organisations from the outset. This led to the formation of a group of twenty active prospective residents and discussion panels to define the project's goals. Over forty civil society organisations, experts and different local governments signed a charter to establish CLT Ghent.

In July 2013, CLT Ghent hosted an international conference that attracted interest from across Europe and featured key figures from the CLT movement. By bringing other organisations on board, including the social housing company WoninGent, the Flemish Chief Architect,[10] the local public welfare centre OCMW Ghent and the non-profit SIVI,[11] Saamo sought to take CLT Ghent's development to a new level.

By December 2013, CLT Ghent was legally established as a non-profit, though financial support from the Flemish government was lacking, slowing the development of a foundation to manage the land. Despite this, CLT Ghent continued its efforts, particularly with a renovation programme called 'Dampoort knapT OP!' This project aimed to help 'emergency buyers' (Bolt and Van Kempen, 2002) – those who purchase homes as long-term investments but lack the funds for necessary renovations – by using a rolling fund allowing the reuse of state subsidies for future renovations. This initiative, initiated in the neighbourhood of Dampoort, successfully progressed from early 2014 to June 2016, supporting lower-income residents and contributing to climate goals by improving energy efficiency in vulnerable households. Based on the initiative and a subsequent EU project,[12] the city upscaled the principle by installing a similar programme at the scale of the city for the period of 2022–26.

CLT Ghent's profile grew significantly with its participation in the above-mentioned SHICC project. The increasing recognition of CLT Ghent led to the formation of the Flemish CLT Coalition, a group of fifteen civil society organisations aimed at promoting the CLT model regionally. However, the coalition's activities were put on hold when CLT Ghent focused on its first housing project, avoiding potential conflicts with policymakers.

CLT Ghent's first major project involved developing a site in the neighbourhood of Meulestede. Despite initial enthusiasm, the project faced numerous delays. It took seven years to establish the necessary financial and legal frameworks and secure a building permit. In 2013, the city of Ghent proposed a leasehold on the Meulestede site as part of the broader redevelopment project, Muide Meulestede Morgen. During the long wait for the project to move forward, CLT Ghent, in collaboration with the association Saamo, fuelled community engagement by, among others, developing Supermerkade, a community-oriented affordable supermarket.

In December 2017, CLT Ghent officially created its public utility foundation, enabling it to manage land. Shortly after, the Flemish parliament launched a project to promote alternative housing forms, and CLT Ghent was selected, gaining temporary legal flexibility to advance its project. The Meulestede site became the property of SoGent, the public service autonomous urban development company, which agreed to lease the land to CLT Ghent under specific conditions, preserving the CLT's democratic structure while providing land security. The planned development features thirty-four housing units with private gardens, collective spaces and energy-efficient construction in line with nearly-zero energy (NZE) standards. The foundation stone was laid in October 2022, with the project expected to be completed by 2024 (see Figure 3.2).

The success of the renovation programme 'Dampoort knapT OP!' and CLT Ghent's involvement in the above-mentioned SHICC programme contributed to growing political support. In the 2018 local elections, all political parties in Ghent included the CLT model in their programmes. After the election, the Ghent city government – comprising the then-leading coalition of the Socialist and Green Party SP.A-Groen, the Liberal Party Open VLD and the Christian-Democratic Party CD&V – incorporated the CLT model into its policy agenda, providing additional subsidies for CLT Ghent's operations.

As CLT Ghent continues to develop, it is exploring new projects, including a smaller initiative in the neighbourhood of Mariakerke. Here, a private landowner offered a plot of land to CLT Ghent, enabling the construction

Figure 3.2 The first project of the CLT of Ghent, 2024. Photo © CLT Ghent, all rights reserved.

of two housing units. This project aims to attract private investors by demonstrating that the CLT model can be both socially beneficial and financially viable. With 140 members in 2020, including prospective inhabitants, supporting members and partner non-profits, CLT Ghent is gradually becoming a part of Ghent's social and housing landscape, showcasing both the potential and challenges of collaborative efforts in embedding the model (SHICC, 2020).

A community land trust for middle-income households: CLT Leuven

Leuven became interested in the CLT model due to the success of CLTB and CLT Ghent and broader implementation of the model in the United Kingdom and France. The first significant steps toward establishing a CLT in Leuven were taken in 2019, though initial interest was sparked in 2013 by Jong Groen, the youth wing of the Flemish Green Party, which advocated for CLTs as a solution to housing problems.

In 2019, after the 2018 elections, the Green Party alderman for housing global policy and equal opportunity, Lies Corneillie, played a crucial role in incorporating CLTs into the city's policy document for 2019–25. The document aimed to explore CLTs as a tool to address the needs of emergency buyers and proposed the city's active involvement in developing CLT projects on city-owned land. This commitment was further solidified in the city's multiyear plan, which allocated €5 million to establishing the CLT, supporting its operations and funding the first project. The alderman, who was also chairman of Leuven's public service autonomous urban development company AGSL,[13] commissioned a feasibility study on a CLT in Leuven, conducted from March 2019 to March 2020 by CLTB and the Vrije Universiteit Brussel's research group Cosmopolis, in collaboration with the city.

A steering committee was formed to oversee the study, comprising municipal actors such as the city of Leuven, AGSL and the public welfare centre (OCMW), and six associations. The feasibility study was published in 2020 and followed the structure of similar studies in Brussels and Ghent. It proposed a first CLT project on a site near the railway in the neighbourhood of Kleine Rijsel. In particular, the study identified the 'missing middle' (the third income quintile) as the primary target group: those who earn too much for social housing but not enough to purchase quality housing in Leuven. By focusing on this 'missing middle', the CLT could indirectly benefit lower-income groups by freeing up space on the rental market. The city fast-tracked approval for the chosen site, and in October 2020, a coordinator was appointed for the CLT project in Kleine Rijsel. This project, developed by AGSL, involved extensive stakeholder engagement through workshops, meetings and public information sessions (see Figure 3.3). By October 2021, a general information day attracted around sixty organisations from Leuven, Ghent, Antwerp and Amsterdam. Following these events, the project was structured into social and business parts, with the involvement of civil society organisations and businesses.

On 29 September 2022, the CLT Leuven non-profit organisation was established officially, involving thirty-two organisations. The association has a structure similar to that of CLTB and CLT Ghent, combining a non-profit for daily management with a public benefit foundation (SON) to acquire land. The CLT plans to construct nine residences with a communal space on the Kleine Rijsel site, for which a project was selected in March 2023. Construction work is supposed to begin in the summer of 2025. CLT Leuven has the ambitious plan to build 100 residences by 2030.

Community agency, partnerships and political will

The geneses and development processes of the three cases show that CLTs in Belgium emerged as multi-layered platforms, combining public,

Figure 3.3 Role-play gaming session with Leuven's local actors, KU Leuven students and academics, 2024. Photo © insist.earth, all rights reserved.

public-private, private and collective entities as an expression of community agency *vis-à-vis* the issue of the accessibility of affordable housing. Political will and partnerships can be identified as two operational and environmental conditions crucially defining community agency by compressing or expanding the possibilities of CLTs. Securing political support is essential for the CLTs developments and can take various forms. However, it is never guaranteed. Even when included in a party's election programme, the model may not be prioritised in government actions unless it is part of the governmental decision-making agenda. The other key factor in the development of CLTs is partnerships. Given the wide range of technical aspects involved in project realisation, these partnerships can be quite wide-ranging and have different roles, such as providing expertise, fostering accountability, driving innovation, securing resources – whether financial or in the form of expertise – and expanding networks.

These two factors are interwoven, continually reinforcing one another. Partnerships with well-established organisations have been crucial in convincing the government to support the CLTs, as these alliances enabled new CLTs to leverage existing expertise and networks to build trust and influence. While the development of partnerships is a result of CLTs' proactivity and agency, political support can be perceived as an external operational condition, though it is not completely unaffected by CLTs' scope of action. The CLTs employed various advocacy tactics, such as using (inter)national recognition and awards to influence government decisions, aligning their messaging with political frameworks and attracting government interest by enhancing their public image. Ultimately, we argue, political support is an outcome of the transformative political nature of CLTs and their political impact.

In the next section, we will address the political impact of CLTs by focusing on collective capabilities as inherently transformative functionings of collective organisations. Specifically, we suggest that collective capabilities are developed by CLTs to deliver affordable housing – thus realising community agency – while (strategically) dealing with operational conditions such as political will and partnerships. In particular, we introduce a specific category of capabilities that we call 'institutional capabilities'.

The transformative role of institutional capabilities

The tripartite governance of CLTs, by distributing equal decisional power to private citizens, civil society organisations and local state authorities, is a statement about housing as a political matter, a matter of urban governance and of public accountability, confirmed by the recognition of the *utilité publique* or public interest of CLT missions. Additionally, the very histories mentioned in the previous paragraphs reveal the role of local actors and communities operating with a political stance, addressing the housing question beyond the here and now of a specific community or group of citizens. Similarly, through the capability approach lens, a given functioning, a given being or doing, is a societal endeavour, as its success is not the responsibility of an isolated entity or individual. Because of the political dimension this opens, the capability approach therefore seems appropriate for discussing CLTs' political impact.

Assessing and affecting environmental conditions

The capability approach, developed by Amartya Sen and Martha Nussbaum in the 1970s (Nussbaum, 1988; 1992; Sen, 1993; 1999; Walsh, 2000), revolves around assessing the actual chances of realising valued beings and doings *vis-à-vis* the concrete conditions a given subject has to deal with. Identifying these conditions makes it possible to distinguish the factors that are in the hands of concerned subjects from those that are in the hands of other actors.

According to Sen's theorisations, the concept of capability is strictly interconnected with the concept of agency. Agency reflects the capacity of individuals to realise their goals following their values by effectively and proactively shaping their destiny and social environment (Sen, 1999; Alkire, 2008; Crocker and Robeyns, 2010; Pelenc, Bazile and Ceruti, 2015). Capabilities are the specific functionings that realise and make agency concrete and measure the effectiveness of a subject's doings and beings in achieving desired or valued purposes. By indicating the environmental conditions that make actions successful, capabilities question the context and highlight what needs to change for actions to be successful, as well as the responsible actors, pointing to expanding or reinforcing agency when capabilities are not available. The normative goal of human development can be subsumed to the improvement of people's capabilities through the exercise of their agency. Therefore, capabilities can be considered transformative indicators, continuously pointing at and triggering the transformation of the organisation or of the context towards more effective functionings, thus expanding agency.

While most attention has been dedicated to individual capabilities, more recently scholars have started to address collective capabilities as a category in and of itself, different from the sum of individual capabilities (Stewart, 2005; Deneulin, 2006; Ibrahim, 2006; Ballet, Dubois and Mahieu, 2007; Volkert, 2013). Collective capabilities can be defined as those capabilities exercised by a group – or more generally by a collective subject – that acts 'in order to secure a capability for the members of that group' (Robeyns, 2017: 116). The interaction of a group of people makes it possible to carry out actions and achieve states of being that would be impossible if individuals acted alone (Ballet, Dubois and Mahieu, 2007; Pelenc, Bazile and Ceruti, 2015).

A relevant question addressed in the literature on the capabilities approach is: how do collective initiatives and collective agency serve individual agencies? While the seed for community-oriented action is already embedded in individual motivations[14] and goals, collective initiatives enable people not only to formulate new, collectively valued goals and purposes but also to create conditions that are favourable to taking action, thus expanding and orienting individual agency towards collectively valued goals. 'Collective capabilities affect individual choices in two ways: first, they affect the individual's perception of the good (i.e., what constitutes a "valuable functioning" for him/her) and, secondly, they determine his/her ability to achieve these functionings' (Ibrahim, 2006: 404). Therefore, organisations can be seen as a means to expand individuals' agency through the emergence and performance of collective capabilities.[15] CLTs were created as a way to collectively deliver affordable housing while implementing a non-speculative model by joining the capacities and agencies of the interested communities with those of local actors and organisations.

Towards this purpose and based on the literature, collective capabilities serve individuals and individual entities by operating at two different levels, necessarily interweaving with and reinforcing each other. On one level, they ensure and support the capabilities of singular entities involved – groups and people (Pelenc, Bazile and Ceruti, 2015; Robeyns, 2017). This is also possible because, almost by definition, on a second level, collective organisations can achieve results that individuals or single entities alone would not be able to realise (Ibrahim, 2006; Ballet, Dubois and Mahieu, 2007; Pelenc, Bazile and Ceruti, 2015). They do so by pooling resources and forms of expertise but also by reshaping their goals and valued doings in consideration of a different organisational setting, converging programmes, increased capacities and critical mass.

CLTs from the angle of the capability approach

Building on this understanding, we recognise three forms of collective capabilities that enable CLTs to pursue their goals, thus expanding the agency of the involved actors concerning the right to housing: i) capabilities that ensure the functioning of each entity; ii) capabilities which respond to the needs and collective agency of several organisations coming together for a shared goal; and iii) capabilities that we call 'institutional capabilities'. The latter go beyond the organisational level and respond to CLTs' inherent political mission.

The capability to realise new housing projects and deliver affordable housing units and the capability to involve concerned local communities in the process are examples of the first dimension of collective capabilities. Greater than the sum of capacities and forms of expertise provided by each involved entity, the result secures the diverse range of capabilities expected by each involved entity: private individuals, civil society organisations and public actors. From this perspective, the abstract right to housing is fulfilled by CLTs through a bundle of different functionings, realising the agency of the different actors concerned and involved. For example, being able to access affordable housing is a desired capability of future residents. Being able to deliver affordable housing units for the target groups is a functioning of the public actors and of specific civil society organisations. Finally, for collective actors and local stakeholders, the desired functioning would be to be able to steward the common good of a given neighbourhood hosting a new CLT project. The multilayered structure of CLTs, by combining different capacities, sustains multiple functionings of the different involved actors and individuals, while redefining them towards their shared purposes.

The capabilities belonging to the second dimension are those that the single involved entities would not be able to attain without the CLTs' collective setting and that respond to CLTs' collective organisational needs. Examples of these capabilities are: guaranteeing access to credit under favourable conditions, reclaiming and renovating an abandoned building to realise affordable housing units, creating empowering and inclusive living environments that support individual emancipation, and setting up a governance structure that protects affordability in perpetuity and prevents speculative processes.

In addition to these, the capabilities of the third dimension, while relying on the combination of capacities of single entities involved and their existing agency, purposely seek to transform the operational conditions of CLTs by transforming their environment at the fundamental level of values, instigating a cultural paradigm shift around land tenure and ownership models. Some examples of these functionings are: establishing strategic partnerships, promoting dissemination, research and innovation on their projects, realising sustainably successful projects, adapting narratives to the needs of local policymakers and political entities, proving the flexibility of the model by adapting the projects to a variety of conditions, and seeking official recognition by applying for awards and acknowledgements.

All these are collective capabilities, as they describe collective functionings that enable CLTs to achieve the expected results and realise their agency. Additionally, as capabilities, they describe functionings which are also necessarily impacted by environmental and operational conditions, such as the availability of resources and expertise to successfully develop the projects, networking capacity to access research project consortia and the resources required for organisational growth. All collective capabilities of this third category have in common the attempt to increase the trust – and, as a result, the support – of local actors in both the CLT model and its underlying values and the organisations that are supposed to realise this model at a specific site.

At a fundamental level, what these capabilities achieve contributes to realising a fundamental and implicit purpose of CLTs: to sustain and institute a new culture of homeownership and land tenure. This can be seen as the long-term institutional goal of CLTs, which is at the same time an end and a means. It is an end because what ultimately matters and constitutes the core mission of CLTs, realised through their diverse configurations and formulas, is to establish more just and more sustainable homeownership and land tenure institutions. As demonstrated through their various projects and international collaborations, CLTs are strongly inclined to adapt and hybridise their model while responding to site-specific conditions, as long as this allows them to further push the agenda of affordable housing and non-speculative land tenure. Moreover, CLTs' goal is a means because, by progressively planting the seeds of such a culture, CLTs transform the environmental and operational conditions, thus supporting their overall capacity to realise their projects. In a virtuous cycle, the more projects can be realised, the more the CLTs' culture of homeownership and land tenure is proved and reinforced, and the more local actors and policymakers will be convinced and sustain their model and projects.[16]

We therefore introduce and define institutional capabilities as those collective capabilities that are developed to transform existing institutions that are addressed by the mission of a given collective entity, thus expanding the agency of the collective and, simultaneously, of the individual entities involved. In the case of CLTs, the institutions under transformation are homeownership and land tenure.

By operating at the core level of values and cultural paradigm, these capabilities deeply affect societal preferences and desires, thus impacting political will and strategic partnerships in a much more substantial way than any temporary agreement or exchanged promise. Their transformative dynamic results in a continuously expanding agency of CLTs and of the involved entities: public, private and collective.

Conclusion: Community-led housing initiatives and institutional transformation

In this chapter, we conceptualised the establishment and development of Belgian CLTs as the result of a dynamic, evolving relationship between community agency around a collectively valued purpose – in this case, providing perpetual accessibility to affordable housing – and environmental and operational conditions, specifically political will and partnerships in the case of CLTs. CLTs develop collective capabilities to respond to both, and institutional capabilities in particular have been introduced as agents of environmental and societal change, aimed at transforming existing land tenure and (home)ownership culture and institutions. From this angle, the impact of CLTs can be assessed not only in quantitative terms (number of housing units being realised), as a frequently criticised limitation, but also in terms of institutional transformation, care or institutional work (Beauregard, 2005; Healey, 2005; Lawrence and Suddaby, 2006; De Leonardis, 2011). From this perspective, political will is not simply passively accepted but is shaped at a cultural level. And, complementarily, partnerships can be understood not only as pragmatically supporting the implementation of the projects but also as transformative practices: through a diverse range of collaborations, the culture of homeownership and land tenure, the *modi operandi*, are reworked at the level of underlying values, fuelled by increased trust in the model.

While the context and occasion of this chapter do not allow for further exploration of this concept, we conclude by positing the working hypothesis that institutional capabilities may be part and parcel of any collective initiative with political, transformative purposes, such as community-led housing initiatives fighting to realise the right to housing. This opens new areas of investigation, exploring to what extent and how these organisations actively pursue institutional transformation and have an impact on a political level, beyond and besides the successful realisation of their projects and relieving the housing needs of a specific target community.

Research Funding

This research was supported by Vrije Universiteit Brussel.

Acknowledgements

We want to thank and acknowledge Petry Brand, who provided substantial input for the empirical discussion of the three CLTs through his master's thesis: Petry, B. (2023), 'The bumpy road to a Community Land Trust. An analysis of the obstacles in the development of CLTs in Brussel, Ghent and Leuven', Master's Thesis, Vrije Universiteit Brussel.

Notes

1 See, for instance, https://portico.urban-initiative.eu/urban-stories/uia/ghent-knapt-op-journal-4-final-updates-and-new-beginnings-ghents-housing-renovation-project (accessed 19 March 2026); CLT Gent vzw and OCMW Gent, 2016.
2 The underlying empirical data is mostly based on the master's thesis by Petry (2023), who studied the obstacles in the development of CLTs in Brussels, Ghent and Leuven at Vrije Universiteit Brussel.
3 We use the word 'environment' in the sense in which it is defined in complex systems theories (Weaver, 1948; Simon, 1962).
4 We define institutions from a sociological point of view (De Leonardis, 1998; 2011) as 'social practices structured by – and generative of – shared norms, cultures, and meanings. In this key, institutions are constructs of social intelligence: domains in which this is deposited, partly crystallised in routines, and employed in elaborating shared versions of common goods, problems and solutions; and therefore, as domains of possible, further social learning' (De Leonardis, 1998: 25).
5 For more details on the beginning of CLTB, see Lenna (2019b); De Pauw and Aernouts (2020); Petry (2023).
6 https://vb.nweurope.eu/projects/project-search/shicc-sustainable-housing-for-inclusive-and-cohesive-cities/ (accessed 19 March 2026).
7 Formerly known as Urban Innovative Actions (UIA) and today renamed as European Urban Initiative, it is an Initiative of the European Union (EU) 'that provides urban areas throughout the EU with resources to test new and unproven solutions to address urban challenges'.
8 These include the Societal Housing Network (SoHoNet), a network aiming to promote and support the design, financing, creation or acquisition and management of housing in Belgium to improve access to decent and sustainable housing for vulnerable groups; see https://sohonet.be (accessed 19 March 2026).
9 Among others, the World Habitat Award went to CLTB in 2021.
10 The Flemish Government Architect is an independent government entity aiming to promote a high-quality built environment by developing a long-term spatial vision in collaboration with various administrations and external stakeholders.
11 SIVI is a Ghent's Dampoort neighbourhood non-profit organisation addressing structural poverty while also meeting immediate needs. They help vulnerable individuals regain stability in their lives, while simultaneously engaging them in policymaking to create long-term, inclusive solutions.
12 This programme was initiated by the city of Ghent, SAAMO, and various other public and academic institutions and awarded by Urban Innovative Actions, applying the Dampoort knapT OP principles to the scale of the city. See https://uia-initiative.eu/en/uia-cities/ghent-call3 (accessed 19 March 2026).

13 AGSL is 'a subsidiary of the city of Leuven. It develops and manages, in an independent and corporate manner, real estate in the general urban interest'; see www.leuven.be/agsl (accessed 19 March 2026).

14 According to Sen (Pelenc et al., 2013; Rauschmayer, Bauler and Schäpke, 2013), beyond the ability to act in pursuit of self-interested goals, agency also includes the capacity to achieve objectives that extend beyond personal well-being, such as participating in community development and efforts to reduce poverty (Deneulin and Alkire, 2009), environmental protection (Sen, 2008) and local sustainable development. Qualities such as sympathy, generosity and responsibility are at the core of such a non-individualistic attitude.

15 This is how Pelenc et al. (2015) explain the relationship between individual capabilities, collective agency and collective capabilities: 'Collective agency is the capacity of the group to define common goals and the freedom to act to reach the chosen goals .... The notion of collective capability refers to the real opportunities available to a group of interacting people to achieve a set of functionings that is defined collectively as valuable, ... consistent with the goal set through the process of collective agency. Once collective agency is constructed through a process of interaction between individual agencies, a common goal and a set of shared representations are defined. It is then possible for the group to coordinate the pooling of resources (time, money, goods, services, skills, etc.) as a common set that represents the "material" basis for collective agency. By undertaking collective action, the group will achieve the collective capabilities. Depending on the result of collective action there will be a positive or negative impact on the collective agency and to a certain extent on the agency of the individual members' (Pelenc, Bazile and Ceruti, 2015: 229).

16 The integration of the CLT model into existing social housing policies has proved essential for its development beyond just securing financial resources.

References

Aernouts, N., and M. Ryckewaert (2018), 'Beyond housing: on the role of commoning in the establishment of a Community Land Trust project', *International Journal of Housing Policy*, 18:4, 503–21, https://doi.org/10.1080/19491247.2017.1331592

Alkire, S. (2008), *Concepts and measures of agency*, Oxford Poverty & Human Development Initiative (OPHI), https://ora.ox.ac.uk/objects/uuid:cdecbaca-447c-43b7-8e3f-851517b5ff97/files/m2f8754b8ca7c1d479472d984ad9c1037 (accessed 11 March 2026).

Ballet, J., J. Dubois, and F. Mahieu (2007), 'Responsibility for Each Other's Freedom: Agency as the Source of Collective Capability', *Journal of Human Development*, 8:2, 185–201, https://doi.org/10.1080/14649880701371000

Beauregard, R. A. (2005), 'Introduction: Institutional Transformations', *Planning Theory*, 4:3, 203–07.

Bolt, G., and R. Van Kempen (2002), 'Moving up or moving down? Housing careers of Turks and Moroccans in Utrecht, the Netherlands', *Housing Studies*, 17:3, 401–22.

Crocker, D., and I. Robeyns (2010), 'Capability and Agency', in C. Morris (ed.), *Amartya Sen* (Cambridge: Cambridge University Press).

Davis, J. E. (ed.) (2010), *The Community Land Trust Reader* (Cambridge, MA: Lincoln Institute of Land Policy).

Davis, J. E., L. Algoed, and M. E. Hernández-Torrales (eds) (2020), *On Common Ground: International Perspectives on the Community Land Trust* (Madison, WI: Terra Nostra Press).

De Leonardis, O. (1998), *In un diverso welfare. Sogni e incubi* (Milano: Feltrinelli).

De Leonardis, O. (2011), *La istituzioni: come e perché parlarne* (Roma: Carocci).

De Pauw, G., and N. Aernouts (2020), 'From Pressure Group to Government Partner: The Story of the Brussels Community Land Trust', in J. E. Davis (ed.), *On Common Ground: International Perspectives on the Community Land Trust* (Madison, WI: Terra Nostra Press).

Deneulin, S. (2006), *The Capability Approach and the Praxis of Development* (Houndmills: Palgrave Macmillan).

Deneulin, S., and S. Alkire (2009), *An Introduction to the Human Development and Capability Approach: Freedom and Agency* (London: Earthscan).

Healey, P. (2005), 'On the project of "institutional transformation" in the planning field: commentary on the contributions', *Planning Theory*, 4:3, 301–10.

Ibrahim, S. S. (2006), 'From Individual to Collective Capabilities: The Capability Approach as a Conceptual Framework for Self-Help', *Journal of Human Development*, 7:3, 397–416, https://doi.org/10.1080/14649880600815982

Lawrence, T. B., and R. Suddaby (2006), 'Institutions and Institutional Work', in S. Clegg et al. (eds), *The SAGE Handbook of Organization Studies* (London: Sage), pp. 215–54, https://doi.org/10.4135/9781848608030.n7

Lenna, V. (2019a), 'Riconoscimento e responsabilità. Il ruolo del progetto nel Community Land Trust di Bruxelles', *Ardeth*, 4:1, 31, https://doi.org/10.17454/ARDETH04.03

Lenna, V. (2019b), 'The Project of Property as Emancipation. A Community Land Trust in Brussels' (PhD diss., IUAV Venice and KU Leuven). Available at https://air.iuav.it/bitstream/11578/319386/2/PDFa-Verena%20Lenna%20PhD%20dissertation.pdf (accessed 8 April 2026).

Lenna, V. (2024), 'The Publicness of Urban Commons. Insights from the Brussels Commoning Scene', AESOP Annual Congress Proceedings, 36th AESOP Annual Congress, 2024.

Nussbaum, M. (1988), 'Nature, Functioning and Capability: Aristotle on Political Distribution', in *Oxford Studies in Ancient Philosophy*, pp. 145–84.

Nussbaum, M. C. (1992), 'Human Functioning and Social Justice: In Defense of Aristotelian Essentialism', *Political Theory*, 20:2, 202–46, https://doi.org/10.1177/0090591792020002002

Pelenc, J., D. Bazile, and C. Ceruti (2015), 'Collective capability and collective agency for sustainability: A case study', *Ecological Economics*, 118, 226–39, https://doi.org/10.1016/j.ecolecon.2015.07.001

Petry, B. (2023), 'The Bumpy Road to a Community Land Trust: An Analysis of the Obstacles in the Development of CLTs in Brussel, Ghent and Leuven' (Master's thesis, Vrije Universiteit Brussel).

Rauschmayer, F., T. Bauler, and N. Schäpke (2013), 'Towards a Governance of Sustainability Transitions: Giving Place to Individuals' (Conference Paper: SCORAI Europe Workshop). Available at www.researchgate.net/publication/262378808_Towards_a_governance_of_sustainability_transitions_Giving_place_to_individuals (accessed 8 April 2026).

Robeyns, I. (2017), *Wellbeing, Freedom and Social Justice: The Capability Approach Re-Examined* (Cambridge: Open Book Publishers), https://doi.org/10.11647/OBP.0130

Sen, A. (1993), 'Capability and Well-being', in A. Sen and M. Nussbaum (eds), *The Quality of Life* (Oxford: Clarendon Press).

Sen, A. (1999), *Development as Freedom* (New York: Knopf).

Sen, A. (2008), 'The Idea of Justice', *Journal of Human Development*, 9:3, 331–42, https://doi.org/10.1080/14649880802236540

SHICC (2020), 'Stedelijke Community Land Trusts in Europa: naar een transnationale beweging', *Interreg North-West Europe*, p. 48.

Simon, H. A. (1962), 'The Architecture of Complexity', *Proceedings of the American Philosophical Society*, 106:6, 467–82.

Smetcoren, A. S., et al. (2022), *Care and Living in Community, CALICO. End Evaluation Report* (SARLab and Cosmopolis VUB).

Stewart, F. (2005), 'Groups and Capabilities', *Journal of Human Development*, 6:2, 185–204, https://doi.org/10.1080/14649880500120517

Vercellone, A. (2020), *Il Community Land Trust: Autonomia Privata, Conformazione della Proprietà, Distribuzione della Rendita Urbana* (Milano: Giuffrè Francis Lefebvre).

Volkert, J. (2013), Concepts of Agency, Sustainable Human Development and Collective Abilities (unpublished), https://doi.org/10.13140/RG.2.1.1460.5524

Walsh, V. (2000), 'Smith After Sen', *Review of Political Economy*, 12:1, 5–25, https://doi.org/10.1080/095382500106795

Weaver, W. (1948), 'Science and Complexity', *American Scientist*, 36:4, 536–44.

4

Between provision and self-determination: New forms and networks of self-governance in public and collectively owned housing in Germany

Bettina Barthel, Anna Heilgemeir

Introduction

In Germany, a wide variety of legal and organisational arrangements for self- or co-determination in housing can be found. The oldest forms of self-governance in housing are likely the *Wohnungsbaugenossenschaften*, (large-scale) housing cooperatives, which have existed since the nineteenth century (Novy, 1982), while the most recent and ambitious political initiative calling for co-determination in public housing is certainly the campaign to socialise large private housing companies in Berlin, *Deutsche Wohnen & Co enteignen*.[1] This chapter, however, aims to present two other, related strands that deserve their own attention.

A common criticism of publicly owned housing is that it represents a centralised and paternalistic form of housing provision – despite the fact that tenants do have some co-determination rights, for example in the form of tenant councils. In light of this, and in particular as of 2013–14, various urban policy initiatives have come together in Berlin to demand more co-determination in the context of municipal housing provision.[2] In 2015 they campaigned for a referendum to change Berlin's *Wohnraumversorgungsgesetz* (Housing Supply Act), which was withdrawn after parts of it were implemented by the local government. Several grassroots tenants' rights initiatives that arose in this context remained active at the time, including the initiative for Self-Governance in Public Housing (*Kommunal & Selbstverwaltet Wohnen*), which is discussed as the first strand in this chapter.

The second strand sheds light on the many forms of independently self-governed, collectively owned housing existing in Germany today. Some of these projects, which grew out of the squatting movement, came together in the 1990s to form a grassroots democratic network of self-organised housing projects: the *Mietshäuser Syndikat* (Tenement Syndicate). Since the aim of this edited volume is to present new community-led or grassroots housing models that have emerged in Europe over the last two decades, we contribute to this aim by outlining those new forms of housing self-governance in Germany that have evolved during this period. To distinguish between the two strands of self-governance, we refer to them as *self-governance in publicly owned housing* and *self-governance in collectively owned housing*.

We interpret the development of these new forms as practical experiments to increase the accessibility of self-governed housing. By this, we mean increasing the accessibility of decision-making and the possibility for residents to shape the living environment within the context of public housing. In the context of autonomous self-organisation, there is an ongoing internal debate among activists about accessibility due to self-organisation's seemingly contradictory role. On the one hand, self-organisation in the form of self-help or mutual aid is a form of empowerment that was and is often born out of necessity: urgent needs of parts of the population may not be met by public institutions, or specific groups may suffer from state repression (Raha, 2024: 130 ff.). On the other hand, the current context in Germany is shaped by rising speculative property prices, rising construction costs, supply problems, inflation, rising interest rates and the energy crisis (Barthel et al., 2023). Activists recognise that under such unfavourable conditions, self-organisation in housing requires certain skills, abilities and resources that only parts of the population actually have. This raises the question of whether self-governed housing is becoming a privilege of a (white) middle class (even as this very middle class is also affected by precarisation, see Vollmer and Scheller, 2018). In this sense, the question of accessibility in the context of self-governed housing encompasses various aspects, from availability in numbers to financial affordability, organisational capacities, barrier-free access, (sub)cultural, political and social selection criteria, and decision-making structures.

In this article, therefore, we will present new variations of housing self-governance in Germany and explore ambitions and challenges in the field of tension between accessibility and collective self-determination. The current new organisational variations can best be understood as transformations of older forms under changing political-economic conditions (Uhlig and Novy, 1981: 113). We will therefore in the following section situate them within historical traditions of self-governance and characterise them as part of post-autonomous politics. To deepen our understanding of their contexts and organisational aspects, we conducted a qualitative interview study. After briefly describing the study we present the findings from this research in three steps. Firstly, we systematise the diverse forms that can be found in the two strands of publicly and collectively owned housing through a typology. For each strand, we present one project in more detail as an example. Secondly, we investigate the form and role of networks in the field, noting the focus on regional and neighbourhood integration. Thirdly, we offer a closer look at some of the organisational changes and challenges that we have identified as typical of self-governance, including issues of professionalisation, hierarchies and the role of public institutions and the state. The conclusion briefly reflects on the key findings.

Historical context of current self-governance approaches

The notion of self-governance has historically oscillated between top-down administration and political emancipation, conceptualised both within and as a counter-concept to the state. The German historian Hans-Ulrich Thamer characterises self-governance as a core element of nineteenth-century liberal concepts of the modern bourgeois state at both national and municipal levels (Thamer, 2000),[3] while in the context of the anarchist movement, concepts of self-management and social organisation without the state were developed and propagated by thinkers such as Pierre-Joseph Proudhon (1851). In the second half of the nineteenth century, as capitalism, industrialisation, impoverishment and rural-urban migration increased social inequality and the polarisation of society, the social question became the dominant issue. The urban non-profit housing sector developed as a response to the social question. In Germany, 'in the tradition of paternalistic care for the poor, a municipal housing welfare system emerged that created asylums, homes, and finally flats' (Uhlig and Novy, 1981: 110, translation by the authors). Since then, public housing provision has always developed in parallel with cooperative and private ownership models. Both the very first public as well as cooperative housing companies were initiated in the mid-nineteenth century, but the majority of them were established later, at the beginning of the twentieth century (Novy, 1982: 47). Public housing companies develop, own and manage housing stock, mostly at the municipal level. Initially, both public and cooperative housing provision tended to operate with a top-down structure until democratic elements emerged in the context of the 1918 revolution (Mersmann, 1993).

With regard to housing in post-war West Germany, the focus was on quantitative reconstruction under the Fordist mode of production. The *Wohnungsgemeinnützigkeit* was established, a legal framework that promoted affordable housing through tax reductions. Additionally, subsidies could be used by public, private and cooperative investors to build housing if they provided social housing over a limited timeframe in return. The cooperative researcher Klaus Novy describes this phase as a decades-long depoliticisation of the housing issue, reducing housing to a mere question of supply (see also Mersmann, 1993: 33). This changed under the influence of the 1968 movement, when the concept of *autogestion,* a common slogan of students and workers in Paris, became popular and was theoretically elaborated by the French intellectual Henri Lefebvre (Lefebvre, 1966; Mullis, 2014). For him, everyday life was the central site of political change, and the central group of actors shall be those affected by the politics (Ronneberger, 2008). Critical of representative democracy, Lefebvre argued that the diverse interests of the grassroots had to be present, not 'represented'. As a spatial theorist, he also assumed that there could be no egalitarian social organisation without the practice of spatial production (Mullis, 2014: 79). He understood grassroots movements such as the feminist, alternative and peace movements, or neighbourhood committees, as producing space as a form of resistance. These ideas were influential for the Italian autonomist movement (Mullis, 2014: 73) and the squatting movements of the 1980s in West Germany. Here, after the successful legalisation of squats in the 1980s and 1990s, a number of independent collective housing structures emerged in different legal forms with the aim of self-determination through self-governance. From this, the *Mietshäuser Syndikat* (MHS) was founded in Freiburg in the early 1990s. Since then, around 200 self-organised housing projects have joined the network throughout Germany. Some are large (with more than 280 people), others are small (six people). The projects are located in rural and urban areas; some are kept exclusively for housing, while others include commercial spaces, or spaces for neighbourhood, social, political and cultural activities (Barthel, 2020) (see Figure 4.1).

The 1968 movement and Lefebvre's theories on the city were also taken up at different scales within the field of architecture, with the aim of overcoming the functionalist logic of twentieth-century urban planning and its links to the Fordist mode of production. In the 1970s, new concepts for spatial structures emerged that aimed to enable appropriation and self-governance by residents (Reuschling, 2018), thus opening out towards new practices of self-governance in public housing. The most relevant example is the Steilshoop project, which was part of a newly built public housing estate in Hamburg. A self-managed tenants' association acted as the general tenant for a block planned for 200 inhabitants and made decisions regarding design and functionality, as well as the selection of residents. This made Steilshoop, according to current research, the first self-managed project under municipal ownership in Germany (Reuschling, 2018: 162).

In the frame of neoliberal policies in the 1990s, *Wohnungsgemeinnützigkeit* was abolished. In addition, since 2010, many temporary subsidy contracts for social housing have expired, leading to huge rent increases in both the private and public social housing sectors. Furthermore, there was also a massive sell-off and privatisation of the social housing stock. Berlin was particularly affected by these developments, among other reasons because it still has a particularly high proportion of rented dwellings (84%).[4] Between 1990 and 2010, over 300,000 public housing apartments (around 50%)

The Mietshäuser Syndikat (MHS)

The MHS structure combines a high degree of autonomy for each project with the most possible protection against re-privatisation. Each building is owned by a limited liability company with two shareholders: the tenants' association, and an overarching limited liability company, Mietshäuser Syndikat GmbH. The tenants' association is the majority shareholder in each project. The tenants are autonomous in all matters relating to construction and renovation, as well as everyday concerns such as the distribution of rental costs and internal organisation. Tenant autonomy is limited only in decisions concerning the property. The second shareholder, Mietshäuser Syndikat GmbH, has a veto right in property-related matters. For example, the sale of a building requires the approval of both shareholders. The sole shareholder of Mietshäuser Syndikat GmbH is the MHS association. All the MHS housing projects, as well as additional individuals, are members of this association. The more members the MHS association has as a second shareholder, the less likely it is that the MHS and the tenants' association will agree to a sale. In addition to the principles of decommodification and self-organisation (of the individual projects as well as the network as a whole), the MHS structure is based on mutual self-help in the form of knowledge transfer as well as a degree of financial support (Hurlin, 2018; Heilgemeir, 2020).

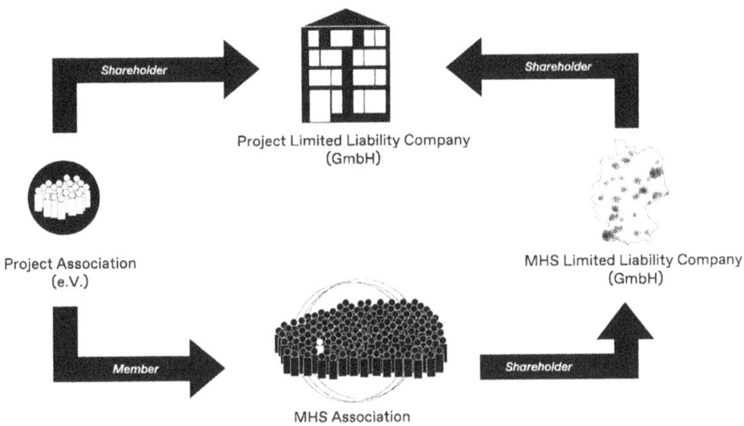

Figure 4.1 Structure of the Mietshäuser Syndikat, 2024. Graph © Anna Heilgemeir, all rights reserved.

were privatised (Holm, 2020), while the expiry of subsidy contracts after 2010 has affected around 140,000 flats so far. At present, Berlin's six public housing companies hold approximately 20% of housing stock, but only a part of this is still designated as social housing (Holm, 2022: 7).

While the first big housing movement in Berlin after the fall of the wall was the *Wir bleiben alle* movement (we stay all, 1992), the housing issue took central stage as a political topic in the 2010s, complemented by a critique of neoliberalism and gentrification. Following the financial and real estate crisis of 2007, the increasing financialisation of the housing sector and the massive increase in the cost of urban housing has led to a re-politicisation of urban social movements (Vollmer and Scheller, 2018). Berlin became a central field of action (see Holm, 2014).[5] The network *Kommunal & Selbstverwaltet Wohnen* (kusWo) was founded in Berlin when various tenants' initiatives joined forces in 2017 (kusWo, 2020). They demanded not only rent freezes, protection from eviction and the preservation of their housing communities and neighbourhoods, but also co-determination rights in the (further) development and operation of public housing stock as a basis for a 'socially just housing provision' (kusWo, 2018: 4) (see Figure 4.2).

Bündnis kommunal & selbstverwaltet Wohnen (Alliance for Self-Governance in Public Housing kusWo)

Seven tenants' and urban activist initiatives decided to form a network for more co-determination in public housing and development. Their goal was to increase the visibility of the already existing forms of self- and co-determination in their own practice and transform them into models for more self-governance in public housing. They therefore published a brochure presenting the different tenants' communities in publicly owned housing (kusWo 2018: 19ff), together with the idea of developing a modular system that differentiates between different levels of tenants' participation, outlining a number of issues considered to be closely related to housing. In addition to the mere provision of living space, kusWo identified the following *Bausteine* (building blocks or fields of action): commercial or social use, maintenance and renovation, neighbourhood integration, administration, and property rights (see kusWo 2018: 9). The political demand was that within the fields of action self-governance should be shaped differently 'depending on the initial conditions and the degree of organisation among the tenants' (ibid.). Tenants should then have the right to determine the extent to which they want to have a say in these areas. The more say they have, the more responsibility they take on. It should be possible to have full self-government through general tenancy agreements as well as normal tenancy agreements with a veto right against re-privatisation. Existing examples as well as historical and international references served as a blueprint and argument. In order to be able to represent and negotiate the tenants' interests vis-à-vis the public housing companies, the concept included a call for financial resources and advice from public bodies (ibid.).

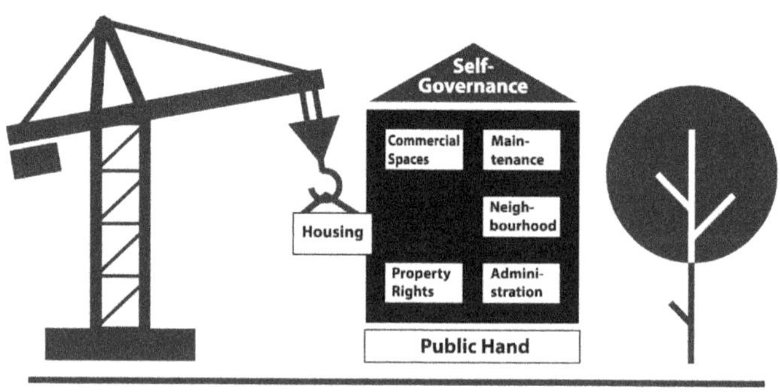

Figure 4.2 Modular system as envisaged, 2018. Graph © *Kommunal & Selbstverwaltet Wohnen*, translated by the authors, all rights reserved.

According to Vollmer and Scheller (2018), in this political-economic context, urban movements responded with a new, post-autonomous and post-identitarian orientation, converging institutional and autonomous strategies: 'They clearly distance themselves from existing party politics, do not want to be appropriated by them, and also resist being subsumed by participatory formats.' (Vollmer and Scheller, 2018: 149, translation by the authors.) At the same time, however, urban movements make very specific demands on public institutions and the state. Vollmer and Scheller consider the approaches of both the MHS and kusWo to be examples of post-autonomous strategies (Vollmer and Scheller, 2018: 147, with reference to Vey, 2016).

Methods and empirical sources

In order to deepen our understanding of the organisational characteristics and new forms of grassroots housing and self-governance in public housing in Germany, and to complement our literature review on past and present forms of self-governance, in spring and summer 2024 we conducted interviews and group discussions with twelve people who are involved in one or more projects and initiatives. This included members of the regional advisory group of the MHS from Berlin, which advises existing and new projects. We also spoke to residents of three different housing projects – including Kumi*13, which provides housing for existing tenants and refugees[6] – and two groups that self-organise co-housing for people with experiences of forced migration. One of them, Campus Cosmopolis, began as an initiative of the MHS before forming its own small cooperative (Campus Cosmopolis, n.d). The other is in the process of joining the MHS and prefers to remain anonymous (Project X). We additionally integrate the perspectives of P99 and Zusammenhaus, both professionalised providers of property management services for self-governed housing projects. We spoke with two spin-offs of the MHS that operate both as non-profit companies for project development, property management, and form collective ownership structures: the Likedeelerei (Hamburg) and the SauRiassl Syndikat (based in south-eastern Upper Bavaria). Interview partners also included two members of kusWo: a policy advisor to the public sector who has been involved in negotiations between former squats that are now owned by public housing companies; and a former social housing tenant and urban development activist. Lastly, we interviewed two representatives of *Rad und Tat* (RuT), a self-organised group and cultural and housing project for lesbian and queer women that has been cooperating with a public housing company from 2019.

Our interviewees have developed ideas, fought for them politically, and implemented them. They operate in different ways at the interface between the production of housing, its maintenance and management, and the production of space in everyday life. It is therefore more of a 'maker' rather than a resident perspective that emerges from the interviews. Our interviewees discussed their motivations with us, as well as the initiation of their organisations, the legal and organisational structures, and the advantages and challenges of self-governance in housing. We approached these interviews as fellow-activists, academics and peers, insofar as we as authors have been active in self-governed housing structures ourselves for many years, while also carrying out research on this topic within the social sciences and architecture/urban planning. Our knowledge of the field thus complements the information gleaned from the interviews, the organisations' and initiative's websites and other published material such as brochures.

The organisations and structures we include in our analysis differ both in their geographical spread (kusWo is active only in Berlin, whereas the MHS and its spin-offs are based in various locations throughout Germany) and their scale. Our analysis does not aim for a symmetrical comparison of projects of the same scale and purpose, but rather, explores new developments and tendencies within two strands of the movement.

New forms of housing self-governance in Germany: Types – networks – organisation

Two strands of housing self-governance – a typology

A key feature of self-governed housing, as of self-organisation in general, is the diversity of structures and forms of organisation specific to time, place, context of origin, motivation and structural constraints or opportunities. Self-governed housing in Germany appears to be no exception in this regard. In order to provide an overview and identify possible trends, we have developed a tentative typology across new forms of self-governance in publicly and collectively owned housing. Based on our empirical analysis, we identify the following types of self-governance in public housing (Table 4.1):

Table 4.1 Typology of self-governance in publicly owned housing (based on the types of communal and self-managed housing presented in kusWo 2018, supplemented by the authors).

I Self-governance in publicly owned housing	
I.a	**Leasehold buildings** (*Pachthäuser*)
	These are formerly squatted buildings that were either taken over directly by the public housing companies (PHCs) during the legalisation phase in the 1980s or 1990s, or buildings that were re-municipalised through buy-backs under Berlin's *SPD-Grüne-Linke* (Social Democratic Party/ Green Party, Leftist Party) coalition in Berlin between 2017 and 2021. The inhabitants,

organised as associations, have extensive rights and obligations to self-govern, which are regulated in general rental or lease agreements with the PHC. Such contracts have limited terms of fifteen to twenty years (kusWo, Int. 31 July 2024), after which they must be renegotiated. This means that the buildings have to fight to maintain their capacity to self-govern.

I.b **Re-municipalised social housing complexes** (*Rekommunalisierte Großwohnsiedlungen*)*
This category refers to large housing complexes built with the aid of public funds by private investors in the 1970s and 1980s, or privatised publicly owned and publicly funded housing complexes later bought or repurchased by PHCs due to pressure from tenants during Berlin's *SPD-Grüne-Linke* government. The diverse tenants' communities had been organising and fighting for their rights since 2014 (see Kotti & Co., n.d.), and continued to do so after the buy-back of their housing stock. Tenants fear rising rents, displacement from their neighbourhoods and reprivatisation. In addition, centralised and bureaucratic administration have led to inadequate maintenance, rigid rental practices that do not take into account family or neighbourhood ties and the inadequate allocation of commercial units (kusWo, int. 31 July 2024). A key example of this is the Neues Kreuzberger Zentrum at Kottbusser Tor (Mieterrat Neues Kreuzberger Zentrum, n.d.). Deutsche Wohnen & Co. enteignen (2020) also refers to the idea of co-determination via tenants' councils.

I.c **Pre-emptive acquisitions** (*Vorkaufshäuser*)
These are apartment buildings in social preservation areas (*Milieuschutzgebiete*)**, that have been acquired by public housing companies through the municipal pre-emptive right to buy as applied between 2015 and 2021 in Berlin. The district occasionally drew on its pre-emptive rights after tenants had found out about the sale of their building and begun to self-organise, fighting hard to prevent the sale. These heterogeneous but now self-organised tenant communities often had a strong interest in self-management in order to keep maintenance costs low, prevent resale, or rent out commercial space according to the needs of the neighbourhood.

I.d **Model projects of public-civil society cooperation** (*Modellprojekte*)
Empty or sparsely built-up areas with iconic buildings that have been re-municipalised or retained in the public housing stock as a result of pressure from urban activist groups (e.g., Stadt von Unten, n.d.). In some cases, this has led to the implementation of so-called model projects, in which local authorities and self-organised groups work together on urban planning on a larger scale to plan entire blocks or neighbourhoods (see for example: Modellprojekt Rathausblock, n.d.; Haus der Statistik, n.d.; Wohnungsbaugesellschaft Mitte (n.d.); Wall et al., 2024).

(*continued*)

Table 4.1 (Cont.)

I Self-governance in publicly owned housing	
I.e	**Co-housing initiatives in the construction of new public housing** In these cases, self-organised groups search for suitable space for collective living and approach PHCs in order to set up cooperations. On the one hand, as these groups often include marginalised individuals, they do not possess the necessary resources to build independently. On the other hand, standard municipal housing often does not meet their needs. In order to overcome these deficits, such groups aim for cooperative project developments on plots of land that have been set aside by the city for new developments. They aim for self-management and general leases (e.g., RuT).

* Some leasehold buildings are no longer in the public hand due to the privatisation of public housing stock. The same applies to a number of the social housing complexes. Although such buildings belong to private investors, tenants also joined the kusWo network in order to demand remunicipalisation.

** A category in German Building Law (§ 172 Abs. 1 Nr. 2, Abs. 4 BauGB) set up to prevent the composition of a given area's population from being completely changed in view of expected modernisation measures. In particular, this law should protect groups with low income from displacement.

To gain a clearer idea of how self-organised groups collaborate with public housing providers in the project development phase, we spoke to the lesbian and queer cultural and housing project RuT (Type I.e). The initiative grew out of a self-help counselling structure and cultural centre for lesbians that started in the late 1980s. With the aim of creating a non-discriminatory and intergenerational housing and living space for lesbian and queer women with and without disabilities, a group of women had been looking for a building or plot of land since 2008. They wanted to realise an alternative housing concept to that of the heteronormative nuclear family and enable alternative forms of care. The group originally aimed to realise the project as an independent, self-governed cooperative. Years of futile efforts led the group to the conclusion that they would not be able to find land or a building if they financed the project on their own. After years of lobbying, RuT was selected for a cooperation with a public housing company for the construction of a new building in a central district in Berlin in 2019. The building is due to be completed in 2025. RuT was not part of the alliance *Kommunal & Selbstverwaltet Wohnen* (kusWo), but it can be regarded as a model for self-governance in public housing development.

Turning now to the strand of independent, self-governed and collectively owned housing, we can roughly identify five forms of organising within the MHS, its networks or spin-offs (Table 4.2).

Table 4.2 Typology of self-governance in collectively owned housing (developed by the authors).

II Self-governance in collectively owned housing	
II.a	**Typical self-organised MHS project** A self-organised group that buys and renovates or builds a house. They are advised and supported by the peer-to-peer MHS support structures, but the group members autonomously decide and implement all matters relating to daily life, administration and the group's structures in accordance with grassroots democratic organising. They become embedded in the MHS network. Formally, the MHS umbrella organisation can only veto the re-privatisation of properties. Some of these projects also provide apartments or rooms for people in need who are not necessarily involved in its self-administration.
II.b	**Collectively owned projects that outsource administrative tasks to property management companies** This model is used by some MHS projects, although it originated in the context of self-help cooperatives in the 1990s. An external 'service provider' (collective or owner-operated company) offers paid services, ranging from book-keeping, managing rental accounts and operating cost accounting to economic and financial planning, property management and caretaker services. As these companies (such as *P99* and *Zusammenhaus)* emerged from the context of self-organised housing, there is a shared understanding of collective processes and autonomy (Zusammenhaus GmbH, n.d.): 'The autonomy and responsibility of the projects should not be affected' (P99, n.d.).
II.c	**Collectively owned projects providing for original tenants** In these cases, self-organised groups buy partially occupied apartment buildings, so that, as a result, the building is in part a self-managed project and partly occupied by the original tenants. This can also include projects that specifically provide housing for people who are discriminated against in the housing market. The original tenants may stay on, becoming part of the group and participating in its self-management structures; or they get managed. The latter means that the self-organised group takes on the classic role of landlord, creating a hierarchy within the building.
II.d	**Self-organised cohousing with marginalised communities** These projects aim to create self-managed housing for marginalised groups, but rather than 'managing' it, they seek to bring people together. A core group develops and organises the project for people who would not otherwise have access to self-managed housing (Campus Cosmopolis, Project X). The group is thus divided into those who do the organisation and administration (making most of the decisions about legal structure and funding) and those who are provided with housing through this structure. The idea, however, is that all the residents take care of the building and are involved in decisions about daily life.

(continued)

Table 4.2 (Cont.)

II Self-governance in collectively owned housing	
II.e	**Non-profit project developers with collective ownership structures** These recently established new organisational arrangements aim at coordinating collective housing based less on self-organisation and more on paid labour and professionalisation. Examples include the SoWo Leipzig (founded in 2018) (SoWo Leipzig, n.d.), the SauRiassl Syndikat in Bavaria (founded in 2018) (SauRiassl Syndikat, n.d.) and the Likedeelerei in Hamburg (founded in 2021) (Likedeelerei, n.d.). They originate from the MHS network and combine professionalisation in project development and administration with opportunities for co-determination and co-design by tenants, and include external controls to maintain decommodification. Taken together, the structures of this type support nineteen buildings, the majority of which are apartment buildings with a surface area of 400 and 1,900 square metres and 4–40 inhabitants, as well as some single-family or duplex buildings, and some individual apartments so far (2024).

To gain a better understanding of the non-profit project developers of Type II.e, we take a closer look at SauRiassl Syndikat. Members of a typical MHS project developed this new concept after several years of experience as group and members of the MHS network. They gained the impression that self-organisation appeared to require too much energy and time to 'carry the model into the breadth of society' and 'to start a property revolution' (Interview SauRiassl, 12 August 2024). In particular, the start-up phase of a project, and the process of development, purchase and renovation, proved to be challenges in terms of accessibility. They aim to implement more projects faster, assuming that this would increase their impact at the neighbourhood and community level, and ultimately on society as a whole.

While the legal form of SauRiassl is similar to that of the MHS insofar as de-commodification is ensured by an external guardian organisation, it differs in its division of tasks and decision-making structures and follows a more holistic approach to challenges of urban and regional planning. An association (founded in 2018) decides on the purchase of new properties at annual general meetings, appoints the management of its company, SauRiassl GmbH, and ensures compliance with the basic principles of self-determination, ecology, community and solidarity. Project development, construction, renovation and day-to-day administration are carried out by a team of employees and a partner architect firm. By 2024 SauRiassl GmbH owns seven properties containing between two and seven residential units.

Overall, the initiatives operating within public as well as collectively self-governed housing tend to share similar motivations and objectives. In addition to creating and maintaining long-term safe and affordable housing, they aim for a structural change in ownership towards the de-commodification and democratisation of economic resources. The activists hope to bring about a change in financing systems, construction methods, land allocation etc., either by appealing to state structures as in the case of kusWo, or by directly implementing new approaches. However, new forms seem to be shifting in different directions within each of the two strands. While there seems to be a trend to demand more self-governance in the context of publicly owned housing, the strand of collectively owned housing evinces new forms that involve less self-governance.

International inspiration and regional and neighbourhood integration

Taking up the anthology's question about forms of networking, three aspects emerge as relevant: the combination of transregional networking and local integration, the role and quality of networks, and the nature of international links. The structures investigated in this text tend to favour regional approaches and decentralisation as structural principles. The MHS was not established with the intention to expand across Germany as it has over the past thirty years; however, the concept attracted a lot of interest and enquiries from other cities and regions. The result is a highly integrated and lively network with a focus on knowledge exchange, support in setting up new projects, and above all de-commodification, as each project within the MHS acts as an external guardian for the other projects. The independent and newly established structures (Type II.e) that have emerged from the MHS context are explicitly more local, limiting their sphere of activity to a specific city or, in the case of rural projects such as SauRiassl, to the region. As the example of SauRiassl shows, focusing on regional integration has advantages: as property developer, SauRiassl receives regular property offers and has access to a stable network of construction companies and local planners, easing the cooperative processes. Their involvement in local politics strengthens their relationship with municipal structures. This is in line with SauRiassl's comprehensive socio-ecological approach, which includes several other key areas of rural-urban development, such as mobility transition, solidarity-based agriculture, electricity for tenants and more. Only the protection against privatisation is organised translocally or transregionally in this model: sister structures such as the Likedeelerei and the MHS are afforded the legal right to veto the sale of SauRiassl's properties. SauRiassl supports other groups with similar goals in other places in order to allow a mutually supportive network of local structures to emerge (SauRiassl, Int. 12 August 2024). For the kusWo network and the case of the public housing, although funding and legislation are defined at the federal level, the relevant political arena is similarly the municipal level because this is where public housing companies operate and where final political decisions on project implementation are taken.

Regarding the second aspect, the role and quality of the networks, social integration into the neighbourhood is a central motivation for most projects within both strands. The neighbourhood is seen as an area of care, as many people organise joint care work at a local level in order to support one another in everyday life (RuT, Int. 31 July 2024, Type I.e). The concept of the *Likedeelerei* (Type II.e), for example, grew out of a practice of providing legal and social assistance for unemployed people of the local community. Many collectively owned projects offer community spaces that are accessible to neighbours, or they participate in and provide infrastructure for neighbourhood activities such as flea markets or community kitchens (Type II.a, c, d; Kumi*13; Campus Cosmopolis). The aim behind the interweaving of housing, community work and neighbourhood activities is to 'turn the building into a tool for more' (Kumi*13, Int. 21 August 2024). Within public housing companies, too, sociocultural spaces such as bicycle repair shops or self-organised cafés are able to exist (kusWo, Int. 30 July 2024, Type I.a). For large public housing complexes with a tenants' council (Type I.b), buildings where the municipality has exerted its pre-emptive right to buy (Type I.c) and large-scale public development projects (Type I.d), a street front communal and community-based area at the ground floor is an important requirement that is upheld within the publicly owned housing companies (kusWo, Int. 30 July 2024). For both strands, however, the aim to strengthen neighbourhood networks is increasingly difficult to realise due to rising costs and competition for use between housing and community space (Kumi*13, Int. 21 August 2024; kusWo, Int. 30 July 2024, RuT, Int. 31 July 2024).

We notice a difference in the strength of the networks between independent structures of collectively owned housing and self-governed structures within publicly owned housing. The composition of the initiatives organised within the kusWo network in Berlin appears to be unique (see Table 4.1); as far as we know, similar structures have not emerged in other cities. Nonetheless, as a political alliance with the aim of representing shared political interests and carrying out grassroots urban activism, kusWo itself seems to have slowed down after a few years of activity. That said, viewed in context, its activities have a longer reach. KusWo can be viewed as an extension of earlier activities in the field of rental policy activism, such as the initiative for a tenants' referendum in 2015. Moreover, the ideas and strategies developed within kusWo are carried forward in further shifting constellations and networks (for example the campaign to socialise large private housing companies in Berlin, *Deutsche Wohnen & Co enteignen*) (Deutsche Wohnen & Co enteignen, n.d.). However, it is certainly remarkable that existing individual model projects do not maintain intensive networking activities and are not even in contact with the overarching activist networks (RuT, Int. 31 July 2024). This may be because the groups are already heavily involved in cooperating with public housing companies, as they directly depend on them and have to concentrate their efforts on this relationship in order to assert their interests. In this respect, RuT argues that networking and dissemination are not covered by their publicly funded budget (RuT, Int. 31 July 2024). In contrast, the networks maintained between collectively owned projects are far more materially interconnected; their interrelatedness is deeply structural and as such fulfils various functions. Such networks protect each project from privatisation, enable growth through knowledge transfer and serve as financial support structures. The difference in terms of networking between the two strands could therefore be attributed to the difference between the self-organised management of material resources held in common, such as buildings and land, and those forms of political struggle in which initiatives do not have such resources at their disposal, but demand the fulfilment of their needs and cooperation from powerful opposing actors, thus sometimes having to navigate conflicting interests.

Thirdly, while regional and local networks are key at a day-to-day and structural level, international housing activist networks are comparatively less relevant. Their main role is to provide inspiration,[7] although advice and knowledge transfer are also important. The international working group of the MHS supports spin-off initiatives in neighbouring countries such as the Netherlands, Austria, France and the Czech Republic (e.g., VrijCoop or HabiTAT, see Hölzl, 2022). However, the varying legal and economic frameworks from country to country make a simple transfer of structures impossible. Rather, the aim is to exchange patterns of successful self-organisation and to strengthen these networks (e.g., through the Commoning Spaces Network, see Chapter 14).

With regard to the strand of self-governance in publicly owned housing, our research shows that above all historical examples provide inspiration, such as the *Wiener Siedlerbewegung* (Vienna Settlement Movement, as researched by Klaus Novy, see for example Novy and Förster, 1985; Novy, 2019 (reprint)). Research on public housing has recently revived a tradition that disappeared with the epistemic rupture of the collapse of the Eastern Bloc, such as practices of *autogestion* or self-management in Yugoslavian social property (Marčetić, 2021: 26 ff; Jovanović, 2022) or self-help elements in the housing sector of the former GDR (Göngrich and Hegewald,

2017). Knowledge about these historical but also recent practices circulate at the interface between research, architecture, art and urban activism. It is made available to a broader public through flyers and brochures (see Kotti & Co., Berliner Bündnis Sozialmieter.de and Selbstuniversität e.V., 2014), or through transdisciplinary teaching projects. The research of historical and present projects inspired for example Campus Cosmopolis to implement their own projects (see Campus Cosmopolis, Int. 31 July 2024).[8] In this way, rethinking and reassembling utopian ideas, historical references and recent examples bridge space and time in order to increase accessibility.

Transforming grassroots democracy and professionalising self-governance?

In 2018, the kusWo initiative hoped for a learning process among local authorities and a different attitude towards tenants – a recognition that 'responsibility for the building can actually be much closer to the people' (kusWo, Int. 31 July 2024). They aimed for more co-determination and less paternalism in the provision of housing. As the example of RuT shows, this is an uphill struggle. The group's architectural ideas did not fit into the public housing company's typical standardised building typologies. As the group was not able to contribute enough equity to the construction costs, structural measures to enable communal living were implemented only to a very limited extent. However, the group was able to bring in their own architects and participate in the layout and interior design of the communal spaces. Negotiations proved difficult due to the asymmetrical power relations between the group and the public housing company, which were particularly evident in the lack of transparency and knowledge hierarchies. The group's original plan to implement the housing project as a leasehold house (Type I.a) was not approved; the current planning status is for individual leases on each apartment. This means that the public housing company remains the contractual rental body, with the exception of a shared care home and the ground floor space. Over the frustrating fourteen-year planning period, the original group has mostly disintegrated; in 2024, three people with paid project development positions and a handful of volunteers remain (RuT, Int. 31 July 2024). This frustration is shared by other initiatives in the field of self-governance in public housing: even leasehold buildings (Type I.a), which enjoy the greatest autonomy, are subject to certain restrictions in the design of their living spaces, and have to fight to maintain their status and freedoms (kusWo, Int. 31 July 2024).

Grassroots structures, on the other hand, are based on full-scale democratic self-governance. This generally means that the people involved in the project do everything themselves on an equal footing, discussing and deciding everything together. However, as one of our interviewees put it, 'discussing everything can be an unfair method when some have never been to school and others have studied politics' (Campus Cosmopolis, Int. 31 July 2024). Reuschling (2018) also notes challenges: 'There are also inherent dynamics that make self-organisation difficult as a permanent structure because, as unpaid work, it always tends to conflict with time for paid work and other commitments' (170). In response to these problems, we observed in some cases a deliberate abandonment of certain basic democratic elements in order to compensate for inequalities and increase accessibility. The two main issues here are *hierarchical elements* and *professionalisation.*

In some projects, decision-making structures are no longer entirely based on consensus, but include elements of majority rule, such as simple or two-thirds majorities, 'because this is a mode that everyone knows' (Campus Cosmopolis, Int. 31 July 2024). Additionally, they may set up hierarchical structures of responsibility: 'It is self-governance, but hierarchically structured' (Campus Cosmopolis, Int. 31 July 2024). These could involve limited transparency (e.g., financial transparency, Campus Cosmopolis, Int. 31 July 2024) and communication (Type II.e, SauRiassl, Int. 12 August 2024.). In such cases, not everyone is involved in all decisions, and not all meetings are open to everyone. Campus Cosmopolis, which organises co-housing for refugees and non-refugees, argues that limiting formal (financial and legal) responsibilities to a few people allows for the participation of those who could not carry this burden (Campus Cosmopolis, Int. 31 July 2024, Type II.d). As a consequence, those who take on responsibility are sometimes perceived as 'landlords' (SauRiassl, Int. 12 August 2024, Type II.e), or as a 'boss or service provider' (Type II.d, Project X, Int. 16 August 2024). Some projects try to buffer this relationship by working with professionalised but movement-related management structures (Type II.b, Zusammenhaus, Int. 16 August 2024), while others mediate such differences within the group itself (Project X, Int. 16 August 2024). Social proximity serves as a counterbalance: co-housing, regionality, staying small, being approachable and knowing one another at a personal, day-to-day level enables familiarity and trust. Such structures still allow for and demand participation and collective decision-making in matters of daily and community life.

Hierarchical elements also play a role in the second set of themes relating to the division of labour, DIY and professionalisation. Professionalised project developers or property management service providers do bring some advantages. Work processes become more efficient, while errors can be avoided. Novy developed concepts regarding this issue already back in the 1980s:

> The low organisational capacity and the overwhelming complexity of the matter would have to be compensated for by organisational offers that are below

> the level of the previous owner and that come close to those affected without over- or under-challenging them. This seems most likely to be possible … through the organisational separation of functions in need of professionalisation, such as land acquisition, financing, planning, etc. (Novy, 1982: 121, translation by the authors)

This separation of production and maintenance is a structural feature of the collectively owned, self-governed housing provision of Type II.e (SauRiassl and Likedeelerei), as well as in the context of self-governance in publicly owned housing. In this arrangement, the co-design of living space is possible.

However, from a self-governance perspective, professional project development creates certain structural tensions. According to the MHS approach, for self-organisation to be effective, first a collective or group effort must exist. Each group can then be supported by the peer-to-peer support structure, but the group itself must take all the necessary steps themselves, from finding a house or building, to setting up finances, developing their own rules, etc. Professional project development, which begins with a site or a building rather than a group of users, is understood to run the risk of delimiting the development of self-organising capacity of future users. The capacity to self-organise is a prerequisite for self-governance, and the existence of the MHS network depends on it. Doing things in collective self-organisation – DIY – is an intensive learning process that involves appropriation of the structures, practices and knowledge. This is a central element of self-empowerment in self-governance and a structural feature of the MHS that enables the network's growth. In our interviews, it became clear that many of those who now offer paid services in the field have acquired their skills as part of their activism in the MHS, as well as in other forms of self-organisation (renovating squatted buildings, self-organised youth centres, queer self-help, SauRiassl Int. 12 August 2024, Zusammenhaus, P99, Int. 16 August 2024). In other words, they have apprenticed in self-organisation, in structures that enable political and practical self-education, because such structures are error-friendly by not being too efficiency-oriented. Some have underpinned these skills with professional training, others have not. It appears that professionalised structures are thus fed by the grassroots contexts, and depend on them to remain rooted in emancipatory ideas. It seems to us that each side needs the other in order to increase accessibility in terms of diversification and growth.

The new forms of self-governed and collectively owned housing that we have presented are sometimes criticised within the self-organised housing scene as being too commercial or too state-oriented; however, the intensity of these debates cannot be compared to the disputes within the squatting movement in the 1980s, when deep conflicts and frictions separated the 'negotiators' and the radical revolutionary fraction (Kuhn, 2014: 209).

Nowadays, we perceive far more pragmatism with regard to the question of whether self-governed, collectively owned housing is preferable to living under the roof of a public housing company. At least when it comes to housing, the state is seen as a structure of neglect and failure rather than an authoritarian power structure (as in Lefebvre's time), and the public housing sector is seen as a field of action: something to be transformed. Groups tend to take the option that allows them to realise their aim to create living space for those who are marginalised in multiple ways, enabling forms of collective co-housing or collective care. There is a shift towards self-organisation when the state fails to meet certain needs. However, as the example of RuT shows, in the face of limited group resources, the path leads back to the state and the attempt to achieve the fulfilment of people's needs by organising and exerting pressure within the public sector's asymmetrical power structures. Quite a few engaged people are involved in both spheres at the same time, combining struggles within public housing as well as collectively owned housing.

This aligns with the above-mentioned post-autonomous strategies (see Vollmer and Scheller, 2018). KusWo continues to hold the state responsible for providing resources, while also trying to implement aspects of self-governance in these structures. Some collectively owned self-governed projects see themselves as a repair structure for the state's deficits in providing adequate quality and self-determined housing (Campus Cosmopolis, Int. 31 July 2024).[9] However, they also consider it appropriate to receive public funding for self-governed forms of housing, as they see themselves as acting in the public interest by providing long-term, secure and affordable housing (Campus Cosmopolis, Int. 31 July 2024).

Conclusion: Self-governance as a continuing search in practice

This chapter aimed to present and outline new forms of self-governance in collectively owned and publicly owned housing, considering these as models for affordable, neighbourhood-based and secure housing that is accessible to higher numbers and a more diverse range of people. In doing so, it aimed to describe the practices and challenges of self-governance in housing. Self-governance is described as being in decline since the end of the 1980s (Ronneberger, 2008), yet it has not ceased to exist. Instead, there is a relatively small but lively world of self-governance in the making. We observe a diversification of organisational models with different approaches to self-organisation and de-commodification, which should be understood as interrelated. Rather than providing only one solution to the housing problem, tailor-made new forms are being developed that are more likely to emerge from local contexts, the experiences of stakeholders and the demands of tenant communities. We see these forms as a result of collective processes of searching for, and continuously refining, self-management strategies in housing policy. We understand them as elements of the post-autonomous phase of urban movements. Self-reflection on the exclusivity and limited reach of autonomous mobilisation, as well as on middle-class privilege, may have contributed towards increased efforts for more accessibility in self-governed housing. While the aim is to reduce existing inequalities, aspects of these structures are (self-)criticised as paternalistic (Campus Cosmopolis, Int. 31 July 2024). The groups reflect on and take up this ambivalent position.

At the same time, they are also confronted with their own limited capacity as the effort required to achieve immediate goals can often seem too time-consuming and resource-intensive under increasingly difficult economic conditions. Meanwhile, public housing tenants remain challenged by the asymmetrical power relations and efficiency-oriented, inflexible forms of provision in public housing. They are trying to slowly penetrate the sphere of public housing provision with practices of self-governance. Writing in 1993, the cooperative researcher Arno Mersmann's words resonate with the current moment when he describes an irreconcilable contradiction between the bottom and the top. Companies (be they large-scale cooperatives, public housing companies, or even private investors) feel disrupted in their day-to-day business by demands for co-determination, while small groups fight against bureaucracy and (state) funding guidelines that do not cater to their needs (Mersmann, 1993: 13).

The desire for state support is just as present as the desire for independence and creative freedom for experimental approaches. The history and forms of self-governance continue to evolve, oscillating between limitation by state power and self-organised exhaustion, between provision and self-determination.

Research Funding

This research was partly funded by the Deutsche Forschungsgemeinschaft (DFG, German Research Foundation) – FOR 2265.

Notes

1 As of 2018, the initiative pushes for the expropriation of large private companies in the housing sector and the transferral of the housing stock into common

ownership under a public-law institution that allows for tenant participation. https://dwenteignen.de/en/ (accessed 9 October 2024).

2 For example the *Initiative neuer kommunaler Wohnungsbau* (Initiative for New Municipal Housing), active since 2014 (www.inkw-berlin.de/, accessed 29 November 2024) and the *Initiative Mietenvolksentscheid* (Tenants' Referendum Initiative), active 2014–15.

3 Following Thamer (2000) the German word *Selbstverwaltung* (self-governance) first appeared in the *Konstitutionsergänzungsakte* (Constitutional Supplementary Act) of 1816 for Frankfurt (Main). The concept is rooted in the medieval tradition of municipal freedoms.

4 www.statistik-berlin-brandenburg.de/f-i-2-4j (accessed 4 December 2024).

5 In Berlin in particular, an urban policy focus on municipal housing construction has taken shape in the form of tenant protests (e.g., Kotti & Co. from 2011), the 2015 rent referendum (*Mietenvolksentscheid*), and the referendum on the expropriation of large corporations (Deutsche Wohnen & Co. Enteignen, since 2018), as well ongoing debates on federal laws such as the rent freeze (*Mietpreisbremse*), the rent cap (*Mietendeckel*) or the re-introduction of the above-mentioned *Wohnungsgemeinnützigkeit* clause, which was abolished in 1990.

6 http://kumi13.org/the-house-project-kumi13/ (accessed 16 October 2024).

7 For example, the Salzburg Housing Fund today inspires Berlin's tenant movement (Kotti & Co, 2014), while structural features of self-determination from the MHS are used to criticise the Austrian state-regulated housing industry, which functions well in terms of numbers and rent levels, but is described as being too paternalistic, having exclusionary allocation criteria or offering little room for alternative living models (Heindl, 2022).

8 An important reference for these theses was the Grand Hotel Cosmopolis in Augsburg, a public refugee home run by a civic association. In a former elderly home, a mixture between housing for asylum seekers, artists' studios, and a hotel is assembled into a 'social sculpture' (https://grandhotel-cosmopolis.org/, accessed 28 November 2024).

9 Given the prevailing racist and xenophobic government policies, it is probably no coincidence that the projects that create housing for refugees are those that are independently self-organised and collectively owned.

References

Barthel, B. (2020), 'Legal hacking und seine praktischen Dimensionen am Beispiel des Mietshäuser Syndikats', *juridikum – Zeitschrift für Kritik | Recht | Gesellschaft*, 3, 366–75, https://doi.org/10.33196/juridikum202003036601

Barthel, B., J. Schmidt, R. Weilert, and L. Hurlin (2023), '(Wie) geht's noch? Hausprojekte selbst organisieren unter erschwerten Bedingungen', *Común – Magazin für stadtpolitische Interventionen*, 7. Available at https://comun-magazin.org/wie-gehts-noch/ (accessed 31 August 2024).

Campus Cosmopolis (n.d.), *A Platform for Urban Alternatives*. Available at http://campuscosmopolis.de/de_DE/ (accessed 28 November 2024).

Deutsche Wohnen & Co Enteignen (2020), *Vergesellschaftung und Gemeinwirtschaft: Lösungen für die Berliner Wohnungskrise*, 2nd edn (Berlin). Available at https://dwenteignen.de/material (accessed 28 November 2024).

Deutsche Wohnen enteignen (n.d.), *Official Campaign Website*. Available at https://dwenteignen.de/en/ (accessed 9 October 2024).

Göngrich, E., and C. Hegewald (2017), *Subbotnik: Lenin und die Grünplanung in Marzahn-Hellersdorf* (Berlin: IGA).

Haus der Statistik (n.d.), *Modellprojekt Haus der Statistik*. Available at https://hausderstatistik.org/ (accessed 5 September 2024).

Heilgemeir, A. (2020), 'The Mietshäuser Syndikat: A Structural Answer to Anti-speculative and Self-Governed Housing Production', in S. Delz, R. Hehl, and P. Ventura (eds), *Housing the Co-op: A Micropolitical Manifesto* (Berlin: Ruby Press), pp. 135–47.

Heindl, G. (2022), *Stadtkonflikte: Radikale Demokratie in Architektur und Stadtplanung* (Wien: Mandelbaum Verlag).

Holm, A. (2014), *Reclaim Berlin: Soziale Kämpfe in der neoliberalen Stadt* (Berlin: Assoziation A).

Holm, A. (2020), 'Privatisierungspolitik in Berlin seit 1990', *Arch+*, 12, *Berlin Theorie – Politik des Raums im Neuen Berlin*, 96–103.

Holm, A. (2022), 'Die Lage der sozialen Wohnraumversorgung in Berlin: Stellungnahme für die Expertenkom mission zum Volksentscheid' *Vergesellschaftung großer Wohnungsunternehmen*, Berlin: Rosa Luxemburg Stiftung. Available at https://www.rosalux.de/fileadmin/rls_uploads/pdfs/Artikel/3-22_Onl-Publ_Wohnraumversorgung.pdf (accessed 24 September 2024).

Hölzl, C., and D. Hölzl (2022), 'Establishing new housing commons in Vienna in the context of translocal networks', *Housing Studies*, 39:5, 1152–1175. https://doi.org/10.1080/02673037.2022.2104820

Hurlin, L. (2018), 'Mietshäuser Syndikat: Collective Ownership, the "Housing Question" and Degrowth', in A. Nelson and F. Schneider (eds), *Housing for Degrowth* (London: Routledge), pp. 233–43.

Jovanović, J. (2022), 'Materializing the Self-management: Tracking the Commons in Yugoslav Housing Economy', in S. Stavrides and P. Travlou (eds), *Housing as Commons* (London: Bloomsbury Academic), pp. 209–33.

Kommunal & Selbstverwaltet Wohnen (2018), *Bezahlbaren Wohnraum sichern, Privatisierung ausschließen: Kommunal und selbstverwaltet für eine sozial gerechte Wohnraumversorgung*. Available at https://kommunal-selbstverwaltet-wohnen.de/2018_kuswo_broschuere.pdf (accessed 31 August 2024).

Kommunal & Selbstverwaltet Wohnen (2020), 'Öffentliche Hand und alles gut?: Mieter*innen für die Demokratisierung der öffentlichen Wohnraumversorgung', in B. Schönig and L. Vollmer (eds), *Wohnungsfragen ohne Ende?! Ressourcen für eine soziale Wohnraumversorgung* (Bielefeld: transcript Verlag), pp. 177–90, https://doi.org/10.1515/9783839445082-011

Kotti & Co. (n.d.), *Die Mietergemeinschaft am Kottbusser Tor*. Available at https://kottiundco.net/ (accessed 24 September 2024).

Kotti & Co., Berliner Bündnis Sozialmieter.de and Selbstuniversität e.V. (eds) (2014), *Nichts läuft hier richtig: Informationen zum sozialen Wohnungsbau* (Berlin).

Kuhn, A. (2014), 'Selbstverwaltete Wohnprojekte im Wandel', in B. Belina, M. Naumann, and A. Strüver (eds), *Handbuch für kritische Stadtgeographie* (Münster: Westfälisches Dampfboot), pp. 206–11.

Kumi*13 (n.d.), *A Self-governed Housing Project*. Available at http://kumi13.org/the-house-project-kumi13/ (accessed 16 October 2024).

Lefebvre, H. (1966), 'Henri Lefebvre ouvre le débat sur la théorie de l'autogestion', *Autogestion: Études, Débats, Documents*, 1, 59–70, https://doi.org/10.3406/autog.1966.886

Likedeelerei (n.d.), *Syndikat für solidarisches Wohnen*. Available at https://likedeelerei.org/ (accessed 24 September 2024).

Marčetić, I. (2021), *Housing Policies in the Service of Social and Spatial (In)Equality* (Zagreb: Pravo na Grad).

Mersmann, A. (1993), *Nachbarschaftliches Wohnen Mitgestalten: Bewohner-Beteiligung und ihre Integration in das soziale Management von Wohnungsunternehmen* (Frankfurt/M: Wohnbund).

Mieterrat Neues Kreuzberger Zentrum (n.d.), *Platform for Tenant Advocacy*. Available at http://mieterratnkz.de/ (accessed 24 September 2024).

Mullis, D. (2014), *Recht auf die Stadt: Von Selbstverwaltung und radikaler Demokratie* (Münster: Unrast Verlag).

Novy, K. (1982), 'Wohnungswirtschaftliche Selbstverwaltung und Selbstfinanzierung: Eine ideengeschichtliche Montage', *Leviathan*, 10:1, 41–67.

Novy, K. (2019), 'Die Pioniere vom Rosenhügel: Zur wirklichen Revolution des ArbeiterInnenwohnens durch die Wiener SiedlerInnen', *dérive*, 77, 39–45.

Novy, K., and W. Förster (1985), *Einfach bauen: Genossenschaftliche Selbsthilfe nach der Jahrhundertwende* (Wien: Verein für moderne Kommunalpolitik).

P99 (n.d.), *Gebäudeverwaltung*. Available at https://p-99.de/ (accessed 16 November 2024).

Proudhon, P. J. (1851), *Idée générale de la révolution au XIXe siècle: Choix d'études sur la pratique révolutionnaire et industrielle* (Paris: Garnier Frères).

Raha, N. (2024), 'Ein queer-marxistischer Transfeminismus: Zur queeren und trans sozialen Reproduktion', in F. Beier (ed.), *Materialistischer Queerfeminismus: Theorien zu Geschlecht und Sexualität im Kapitalismus* (Münster: Unrast), pp. 105–40.

Reuschling, F. (2018), 'Soziale Wohnutopien 68', *Suburban*, 2:3, 159–71.

Ronneberger, K. (2008), 'Henri Lefebvre and urban everyday life: In search of the possible'. In *Space, Difference, Everyday Life* (Abingdon: Routledge), pp. 148–60.

SauRiassl Syndikat (n.d.), *Housing Cooperative Projects*. Available at www.sauriassl.org/ (accessed 24 September 2024).

SoWo Leipzig eG (n.d.), *Solidarische Wohngenossenschaft*. Available at https://sowo-eg.org/ (accessed 21 September 2024).

Stadt von Unten (n.d.), *Initiative for Cooperative Housing*. Available at https://stadtvonunten.de/ (accessed 24 September 2024).

Thamer, H.-U. (2000), 'Der Citoyen und die Selbstverwaltung des 19. Jahrhunderts', in *Engagierte Bürgerschaft* (Wiesbaden: VS Verlag für Sozialwissenschaften), pp. 289–302.

Uhlig, G., and K. Novy (1981), 'Zur Organisationsdynamik wohnungspolitischer Selbsthilfeinitiativen. Problemskizze zur Geschichte lokaler Wohnungspolitik in Deutschland'. Available at https://orlis.difu.de/handle/difu/493502 (accessed 1 April 2026).

Vernetzungstreffen Rathausblock (n.d.), *Plattform aktiver Initiativen im Rathausblock*. Available at https://rathausblock.org/ueber-uns/modellprojekt/ (accessed 5 September 2024).

Vey, J. (2016), 'Crisis Protests in Germany, Occupy Wall Street, and Mietshäuser Syndikat: Antinomies of Current Marxist- and Anarchist-inspired Movements and their Convergence', *Capital & Class*, 40:1, 59–74.

Vollmer, L., and D. Scheller (2018), 'Postautonome und postidentitäre Mieter_innenproteste in Berlin und New York', in A. Schoch and R. Bürgin (eds), *Urbane Widerstände – Urban Resistance* (Bern: Peter Lang), pp. 139–57.

Wall, R., F. Marlow, and I. Farías (2024), *Zaudern ums Gemeinwohl: Produktive Missverständnisse in der kooperativen Stadtentwicklung* (Hamburg: adocs).

Wohnungsbaugesellschaft Mitte (n.d.), *Modellprojekt Haus der Statistik*. Available at www.wbm.de/neubau-berlin/mitte/haus-der-statistik/ (accessed 5 September 2024).

Zusammenhaus GmbH (n.d.), *Building management company*. Available at https://zusammenhaus.berlin/ (accessed 21 August 2024).

Interviews and group discussions

Group discussion at a Mietshäuser Syndikats assembly with two members of the Likedeelerei, 13 April 2024 (GD 13 April 2024).

Interview with a member of Kommunal & Selbstverwaltet Wohnen, 30 July 2024 (Int. 30 July 2024).

Interview with an executive board member of SauRiassl, 12 August 2024 (Int. 12 August 2024).

Interview with a member of Kommunal & Selbstverwaltet Wohnen and two members of Wohnprojekt RuT-Rad und Tat Berlin, 31 July 2024 (Int. 31 July 2024).

Interview with a member of Campus Cosmopolis, 31 July 2024 (Int. 31 July 2024).

Group Interview and discussion with two people from the building management company Zusammenhaus (one of them also an inhabitant of a Mietshäuser Syndikat Project) and one person from the building management company P99 and a member of Project X, 31 July 2024 (Int. 31 July 2024).

Interview with the Mietshäuser Syndikat Project Kumi*13, Int. 21 August 2024 (Int. 21 August 2024).

5

Housing cooperatives in Italy: A discontinuous tradition amid crisis and re-emerging public-cooperative synergies

Silvia Cafora, Rossella Ferro

Introduction

Italian cooperatives have a rich history, stemming from the mutualist workers' movement and philanthropic socialism of the late nineteenth century between the Piedmont and Lombardy regions in northern Italy. Cooperatives built many of the first working-class districts in cities prior to the large-scale programmes of state production. Over the decades, cooperative housing evolved as a deep-rooted yet discontinuous tradition, eventually becoming entangled in a residual-familiaristic welfare regime (Kemney, 2001).

Today, Italy's housing system is heavily commodified. It is characterised by a high homeownership rate of 62.6% compared to 32% for renters (Cafora et al., 2024). The system is dominated by a liberal market that exacerbates inequalities and has created a structural crisis of affordable housing (Arbaci, 2023). Since the 1990s, the public housing stock has steadily declined (with a more than 22% loss of assets) due to sales programmes promoting homeownership and efforts to rebalance the budgets of public housing agencies (Freguja, 2022). Additionally, a portion of the public housing stock remains unused and often in deteriorated conditions.

The mutualist movement left a lasting imprint on the cooperative housing system, influencing both its social dynamics and architectural features. Commonly, cooperative housing still includes self-managed community spaces for cultural and social activities and services designed to support members facing economic or personal challenges. Today, Italy is home to 8,125 housing cooperatives which have historically been intertwined with public housing campaigns aimed at supporting vulnerable populations (Pavesi, 2022: 17). Among the various forms of Italian housing cooperatives, those with undivided ownership stand out for their ability to provide affordable, below-market rents. Alongside undivided ownership cooperatives, Italy also recognises privately owned and hybrid cooperative models.

This chapter focuses on undivided ownership cooperatives, examining their long-term impact on housing affordability, exploring the historical, social and political factors that have contributed to their marginalisation in recent decades and their current capacity to resist ongoing housing commodification. In undivided ownership cooperatives, the legal title to the property is held by the cooperative itself, while residents participate as cooperative members and collective shareholders.[1] Members pay an admission fee and a monthly fee for the right to live in their assigned units. Thus, it is a combined model between collective ownership and assignment, in which residents, as long as they are cooperative members, have the permanent right to enjoy residence. When members relinquish their units, they revert to the cooperative's asset pool to be reassigned based on criteria outlined in the cooperative's statutes. In view of the recent rise of housing cooperatives across Europe, the model is comparable with rental and right-to-use cooperative housing schemes. In this context, the century-old Italian cooperative tradition offers a significant case study, as it has evolved over time by increasingly structuring its internal governance and administrative frameworks.

This research links to growing academic interest in the emerging global role of cooperatives and new public–cooperative partnerships in the development of affordable rental housing across countries (Crabtree et al., 2019; Cabré, 2018; Ferreri and Vidal, 2022). In Italy, the housing debate is currently at a transitional juncture shaped by a worsening housing crisis, in which 8.7% of the population is overburdened by housing costs and evictions are on the rise, with 50,000 cases recorded in 2023 (Cafora et al., 2024: 3). The production of below-market rental housing has become a central concern in both public and political discourse. After several decades of marginalisation, housing cooperatives are regaining visibility and relevance.

Nevertheless, despite this renewed interest, there is a significant gap in the literature on housing cooperatives in Italy – both from national and international perspectives. To date, no comprehensive study has fully traced the historical evolution of the Italian cooperative housing system and its development to the present day. As Caruso (2017: 10) notes, 'Southern Europe was rarely included in academic comparative housing studies'. In Italy, knowledge about cooperative housing remains fragmented within housing studies, and specialised research is often promoted directly by the cooperatives themselves or by the federations supporting them (Gaeta, 2017). As a result, much of the relevant research risks being confined to archives and local studies.

Accordingly, one of the key objectives of this research is to reconstruct the historical and socio-economic aetiology of undivided-ownership housing cooperatives. Thus, their continued potential as a viable alternative to the dominant housing market model would be critically assessed despite the erosion of some of their original values over time. Historically, they played a significant role in shaping Italy's housing system. Today, they continue to maintain an important building heritage and offer the most promising solutions for addressing the current housing crisis. In 2023, Legacoop Abitanti (the national alliance of housing cooperatives) started working on the renewal of the national housing cooperative movement aimed at addressing the needs of the most disadvantaged communities.

The geographical focus of this research is primarily on the regions of Milan in Lombardy, Turin in Piedmont and Bologna in Emilia-Romagna, located in northern and central Italy. Cooperatives are most strongly represented in these areas, which allows for a more accurate analysis of the phenomenon. This research adopts a qualitative mixed-methods approach, combining historical reconstruction, literature review and semi-structured interviews. The study also considers current data, including censuses of residents, reports from cooperative federations and financial statements. National and municipal planning documents were also analysed. Interviews with cooperative representatives from the Milan area (Cooperativa Abitare and Cooperativa Uniabita of Cinisello Balsamo) and from national and regional leaders of Legacoop Abitanti in 2023 have been integral to understanding the state of the cooperative housing system. Quantifying the assets of undivided ownership cooperatives, however, proves to be a challenging task. A comprehensive and organised public database is currently lacking, despite the fact that cooperatives must report property and financial information annually to the Ministry of Enterprises in order to maintain their legal status. To overcome this issue, this research initiated a quantitative survey in collaboration with Legacoop Lombardia, Piedmont and Emilia-Romagna. The aim is to collect data on the number of cooperatives, housing units, resident members and average rent costs in these regions. However, the analysis of these results is still ongoing and this chapter includes some initial findings.

The chapter is structured as follows. The next section reviews the state of the art in Italy's undivided ownership cooperatives. Section 3 traces the historical and ideological conditions that supported the spread of this model during the industrial revolution. The subsequent sections discuss the resurgence of cooperative housing in national and European debates, focusing on its role in addressing housing affordability. The chapter concludes with a summary of findings and a brief outlook on the future of cooperative housing in Italy.

Italian cooperative housing, a gap in academic knowledge. A comprehensive overview of the phenomenon

The research has compiled various available datasets to present an overview of the undivided ownership cooperative model. According to Legacoop

Abitanti, 96% of the undivided ownership cooperatives are located in three out of Italy's twenty regions: Lombardy, Emilia-Romagna and Piedmont. Not surprisingly, these areas also coincide with the regions where industrialisation and the workers' movement gained significant traction in the second half of the twentieth century. Founded in 1961, Legacoop Abitanti, the largest national federation of undivided ownership housing cooperatives, whose main efforts are to implement national and international advocacy to support the housing coops, manages approximately 40,000 units at the national level. These units are found throughout almost all the Italian regions, with estimates reaching up to 45,000 when considering the total stock across the three major cooperative consortia: Legacoop Abitanti, Confcooperative Habitat and AGCI Ambiente e Sviluppo Urbano. The three federations were established between the 1950s and early 1960s and have constituted the Alleanza delle Cooperative Italiane (ACI), a strategic alliance intended to enhance the role of cooperatives as key actors in fostering a more just, inclusive and sustainable socio-economic and spatial order (Rossini, 2020).

Within Lombardy, Legacoop Abitanti oversees seventy-two cooperatives. Its 17,000 units constitute almost 50% of the region's cooperative housing in undivided ownership. Nearly 92% of these cooperatives are concentrated in the metropolitan area of Milan where they comprise a stock of 9,000 flats. In Bologna, two key housing cooperatives (Dozza and Risanamento) manage around 3,000 units, with an annual turnover of 300 reassignments (City of Bologna, 2020). According to its social and financial statement from 2017, the Di Vittorio cooperative in Piedmont oversees 3,170 dwellings across twenty-five municipalities, with 218 new units built after 2017. The cooperative housing stock was mainly set up between the 1950s and 1970s.

The fees for enjoying a cooperative unit vary but are significantly more affordable than on the free rental market. For example, residents of Cooperativa Abitare in Milan, with over 2,700 flats, pay €33 to €75 per square metre per year. For a 67-square-metre unit, this results in a monthly fee ranging between €185 and €420, excluding utilities. In comparison, the average monthly rent for a similar apartment on the open market is approximately €1,000, more than double the cooperative fee (Scenari Immobiliari, 2023).

Undivided ownership cooperatives, particularly in Milan, Bologna and Turin, have preserved large housing stocks over time. These cooperatives remain managed collectively for social purposes, benefiting from economies of scale and a commitment to mutualistic ideals. Despite their relatively small size, they play a critical role in offering affordable housing options. In the past, the building costs were covered through membership fees, individual contributions, loans and significant public funding. All profits are reinvested into maintaining and managing the cooperative, as well as providing additional services to improve the residents' quality of life. For instance, a representative of Cooperativa Abitare stated in the interview: 'We have a comprehensive internal assistance plan, including help for people with disabilities, the elderly and those in fragile situations. Our services include accompaniment to medical appointments, warm meal delivery and home medication assistance, benefiting approximately 250 households – or 10% of our members'. In fact, the housing cooperative system has historically interacted and collaborated with other branches of the cooperative movement – such as social, food and labour cooperatives – in pursuit of mutualistic goals.

Since 2008, major Italian cities have been exploring various political and economic strategies to produce affordable and inclusive housing. These efforts often focus on public-private collaborations aimed at developing social housing, while public housing has been sold off at the same time. In this context, housing cooperatives have played a marginal role despite their long-standing tradition and the growing European interest in cooperatives as a potential solution to the housing crisis. The undivided ownership model, though somewhat neglected since the 1970s, still holds great potential for fostering affordable housing and contributing to welfare redistribution in Italy's housing system.

From the roots of the mutualist and workers' movement to the complex evolution of cooperative housing in the nineteenth and twentieth centuries

To understand why undivided ownership housing cooperatives play a marginal role in today's Italian housing system, we must briefly examine the historical evolution of the phenomenon and the political ideologies and values that either supported or hampered their spread. Some historical factors dating back from 1879 to the 1960s and having contributed to the emergence, diffusion and success of this cooperative model were: (1) national and international grassroots and democratic movements claiming or attentive to working-class housing needs corresponding to a lack of adequacy and accessibility of housing in growing urban areas, (2) a parliamentarian body from various political stances, social democrat, Catholic or moderate liberal, which was sensitive to the expression of the cooperative movement, and (3) public policy schemes, including land policies, to legally recognise and fiscally support the development of new undivided ownership projects. When homeownership-oriented perspectives established themselves as a political and cultural marker from the late 1970s and more explicitly in the

1980s–1990s, undivided ownership was limited or forced to pursue the diffusion of private property.

The early examples of cooperative housing were pioneering and experimental. They emerged in the second half of the nineteenth century, building on the experiences of workers' societies, which evolved to become the cooperative and union movements (Meriggi, 1986). These movements transferred two key principles to Italian cooperatives: mutual aid and active participation (Battilani, 2014). Although mutualism and participation were central to the original idea of Italian cooperativism, the first legal codification[2] in 1882 overlooked the value-based aspects of the movement. Franco Belli described this as 'a kind of original sin, ... a dualistic approach hinged precisely on the separation of form and substance of the cooperative phenomenon, which, amidst ups and downs, has ultimately accompanied us until today'[3] (Belli, 2005: 10).

The first Italian housing cooperative, the Società Edificatrice Abitazioni Operaie (SEAO), i.e., the Workers' Housing Construction Society, was founded in 1879 within the Milanese Workers' Consulate, an association aimed at coordinating action taken by the workers' societies as directed by a group of democratic radicals and moderate liberals from the petty bourgeoisie. They aimed to respond to the emerging housing crisis of the working class with a housing model oriented toward improving conditions of hygiene and comfort. Their philanthropic goals were in part oriented to prevent the exacerbation of growing social tensions (Rossetti, 1986). The figure of the worker-owner was at the centre of this model (Hunecke, 1976), promoting the idea that individual savings from the housing cooperative members could flow into the constitution of capital to invest in housing construction and to pay back construction loans. Ideally, the worker could become the apartment owner by paying a low annual amortisation fee in addition to rent. Actually, the development projects encountered severe economic difficulties, and most workers failed to meet the stipulated contractual conditions, with the cooperative repossessing the housing units. So, the SEAO, initially conceived as a hybrid-tenure housing cooperative oriented to homeownership (Quinzii and Terna, 2012), changed its status in 1898 to undivided ownership, in which each member owned a portion of the whole rather than a single unit.

In some other cases, cooperative projects were directly conceived as undivided ownership from the outset, reflecting the spirit and needs of the workers' movement. For example, the founding members of Cooperativa Abitare in Milan, as one of its representatives stated, were farmhands, bricklayers and day labourers from the northern Milan area. They built the first living units with scrap materials on their weekends and in their spare time. These self-built homes included design innovations tailored to the needs of working-class families, such as larger bedrooms to accommodate large households and shared ground floor spaces for social halls, flour stores and adult literacy classrooms. These spaces fostered both socio-political activities and self-sufficiency. Internal financing mechanisms, such as members' income shares and voluntary labour, were vital to sustaining these community-driven projects (cf. Figure 5.1).

Throughout the late nineteenth and early twentieth centuries, numerous undivided ownership projects were initiated despite material difficulties, lack of technical expertise and financial constraints. The cooperative movement called for public intervention and municipalisation to support these efforts. In response, the 1903 Luzzatti Law[4] was enacted, which introduced low-income housing policies, offering credit reliefs and tax incentives to encourage the construction of homes for the working class. Under this law, cooperatives and mutual aid societies were privileged entities eligible for specific support, and municipalities were empowered to allocate land for low-income housing at cost price. This law marked the first formal collaboration between cooperative housing and public policy. While the 1903 Law regulated early cooperative housing experiences, it also laid the groundwork for the future public housing system. Despite the benefits provided by this law, cooperative housing production did not take off until the late 1910s, following the introduction of further reforms, including additional tax and credit reliefs and a renewed alliance between the cooperative movement and socialist circles (Rossetti, 1986). This period saw the first major expansion of cooperative housing.

Figure 5.1 Cooperative Umanitaria Milan, 1940 and Cooperativa SEAO Milano, 100th anniversary, 2019. Photo © Legacoop Archive, all rights reserved.

Under fascism, the cooperative movement faced significant repression, with several undivided ownership cooperatives placed under receivership and pressured to privatise their assets. The fascist regime sought to weaken the cooperative movement, coopting and controlling it rather than dismantling it entirely (Nejrotti, 1986). The regime favoured privately owned cooperatives in line with its pro-homeownership stance, while mutualistic ideals were replaced by a corporatist view of low-income housing, based on interest groups such as military personnel, war invalids, pensioners and railroad workers. Only after the liberation from the fascist regime, with the 1947 Basevi Law and the simultaneous drafting of Article 45 of the new constitution, was 'the cooperatives' social function of a mutual nature and without purposes of private speculation'[5] fully recognised.

In the post-war period, housing cooperatives played a crucial role in urban and economic reconstruction. The 1949 Piano Fanfani, also known as the INA-Casa scheme, marked a significant expansion of low-income housing initiatives and aimed to accommodate migration to urban centres linked to post-war industrialisation. This period ushered in a new era of public policies that viewed cooperatives as privileged partners in the development of affordable housing, both for privately owned and undivided ownership models (Sapelli, 1986). In 1962, Law 167 further reinforced this public-cooperative partnership, requiring municipalities to plan for building areas to be granted to cooperatives for social housing. Additionally, Law 865 of 1971 introduced the so-called 'leasehold', a policy tool that allowed to separate the ownership of land from the ownership of the buildings put up on it, with the aim to protect land from speculation and to make public-cooperative housing developments possible with greater economic sustainability.

However, the public policies that facilitated access to affordable land for cooperatives have no longer been in place since the 1980s (Granata, 2002: 14). Public investment has shifted toward public-private partnerships and policies favouring homeownership rather than rental housing. The repeal of subsidies and tax reliefs in the late 1980s, coinciding with the rise of neoliberalism, led housing cooperatives to compete in a market where social loans from members could no longer fund new construction. A significant turning point came with the Ferrarini-Botta Law of 1992, which allowed cooperatives to sell apartments to their members, followed in 1993 by Law 560 which facilitated the privatisation of public social housing.

The Italian cooperative housing system can rely on a long tradition of tools and a vast know-how heritage concerning housing decommodification and accessibility – especially through the undivided ownership tenure – which is rooted in the values of mutualism and democratic participation. The dismantling of some of these tools, the public disinvestments in housing cooperatives and their consequent position of marginality in the Italian housing system cannot be understood without considering the general ideological shift to neoliberalism. Also, the cooperative system itself frequently drifted away from its foundational social values, adapting to the rise of individualistic stances over collective ones. It is the same path of disillusion and disaffection with politics shown, for example, by growing electoral abstention and meso-level institutions' loss of representativeness.

Current developments of cooperative housing in Italy

The current impasse for cooperative housing becomes even more critical when considered within the broader context of the affordability and adequacy challenges affecting the Italian housing system. Recent Eurostat data (Eurostat, 2025) highlights a growing trend of housing deprivation and segregation in Italy, alongside a shortage of public housing stock and a reduction in affordable rental housing. Approximately 8.7% of the population, or 5.2 million people, experience housing hardship, with housing costs accounting for more than 40% of disposable income. Additionally, 5.3% of the population live in severe housing deprivation.

In Milan, a city historically associated with cooperative housing but now facing one of the most severe housing crises in Italy, the availability of affordable housing is insufficient and the income gap between the social classes continues to widen. A mere 8.2% of taxpayers earning over €75,000 annually generate more than 40% of the total income, illustrating the growing polarisation between the 'rich' and the 'poor', with the so-called 'middle class' shrinking (Municipality of Milan, 2023). The demand for public social housing now outstrips supply, with waiting lists increasingly dense and unmet. Of the 28,000 municipal public units, 4,200 are awaiting maintenance. In the last two decades, the number of public units of the Aziende Lombarde per l'Edilizia Residenziale (Lombardy Company for Residential Construction, ALER) (regional owned and municipal managed public housing) has decreased from approximately 100,000 to 70,000, largely due to sale plans (Municipality of Milan, 2023).

These outcomes are largely the result of a gradual shift, since the 1990s, in housing policy away from the issue of housing rights, leaving us with weak housing policies and no clear vision for reform or a revitalisation of the public and social housing sectors. The last major housing initiatives, the National Housing Plans of 2009 and 2013, had reduced objectives and limited impact on rental housing affordability. Since then, while the cooperative culture has significantly weakened in terms of social and political recognition, the government has increasingly supported public-private partnerships to address housing production. The 2009 National Housing Plan (Prime Minister's Decree/DPCM of 16 July 2009) introduced the Integrated System of Real Estate Funds (SIF), which aimed to create housing for rent or to promote innovative financial instruments in partnership with public and private actors, ultimately increasing housing supply for rental purposes (Ferri, 2020: 118). These housing projects have come to be known as Italian social housing[6] (Caruso, 2017; Pavesi, 2022), consisting of developments primarily on public land, where some units are sold at subsidised prices while others are offered at below-market rents.

However, this strategy does not prioritise or produce new common goods, as it focuses on a mix of tenures primarily geared toward homeownership, with price caps only in place for the first ten years after construction. Its goal is to expand the housing and services market for the so-called 'Grey Band' – people who cannot access the private housing market but are also ineligible for public social housing. Italian social housing has become a distinct part of the country's housing policies, significantly altering public attitudes toward social housing and often in ways that diverge from its original public objectives (Pavesi, 2022). The trajectory of housing policies in Italy illustrates missed opportunities to create durable, affordable housing, culminating in the near exclusion of housing issues from the post-pandemic Recovery Plan and the relatively low level of social investment on public expenditure (Peverini et al., 2023).

The role cooperatives play in this new public-private housing development framework is marginal and often limited to acting as builders or housing managers in SIF projects, despite their potential to bring about affordable housing (Pavesi, 2022). While Italian social housing and undivided ownership cooperatives share the goal of producing affordable housing through collective private strategies, cooperatives are no longer considered key partners in recent housing policies. Public support for undivided ownership cooperatives has dwindled, and no subsidies are available to promote the development of new cooperative projects. As the president of Legacoop Abitanti noted in the interview, the unravelling of the public-cooperative relationship has weakened the traditional advocacy role once held by housing cooperatives.

Cooperative leaders in Milan explained in the interview that, since the early 2000s, undivided ownership cooperatives have shifted towards asset protection, grappling with rising construction costs, particularly in recent years. Without land policies offering affordable building sites and public subsidies, cooperatives now face competition from the market where members' social loans no longer suffice to cover the costs of new construction (interview, president of Uniabita, Cinisello Balsamo). Although cooperatives continue to rely on internal lending, many directors are now considering alternative financial instruments, including bank debt. However, banks are hesitant to provide the necessary credit for new housing projects, as undivided ownership requires long periods to recoup initial investments. Consequently, cooperatives often offset their investments by selling part of the developed land, thereby dispersing the principles of undivided ownership (interview, representative, Cooperativa Abitare). Despite attempts to adapt to new market conditions since the 1990s, cooperatives have yet to devise an organic strategy to meet the evolving demands of society, the market and politics (Granata, 2002: 14).

The weakening of the cooperative model is also reflected in the decline of mutualistic culture, accompanied by a fragmentation of the social base and diminished participation in assembly meetings and community space management, as a representative of Cooperativa Abitare stated in the interview. The social mechanisms that once sustained housing cooperatives, such as social lending and generational turnover, have stalled. Families increasingly prefer investing their savings in private homeownership rather than reinvesting in cooperative housing, and members are becoming less engaged with the cooperative's political and economic challenges.

Since 2020, cooperatives have begun to reconsider their future role, particularly in light of the growing housing crisis in Italy's most desirable cities and the evident collapse of the private homeownership-based housing system. These discussions involve cooperatives, grassroots movements and both local and national governments, all searching for solutions. As noted in interviews, many cooperatives are finding renewed motivation to address critical housing issues, aided by a rise in available capital due to generational shift and rent adjustments following market inflation (cf. Figure 5.2).

To overcome financial constraints, cooperatives are working to update their business models, improving asset management and reinvesting profits. One innovation promoted by cooperative federations is the emphasis on non-housing functions to generate profits for reinvestment in undivided ownership projects (interview, president of Legacoop Abitanti). For example, the reuse of ground-floor commercial spaces in cooperative housing buildings – often left vacant for years – has led to their revitalisation through new cooperative initiatives, such as bookstores, cafés and community spaces. At the same time, they seek to reaffirm their mutualistic principles, working to restore a sense of community and belonging among members, which is essential for cooperative movements to survive (Quinzii and Terna, 2012: 21). They are also exploring new alliances with other cooperative sectors, the non-profit sector, private actors and, crucially, the public sector.

The inability to implement new undivided ownership assets in Italy is particularly stark when viewed from a European perspective. Across Europe, neo-cooperativism has seen a resurgence of undivided ownership and rental models as a response to the housing crisis and urban planning challenges.

Figure 5.2 Cooperators in Milan, 1958. Photo © Legacoop Archive, all rights reserved.

Countries with both strong and emerging cooperative traditions are developing policies that emphasise the social value of land, aiming to combat housing financialisation and speculation by promoting collective ownership models. For instance, in Barcelona, the cooperative movement draws inspiration from the Danish Andel Model for undivided ownership, while Zurich has experienced a renewal of cooperativism with a new wave of self-help cooperatives and supportive public policies at the local and regional levels. Other examples include Austria and Germany, where cooperative housing remains a significant part of the rental market, with new pushes for cooperative models since the 1980s and late 2000s (Hölzl et al., 2023).

This comparison highlights the paradox of Italy's underutilised and marginalised cooperative system, which other European municipalities have often viewed as a model to emulate. As the interviewed president of Legacoop Abitanti Emilia-Romagna noted, some European cities regard Italy's cooperative housing system as an exemplary practice. Against this background and increasing housing shortage in Italy's most attractive cities, Legacoop has re-engaged in dialogue with local and national public authorities, positioning itself as a partner in a new affordable housing supply chain. In early 2024, they proposed a National Housing Plan aimed at revitalising housing cooperatives as strategic partners in addressing the housing crisis.

Legacoop Abitanti's National Housing Plan proposes the creation of 50,000 social housing units, with 30% of the rents reduced compared to market rates. Legacoop aims to build 10% of these units (5,000 units) through public-private co-design partnerships, thereby freeing up resources for public housing for the most disadvantaged. The plan estimates a total investment of €206.6 million, with 39% financed by public resources (approximately €80.6 million) and 61% (€126 million) from cooperative resources. The plan also involves collaboration with the European Investment Bank (EIB) and the Council of Europe Development Bank (CEB). Housing units will be produced through urban regeneration and rehabilitation projects, thus avoiding new land consumption. The main efforts are aimed at gaining recognition from public authorities as a potential ally in making below-market rental housing available and at re-integrating – much as in the past – an economic and policy strategy capable of supporting the development of new housing cooperatives.

Moreover, since 2019, Legacoop has engaged in significant advocacy and networking efforts at the national and European levels, joining key networks such as Housing Europe, Co-habitat Network and World Habitat. It has actively contributed to debates on European housing policies and emerging housing task forces, while also inviting members of the European Parliament to participate in national cooperative assemblies. While the debate on Italy's housing crisis is gaining traction among national actors, the responses remain unclear and fragmented. Despite some minor openness, housing cooperatives continue to be sidelined in favour of private sector partnerships. However, in the interview, the president of Legacoop Abitanti confirmed that increasing recognition from European counterparts fosters Italian housing cooperatives to become more aware of their potential role and motivates them to actively work on strategies, plans and proposals to reorganise their management and finance with an objective to influence housing policies more effectively.

Conclusion and outlook

The contributions of this study are twofold. First, we aimed to quantify the current extent of undivided ownership housing cooperatives and provide a comprehensive overview of the phenomenon in Italy. We traced key phases in its evolution to better understand the potential and limitations of this affordable housing model, as well as the social and political factors that either support or hamper it. The study highlights how grassroots solidarity movements, the political representation of the cooperative movement and the existence of supportive public policies were crucial in the past to the success of cooperative housing. As a result, we conclude that undivided ownership cooperatives are currently a stalled mechanism in Italy, with little room for development in their present state. The research also underscores the recent shift towards new housing solutions initiated by cooperative federations and executives.

Second, the study contributes to practice-oriented approaches by recognising the transition that cooperatives and the broader housing system in Italy are undergoing. From this perspective, the chapter identifies the efforts of various actors seeking a new configuration to address current needs and challenges. Accordingly, the authors aim to support this transition through the findings and approach presented. For example, the research prompted the establishment of a national data collection on cooperatives, aiming to provide a more comprehensive and accurate overview of the state of undivided ownership housing cooperatives in Italy. In 2023, together with Legacoop, we conducted a census of these cooperatives in Lombardy, Piedmont and Emilia-Romagna with plans to extend the study across the entire country. This work emphasises the importance of improving the acquisition of quantitative data to increase awareness of the phenomenon among cooperators and at the national level. Legacoop aims to strengthen the national debate on cooperative culture and explore the potential for fostering housing affordability and the decommodification of public and cooperative assets, as has occurred at various points in the past. Legacoop's ongoing work is charting new paths for development and advocacy, both nationally and internationally. They are engaging in discussions with other European cooperative networks and economic and financial institutions. Their goal is to expand the network and create a platform that can attract EU funding opportunities. Legacoop is currently involved in several EU networks, including Housing Europe, the CoHabitat Network and the European Network for Housing Research (ENHR) (see Chapter 13). Finally, there is a new momentum from younger generations to actively engage with the cooperative movement, alongside a fresh outlook from established Italian housing cooperatives.

Acknowledgments

This work is dedicated to the memory of Davide Ostoni, young soul of the historical Abitare cooperative in Milan.

Notes

1 As established by the national Consolidation Act of 1938.

2 The 1882 Commerce Code first codified cooperative societies in Italy, defining them as companies with variable capital (thus allowing free entry and exit of members) regulated by the principle 'one head, one vote'.

3 Translated by the authors.
4 Luigi Luzzatti was an Italian politician and parliamentarian who was part of the Milanese Workers' Consulate. He promoted the first Italian housing cooperative in 1879 and is considered a political father of cooperative and public housing.
5 www.senato.it/istituzione/la-costituzione/parte-i/titolo-iii/articolo-45 (accessed 8 January 2025); translated by the authors.
6 While in Europe, social housing (also) includes the housing stock that answer to the housing needs of the most fragile part of the community, Italian social housing, as named by Caruso (2017), is a public-private operation aimed at producing housing answers for the so-called grey band of the community. The property of the stock is mostly in private real estate that is leased for twenty to forty years at affordable prices.

References

Arbaci, S. (2023), 'Looking back into the future: European housing system of social market economy', in S. Cafora (ed.), *Abitare Alternativo, modelli in azione* (Milano: Feltrinelli).

Battilani, P. (2014), 'Mutualità e scambio mutualistico nella storia della Cooperazione italiana', *Quaderni Fondazione Ivano Barberini*. Available at https://fondazionebarberini.it/old/PDF/ricerca/Mutualita_Battilani.pdf (accessed 8 April 2026).

Belli, F. (2005), 'Spunti e riflessioni sull'evoluzione della legislazione in materia cooperativa', in A. Siena (ed.), *Le opportunità del nuovo diritto societario per le imprese cooperative*, pp. 7–22. Available at www.regione.toscana.it/documents/10180/70188/Le%20opportunita%60%20del%20nuovo%20diritto%20societario%20per%20le%20cooperative_78667/6534fbc7-8574-46ae-b6b7-4464255e90b6 (accessed 8 April 2026).

Cabré, E., and A. Andres (2018), 'La Borda: a case study on the implementation of cooperative housing in Catalonia', *International Journal of Housing Policy*, 18:3, 412–32, https://doi.org/10.1080/19491247.2017.1331591

Cafora, S., J. Lareno, and T. Vitale (2024), 'Policies to decommodify and revive the right to housing in Italy', *Fondazione Feltrinelli*, https://doi.org/10.31235/osf.io/865t9

Caruso, N. (2017), 'Policies and practices in Italian welfare housing', *Springer*, 8, 7–23.

City of Bologna (2020), *General Urban Plan 2020 of Bologna*. Available at http://dru.iperbole.bologna.it/piano-urbanistico-generale (accessed 13 March 2026).

Crabtree, L., N. Perry, S. Grimstad, and J. McNeill (2019), 'Impediments and opportunities for growing the cooperative housing sector: An Australian case study', *International Journal of Housing Policy*, 21:1, 138–52, https://doi.org/10.1080/19491247.2019.1658916

Eurostat (2025), 'Living conditions in Europe – housing'. Available at https://ec.europa.eu/eurostat/statistics-explained/index.php?title=Living_conditions_in_Europe_-_housing (accessed 8 April 2026).

Ferreri, M., and L. Vidal (2022), 'Public-cooperative policy mechanisms for housing commons', *International Journal of Housing Policy*, 22:2, 149–73, https://doi.org/10.1080/19491247.2021.1924908

Ferri, G. (2020), 'Strumenti economici e giuridici dell'housing sociale a confronto con quelli dei modelli pionieri', in S. Cafora (ed.), *Abitare Pioniere* (Milano: Feltrinelli), pp. 13–24.
Freguja, C. (2022), 'Audizione dell'Istituto Nazionale di Statistica', *Gruppo di lavoro sulle politiche per la casa e l'emergenza abitativa* (Istat). Available at www.istat.it/it/files/2022/09/Istat-Audizione-Politiche-per-la-Casa_06_09_22.pdf (accessed 13 March 2026).
Gaeta, L. (2017), 'I grandi proprietari milanesi di edilizia residenziale: questi sconosciuti', in F. Cognetti and A. Delera (eds), *For Rent. Politiche e progetti per la casa accessibile a Milano* (Milano: Mimesis), pp. 123–33.
Granata, M. (2002), *La Lombardia cooperativa. La Lega nazionale cooperative e mutue nel secondo dopoguerra* (Milano: FrancoAngeli).
Hölzl, C., H. Nuissl, F. Beran, and T. Kormeyer (2023), 'Nonprofit Landlord Types on the Housing Market – A Key to Rising Displacement in Berlin?', *Housing Policy Debate*, 35:1, 1–21, https://doi.org/10.1080/10511482.2023.2271898
Hunecke, V. (1976), 'Comune e classe operaia a Milano (1859–1898)', *Studi Storici*, 17:3, 63–96.
Meriggi, M. (1986), 'Solidarietà e organizzazione. Le società di mutuo soccorso', in G. Sapelli and M. Degl'Innocenzi, *Cooperative in Lombardia dal 1886* (Milano: Edizioni Unicopli), pp. 155–75.
Municipality of Milan (2023), 'New housing strategy'. Available at www.comune.milano.it/en/w/forum-abitare.-presentata-la-nuova-strategia-per-la-casa (accessed 8 April 2026).
Nejrotti, M. (1986), 'Fascismo: la cooperazione compressa e snaturata', in G. Sapelli and M. Degl'Innocenzi, *Cooperative in Lombardia dal 1886* (Milano: Edizioni Unicopli), pp. 85–110.
Pavesi, A. S. (2022), 'Introduzione. Dalla rigenerazione urbana alle pratiche di coprogettazione per un welfare di filiera cooperativa', in M. Vignudelli (ed.), *Transizioni Urbane cooperative. Generare valore sociale nell'abitare e nelle prospettive di rigenerazione urbana* (Bologna: Fondazione Barberini), pp. 16–22.
Peverini, M., M. Friesenecker, R. Cavicchia, L. M. Munson, K. W. De Jesus, and A. Susani (2023), 'Greener housing, but affordable? A study of synergies and conflicts between environmental policy instruments and access to housing'.
Quinzii, C., and D. Terna (2012), *Ritorno all'abitare: una cooperativa in città* (Siracusa: LetteraVentidue).
Rossetti, V. (1986), 'La soluzione cooperativa al problema della casa', in G. Sapelli and M. Degl'Innocenzi (eds), *Cooperative in Lombardia dal 1886* (Milano: Edizioni Unicopli), pp. 239–69.
Rossini, L. (2020), 'Lazio (Italy)', in C. Baiges, M. Ferreri, and L. Vidal, *International Policies to Promote Cooperative Housing* (Barcelona: La Dinamo), pp. 59–64.
Sapelli, G. (1986), 'Il secondo dopoguerra. Verso la maturità del sistema', in G. Sapelli and M. Degl'Innocenzi (eds), *Cooperative in Lombardia dal 1886* (Milano: Edizioni Unicopli), pp. 111–30.
Scenari Immobiliari (2023), 'La casa in locazione in Italia e in Europa – Focus Milano e Lombardia', 8 March 2023.

6

Collaborative housing in the Czech Republic: Focusing on the layers of obduracy

Tomáš Hoření Samec, Petr Kodenko Kubala, Václav Orcígr, Jan Malý Blažek

Introduction

This chapter reflects an applied research project focusing on the introduction of collaborative housing in the Czech Republic, where despite a significant housing affordability crisis (Hoření Samec and Kubala, 2024), collaborative housing has not developed on a scale comparable to other European countries (Tummers, 2016). We understand collaborative housing as an umbrella term for housing which encompasses the voluntary, democratic and deliberate cooperation of households on the development and management of housing (Czischke, Carriou and Lang, 2020; Malý Blažek et al., 2023). By focusing on the Czech Republic, we contribute to the discussion on the dynamics of collaborative housing (re)development beyond the Western, Northern and German-speaking European countries. Specifically, we advance further discussions on the possibilities of introducing collaborative housing and scaling it in Central (and) Eastern Europe (Pósfai et al., 2022; Kodenko Kubala et al., 2023; Lis et al., 2023; Pósfai et al., 2024; Hölzl, 2025). Our contribution is to deepen and widen these discussions while specifically trying to show that clear-cut interpretations of why collaborative housing is not developing are missing the point. We argue that the issue is more complex and ambivalent, and the absence of development does not have to be a historical necessity (in the form of a 'post-socialist legacy') but an interplay between lacking infrastructures, prevailing discourses and a neoliberal housing regime which accentuates the asset function of housing.

The Czech housing system and housing discourse represent the Central (and) Eastern European model, which has common structural features – the majority of tenure is private homeownership that is rather often unmortgaged due to the privatisation of the formerly public housing stock in the 1990s and 2000s. The Czech housing system is characterised by residual public housing and a reliance on market-oriented private individual ownership, with a strong role of families in housing acquisition (Kubala and Hoření Samec, 2021) and the private rental market. Between 2017 and 2022, property prices in the Czech Republic more than doubled (Czech Statistical Office, 2024), together with increases in the offered rents, which outpaced rises in household income (Orcígr et al., 2024). Housing became increasingly unaffordable for vulnerable households, especially for those struggling on the job market, people with disabilities, single-income households, older people or young adults. A 2021 study estimated that approximately half a million Czech households, comprising nearly a million people, faced excessive housing costs (more than 40% of their incomes), risked losing their homes or were in housing distress (Klusáček et al., 2021: 8). Such a housing crisis is by no means limited to the Czech Republic but has been experienced in Hungary (Gagyi et al., 2021), Slovakia (Gresakova et al., 2020) and Poland (Kajta et al., 2022) as well. This makes our case relevant to the broader Central Eastern European context due to similar structural features in the housing regimes, but also owing to the cultural similarities in the perception of homeownership across the countries of Central and (South-)Eastern Europe.

In reaction to the housing crisis, some political parties in various Czech municipalities have promised to develop new housing policies tackling the issue. These include the production of more public, cooperative or private rental housing. The research project reflected in this chapter focused on the intersections between top-down (municipal-led) and bottom-up (community-led) possibilities for collaboration between public and civic actors. The project explored and fostered cooperation between municipalities and their residents, with one of its goals being to help to initiate collaborative housing projects. Over time, as research progressed, we began to experience a range of barriers to the introduction of collaborative housing, including a lack of political willingness and capacity among municipalities. Focusing here on discussing these barriers and limitations rather than positive outcomes and outputs, we firstly introduce the theoretical framing based on Anique Hommels' (2005) adoption of the urban-assemblages approach: the concept of obduracy. We then present our methods of data (co)creation and analysis, followed by our findings as they relate to the identified limitations faced by municipalities and residents, respectively. In the concluding discussion, we relate our argument to the existing literature: the insufficient development of collaborative housing is linked to underdeveloped institutional infrastructure which would enable the financing and management of the project as well as insufficient (in)formal communication between actors involving representatives of public and civic spheres: public servants, residents, but also us as researchers.

Theoretical framing: Concept of obduracy

The main source of theoretical inspiration for this chapter is a body of work in housing studies informed by actor-network theory resulting in the 'urban assemblages' approach (Gabriel and Jacobs, 2008; Farías and Bender, 2010; Cook, Smith and Searle, 2013; Blok and Farías, 2016; Färber, 2019). On the ontological level, this stream of literature is based on the assumption of the processual nature of the world, which understands it as a place of constant change, flows and developments (Law, 1994; 2003). If we accept such an ontological stance, a fundamental question arises: how is it possible that something endures despite continuous change? From this perspective, any endurance requires daily effort. No institution, convention or established procedure could persist without sufficient daily effort dedicated to its preservation. The second major question would be how it is possible that something endures, even when 'the life is elsewhere', the world has already moved on. Everything changes and seems to want to go in a different direction, yet a part of social reality apparently resists these changes. This kind of endurance is captured by the concept of *obduracy* in Science and Technology Studies (Law, 2003; Hommels, 2005; 2020). For our context, we are inspired by the work of Anique Hommels. According to her, the city is the sediment and interconnection of urban assemblages, which are constantly in the process of change: rebuilt, renovated, reconstructed. At the same time, it resists the process of change. When discussing the paradoxical nature of such processualism in her theoretical intervention, Hommels (2005) introduces the concept of obduracy and distinguishes its three layers: frames, embeddedness and persistent tradition. In this chapter, we only employ frames and persistent tradition to make sense of our field data.

Using attempts to rebuild the Hoog Catharijne (a shopping mall in Utrecht) as an example, Hommels shows that it is not solely the materiality of buildings that hinders change. In that case, Hoog Catharijne should have been rebuilt roughly twenty years earlier than its actual reconstruction (completed in 1993). However, two competing reconstruction plans backed by strong institutions and interests led to a dead end and, thus, blocked the reconstruction for decades. The *frames*, conceptualised as established ways of thinking and doing that different groups carry in their heads and bodies, are to blame here. It is difficult to enforce something that exists outside of these frames. The frames model stresses the role of *obduracy* in design processes. Studying obduracy in urban redesign involves the identification of the actors involved in local town-planning and redesign activities as well as the analysis of their (potentially opposite) ways of thinking (Hommels,

2005: 344). In our analytical framework, the frames are the conceptions, capacities and established (expected) roles of public institutions – state and municipalities.

The *persistent tradition* of obduracy refers to the widely shared collective ideas and values within a society that dictate what should be, what is considered right and what constitutes a good life. These shared beliefs deeply influence urban planning and development, establishing norms that guide not only the physical construction of cities but also the social expectations tied to them. A focus on persistent traditions highlights how culturally embedded and collective traditions that persist over a longer period of time and transcend local contexts contribute to the obduracy of urban structures (Hommels, 2005: 344). The difference with frames is in the emphasis on 'shared visions'; frames place attention on the differences among human actors (such as collaborative housing groups) and not on the cultural and symbolic factors that play a crucial role in the constitution of the obduracy of urban structures, as persistent tradition does. In our view, the persistent tradition thus consists of (1) conceptions, imaginaries and discourses of what good and desirable housing should look like, and (2) the legal framework, state regulations, subsidy programmes and supporting infrastructure for the specific types of housing.

Methods

The research project focused on opportunities for and barriers to the introduction of collaborative housing in the Czech context. During the project, six municipalities were engaged as sites for research and advocacy; these involved participatory and multi-stakeholder workshops, a survey with residents, and meetings and roundtables with local politicians and administration. Furthermore, during the course of the research project (2021–23), we contacted the Ministry of Regional Affairs of the Czech Republic to report our results. The partner municipalities were either regional centres (Jihlava, Liberec, Opava and Pardubice) or smaller-scale municipalities within close distance of regional centres (Psáry, Hrádek and Nisou). In these municipalities, we conducted fourteen research workshops with local residents and four multi-stakeholder workshops for residents and politicians where we presented our (working) results. The participants were diverse in terms of their social and economic background in the various cities; for instance, in Liberec, the recruiting process was related to one of the project partners, the Technical University, which resulted in above-average attendance among their graduates. In Jihlava meanwhile, the participants were rather 'ordinary' people who were attracted by the promise of 'getting housing from the municipality'. However, we neither scanned nor collected their social and demographic status, inferring these characteristics from their qualitative self-description during the workshops.

The workshops had three aims:

1. introduce participants to the concept of collaborative housing, defined as an umbrella term for diverse forms of housing that have in common multiple households participating purposefully, actively and democratically in the development and management of their housing (Malý Blažek et al., 2023);
2. explore and discuss their housing preferences, particularly, preferences related to collaboration and sharing; and
3. simulate the formation of a collaborative housing project group and thereby help to initiate the process of creating a collaborative housing project in the respective city.

The workshops were designed as a series of three 3-hour sessions, with 176 participants attending in total. Participants were recruited through various information channels – via a public campaign combining advertisements in local media and relevant Facebook groups, posters in public spaces and information dissemination through official city channels (websites, newsletters and city bulletins). Invitations to the workshops were formulated in all cases as a request for 'participation in collaborative housing research'. However, the information contained a general promise by the municipalities to introduce some form of collaborative housing into their housing policies. The workshops were recorded, transcribed and subsequently analysed. The analysis was inspired by the inductive Grounded Theory approach (Strauss and Corbin, 1990), which initially involved open coding followed by axial coding. Throughout the analysis, a set of 113 codes was created, which helped us to systematise the data. We also ran an exploratory online survey which mapped needs, opinions and preferences regarding collaboration in housing in the Czech Republic. A total of 1,012 respondents completed the survey. For the purpose of this chapter, the survey data rather serves as supplementary and contextual material. In addition to the central methodological instruments described above in the form of questionnaires and workshops, we also employed participant observation. Notes from the meetings with local politicians as well as state institutions were taken and discussed widely during our regular project-team meetings.

Findings: Layers of obduracy

Representatives of public institutions

One of the first encounters within the research field began by organising roundtables in our partner municipalities. These usually included our contact persons – local politician(s) who previously agreed to sign a memorandum of cooperation – and municipal officials, typically from the department of spatial planning / architecture. During the course of these meetings, we presented the concept of collaborative housing with various international examples. We also tried to ascertain the municipalities' specific intentions or possible strategies in relation to housing and urban planning policy. Apparently, in all municipalities, the actors were tentatively interested in the concept of collaborative housing, often arguing that housing is indeed unaffordable even for middle-income households. Furthermore, all cities possessed land (often 'brownfield-like' plots) which could 'somehow' be used for building up municipal or collaborative housing. Although all cities, represented by their politicians (in some cases their mayors or council members responsible for housing and/or urban development), rhetorically supported the idea and the project, even the first step inviting local residents to attend an introductory workshop proved rather demanding. For example, it took an enormous communication effort to just prepare and publish an article for municipal newspapers/bulletins inviting local people to the workshops. Providing such coordinated PR support to the research project could be perceived as being outside the frame; nevertheless, we expected that the cities would see it as potentially beneficial. However, it could also have been seen as too binding for the cities, as they are also embedded in the current housing regime, with the individual eventually being responsible for housing.

An example of a city where residents attended the workshops in large numbers was Jihlava, a regional capital located between the metropolises of Prague and Brno where the local vice-mayor went viral with a video presenting the city as one that will build hundreds of cooperative housing units. During the 2018–22 legislative period, the local government coalition attempted to develop complex municipal housing policies encompassing collaborative housing development. From our perspective, the politicians seemed motivated to incorporate some form of collaborative housing into their local housing policies, and the workshops were successful in terms of the number of participants. However, the process radically changed following elections in which the coalition lost its position. The political change brought with it changes in the imagination of who is responsible for housing provision. This shift is exemplified by a particular situation from a multi-stakeholder workshop to which we had invited the newly elected politician responsible for housing. After presenting the analysis of the survey and data from the participatory workshop, the politician made a speech, which could be paraphrased as follows: 'People, you know, the previous coalition promised that it would give people housing … but, this is not possible, so do not think that anything like that might happen now'. For the residents, it was quite a shocking U-turn in the approach of the political representation and revealed that the change of the housing system is contingent upon a wide array of factors, all of which could nonetheless be hindered by one 'small' reverse back towards the obdurate frames and persistent traditions embedded in the existing housing regime.

The obduracy of how 'things are done' colliding with insufficient city administration capacity embedded in the neoliberal housing regime was made apparent in the perceived role of the research team in the process. The team had been an active initiator of the whole process and, at the same time, the main workshop organiser. This gave the impression that the research team itself would achieve more than was realistic, for example, that it would bring specific project documentation and, thus, set in motion the construction itself. In this sense, the framing is that the research has value for the municipalities, not in delivering conceptual knowledge per se, but in tangible results which could be embedded into the existing housing development practice. The persistent tradition about what housing should 'look like' was, on the other hand, manifested in internalised scepticism towards some attributes of collaborative housing. In this respect, collaborative housing could have been an undesirable risk considered similar to a return to state socialism, which is among certain politicians perceived and performed as a spectre which haunts anything resembling collective action. Some political actors connected collaborative housing to social or community housing, which might have negative connotation in the Czech context as housing forms for the most vulnerable households. They believed the public would see it as a factor contributing to the immigration of 'risky' households, resonating with moralising housing discourses related to housing 'undesirable' households (Hoření Samec, Decker and Trlifajová, 2024). The persistent tradition of housing as a private matter together with the lack of tools, capacity, procedures and knowledge of how to deal with housing innovations resulted in municipal inaction and an inability to intervene effectively in this area or to support collaborative housing development. Importantly, as we illustrate below, these perceptions were not limited only to the city representatives. Although they were not always held by the majority of actors, such accounts influenced the discussions and meetings and, as we see it, productively contributed to the obduracy and cemented the housing status quo.

Citizens and potential residents

From the analysis of the survey and workshops, it is evident that participants perceived collaborative housing as complex and ambiguous. It is a form of housing that has advantages and attractiveness for many, but, contrariwise, was associated with doubts and uncertainties. In the following sections, we describe this multiplicity and ambiguity by summarising the most important advantages or doubts and uncertainties that illustrate the frames and persistent traditions as well as the ways in which non-institutional actors (citizens) are embedded in the existing housing regime.

The workshops revealed that there are two main reasons why collaborative housing has been considered housing that brings benefits to its residents. Firstly, it was seen as a potentially more affordable form of housing. Secondly, the idea of living in collaborative housing that emphasises neighbourhood or community aspects had appeal in terms of opportunities for mutual care, shared belongings or as a prevention of loneliness. Such a view goes against the persistent tradition found in the prevailing discourse among Czech homebuyers, where housing is seen as an individual and familial issue (Samec, 2018). Other perceived benefits included the opportunity to achieve a higher standard of living through collaborative housing, as well as the ability to actively take decisions with others on the overall shape of housing: 'The availability, the financing, that's great. Even the fact that you can speak to the project, what it could look like, if there would be a pond or if there would be a playground. Yeah, like, it's good' (Workshop participant, Jihlava).

Therefore, the participants found the idea of collaborative housing appealing, especially in terms of its potential for economic savings, which resonates with the current housing situation and the pressure felt by (potential) market newcomers in the Czech context. Furthermore, collaborative housing was seen as potentially embedding its inhabitants in the relationship networks that arise from neighbourhood-type housing and providing them with the conditions for mutual care or assistance. Last but not least, it was felt that a collaborative house would allow the opportunity to be active co-creators of the housing project where people would spend a substantial part of their lives.

During the workshops, we also, however, encountered more critical stances, which we placed into three categories: (a) negative associations in the public discourse; (b) uncertainties in the 'preparatory phase'; and (c) problems and conflicts 'after moving in', which we understand as related to certain frames of how people are used to dealing with housing but also in part to the persistent tradition blurring the conceptual lines between housing discourses and practices. The first set of doubts was connected to the level of ideas, stories or visions circulating in the public space. Some workshop participants related collaborative housing to collective-memory-like negative associations of the 'past [socialist] regime', similar to the views of some above-mentioned politicians: 'Well, what I've heard here from the workshops recently is so idealistic, it seems to me that we're going back a bit to the times of communism, right, the communal laundries and such, that which used to be, but I think the people here are not so set up for that' (Workshop participant, Jihlava).

These attitudes could be related to the (lack of) direct experience with the state socialist regime, resembling what Chelcea and Druta (2016) conceptualise as 'zombie socialism'. We observed that this rhetoric permeates not only political and economic elites but also some of the citizenry. Collaborative housing was perceived within this discourse as something resembling the past regime (sharing, cooperation, common spaces and community life). These features might be enough for the idea to lose attractiveness among a section of society. For individuals, collaborative housing was also associated in some cases with negative personal memories – multi-generational cohabitation, student flatmate cohabitation or student dormitories, which resonated and legitimised the negative reference to 'socialism', the 'socialist past' or the 'socialist character of participatory housing'.

Collaborative housing was also associated with a type of 'shared ownership' of housing that was in opposition to the prevailing persistent tradition of aspirations related to private ownership. All of these associations may make this form of housing less attractive. A whole series of questions and concerns were therefore further directed towards the possible purchase of a share of collaborative housing: 'So, I don't know what to say about that. The concerns are clearly about the finances – everyone has that, they would like to know what it will be. So, if one decides to buy it, the apartments will then be ours. Because I've also heard a lot of opinions that no [that is not the case]' (Workshop participant, Jihlava).

The aspiration for individual private homeownership is embedded into the neoliberal system of welfare provision, where housing serves as an economic securitisation vehicle for social reproduction (for retirement and future generations). In this context, for many, it was difficult to 'erase' the asset function of housing and accentuate the use-value, especially when the political and economic system supports housing arsenalisation.

For some workshop participants, living in collaborative housing was perceived as too demanding in terms of time, effort and energy as regards a lack of tested practices, procedures and supporting infrastructure. Specifically, they highlighted the unprepared legal environment, the lack of support in terms of financing from both public and private actors and institutions and the absence of available project management, coordination, advice in different areas or conflict facilitation and mediation: 'I will ask again the question, slash, a small concern, ... whether the banks will finance it and the state will finance it? Or is it about the agreement between these people, if they will be able to come to an agreement?' (Workshop participant, Jihlava).

Developing a new frame on how to do something almost completely new proved quite demanding for many participants; their concerns were often transformed into calls for support from various experts and external services, for example, project management, coordination, legal advice and financial advice. The research participants were aware of the advantage of involving external experts (project managers, facilitators, mediators, etc.) to help with setting the cohabitation conditions, house rules and ways of resolving conflicts.

Such expertise could make the phases easier before and after moving in, but, during the workshops, it was expressed that collaborative housing projects did not sufficiently reflect certain 'social laws' according to which our respondents believe the world works: 'The fewer households/people, the fewer problems'; 'one hundred people – one hundred tastes' (Kodenko Kubala et al., 2023). Importantly, despite the fact that a great and deliberate effort was made to present collaborative housing as a concept that includes a whole range of different settings and intensities of coexistence, the perception of research participants tended to imagine collaborative housing as a form of coexistence that creates very intimate relationships between cohabitants. It might be the case that the persistent tradition of housing as a private matter limits the imagination of alternatives, which sometimes tend to be 'over-burned' by imagining complete collaboration in all aspects, which then makes it easier to be dismissed as too demanding.

Concluding discussion

The chapter aimed to highlight the complexity of introducing collaborative housing in the Czech Republic and contribute to an emerging academic discussion in the Central Eastern European setting. We used the concept of obduracy to illustrate that *frames* of the existing housing regime enacted through the *persistent tradition* in individual perceptions and the collectively shared imagination of housing reinforce each other, preventing the scaled development of collaborative housing projects in the Czech Republic. Empirically, we observed an ambivalent perception of collaborative housing, with its novelty proving to be both advantageous and disadvantageous. For representatives of public institutions, collaborative housing represents a promissory tool which, under certain circumstances, could help to mitigate the housing affordability crisis (see Chapter 9). For engaged citizens, it similarly promises financial savings, community living and a higher standard of living. In sum, we can state sympathy for this type of housing on all sides.

Nevertheless, the novelty of collaborative housing also functions as an obstacle. Public institutions lack sufficient knowledge of the collaborative housing concept and do not have the capacity to effectively initiate or support such housing types. In regard to Hommels' (2005) framework, this might be perceived on a layer of frames, where re-embedding the housing regime through new innovation (i.e., collaborative housing) might be perceived as demanding and costly. This difficulty is compounded when existing traditions in how housing is imagined as an individual matter are used as an excuse to avoid dedicating the resources needed to change. Citizens in workshops similarly pointed to the overall unpreparedness of the entire environment, highlighting the lack of supportive city infrastructure, the absence of a legal entity, non-existent banking products or other types of financing, and the absence of state subsidy titles and support programmes. They also discussed the lack of various types of counselling and support in terms of project management, coordination and mediation. Insufficient infrastructure was recognisable from both sides of the possible implementation. Likewise, in research outside the Central European context, institutional infrastructure is argued as crucial to collaborative housing development. Lang and Mullins (2020) argued that in their case, the lack of specialised institutions providing knowledge and resources causes the absence of a more widespread adoption of collaborative housing forms. Helamaa (2019), in the Finnish context, identified underdeveloped support systems as the biggest obstacle to the development of collaborative housing. Similarly, Lang, Chatterton and Mullins (2020) emphasise the role of intermediary institutions and the institutional context in the expansion of grassroots initiatives (see also Lang and Stoeger, 2018; Hölzl and Hölzl, 2022).

However, apart from the relevance of institutional infrastructure, our research points to the crucial interdependence between this and housing discourses which are reproduced by the involved actors-politicians, officials and residents. Such housing discourses present and perform individual homeownership as intrinsically preferable, stated in an unquestionable way which indeed resembles a *persistent tradition* of thinking collectively. However, we interpret that as more than a purely discursive matter of homeownership normalisation (Hoření Samec and Kubala, 2024), but of the broader assemblage of the neoliberal housing regime as well, where private homeownership serves as a crucial means to secure one's (and one's family's) social and economic position today and in the future (Samec, 2018). In that framing, other forms of tenure might be suspicious and not 'effective' in performing housing as an asset. While such framing is not an inherent social fact and might be challenged (Pósfai et al., 2022; 2024), the current situation resembles a 'stuck wheel'. The lack of infrastructure enabling the time and resources needed to develop effective collaborative housing, such as proper legal forms, financial instruments and project management, resonates in the hesitant voices. These voices may raise the spectre of the socialist past or scepticism about cooperation between people, creating, in a way, a self-fulfilling prophecy, revealing the obduracy of actors and their interconnections.

In conclusion, we do not suggest that one of these identified explanations (or layers of obduracy) is dominant and that others derive from it. Rather, we argue that one layer reinforces another; they are interwoven and interconnected in various and dynamic ways. Together, they create the complex obduracy of the current housing regime. If these conditions are not changed by deliberate and publicly backed strategies, attempts to (re)introduce collaborative housing into the Czech housing context will represent only a flicker in the wind with the hope of creating a small fire under the smothered terrain of the relatively well-established interconnection of private capital and private actors of different types.

Research Funding

The research was supported by the Technology Agency of the Czech Republic (SS03010221) and the language proofreading of the manuscript was supported by the Brno University of Technology, Faculty of Architecture. The open access fee for this chapter was supported by the Faculty of Architecture, Czech Technical University in Prague, through the Academic Competition for Support of Creative and Publication Activities programme. The work of Petr Kodenko Kubala was supported by the Czech Science Foundation under the grant 'Affordable Housing within "Planetary Boundaries": Theories, Practices, Infrastructures'; Grantová agentura České republiky, grant number: 24-10190O.

Acknowledgement

We would like to thank our project team members who participated in the field research and team meetings, Anna Vinklárková, Jana Kubcová, Markéta Káňová, Radek Suchánek, Lukáš Houser, David Tichý and Michal Kohout and Bradley McGregor for language editing.

References

Blok, A., and I. Farias (2016), *Urban Cosmopolitics : Agencements, Assemblies, Atmospheres* (Routledge), https://doi.org/10.4324/9781315748177

Chelcea, L., and O. Druţă (2016), 'The specter of zombie socialism and the rise of neoliberalism in post-socialist Central and Eastern Europe', *Eurasian Geography and Economics*, 57:4, 1–24, https://doi.org/10.1080/15387216.2016.1266273

Cook, N., S. J. Smith, and B. A. Searle (2013), 'Debted objects: Homemaking in an era of mortgage-enabled consumption', *Housing, Theory and Society*, 30:3, 293–311, https://doi.org/10.1080/14036096.2013.767280

Czech Statistical Office (2024), 'Indices of realized flat prices – 4th quarter of 2023'. Available at www.czso.cz/csu/czso/house-price-index-owner-occupied-housing-price-index-4-quarter-of-2023 (accessed 24 June 2024).

Czischke, D., C. Carriou, and R. Lang (2020), 'Collaborative housing in Europe: Conceptualizing the field', *Housing, Theory and Society*, 37:1, 1–9, https://doi.org/10.1080/14036096.2020.1703611

Färber, A. (2019), 'How does ANT help us to rethink the city and its promises?', in A. Blok, I. Farías, and C. Roberts (eds), *The Routledge Companion to Actor-Network Theory* (London: Routledge), pp. 264–72.

Farías, I., and T. Bender (2010), *Urban Assemblages: How Actor-Network Theory Changes Urban Studies* (London: Routledge).

Gabriel, M., and K. Jacobs (2008), 'The post-social turn: Challenges for housing research', *Housing Studies*, 23:4, 527–40, https://doi.org/10.1080/02673030802101666

Gagyi, Á., C. Jelinek, Z. Pósfai, and A.Vigvári (2021), 'Semi-peripheral financialization and informal household solutions: Embedded scales of uneven development in Hungarian urban fringes', in M. Mikuš and P. Rodik (eds), *Households and Financialization in Europe* (London: Routledge), pp. 81–103.

Gresakova, L., Z. Tabackova, and Z. Reveszova (2020), 'Mapping with care as an outline for post-neoliberal architecture methodologies – Tools of the Never-Never School', *Architektúra & Urbanizmus*, 54:1–2, 7–19, https://doi.org/10.31577/archandurb.2020.54.1-2.1

Helamaa, A. (2019), 'From marginal to mainstream? Analysing translations between the CH niche and the established housing sector in Finland', *Built Environment*, 45:3, 364–81.

Hölzl, C. (2025), 'Cooperative housing pioneers in Central and South-Eastern Europe: Mainstreaming alternatives through translocal networks', *Critical Housing Analysis*, 12:1, 115–30, https://doi.org/10.13060/23362839.2025.12.1.591

Hölzl, C., and D. Hölzl (2022), 'Establishing new housing commons in Vienna in the context of translocal networks', *Housing Studies*, 39:5, 1152–75, https://doi.org/10.1080/02673037.2022.2104820

Hommels, A. (2005), 'Studying obduracy in the city: Toward a productive fusion between technology studies and urban studies', *Science, Technology, & Human Values*, 30:3, 323–51, https://doi.org/10.1177/0162243904271759

Hommels, A. (2020), 'STS and the city: Techno-politics, obduracy and globalisation', *Science as Culture*, 29:3, 410–16, https://doi.org/10.1080/09505431.2019.1710740

Hoření Samec, T., A. Decker, and L. Trlifajová (2024), 'Consumption loans consuming homes: Intersections of housing precarity and personal overindebtedness', *International Journal of Housing Policy*, 24:3, 501–20, https://doi.org/10.1080/19491247.2024.2350134

Hoření Samec, T., and P. Kubala (2024), 'Dual responsibilization for housing in a housing crisis: Young adults in the Czech Republic', *Housing Studies*, 39:4, 857–76, https://doi.org/10.1080/02673037.2022.2091115

Kajta, J., P. Pustulka, and J. Radzińska (2022), 'Young people and housing transitions during COVID-19: Navigating co-residence with parents and housing autonomy', *Housing Studies*, 38:1, 44–64, https://doi.org/10.1080/02673037.2022.2135171

Klusáček, J., M. Greineder, V. Lesák, I. Kowaliková, and J. Brož (2021), *Bydlení jako problém* (Prague: Iniciativa za bydlení).
Kodenko Kubala, P., J. Malý Blažek, V. Orcígr, T. Hoření Samec, M. Káňová, D. Tichý, and J. Kubcová (2023), 'Traces of obduracy: Imaginaries of "social inertia" in the process of introducing CH in the Czech Republic', *Critical Housing Analysis*, 10:1, 39–49, https://doi.org/10.13060/23362839.2023.10.1.552
Kubala, P., and T. Hoření Samec (2021), 'The pace of "the good life": Connecting past, present, and future in the context of a housing affordability crisis', *Time & Society*, 30:2, 198–222, https://doi.org/10.1177/0961463X20987814
Lang, R., and D. Mullins (2020), 'Field emergence in civil society: A theoretical framework and its application to community-led housing organisations in England', *VOLUNTAS: International Journal of Voluntary and Nonprofit Organizations*, 31, 184–200.
Lang, R., and H. Stoeger (2018), 'The role of the local institutional context in understanding CH models: Empirical evidence from Austria', *International Journal of Housing Policy*, 18:1, 35–54, https://doi.org/10.1080/19491247.2016.1265265
Lang, R., P. Chatterton, and D. Mullins (2020), 'Grassroots innovations in community-led housing in England: The role and evolution of intermediaries', *International Journal of Urban Sustainable Development*, 12:1, 52–72, https://doi.org/10.1080/19463138.2019.1663525
Law, J. (1994), *Organizing Modernity: Social Ordering and Social Theory* (Oxford: Wiley-Blackwell).
Law, J. (2003), 'Ordering and obduracy', Centre for Science Studies, Lancaster University. Available at www.lancaster.ac.uk/fass/resources/sociology-online-papers/papers/law-ordering-and-obduracy.pdf (accessed 6 November 2024).
Lis, P., Z. Rataj, and K. Suszyńska (2023), 'Limitations in the diffusion of CH in Poland: Expectations and beliefs of young generation as potential users', *Journal of Urban Affairs*, 47:3, 1045–621–18, https://doi.org/10.1080/07352166.2023.2206034
Malý Blažek, J., T. Hoření Samec, P. Kubala, and V. Orcígr (2023), 'Participatory housing: A new conceptual framework for democratic forms of housing in the Czech Republic', *Sociologický časopis / Czech Sociological Review*, 59:2, 173–95, https://doi.org/10.13060/csr.2023.029
Orcígr, V. (ed.) (2024), *Pražská bytová krize: Perspektivy a souvislosti* (Praha: Arnika).
Pósfai, Z., C. Jelinek, S. Dević, A. Tomašević, and V. Pavlović (2022), *Catalytic Capital Investment as an Enabler of Affordable Rental and Cooperative Housing in Central and South-Eastern Europe: Full Research Report* (Budapest: Periféria Policy and Research Center).
Pósfai, Z., C. Jelinek, M. Ferreri, and C. Cociña (2024), 'MOBA: Rethinking needs and financing for affordable rental and cooperative housing in Central and South-Eastern Europe', *Radical Housing Journal*, 6:1, 221–35, https://doi.org/10.54825/GZCJ9476
Samec, T. (2018), 'Performing housing debt attachments: Forming semi-financialised subjects', *Journal of Cultural Economy*, 11:6, 549–64, https://doi.org/10.1080/17530350.2018.1493611
Strauss, A., and J. Corbin (1990), *Basics of Qualitative Research: Grounded Theory Procedures and Techniques* (Newbury Park, CA: Sage Publications).
Tummers, L. (2016), *The Re-emergence of Co-housing in Europe* (London: Routledge), https://doi.org/10.4324/9781315659886

Part II

Translocal networks, institutions and solidarity

7

Advocating housing politics transnationally and translocally

Johanna Hoerning, Florin Keuneke

Introduction

Any engagement with housing politics is confronted with fragmentary and at times even contradictory housing realities and markets. On the one hand, we are faced with diverse local settings and constellations of actors, housing stocks, dwellers etc. On the other hand, housing policies are mostly formulated on the national level, and subject to global tendencies of transnational ownership and financialisation (Aalbers, 2016; Jacobs, 2019). The bulk of literature concerned with these questions focuses on actors such as private equity funds, banks, social housing providers and the state on local and national levels, as well as on the role of the European Union as a distinct case and question of supranational housing policies (Priemus and Dieleman, 2002; Doling, 2006; Byrne, 2015; Aalbers et al., 2017). More recently, housing is discussed internationally as being in a process of transnationalisation in terms of ownership (Janoschka et al., 2019; Vargas-Silva and Boccagni, 2023; Lauster and Bergmann, 2023), of housing markets (Paris, 2017; Mendes, 2021), of housing policies (She, 2023) as well as of grassroots organisations and social movements (Herrle et al., 2015; Hölzl and Hölzl, 2022). In order to engage with housing more globally and comparatively, scholars have argued for a closer analysis of 'transnational actors, regulation and markets' (Aalbers, 2022: 1066).

Adding to this literature, our paper looks at different types of advocacy organisations that intersect state, civil society and corporate realms as well as different scales from local, to national, European and global contexts. Within housing research, these actors are only rarely studied as such (e.g., Matznetter, 1992; Czischke, 2007). This may be related to the fact that they represent all interest groups that are otherwise considered to be incommensurable: advocacy is done from the *supply side* (providers) as well as from the *demand side* (tenants) – and of course from the perspective of homeowners. A comparative perspective with regard to these actors who specifically engage in advocacy has great potential to shed further light on divergences and convergences of interests with regard to housing politics. At the same time, such actors are neither fully grassroots, nor state or market driven. As non-governmental and non-profit organisations, they are intermediary actors who at least do not represent singular private interests, but organise them collectively. In order to understand how this is done and what the relevance of scale in this context is, this paper looks at them comparatively from the local to the global scale.

In the context of politics of affordable housing, Anaid Yerena (2015; 2019) has shown that advocacy work in housing is not only broad in terms of activities, but also in terms of scale. Still, she states that the local scale is 'particularly vital to the planning and production of affordable housing in communities' (Yerena, 2015: 844). Considering the growing relevance of transnational actors as stated above, the question remains how advocacy addresses and responds to the relevance of different spatial scales. Restricting ourselves to advocacy organisations in the context of tenant housing and broadening the analysis to advocacy organisations lobbying for *tenants* as well as *tenant housing providers* (associations, individual and corporate owners), we analyse how the relationship between local, national and transnational housing policies is strategically addressed and negotiated by advocacy organisations on these different scales. While *de facto* globally acting advocacy organisations are more or less absent in the context of housing, many are organised transnationally, and the European context is a case in point when it comes to structures and politics of tenancy as well as debates over a more-than-national regulation of housing (Hoerning et al., 2021). In order to be able to grasp the different scales, on a national scale, Germany was chosen as case in point with one of the highest percentages of tenant housing, and Berlin as local case in point, representing one of the most vividly debated contexts for housing policies nationally and internationally. Through our sample we are able to show how political advocacy in the governance of housing is on the one hand based on specific understandings of housing itself, which account for a great deal of the legitimisation of advocacy organisations. On the other hand, advocacy strategically switches between local, translocal, national and transnational references, which form the most flexible part of organisational legitimacy. In the framework of our analysis, we build upon organisational and political research on housing as well as on discussions on the relevance of scale, re-scaling and general processes of transnationalisation. In a combination of these perspectives, we engage in analysing the refiguration (Löw and Knoblauch, 2020) of spatial references in the advocacy of the governance of housing. The concept 'refiguration' refers to processes and dynamics of change in terms of 'social structures, knowledge and imaginations, and everyday actions' (Löw and Knoblauch, 2020: 266) that are mediated and expressed spatially in at times very contradictory processes like nationalisation and globalisation, territorialisation and deterritorialisation, inclusion and exclusion, among others.

Framework of analysis

Housing and housing politics

Housing is a remarkable field of research. It is considered an existential need, a human right, and a prerequisite for individual autonomy (Dawkins, 2017), relating (physical) shelter to individual as well as collective social needs (Foley, 1980). Housing is also a practice we all do every day, albeit under very unequal conditions – which also highlights the fact that housing needs to be addressed relationally (Holm and Metzkow, 2021). As a consumer good, housing is not only consumed, but also produced and traded – it reflects and is an integral part of the circulation of capital (Aalbers and Christophers, 2014: 375). Ownership can be public, private, corporate, communal, cooperative or familial (Schwartz and Seabrooke, 2008: 242); and last but not least, housing has become an 'investment vehicle' (Schwartz and Seabrooke, 2008: 242), the financialisation of housing currently representing a very lively field of investigation in housing research (Aalbers, 2016; Jacobs, 2019). Equally multifaceted as housing itself are the actors involved in housing politics. They range from tenant initiatives and social movement organisations representing slum dwellers, homeless and other marginalised groups, to traditional tenant associations, associations and interest groups in the real estate and construction industry, but also cooperatives and public housing companies, investment funds, credit institutions and banks, through to local authorities and the various levels of government.

Among these different state and non-state, corporate and civil actors, complex, but fairly stable networks of established organisations have formed and represent the context of the governance of housing. The organisational field of housing is characterised by a high degree of institutional complexity (Read and Sedgwick, 2023), corresponding to the multiple logics of housing itself. While the stakeholders involved do not vary greatly, there is a considerable differentiation of institutional environments and respective 'systems of norms, values, beliefs and definitions' (Read and Sedgwick, 2023: 155) these stakeholders act within. Due to the fact that housing involves social, (welfare) state and market aspects that are closely interrelated, the politics of housing and all involved actors respond to these interrelations in one way or another. Thus, our sample is driven by the observation that it is not always the clear assignment of stakeholders to these different spheres that accounts for meaningful differences. Many stakeholders cannot be determined as clearly state, market or civil society actors. Rather, we see the most important differentiation dimensions in *scale*, and the question of whether actors are involved in the *provision* or *tenancy* of housing. Institutional complexity for organisations stems from the pursuit of legitimacy in different fields, and in our research, we are interested in determining how this varies for provision and tenancy-oriented actors on different scales and how this is strategically implemented in the advocacy for specific housing policies.

Not only the organisations, but also the governance of housing itself is multiply contextualised between local practice, regional differentiations, international relations and global interrelations. Primarily nationally defined legal frameworks interact with global economic drivers and the locally specific relationship between supply and demand. Housing policy is therefore not only shaped by the actors, but also by the different spatial scales along which housing, the housing market and housing policy are organised in specific places, territories and networks. In Berlin, this complex situation has recently become most evident. The referendum on the socialisation of the portfolios of large housing companies, 'Deutsche Wohnen & Co. enteignen' (Expropriate Deutsche Wohnen & Co.) raised the political question about the conditions of urban living and decisive power in shaping them. This decisive power is not only an actor-related question, but also a spatial one: what can be decided *in* Berlin *for* Berlin and why is this important? Our research thus combines an actor-related perspective with a spatial, scalar perspective (Hoerning 2021) looking into the dynamics of housing politics with a focus on advocacy organisations at the city, state and international level.

Comparing advocacy organisations on different scales

Drawing on semi-structured interviews and document analysis of housing advocacy organisations (HAOs), representing both housing providers and tenants on the local (Berlin), national (Germany) and European level, we analyse how these actors engage in influencing the governance of housing, shaping housing related policies, and building up networks with political actors in the field of housing. The overall history of HAOs points towards an upscaling of the governance of housing. From the beginnings of interest organisations and cooperatives in the local context in the nineteenth century, HAOs have evolved as organisational networks from local up to international umbrella organisations. While globally acting HAOs are less common, the European context contains a number of different umbrella organisations, representing both housing providers as well as tenants, connecting different national associations and providing a forum for networking. The national associations have in turn self-sufficient and politically independent regional and local associations. Companies, cooperatives and tenants are usually direct members of these regional and local organisations, not of the overarching umbrella organisations.

In order to represent this organisational network structure (Figure 7.1), we will briefly introduce our sample[1] according to its historical emergence, from the local to the European/international level and clustered by interest groups. Starting with the tenant side, the local tenant association Berliner Mieterverein (BMV) is the oldest organisation in our sample, founded in 1888, and describes itself as a political advocacy, tenant solidarity as well as advisory and service organisation. Even though its focus lies on Berlin, the European and national levels are becoming more and more important as they impact local tenants' situations and contextualise local living conditions economically and legally. BMV is one of fifteen regional associations of the German HAO DMB Deutscher Mieterbund (German Tenants' Association). DMB represents the German national umbrella organisation in our sample, mainly advocating in the areas where the national government has jurisdiction: funding state governments for housing promotion as well as tenancy law. In doing so, DMB cooperates with local initiatives and social movements as far as they have mutual aims, but it is more common that DMB collaborates with other institutional actors on the national level. Its predecessor goes as far back as 1900, when the first umbrella organisation of tenant associations was founded in Germany. As early as 1926, during the first international tenant congress in Zürich, the International League of Tenants, as the next step of upscaling of tenant associations, was founded. After World War II, the network was re-established as the International Union of Tenants (IUT) in 1955. Its history as a grassroots and social movement organisation is still important for its self-image and work today. IUT represents the tenant lobby on the European level (as well as more globally, but with a strong focus on Europe), connecting forty-four national, mostly European organisations.

On the supply side, the sample includes on the local level the BBU Verband Berlin-Brandenburgischer Wohnungsunternehmen (Association of Berlin-Brandenburg Housing Companies). BBU lobbies for providers' interests, representing companies, cooperatives and municipally owned corporations from Berlin and the state of Brandenburg. Again, the primordial relevance of the local level is reflected in the histories of the organisations, BBU representing the oldest organisation on the supply side, founded in 1897. BBU acts mostly regionally but also tries to sway housing policy on the very local level, for example, influencing the rent index of specific cities in Brandenburg. Thus, the advocacy organisation combines strongly diverging local housing conditions and respective economic interests of their members and political necessities. The same can be said for BBU's umbrella organisation, the German HAO GdW Bundesverband deutscher Wohnungs- und Immobilienunternehmen (Federal Association of German Housing and Real Estate Enterprises). Including BBU, the national organisation contains thirteen independent and autonomous regional associations and, thereby, around 3,000 housing cooperatives, municipal, church, private, state and federally owned housing and property companies throughout Germany.

Figure 7.1 The different advocacy groups, 2024. Graph © author, all rights reserved.

The GdW has strong ties to European housing policy: not only does it have its own European office, but it was also a founding member of the advocacy group Housing Europe (formerly the Network of European Social Housing Providers, CECODHAS) in 1988. Housing Europe cooperates with a wide range of partners in the housing sector on all advocacy sides, from tenants (IUT) to homeless (FEANTSA) or the European Community Land Trust Network (ECLTN), as well as with others on the providers' side such as UIPI (International Union of Property Owners), an advocacy organisation for private owners.

Our research focuses on the advocacy practices these organisations engage in. Advocacy organisations respond to their members' interests in a number of representative and communicative ways. Representing the members, the lobbyists very literally go to politicians and specific institutions such as the Berlin Senate, the German and the European Parliament, the European Commission or the Committee of the Regions, as well as to specific politicians, for example, parliamentary and party spokespersons for housing. This backdoor lobbying is obviously neither documented nor directly observable, but we have gathered data on this type of advocacy practice through interviews with lobbyists as well as politicians. There is also a type of formalised lobbying in terms of governments relying on the advocacy organisations as informants and legitimising assets for the formulation of new policies, but our focus was on active advocacy practices by the organisations themselves. Apart from face-to-face encounters, HAOs publish statements and policy briefs on specific legal acts in representative function, which are not a regularly issued, but an important type of document for our analysis. Besides these expectable representative functions, the organisations take on a series of communicative tasks. Most organisations publish a journal, addressed to their members, including interviews, opinions and reports of new trends or important events. This publication regime is highly important for their advocacy work and has been a central source of information within our document analysis. A hybrid advocacy practice – both representative and communicative – is to be found in press releases, as they are both oriented towards members as well as towards a general and political public in terms of lobbying.

Overall, our comparison of HAOs is based on interviews with core advocacy staff and important political actors such as party spokespersons (n= 16), as well as a document analysis of press releases, statements, journals, newsletters, year books, position papers, studies and reports. The interviews have been openly coded, and the documents have been systematised in a summarising content analysis.

Advocating for housing transnationally and translocally

Normative understandings of housing and strategic collaborations

The actors and their political positioning are based on diverging normative understandings of what housing actually is or should be. This general understanding has implications for the whole advocacy of the organisation. In order to understand this systematically, it helps to deploy a spatial perspective. Different positionings of the actors are based on their conceptualisation of 'smallest units', and the understandings of housing are spatially scaled and based on different spatial logics. These understandings are also used as a political (even if not entirely conscious) strategy by the organisations.

For tenant associations, i.e., the political players on the demand side, the smallest unit of reference is the *resident* and therefore it is the body and its material and social existence that takes centre stage. Tenant associations focus on use and use value (see also Holm and Metzkow, 2021). First and foremost, it is about understanding the home as a *place of use*. The interests of the demand side are therefore centred on a *logic of place*, based on the importance of the home as the basis of life and guarantor of quality of life. The home is a valuable asset, yet not primarily in financial terms, but as a reference point for opportunities and chances of living. An example of this perspective is provided by one of our interview partners from a tenant HAO:

> Everyone needs a place to live. That means everyone needs a home. That's why it's basically understandable that housing is a basic right, because in our part of the world, housing in the context of a dwelling always means a dwelling, including the seclusion of a dwelling and also the security of having a dwelling as a retreat for private ambitions, for love, for meetings, for all sorts of things. It's a core element of our existence and that's why housing is also part of the provision of basic needs. This is an important point in contrast to the

> interpretation that housing is above all a commodity that should be traded at a very high price. So, this is a fundamentally different assessment. (I45)

For the associations and interest organisations on the providers' side, on the other hand, the smallest unit is the *housing unit* itself, from the perspective of its exchange value as a property. Advocacy organisations on the provider side thus follow a particularly pronounced *network logic* when it comes to representing the interests of their members and member companies. Thus, the conditions of their business area should not be too different for the many different places (cities, regions) they engage in.

This distinction serves as a starting point for the positioning of different actors[2] and it is indicative of the different lobby groups. Still, the distinction is empirically not as clear-cut due to the fact that some stakeholders, such as GdW, blur the lines. They refer to housing as having a use value by being a safe haven for the residents but simultaneously interpret a 'functioning [housing] community' (I44) as a means for maintaining exchange value.

Another core understanding of housing and housing policy within the field does not highlight the differences among the various stakeholders, but, rather, the field's broad scope of topics. A core advocacy staff member of Housing Europe proclaimed that housing 'is at the crossroads of many things for people and also the crossroads of many public policies' (I08). This underlines, on the one hand, the importance of housing, both for people and politics. At the same time, this understanding of housing as an intersection, as a connecting element of many different topics, proves to be a widespread way of understanding housing in the field per se. With this relational understanding, HAOs have a broad spectrum of topics at their disposal, on which they position the interest of their members.

This metaphor of a crossroad hints at the common conceptualisation of advocacy associations as intermediary and brokerage actors between different state and housing segments (I44), which is also acknowledged by the lobbyists themselves. They describe themselves as intermediary actors, translators or interpreters who mediate knowledge about specific (local or national) situations along different levels (I08, I41).

Collaborations between different HAOs within the field are ambiguous and based on mutual topics, values or trust. It is common that the gap between the tenant and provider side is bridged by a mutual topic such as improving energy efficiency (I43) or applying for European funding (I10). Thus, for example, at the EU level, unusual alliances (from a local perspective) emerge between tenant and provision sides. The differences in relation to concrete housing realities in the local context are often strong, but the spatial distance and level of governance increase the degree of abstraction. For example, tenant associations on national and international levels are no longer concerned with individual housing fates. And the providers' associations may sometimes even represent socio-political positions in the interests of tenants – at least as long as they are not in conflict with the business interests of their members – in order to enhance housing policies at large.

Scale and the role of spatial knowledge

Advocacy requires expertise, not only topic-related but also about specific local conditions or regional differences. Thus, spatial knowledge is key for advocacy organisations and serves their legitimacy. The examined organisations pride themselves on the quantity and quality of their knowledge about housing and housing market situations 'on the ground' within different local and regional contexts. This knowledge is used for generalisations as well as for specifications in order to influence policymaking, thereby connecting different scales. Thus, organisations working on supranational levels can be addressed for their expertise on a local level just as local organisations may be requested to inform national policymaking (I45).

There are different ways that advocacy associations produce this kind of spatial knowledge. To be sure, they profit from the Russian doll principle of the organisational landscape of advocacy organisations (umbrella organisations including different national, regional and local organisations), which means that their members and memberships enable specific as well as overarching knowledge. They also publish statements, position and informative papers in their members' journals, which offer proof of these types of knowledge. Another way of producing knowledge is to commission research by academic or private institutions or scholars (I41, 43, 44, 45). In doing so, HAOs may sway the outcome of the studies:

> But these studies also have to be supported somehow, of course. In the [many years] that I have been involved ..., we have always returned them with strong (laughing) requests for revisions. Because, of course, we put a lot of thought into it ourselves and, in my opinion, we also have a high level of scientific quality among the experts, professional quality. And then we don't just take over any studies, but naturally scrutinise all sorts of things. I have completely overturned some ... (I41)

Spatial knowledge is transferred through and along various levels of scale. Firstly, it is very important to interpret how directives from the European level play out at the national or local level. Secondly, spatial knowledge is actually produced by moving back and forth between different scales and through the intersecting issues:

> That means I can tell someone that what you are planning in the Commission or [say] 'Dear Commission, that won't work', but we meet and my colleague from Germany in the field of energy or in the field of digitalisation, my

colleague from France in the field of digitalisation and my colleagues from the Netherlands and Denmark also come and give a picture of what it looks like in reality in our companies or in the municipality. And that's the opportunity we then have. (I44)

Besides producing and transferring knowledge, it is interesting to see what kind of knowledge HAOs deal with. Spatial knowledge is often expressed in numbers. Especially, associations on the provider side rely heavily on econometrics to describe the relevance of spatial conditions and to formulate recommendations. On the European level, policymaking is very related to numbers provided by the Directorate-General for statistics, Eurostat. These numbers are clustered nationally, and regional disparities are averaged out. Negotiating calculation methods – such as requesting the revision of calculation rates or adopting reference values – 'is quite an important part of lobbying. Sounds totally dry, but it is indeed important. Because political decisions are being made based on data' (I10), as one lobbyist emphasised. This metric approach also entails that the local specificity of housing conditions might not be considered in the decision-making process if they are not translated into numbers except for highly improbable contingencies:

And then Directorate-General for Economic and Financial Affairs makes a recommendation to the member states: you must provide more housing. So far, it has only done this once in the UK and then in the Greater London Area, which surprised us all. But we found out that the employee who wrote the report used to live there himself. So, it obviously caught his eye. Otherwise, this is not such an issue for the European Commission. But that's also because ... the data from Eurostat is only ever collected at national level. That means ... all these regional disparities ... [are] averaged out .... So, we said the following. We said, look at the housing-overburden rate, break it down to local housing markets, then you have the reality. And secondly, take a general look at the factors used to calculate this. (I10)

These two examples demonstrate the importance of numbers in European housing policy, the production and selection of those numbers proving to be highly influential. Advocacy organisations thus translate differing conditions into the metric language of the EU institutions in order to represent their interest groups, both harmonising (average) and differentiating (selection) the housing conditions at stake.

At the national level, numerical spatial knowledge is important when it comes to housing funding. The majority of this funding is provided by the federal government of Germany according to the 'Königstein formula': the amount of funding depends on a state's population as well as its econometrics. This is criticised by the German tenant association (I43) based on the account that funding should not only be earmarked for providing housing, but also for its features, such as infrastructural conditions on site, including the number of kindergartens and internet access.

The local level – locations and local conditions – plays an important role when it comes to advocating and dealing with knowledge about housing. First and foremost, this is seen in the strongly accumulated choice of locations for the HAO's offices: if they want to address European policy, they entertain an office in Brussels. If they want to address the German housing policy, they engage lobbyists in Berlin: 'Yes, the importance of that is tremendous. It is just not possible not to be in the closer surroundings of the policymakers' (I43).

But entertaining an office in Berlin or Brussels or any other government's location is not enough since housing realities are produced locally. The local scale becomes more meaningful as soon as it comes to the actual realities of planning, constructing and actual housing. Because knowledge about these realities is paramount for advocacy, the lobbyists require an organisational foot on the ground:

> Well, of course everywhere, where cities are somewhat larger, local housing politics are also shaped by our associations. They try to get involved in project planning. ... The whole planning of what I am going to build can only ever be done locally. This cannot be decided by someone from the Berlin ivory tower ... but only on site. (I43)

The general logic of the relevance of space for the conceptualisations of housing and advocacy strategies can be summed up as follows. Tenant and housing provider advocacy associations differ sharply in their self-perception and organisational legitimacy. While tenant HAOs are based on an understanding of housing in relation to residents as smallest units of relevance and thus rely on an understanding of housing as bound to the specific places of habitat, providers' HAOs are based on an understanding of housing in relation to the housing unit itself as the smallest unit of relevance, creating an understanding of housing as a network of differently placed commodities. Still, basic advocacy strategies and their reliance on spatial knowledge do not differ as sharply. The link is an understanding of housing at the crossroads of scales, sectors, and segments of society, allowing for different alliances and connections. Advocacy strategies converge into transscalar practices of linking locally and regionally specific knowledge to overarching policy expertise.

Translocal and transnational advocacy in housing

Our empirical data reveals that translocal and transnational dynamics emerge when spatial differences are significant. These dynamics may take different forms, especially since the housing sector is defined by various kinds of differences: housing markets, tenants' needs, national policies, competences of governmental bodies, building codes and methods or corporate forms just to name a few.

The embedding of housing markets in global financial cycles (Heeg, 2013) also has very localised effects. For example, housing markets are considered as multi-spatial which makes it more important to focus on local or regional conditions than having a national view. This entails that there is not *one* housing market within a country such as Germany. The unequal differences account for a challenge for housing politics and advocacy alike:

> Germany is a patchwork quilt. ... We have federal states where housing construction activities are not really necessary because there is enough housing. And we have other federal states where it is bitterly necessary because there is by no means enough housing. It is not that easy to turn this into a national policy. (I43)

In that sense, housing exhibits considerable similarities to labour, both fields pointing towards the necessity of understanding structural politics in the context of demographics, infrastructures and socio-economic practices. There is also a structural link between the lack of national policies and local/regional differentiation, as market actors respond a lot more flexibly to those lacunas in regulation, thereby accelerating the dynamics of unequal differentiation. Housing advocacy actors react to the changing structures of the housing markets through translocalisation strategies, i.e., they develop demands and strategies in which the focus remains on the local context (state and/or market), but they also display in their activities that it is becoming increasingly important to address the supra-local and global embedding of housing and to reflect this in networks and alliances (see Chapters 3, 13, 15). For advocacy organisations representing the providers, this is common practice and they also have the resources and personnel to do so. One of the major incentives for networking within the advocacy organisations is to engage in best practice-exchange. Against the backdrop of an evaluating process, taking into account market and political peculiarities on a local scale, the goal is that of upscaling promising business practices (I46). Translocalisation on the demand side has a less economic and primarily political character. For instance, tenant associations recognise the need to see the conditions in Barcelona, Oslo and Berlin as interconnected and advocate for this towards politicians when they push for government countermeasures in the face of the touristification of housing shortage due to Airbnb. In this specific case, there was a local ruling[3] in 2018 obliging Airbnb to hand over landlord data to Munich's city council. This ruling was evaluated by the lobbyist as applying 'to Munich, but in our opinion, this is actually a precedent judgment. This means that it would help many other cities in Europe' (I10).

The local tenant HAO, BMV, is translocally connecting different groups by co-organising activities and events like the Alternative Housing Summit in 2018 or campaigns like 'Mietenstopp' (stop the rent) in 2022 with demonstrations all over Germany demanding housing as a human right (I45). Such collaborations enable the sharing of resources and achieve effects which otherwise would be out of reach since the singular actors are missing the necessary financial and personnel resources.

But not only alliances and networks are forged translocally; knowledge and experience are also transferred from one location to another, sometimes crossing national borders (see Chapter 10). The 2016 Urban Agenda reinforced the urban dimension on the European level. It accounts for an example of both partnerships and knowledge exchange translocally and transnationally. The HAOs have engaged strongly in the development of the Urban Agenda. According to its promotion on the EU's website (European Commission, n.d.), the three main aspects are: better regulation, better funding and better knowledge. The designated initiatives and projects of the Urban Agenda entail translocal exchange, for example easy learnings between municipalities when it comes to funding applications, as a lobbyist explains (I10). Nevertheless, translocal and transnational flows are staunched when it comes to financial aspects: 'The cities take care of the whole provision of public services, but they are not immediately engaged in the financing. This is always done through the national level, and much is lost until it gets down there' (I10).

When it comes to transnational networks and alliances, there has been one tremendously important political event which paved the way for transnational housing advocacy in Europe: the Energy Performance of Buildings Directive which took effect in 2010. Before that, the European level was to a certain extent irrelevant to advocacy organisations as the political competences for housing promotion are largely with the member states, the European Union holding no mandate for the policy field per se. The directive, though, has been recognised as an 'awakening kiss for the housing sector' (I44). This directive has entailed major impacts on the manner of construction, not only on new buildings but also on already existing ones. Plus, directives will be transposed into national law by each nation in its own way. Thus, the directive has changed the sector's awareness: European policy thereby has demonstrated a direct impact on the national housing sector, even if housing promotion itself is managed on other governmental levels. European policy has therefore become important for housing companies, which in turn means that it has become important for their advocacy associations.

To influence European policy, the associations have always emphasised the formation of coalitions with other associations. In order to do that, mutual trust is needed but sometimes missing since prejudices are quite common. According to a core advocacy staff member from GdW, transnational exchange of knowledge builds mutual trust (I44): by meeting in person, those prejudices will be reduced – for example, when they come together to visit (pilot) projects. 'That is this aspect in recent years, where the added value of the European association and the reputation has also grown' (I44).

Tenants' HAOs are also working transnationally: by visiting IUT conferences, regional HAOs connect with other tenant associations around the world. Those transnational ties are considered important for the association's work, whether by learning from other countries or promoting its own initiatives: 'We maintain a lot of contacts. We go to conferences in Vienna. The rent cap, when that was introduced in Berlin, we advocated for it in Spain, France, everywhere, and the Spanish, the Catalan, they adopted the rent cap practically one-to-one. And that is naturally an effect of these international contacts' (I45).

With regard to spatial policies, this shows that HAOs engage in capitalising local and national specificities economically and politically in networking logics. Translocalisation and transnationalisation strategies both transfer knowledge, relate people and harmonise conditions, economically and politically.

Conclusion

Our analysis set off from the assertion that the organisational field of housing is characterised by a high degree of institutional complexity in correspondence with the multiple logics of housing itself. Addressing advocacy organisations lobbying for tenant housing both from the providers' as well as the residents' perspectives, we can affirm the differentiation of institutional environments and respective 'systems of norms, values, beliefs and definitions' (Read and Sedgwick, 2023: 155) between these stakeholders. Tenant and housing providers advocacy associations differ sharply in their self-perception and organisational legitimacy. While tenant HAOs are based on an understanding of housing in relation to residents as smallest units of relevance and thus rely on an understanding of housing as bound to the specific places of habitat, providers' HAOs are based on an understanding of housing in relation to the housing unit itself as smallest unit of relevance, creating an understanding of housing as a network of differently placed commodities.

Still, basic advocacy strategies and their reliance on spatial knowledge do not differ as sharply. The link is an understanding of housing at the crossroads of scales, sectors and segments of society, allowing for different alliances and connections. Advocacy strategies converge into transscalar practices of linking locally and regionally specific knowledge to overarching policy expertise. While housing advocacy organisations often claim to merely respond to market and general political dynamics shaping tenant housing, they contribute both to the unequal differentiation as well as harmonisation dynamics through their lobbying, which corresponds to translocal and transnational processes of convergence and divergence alike.

Government levels are highly institutionalised, but the relationship between those levels and the spatial scale they address is not at all clear. Translocal, transnational and global dynamics have led to the fact that many things clearly cannot be regulated within the boundaries of institutionalised state levels. Shifts between those levels only clumsily respond to these challenges. These dynamics are highly conflictive fields of negotiating spatial refiguration in the context of housing. While the advocacy organisations are commonly organised according to government levels (mostly city, state and national associations), the shifts between those levels have led to the emergence of new European associations as well as a restructuring of particular organisations following the logic of political up-scaling. Therefore, we can observe negotiations of refiguration within and between the organisations.

Housing advocacy is, therefore, neither local nor national or international, but oscillates between local and national specificities, as well as translocal and transnational relations. Processes of transnationalisation are generally understood as 'sustained cross-border ties, events and processes across the borders of several national states' (Faist 2010: 1667), that are shaped by state *and* non-state agents alike. In the field of housing politics, the processes of translocalisation – sustaining cross-local ties, events and processes – and of transnationalisation are to a great extent shaped by advocacy organisations, both from the housing providers as well as tenants.

Research Funding

This research was funded by Deutsche Forschungsgemeinschaft (DFG, German Research Foundation), project number 290045248 – SFB 1265.

Table 7.1 Interview sample

I08	Housing Europe, Brussels, 18 December 2018
I10	International Union of Tenants, IUT, Brussels, 19 December 2018
I39	Party Spokesperson GRÜNE, German Parliament, Berlin, 15 March 2021
I41	GdW Bundesverband deutscher Wohnungs- und Immobilien-unternehmen (Federal Association of German Housing and Real Estate Enterprises), Berlin, 25 March 2021
I43	Deutscher Mieterbund, DMB (German Tenant Association), Berlin, 30 March 2021
I44	GdW Bundesverband deutscher Wohnungs- und Immobilien-unternehmen (Federal Association of German Housing and Real Estate Enterprises), Brussels, 27 April 2021
I45	Berliner Mieterverein, BMV (Berlin Tenants‘ Association), Berlin, 24 June 2021
I46	BBU Verband Berlin-Brandenburgischer Wohnungsunter-nehmen (Associations of Berlin and Brandenburg Housing and Real Estate Enterprises) Berlin, 02 July 2021
I49	Party spokesperson FDP, Berlin Senate, 24 September 2021
I51	Secretary of State, Federal Ministry of Internal Affairs, Berlin, 30 September 2021
I53	European Investment Bank, Brussels, 13 January 2022
I54	Party spokesperson CDU, Berlin, 21 January 2022
I58	Party spokesperson LINKE, Berlin Senate, 08 April 2022

Source: Author's own.

Notes

1 The sample within our research project was wider and included HAOs representing homeowners (Haus & Grund, Germany) as well as the wider real estate market (German Property Federation, ZIA, Germany), and the construction industry (International Housing Association).

2 State actors address housing through administrative units such as neighbourhoods, cities and federal states. These are organised *territorially*. Obviously, they also approach housing in terms of the various social groups for which they (want to) shape policies. These include not only income groups or families or certain professions, but also owners and companies.

3 In 2020, this ruling has been overruled by the Higher Administrative Court of Bavaria in favour of Airbnb (Fuchs, 2020).

References

Aalbers, M. (2016), *The Financialization of Housing. A Political Economy Approach* (London and New York: Routledge).

Aalbers, M. (2022), 'Towards a relational and comparative rather than a contrastive global housing studies', *Housing Studies*, 37:6, 1054–72, https://doi.org/10.1080/02673037.2022.2033176

Aalbers, M., and B. Christophers (2014), 'Centering Housing in Political Economy', *Housing, Theory and Society*, 31:4, 373–94, https://doi.org/10.1080/14036096.2014.947082

Aalbers, M., J. van Loon, and R. Fernandes (2017), 'The Financialization of a Social Housing Provider', *International Journal of Urban and Regional Research*, 41:4, 572–87, https://doi.org/10.1111/1468-2427.12520

Byrne, M. (2015), 'Bad banks: the urban implications of asset management companies', *Urban Research & Practice*, 8:2, 255–62, https://doi.org/10.1080/17535069.2015.1050208

Czischke, D. (2007), 'A Policy Network Perspective on Social Housing Provision in the European Union: The Case of CECODHAS', *Housing, Theory and Society*, 24:1, 63–87, https://doi.org/10.1080/14036090601003056

Dawkins, C. J. (2017), 'Autonomy and Housing Policy', *Housing, Theory and Society*, 34:4, 420–38, https://doi.org/10.1080/14036096.2016.1274679

Doling, J. (2006), 'A European Housing Policy?', *International Journal of Housing Policy*, 6:3, 335–49, https://doi.org/10.1080/14616710600973169

European Commission (n.d.), 'Urban Agenda for the EU'. Available at https://commission.europa.eu/eu-regional-and-urban-development/topics/cities-and-urban-development/urban-agenda-eu_en (accessed 19 November 2024).

Faist, T. (2010), 'Towards Transnational Studies: World Theories, Transnationalisation and Changing Institutions', *Journal of Ethnic and Migration Studies*, 36:10, 1665–87, https://doi.org/10.1080/1369183X.2010.489365

Foley, D. L. (1980), 'The Sociology of Housing', *Annual Review of Sociology*, 6, 457–78.

Fuchs, I. (2020), 'Stadt München unterliegt Airbnb in Streit um Herausgabe von Daten', *Süddeutsche Zeitung*, 4 June 2020.

Heeg, S. (2013), 'Wohnungen als Finanzanlage. Auswirkungen von Responsibilisierung und Finanzialisierung im Bereich des Wohnens', *sub\urban. zeitschrift für kritische stadtforschung*, 1:1, 75–99, https://doi.org/10.36900/suburban.v1i1.71

Herrle, P., A. Ley, and J. Fokdal (eds) (2015), *From Local Action to Global Networks: Housing the Urban Poor* (London and New York: Routledge).

Hoerning, J. (2021), 'Comparing Actors and Scales: Methodological Perspectives from a Political Sociology of the Refiguration of Spaces', *Forum Qualitative Sozialforschung / Forum: Qualitative Social Research*, 22:3, https://doi.org/10.17169/fqs-22.3.3763

Hoerning, J., T. Adenstedt, and P. Welch Guerra (2021), 'Dynamiken und Praktiken räumlicher Restrukturierung: NGOs und Interessensorganisationen in der Wohn- und Asylpolitik', in M. Löw, V. Sayman, J. Schwerer, and H. Wolf (eds), *Am Ende der Globalisierung. Über die Refiguration von Räumen* (Bielefeld: transcript), pp. 83–107.

Holm, A., and K. Metzkow (2021), 'Wohnen als Soziales Verhältnis', in A. Holm (ed.), *Wohnen zwischen Markt, Staat und Gesellschaft. Ein sozialwissenschaftliches Handbuch* (Hamburg: VSA), pp. 151–71.

Hölzl, C., and D. Hölzl (2022), 'Establishing new housing commons in Vienna in the context of translocal networks', *Housing Studies*, 39:5, 1152–75, https://doi.org/10.1080/02673037.2022.2104820

Jacobs, K. (2019), *Neoliberal Housing Policy. An International Perspective* (New York: Routledge).

Janoschka, M., G. Alexandri, H. O. Ramos, and S. Vives-Miró (2019), 'Tracing the socio-spatial logics of transnational landlords' real estate investment: Blackstone in Madrid', *European Urban and Regional Studies*, 27:2, 125–41, https://doi.org/10.1177/0969776418822061

Lauster, N., and J. von Bergmann (2023), 'The rise of Housing Nationalism in Canada and transnational property ownership patterns', *Journal of Ethnic and Migration Studies*, 51:9, 2242–69, https://doi.org/10.1080/1369183x.2023.2293635

Löw, M., and H. Knoblauch (2020), 'The Re-Figuration of Spaces and Refigured Modernity – Concept and Diagnosis', *Historical Social Research*, 45:2, 263–92.

Matznetter, W. (1992), 'Organizational Networks in a Corporatist Housing System Non-Profit Housing Associations and Housing Politics in Vienna, Austria', *Scandinavian Housing and Planning Research*, 9:sup2, 23–35, https://doi.org/10.1080/02815737.1992.10801440

Mendes, L. (2021), 'Transnational gentrification and the housing market during pandemic times, Lisbon style', *Urban Geography*, 42:7, 1003–10, https://doi.org/10.1080/02723638.2021.1949832

Paris, C. (2017), 'The Super-Rich and Transnational Housing Markets: Asians Buying Australian Housing', in R. Forrest, S. Koh, and B. Wissink (eds), *Cities and the Super-Rich. The Contemporary City* (New York: Palgrave Macmillan), pp. 63–83, https://doi.org/10.1057/978-1-137-54834-4_4

Priemus, H., and F. Dieleman (2002), 'Social Housing Policy in the European Union: Past, Present and Perspectives', *Urban Studies*, 39:2, 191–200, https://doi.org/10.1080/00420980120102911

Read, D. C., and D. Sedgwick (2023), 'Competing Logics in the Affordable Housing Industry: A Comparative Analysis of How Various Types of Professionals in the For-Profit and Non-Profit Sectors Conceptualize Their Work and that of Their Companies', *Housing, Theory and Society*, 40:2, 152–69, https://doi.org/10.1080/14036096.2022.2118369

Schwartz, H., and L. Seabrooke (2008), 'Varieties of Residential Capitalism in the International Political Economy: Old Welfare States and the New Politics of Housing', *Comparative European Politics*, 6, 237–61, https://doi.org/10.1057/cep.2008.10

She, X. (2023), 'Global city formation, authoritarian politics, and transnational policy transfer: The case of affordable housing in China', *Asian Politics & Policy*, 15:3, 408–30, https://doi.org/10.1111/aspp.12708

Vargas-Silva, C., and P. Boccagni (2023), 'Dreaming of a Remittance House: Understanding Transnational Housing Aspirations', *International Migration Review*, 58:3, 1226–49, https://doi.org/10.1177/01979183231170812

Yerena, A. (2015), 'The Impact of Advocacy Organizations on Low-Income Housing Policy in U.S. Cities', *Urban Affairs Review*, 51:6, 843–70, https://doi.org/10.1177/1078087415571451

Yerena, A. (2019), 'Strategic Action for Affordable Housing: How Advocacy Organizations Accomplish Policy Change', *Journal of Planning Education and Research*, 43:3, 468–81, https://doi.org/10.1177/0739456X19888000

8

The emergence of student housing cooperatives in the UK: Grassroots activism, translocal networks and situational challenges

Anke Schwittay

Introduction

How do students respond to the financialisation of their housing, which has resulted in unaffordable, inadequate and often unhealthy living conditions in many countries around the world? Academic studies have focused on rent strikes, protests and other forms of direct action that students have taken to fight for better housing (Reynolds, 2022; Sotomayor et al., 2022; Steffens et al., 2022). In this chapter, I explore another response that so far has not received much scholarly attention – the establishment of student housing cooperatives (henceforth SHCs), with a focus on the UK. By setting up SHCs, students are creating housing alternatives that put them in control of the governance, management and maintenance of their homes. In this way, they are building affordable and sustainable homes that contribute to the creation of an urban housing commons through prefigurative practices that address housing problems collectively in the here and now.

Commoning refers to the production of non-commodified public spaces that are collectively maintained outside of private or state ownership structures. From its beginnings in natural resource management (Ostrom, 1990), there has been a growing literature exploring the situated practices of urban commoning (Breshnihan and Byrne, 2015). These practices are characterised by a particular tension: on the one hand, cities are particularly fertile ground for experimentations with direct democracy and post-capitalist values that urban commoners frequently espouse (Chatterton, 2016). On the other, urban spaces are exposed to greater state regulation and capitalist dynamics that create extra obstacles to commoning practices, especially for marginalised groups (Huron, 2018). Nevertheless, many cities around the world have seen a rise in urban commons initiatives, often in response to the enclosure and financialisation of urban space. Housing is one area where these dynamics have been particularly acute, especially after the 2008 financial crisis. In response, creating housing commons has been the focus of many recent activist struggles (Fields, 2015; Di Feliciantonio, 2017; Joubert and Hodkinson, 2018).

Student housing cooperatives, where students collectively govern and manage their own housing, are one example of these struggles (Schwittay, 2025). Following Hodkinson's (2012) typology of three interrelated practices of urban housing commoning, first, student cooperators engage in prefigurative commoning, which is a pragmatic approach that focuses on everyday relationships created through living-in-common and their material and aesthetic forms. Second, they are building 'actually existing commons [that are] live relics of the ideal of the commons; and third, they are never complete and perfect and may even have components that contradict the ideal type' (Eizenberg, 2012: 765). This implies that rather than being pure spaces of resistance, SHCs are partial and hybrid, co-existing with multiple public and private forms of ownership, tenure and governance. In the UK, they most closely resemble tenant housing cooperatives as students do not own their houses outright. Instead, they partner with secondary organisations that own the properties and lease them long-term to the SHCs, which are independent legal entities registered under the UK's Cooperative and Community Benefit Societies Act that all student residents join. However, student cooperators exert practical ownership as they collectively make all decisions related to their houses, including financial, membership and management decisions.

SHCs are most prominent in North America, and especially the US, where the first coop was established in 1873 in Evanston, Illinois, by wealthy women who purchased a house for female college students who were excluded from other housing (Jones, 2019). To keep the rents low, residents had to do their own cooking and cleaning on a cooperative basis, a practice that has remained central to the functioning of SHCs to this day. From these origins they have often aimed to provide housing for marginalised groups, in line with the general cooperative principle of open membership and the activist orientation of many student cooperators (Mericle et al., 1994). More independent coops that were not owned by universities or wealthy benefactors began to appear in response to the Great Depression; the largest of which at the University of California Berkeley now houses over 1,000 students in multiple houses. Across North America, there are dozens of coops that are home to around 10,000 students.

In this chapter, I focus on the student housing coop movement in the UK, which traces its origins to the founding of Student Cooperative Dwellings (SCD – later Sanford Cooperative Dwellings) in London in 1968 (Hands, 2016). SCD lobbied the government for five years to fund a pilot project, by which time the coop had expanded its mission from students to young people in general. The coop is still flourishing as a general housing coop. Nothing much happened for the next thirty years, until in 2002/2003 individual efforts restarted in Manchester, where a local architect began advocating for SHCs. As a result, the UK's National Union of Students (NUS) invited members of the North American Students for Cooperation (NASCO) to learn from their successes (Jones, 2019). The NUS, together with the student unions at several Manchester universities and partially funded by the Co-op, a large mainstream British consumer cooperative, then commissioned a study to develop a potential model for UK student cooperative housing (URBED 2004). Because of leadership changes at the student unions and the general top-down nature of the project, this attempt came to nothing (Jones, 2024). Nevertheless, the translocal relationship between UK and North American student cooperators has played a significant part in the re-emergence of SHCs in the UK, whose founders have been inspired by their own visits to US SHCs, participation in NASCO events and international knowledge exchanges.

The founders' own activist grassroots efforts back home were more successful, resulting in Edinburgh Student Housing Cooperative (ESHC) and Birmingham Student Housing Cooperative (BSHC) opening their doors in 2014. ESHC is the largest SHC in the UK, housing 106 residents in 24 flats in two housing blocks. BSHC has a 9-bedroom house, while a third coop called SEASALT opened in a 7-bedroom house in the Moulsecoomb suburb of Brighton in 2021. After two further coops in Nottingham and Sheffield had to close due to technical and interpersonal reasons, in 2025 the Glasgow Student Housing Cooperative (GSHC) was able to purchase a 5-bedroom house. Together, these four coops house 120 students, with groups in several other student cities actively looking for properties. This means that SHCs provide only a very small part of overall student accommodations, with the bulk supplied by private developers and universities. Still, as I show below, coops are an important alternative to these provisions.

This chapter draws on my ongoing action research with UK student cooperators and their supporters, which began in 2021 and includes secondary research, interviews, on-site participatory observations as well as activist engagement. Contextual knowledge about SHCs was obtained through extensive secondary research of organisational websites, social media pages, newspaper articles and videos. This informed the semi-structured interviews I have to date conducted with thirty-seven key participants, ranging from coop founders, early and current residents to staff in supporting organisations. On-site research has been taking place at ESHC and SEASALT in order to gain a better understanding of physical spaces and to see cooperative living in practice. Wanting to support the work of my research participants, I have increasingly engaged in action research, defined as 'bring[ing] together action and reflection, theory and practice, in participation with others, in the pursuit of practical solutions to issues of pressing concern to people' (Reason and Bradbury, 2001: 1). Inspired equally by the determination of student cooperators and J. K. Gibson-Graham's call (2008) for academics to become subjects of possibility through supporting alternative experiments (Schwittay, 2021), I see action research as particularly suited to exploring the transgressive possibilities of scholarly commitments (Gayá and Brydon-Miller, 2017). To this end, I co-organised a national cooperative gathering at Sussex University, volunteer with two supporting organisations and co-edited a collaborative publication celebrating the tenth anniversary of the UK movement (Schwittay and Hartly, 2024).

Building on this research, my analysis addresses the three central questions of this edited collection. How were the SCHs established through grassroots efforts by student activists? What kinds of translocal networks and partnerships do student cooperators build to enable their work? And what are the challenges that arise from students' unique situatedness as young, transient and often precarious subjects? These questions inform the three main findings sections of the remainder of this chapter.

Grassroots activism

All existing SHCs started with grassroots effort by committed student activists, and in this section I trace their persistent efforts that laid the groundwork for the opening of cooperative homes. As argued in the introduction to this collection, grassroots housing models encompass local communities, self-governance and collective participation, all of which were part of the emergence of SHCs in the UK. Experienced student activists often took the lead and I will begin this section by showing how both ESHC and BSHC grew out of the 2010 student protests against rising tuition fees, coupled with personal experiences of housing exploitation. As a result, student cooperators are consciously modelling housing alternatives, with unique spatial and temporal qualities.

Several of the ESHC and BSHC founders were involved in the 2010 National Campaign against Fees and Cuts, when tens of thousands of students marched through central London and occupied universities around the country to protest against cuts to government education spending and the tripling of tuition fees (Amsler, 2011). As a result of these protests, the founders became 'battle-hardened, stubborn and capable organisers' (Shaw and Farmelo, 2017: 59). Even though they lost the campaign and draconic financial measures were implemented, some activists came away with new energies, increased confidence and a growing interest in self-help, mutuality and cooperatives. These resulted in the establishment of food, bike and re-use coops across university campuses, which in turn generated spaces for critical discussions about capitalism and the marketisation of Higher Education (HE) and housing, as well as alternatives to both (Kallin and Shaw, 2019). In other words, rather than being paralysed by their defeat, student activists looked for novel ways to resist by building alternatives in the cracks of the capitalist system (Holloway, 2010). As a BSHC co-founder explained, 'if we can't stop fees rising and prevent cuts to support, then we will need to find another way to make studying affordable. And that would be housing as another big expense'. He thereby established a direct connection between broader student activism and the cooperative housing movement's emergence, showing activists' innovative abilities to 'switch collective labour that generates rents into alternative forms of housing provision' (Joubert and Hodkinson, 2018: 189).

In addition to their political involvement, many coop founders were motivated by personal horrible housing experiences, which ranged from viewing overpriced and unsafe properties to being forced to live in them. As one ESHC founder recalled: 'I had really experienced some bad housing, partly through the price, so I couldn't afford where I was living for a number of years, which put me in a lot of debt and affected my ability to afford food and the like, which had a significant knock-on effect on my studies and my mental health'. While the founders shared this situation with many – maybe most – other students, they recognised their experiences not as a personal or even collective misfortune, but as caused by the structural forces of the capitalist housing market, the financialisation of student housing and the broader marketisation of UK HE. Going even further, they used this recognition as the motivation to create a new grassroots student housing model. This meant that in addition to more common forms of student protests such as rent strikes or occupations, they also engaged in building new physical and social structures to enable different ways of living together. In doing so, they 'shifted conceptions of resistance as subversion or opposition to one of resistance as transformation, … disrupt[ed] logics of power that are very effective in suffocating hope and [created] mental, physical and temporal spaces for cultivating alternative ways of thinking and acting together' (Amsler, 2011: 77, 78).

Through consciously modelling alternatives to the exploitative student housing market, student housing cooperators also want to help other students imagine what is possible. In the process they are creating a new social imaginary that pushes back against a common totalising discourse of capitalist domination as well. As one early ESHC resident argued, 'we are socialised to believe that without capitalism there would be chaos, violence and disorder, and humanity would descend into anarchy. But the coop is not a chaotic mess, it is a self-managing space [that] provides opportunities for liberating and creative work that brings the best out of the people' (quoted in Perez Ruiz and Shaw, 2019: 183). By speaking back, through collective practical action, to the narrative of no-alternative to capitalism (Gibson-Graham, 2008), student cooperators are building alter-capitalist possibilities in the here and now. Their creations have unique spatial and temporal characteristics.

Spatially, SHCs are located in university towns and therefore intersect with studentification debates. Many UK cities with large student populations have seen a backlash against their 'studentification' and the resulting gentrification and community displacement (Smith, 2005). The popular discourse of students as noisy, messy and generally bad neighbours has led to neighbourhood mobilisations against student homes, such as the National HMO (Houses in Multiple Occupancy) Lobby or more local actions (Sage et al., 2013). Building good neighbourly relations and showing that students can be positive members of the community was therefore an important part of the SHC establishment process for some founders. In Brighton, SEASALT founders went door to door to inform neighbours about the coop and answer any questions they might have, and to this day there are occasional BBQs in the SEASALT garden to which neighbours are invited. In Birmingham, British Sign Language classes, which were started when a hearing-impaired student moved into the coop, were opened up to interested neighbours, and in Edinburgh, the basement converted by students into a social space is also made available to external community groups. As one coop supporter explained, 'if you change the relationship that people have to their property, it empowers them to change the relationship to the community they are in. It's completely the opposite of building a huge block and dumping it in the middle of a neighbourhood and having a lot of students who have no connections to it sort of ambling through'. Building connections with their surrounding neighbourhoods is therefore one aim of SHCs, whose residents want to counter the negative perception of students' presence in the urban landscape and contribute to building 'neighbourhood commons' (Hodkinson, 2012: 438).

SHCs also have a unique temporal dimension of investing in the future, because their founders were often motivated to create better housing not for themselves but for future students. Many of the founders never got to live in the coops they built, usually because they had graduated by the time these opened. They were thus acutely aware that their work was for subsequent generations of students, a belief that continues among current residents. Setting up and taking care of SHCs so that the next cohort of students, which is likely to face the same or worse housing challenges, can find affordable and safe houses is an important motivation for student cooperators. This corresponds to scholarly arguments that coop residents are the stewards of the housing commons with a right to dwell there but also a responsibility to keep it in the commons for other members of society who should have access to it (Bruun, 2015). In other words, at a specific, material scale, housing coops, including SHCs, can meet the immediate needs of their current members, while at a broader social scale they can 'serve as a sort of promise to other would-be-commoners that they, too, will ultimately benefit' (Huron, 2018: 56). All of this shows that the grassroots activism of student cooperators has created alternative student housing models in the UK that aim to disrupt common narratives about capitalism and student neighbours alike. However, they would not have been able to open their cooperative homes without the help of like-minded individuals and organisations, which embeds student cooperators in translocal networks of support.

Diverse actors and translocal networks of support

More than other forms of collaborative housing, SHCs are necessarily 'self-organised/managed and highly mediated through collaboration with state and professional institutions' (Thompson, 2020: 87). The main reason for this is that students do not usually have access to mortgage finance and are therefore dependent on secondary institutions for the purchase of their cooperative properties, which are then leased to the coops on a long-term basis. In addition to this financial support, external institutions also provide professional advice and legitimacy. In this section, I trace the translocal networks in which UK student housing cooperators have embedded themselves, beginning with how support from local cooperative associations, universities, councils, housing associations and community land trusts (CLTs) helped with the purchase of properties. I will then explore two national-level networks created specifically around SHCs and analyse the ambivalent alliances that result from them.

The establishment of ESHC in 2014 had support from the University of Edinburgh's Rector and other senior leaders, one of whom had lived in a US SHC during his own student days. Following a student union referendum where 92% of respondents voted in favour of the coop's establishment, the founders began working with Edinburgh city council and a long-standing member of the Scottish Cooperative Enterprise Hub to find a suitable property. The latter introduced the ESHC founders to Castle Rock Edinvar (CRE), a local housing association, which had two older university halls available and agreed to lease these to ESHC (Shaw, 2024). Having the experienced cooperator in the room during lease negotiations was critical because he bestowed credibility and legitimacy. As an ESHC founder recounted: 'there was a lot of benefit when we got older people from the coop movement who could attend meetings with us, even if they didn't speak much. Just having somebody there with grey hair added a degree of legitimacy and made people take us more seriously'.

BSHC was established at around the same time as ESHC (Farmelo, 2024). Its founders did not have the same university support as in Edinburgh, however, because of a more adversarial relationship between students and Birmingham University managers resulting from local student protests. Instead, the founders were inspired by existing non-student housing cooperatives in the city. They also sought out support from groups like Radical Routes, a grassroots activist UK housing cooperative network, and the Confederation of Cooperative Housing (CCH), the more mainstream national umbrella organisation of housing cooperatives. Most significant was their partnership with Birmingham Cooperative Housing Services, a local cooperative housing and community regeneration agency, where a key supporter remembered that 'it was clear that there was a really capable group of students that organised all sorts of things ... They were used to operating in a democratic fashion and carrying out their decisions quite expertly'. Trusting in the students' abilities, he introduced them to the Phone Coop, an independent consumer cooperative, which eventually purchased the property and leased it to the students. The coop became famous for its Friday night dinners that brought together students interested in cooperative and more general student politics.

While the Sussex SHC started in 2018 as the manifesto pledge of a student union officer, it was a partnership with the Brighton and Hove Community Land Trust (BHCLT) that made the purchase of its home possible. They collaborated on a crowdfunding campaign that raised over £300,000 in low-interest loans for the down payment and accessibility modifications. This collaboration is following a nation-wide trend in the UK where the emergence of CLTs has led the way in building mutual housing alternatives in several cities (Thompson, 2015; Bunce, 2016). Additional funds came from several sources, including the university and the national Community Housing Fund, which paid for a part-time manager and architect (see Chapter 2). The Sussex coop, called SEASALT (South-East Students Autonomously Living Together), opened its doors in the fall of 2021 to students in local universities and further education colleges.

These three origin stories show the diverse networks of support students built to realise their aspirations, which mostly included local institutions supporting the acquisition of the houses. In addition, student cooperators created their own translocal networks. Specifically, ESHC and BSHC founders established Students for Cooperation (SfC) as a national umbrella organisation for student cooperatives of all kinds. When the Cooperative Congress, the yearly event of the national network of British cooperatives, took place in Birmingham in 2014, Birmingham cooperators wearing bright yellow SfC T-shirts talked about their just opened coop and thereby generated much visibility and goodwill from attending older cooperators. For the latter, it is the very renewal of the cooperative movement, with its ageing membership, that is at stake. As one long-term supporter put it starkly, 'the older generation of cooperators know that they will die out without younger members'. Indeed, many former student cooperators stay involved in cooperative activities, for example living in general housing coops, working for cooperative organisations or becoming involved in new cooperative developments.

In 2016, SfC commissioned a study to set up a national body of student housing coops, which identified limited access to finance, lack of cooperative knowledge and skills and high student turnover as the most salient challenges (ACORN, 2016). This study led to the creation of Student Coop Homes, a secondary cooperative that works to increase student cooperative capacity through securing finance and properties and providing financial, management, tax and other technical advice to the SHCs (Woodell, 2024) (see Chapter 15). Obtaining such professional expertise is critical for the success of SHCs, as the legal and tax landscape around cooperative housing in the UK is complex. Making mistakes, which can easily happen to inexperienced student cooperators, can have dramatic financial implications and create extra work and emotional stress for students. In 2021, Student Coop Homes conducted a successful crowdfunding campaign that raised over £300,000 in low-interest loans, including £100,000 from a regional consumer cooperative, £7,000 from a US student housing coop and many smaller contributions from individual cooperative supporters. These funds are one concrete example of translocal supportive networks that encompass established cooperative institutions and individuals at home and abroad. These networks provide financial support, technical expertise, legitimacy and inspiration.

What motivates these manifold forms of support? Many research participants cited the sixth Rochdale principle of cooperation (among cooperatives) as the basis for cooperative networks in which they are embedded. These principles are a set of foundational values for the operation of cooperatives formulated by the founders of the modern cooperative movement in Rochdale (England) in 1844. Another term that was used by some was 'intergenerational solidarity', as a description of what binds different cohorts of cooperators together. A BSHC founder felt that one possible motivation of older cooperators was that the post-war consensus around housing and education has been 'broken by neoliberalism', and they want to support student cooperators who are doing something about it. Older cooperators in turn see benefits in the continued existence of the cooperative movement.

In other words, translocal support networks manifest in mutually beneficial relationships that have enabled the establishment of SHCs and facilitate their continued existence.

However, these partnerships are far from straightforward. Some student cooperators felt that the mainstream cooperative movement had acted too late by not buying properties for students when housing was still (more) affordable in the UK. For others, personal differences mattered more. A SEASALT founder described the UK coop sector as 'very white and … also quite old. That's something I struggled with and it almost made me not want to go to coop events and talk to people'. Such generational and identity fissures can grow when tensions arise around communication and decision-making, especially with the organisations that own the cooperative houses. Here, transparency was often cited as a point of contention and charges of 'behaving like a landlord' were sometimes levelled against the organisations that legally own the houses, especially when difficult financial decisions needed to be negotiated in the context of rising mortgage interest rates and everyday prices. However, it is each student housing cooperative, registered as a legal entity that every incoming resident joins, that is the landlord and sets the rent. This calls for a shift in mindset among residents, who 'need to unlearn their preconceptions of landlordism and take accountability for their own living conditions. [This] can be daunting, especially for young people with minimal training and resources' (von Geyer, 2023: 35). In the case of rents, students themselves decide how to raise the necessary funds to cover higher lease payments, through democratic decision-making processes that are at the heart of SHC's internal governance.

Ambivalent feelings can also arise when these values of direct democracy and alter-capitalism come up against mainstream cooperators' preference for board structures and professional staff. These tensions are by no means unique to SHCs; they can emerge when collaborative organisations of all kinds evolve internally or engage with external institutions (Jacobs, 2023). To balance working with more managerially oriented cooperative organisations, student cooperators are also forming relationships with alternative allies such as the aforementioned Radical Routes and participate in wider struggles for housing rights and justice. Furthermore, the ambivalent alliances student cooperators are building form part of the 'everyday realities of community activism in building commons within neoliberal urban regimes' (Bunce, 2016: 148). They show the complexities and challenges that come with living in actually existing housing commons that are necessarily interlinked with market and government structures. Challenges are exacerbated in SHCs, however, because of students' particular characteristics, which I explore in the next section.

Situational challenges

The unique life situation of students being young, transient and often precarious results in several unique challenges, beginning with high resident turnover in SHCs. This creates the ongoing need to pass on knowledge and skills. Another challenge stems from the politics of accessibility and inclusiveness when selecting new residents. Finally, there is the growth of SHCs, a professed aim of all existing coops that is difficult to realise given the current lack of broader institutional and political support for them.

A defining feature of SHCs is high resident turnover, which results from students' transient nature. By the time many find out about the existence of coops, they are often only a year or two away from graduating. Even though all coops have provisions for students to stay on after they finish their studies, from three months at ESHC to one year at SEASALT, this means that new residents have to be recruited and inducted on a yearly basis, and in turn have to learn quickly to participate in cooperative life. In this context, keeping institutional memories and inspiring origin stories alive is an important part of cooperative culture. Even more significant is the challenge of knowledge management and transfer, when financial and policy documents, meeting notes, presentations and other documentation need to be accessible and specialist expertise and skills must be passed on to new residents. Working out successful systems is part of cooperative learning but also time-consuming and labour-intensive, and coops have experimented with work allocation plans, shadowing systems and rotating responsibilities. When residents leave a SHC halfway through an academic year, which sometimes happens for personal reasons, coops might also have to select residents who are not fully committed to cooperative principles, which creates tensions around the equitable distribution of the necessary labour to make SHCs function.

This work of maintaining daily cooperative life and upkeeping houses, which includes everyday tasks but also recruiting and inducting new residents, holding regular meetings, financial, tax and legal management as well as DIY work, can exacerbate general feelings of 'post-development blues', where the excitement and intensity of founding campaigns gives way to the 'more mundane realities of housing management, rent arrears and maintenance' (Thompson, 2020: 96). Alongside its communal benefits, coop living is time-consuming and demanding. As Huron (2018) has shown for housing cooperators in Washington DC, the pressures experienced by especially precarious residents can put limits on their participation (see Chapter 4). Students, who are subject to the double precarity created by the marketisation of UK HE and student housing, often have to work part-time in addition to full-time studies, which can leave little time for cooperative contributions. In fact, SHCs were partly set up to alleviate these pressures; according to one early BSHC resident lower rents were meant to avoid people having to work several part-time jobs to pay for their rent, thus having more time to carry out the necessary coop work. On the other hand, being involved in cooperative work was seen by all research participants as imparting valuable practical and life skills (Macias and Perez Ruiz, 2018; Motawa, 2024). This includes learning to practice consensus-based decision-making, developing financial and legal expertise, understanding and navigating tax requirements as well as home maintenance skills.

Another challenge is related to resident membership, which for all types of housing cooperatives is characterised by a tension between wanting to create an open and accessible space and forging a more narrow, intentional community of residents. This is echoed in the literature, where a distinction is often drawn between housing cooperatives benefitting their members exclusively and more collaborative forms such as CLTs that are also helping the wider community (Thompson, 2020). While this may technically and legally be true, the notion of stewardship broadens duties of care and responsibility (Thompson, 2015). Furthermore, given the internal autonomy and physical limitations of housing coops, access to them is not available to all potentially interested individuals. Depending on how residents are selected, access can be restricted due to nepotism (Bruun, 2015) or favour those with the necessary time and skills (Arbell, 2021). Indeed, housing cooperatives have been compared to gated communities because of their potential exclusiveness and homogeneity (Chiodelli, 2015).

In SHCs, there is often a self-selection around food choices, sexual identity or political orientation. Given the radical student activism of their founders, some coops have remained very political spaces, although that can change with resident turnover. All coops have a commitment to welcoming marginalised groups, especially around gender orientation, neurodivergence and disabilities. One ESHC resident argued that the coop being a judgment-free space for people from gender minorities makes it radical and prefigurative, especially in the context of their broader societal discrimination. Both ESHC and SEASALT are known as safe spaces where people can experiment with gender orientations and feel accepted and validated, often in contrast to regular student housing. Because this can involve non-conformist practices, both coops are 'subverting heterosexual hegemonies as a collective' (Newhouse, 2022: 29). The feeling of internal safety was sometimes contrasted with dangers outside the coops, which made some residents think about their inevitable departure with trepidation.

However, with such self-selection comes the potential of creating niche communities, which can feed into general stereotypes about SHCs being home to hippies, party people or anarchists and restrict the pool of interested applications. While these stereotypes are based on a lack of knowledge about SHCs among the public and students alike, word-of-mouth recruitment of new residents can also result in more homogeneity (Arbell, 2021). Some founders were acutely aware of these tendencies and actively worked to keep membership broader.

One SEASALT founder argued passionately that coops naturally attract quite alternative people:

> … but I was always very very keen that SEASALT was inclusive because I think alternative doesn't always mean inclusive. At the core of what we wanted was sustainable, democratic, affordable decent housing and for me that shouldn't be mixing with imposing lifestyle choices. In theory, it should be a place where everyone who identifies with the values of the housing coop feels that they can live there … If coops are going to be a viable alternative model, we need to go beyond that bubble.

These tensions between different definitions of what being inclusive means are an expression of the contradictions of actually existing commons (Eizenberg, 2012). Wanting to create safe spaces, especially for marginalised groups, while also adhering to the Rochdale principle of open membership creates debates that speak to the 'messy, everyday practices [that] define participation in political projects where participants attempt to build the future in the present' (Chatterton and Pickerill, 2010: 487). In several interviews, participants explained the need for achieving a balance between the diverse needs of cooperative residents and their homes, a process that is part of the everyday learning taking place in them.

A final challenge relates to the growth of SHCs in the UK, which has been very slow. All founders told me that they wanted larger buildings for their own coops, to make a difference for more students, operate more efficiently or so as not to occupy smaller houses that could be family homes. Most importantly, they wanted to show that SHCs can be a viable alternative to marketised student housing. According to an ESHC founder, upon learning that the buildings offered to the coop had 106 beds, some people felt that it might be too ambitious, to which he replied that '"no, this is a good size" because I was personally not as interested in just starting a small coop, I wanted something that was on a larger scale because we were already thinking of it as a movement'. Currently, ESHC residents are working with local universities, the city council and the Scottish Parliament to start more SHCs in Edinburgh. As one involved resident explained, 'we are the pilot [project] … and have successfully shown that we are a better model than private housing providers'. For him and fellow residents, the success of the coop over the past ten years makes it a legitimate contributor to debates on how to address the acute student housing crisis in Edinburgh. Unfortunately, this is still an uphill struggle in an area dominated by private developers, with adverse effects on students' ability to study and health (Kallin, 2024).

The BSHC founders initially aimed for a several-hundred-bed self-built coop but quickly realised that this was not feasible at the time; their willingness to establish a smaller coop and then add additional bedrooms was one of the things that helped build mutual trust and confidence with early supporters. In Brighton, SEASALT founders were considering several larger properties, and only when these fell through for financial and planning reasons was a former student house purchased. There are also active cooperatives looking for properties in Belfast, Glasgow, Manchester, Nottingham and Bristol. All of these have been in existence for several years and some have come close to finding properties. The Glasgow coop, working with Student Coop Homes, was able to purchase a 5-bedroom house in 2025, but for many other groups that goal remains elusive. This shows the ongoing difficulties students face, especially around finding appropriately sized properties in good enough quality and at an affordable price. Another challenge is accessing financing with reasonable interest rates, with very few banks being willing to lend to small housing coops and their mortgage interest rates remaining sky-high. In addition, unclear tax rules around exemptions show the need for more regulatory clarity and for general political support at all levels of government. However, the perseverance of continuing generations of students and their supporters and the accomplishments of the existing SHCs provide real reasons for hope.

Conclusion

2024 marked the tenth anniversary of ESHC and BSHC opening their doors, which means that while the student housing cooperative movement in the UK is still small, it has a successful track record. This chapter contributes to our understanding of grassroots activism, translocal networks and situational challenges of establishing collaborative housing by and for students in the UK. All SHCs were set up through the persistent efforts of committed, hard-working and savvy students, who used their experiences in national and campus-level student politics to prefigure an alternative student housing model. They were successful in building networks at local, national and transnational levels, foremost among them with cooperative support institutions but also local councils, housing associations, CLTs and universities. While these networks were essential to secure the properties, the relationships to which they gave rise remain ambivalent, because of value, age and identity gaps. Nevertheless, students and supporters alike have learned to collaborate across these gaps and in the process have navigated the manifold challenges that arise from the unique student situation along the way.

SHCs in the UK are providing a grassroots model for a different form of housing provisions, showing fellow students, other cooperators and universities that there are alternatives to the financialisation of student housing that has created an acute student housing crisis in the country. Their founders and residents are very aware that their movement, as it currently exists, does not present, and might never become, a viable mainstream solution to this financialisation. What is more important however, for like-minded students, other cooperators and interested academics in the UK and beyond, is that the existence of SHCs shows that more democratic, affordable, healthy and sustainable housing provisions are possible, even in the adverse circumstances presented by the lack of concerted political support for student and other cooperative housing, which remains a marginal form of housing provision in the UK especially in comparison to some European countries. That this should be the case in the birthplace of the modern cooperative movement strikes many as ironic. Nevertheless, student housing cooperators, in the UK and other countries, are creating a space for imagining and building alternatives that 'offer the first sprouts of the new within the old system, a glimpse of what society could be' (Shaw and Farmelo, 2017: 62).

References

ACORN (2016), *Feasibility study for a national body of student housing coops*. Available at www.acorncoopsupport.org.uk/Feasibility_Study_for_a_National_Body_of_Student_Housing_Coops.pdf (accessed 8 April 2026).

Amsler, S. (2011), 'Beyond all reason: spaces of hope in the struggle for England's universities', *Representations*, 116:1, 62–87.

Arbell, Y. (2021), '"A place that is different from the usual capitalist world": the potential of community-led housing as safe and just spaces', *Spatial Justice*, 16.

Bresnihan, P., and M. Byrne (2015), 'Escape into the city: Everyday practices of commoning and the production of urban space in Dublin', *Antipode*, 47:1, 36–54.

Bruun, M. (2015), 'Communities and the commons: Open access and community ownership of the urban commons', in C. Borch and M. Kornberger (eds), *Urban Commons: Rethinking the City* (London: Routledge), pp. 163–80.

Bunce, S. (2016), 'Pursuing urban commons: Politics and alliances in community land trust activism in East London', *Antipode*, 48:1, 134–50.

Chatterton, P. (2016), 'Building transitions to post-capitalist urban commons', *Transactions of the Institute of British Geographers*, 41:4, 403–15.

Chatterton, P., and J. Pickerill (2010), 'Everyday activism and transitions towards post-capitalist worlds', *Transactions of the Institute of British Geographers*, 35:4, 475–90.

Chiodelli, F. (2015), 'What is really different between cohousing and gated communities?', *European Planning Studies*, 23:12, 2566–81.

Di Feliciantonio, C. (2017), 'Social movements and alternative housing models: Practicing the "politics of possibilities" in Spain', *Housing, Theory and Society*, 34:1, 38–56.

Eizenberg, E. (2012), 'Actually existing commons: Three moments of space of community gardens in New York City', *Antipode*, 44:3, 764–82.

Farmelo, S. (2024), 'Origin of the Student Housing Coop Movement in Birmingham', in A. Schwittay and L. Hartly (eds), *Coop Chronicles: Celebrating 10 years of Student Housing Coops in the UK* (Brighton: University of Sussex/Student Cooperative Homes), pp. 36–39.

Fields, D. (2015), 'Contesting the financialisation of urban space: Community organisations and the struggle to preserve affordable rental housing in New York City', *Journal of Urban Affairs*, 37:2, 144–65.

Gayá, P., and M. Brydon-Miller (2017), 'Carpe the academy: Dismantling higher education and prefiguring critical utopias through action research', *Futures*, 94, 34–44.

Gibson-Graham, J. K. (2008), 'Diverse economies: performative practices for other worlds', *Progress in Human Geography*, 32:5, 613–32.

Hands, J. (2016 [1975]), *Housing Cooperatives* (Castleton: Castleton Publishers).

Hodkinson, S. N. (2012), 'The return of the housing question', *Ephemera: Theory and Politics in Organisation*, 12:4, 423–44.

Holloway, J. (2010), *Crack Capitalism* (London: Pluto Press).

Huron, A. (2018), *Carving Out the Commons: Tenant Organizing and Housing Cooperatives in Washington, DC* (Minneapolis, MN: University of Minnesota Press).

Jacobs, S. (2023), 'Egalitarianism and sustainability at the Centre for Alternative Technologies', *Journal of Cooperative Studies*, 56:1, 29–34.

Jones, J. (2019), *Hasten Slowly and You Will Arrive Soon: The Mysterious Presence of Group Equity Housing Cooperatives* (Ann Arbor, MI: NASCO).

Jones, J. (2024), 'Bridging the borders: A brief history of student housing coops in the UK', in A. Schwittay and L. Hartly (eds), *Coop Chronicles: Celebrating 10 years of Student Housing Coops in the UK* (Brighton: University of Sussex/Student Cooperative Homes), pp. 14–19.

Joubert, T., and S. Hodkinson (2018), 'Beyond the Rent Strike, Towards the Commons: Why the Housing Question Requires Activism that Generates its Own Alternatives', in N. Gray (ed.), *Rent and its Discontents: A Century of Housing Struggles Transforming Capitalism* (London: Rowman and Littlefield International).

Kallin, H. (2024), 'Victims of studentification? Variegated student experiences of housing precarity and homelessness in Edinburgh', *Scottish Geographical Journal*, 141:3–4, 319–37, https://doi.org/10.1080/14702541.2024.2372623

Kallin, H., and M. Shaw (2019), 'Escaping the parasite of the student flat: Reflections on an experiment in cooperative housing', *Radical Housing Journal*, 1:1, 223–26.

Macias, T., and P. Perez Ruiz (2018), 'Cooperation in action: The Edinburgh Student Housing Cooperative as a pedagogical space', *Journal of Cooperative Studies*, 51:1, 54–57.

Mericle, A., S. Wilson, J. Jones, and M. Goldstein (eds) (1994), *In Our Own Hands: A History of Student Housing Cooperatives at the University of Michigan* (Ann Arbor, MI: Inter-Cooperative Council).

Motawa, A. (2024), 'Cooperative learning at ESHC', in A. Schwittay and L. Hartly (eds), *Coop Chronicles: Celebrating 10 years of Student Housing Coops in the UK* (Brighton: University of Sussex/Student Cooperative Homes), pp. 62–63.

Newhouse, M. (2022), 'Gendered Experiences of Edinburgh Student Housing Cooperative: Bringing Horizontal Cooperatives Closer to True Non-hierarchical Organising'. MSc Dissertation, University of Edinburgh.

Ostrom, E. (1990), *Governing the Commons: The Evolution of Institutions for Collective Action* (Cambridge: Cambridge University Press).

Perez Ruiz, P., and M. Shaw (2019), 'The cooperative as site of pedagogy: The example of Edinburgh Student Housing Cooperative', in M. Noble and C. Ross (eds), *Reclaiming the University for the Public Good* (London: Palgrave Macmillan), pp. 169–83.

Reason, P., and H. Bradbury (2001), 'Introduction: Inquiry and participation in search of a world worthy of human aspiration', in P. Reason and H. Bradbury (eds), *Handbook of Action Research* (London: SAGE Publications), pp. 1–14.

Reynolds, A. (2022), 'Contesting the financialisation of student accommodation: Campaigns for the right to housing in Dublin, Ireland', *Housing Studies*, 39:6, 1495–1515.

Reynolds, A. (2022), '"Where does my £9000 go?" Student identities in a marketised British Higher Education Sector', *SN Social Sciences*, 2:8, 125, https://doi.org/10.1007/s43545-022-00432-6

Sage, J., D. Smith, and P. Hubbard (2013), 'New-build studentification: A panacea for balanced communities?', *Urban Studies*, 50:13, 2623–41.

Schwittay, A. (2021), *Creative Universities: Reimagining Education for Global Challenges and Alternative Futures* (Bristol: Policy Press).

Schwittay, A. (2025), 'Students take over: Prefiguring urban commons in student housing cooperatives', *Housing Studies* 40:4, 966–87, https://doi.org/10.1080/02673037.2024.2334816

Schwittay, A. and L. Hartly (eds) (2024), *Coop Chronicles: Celebrating 10 Years of Student Housing Coops in the UK* (Brighton: University of Sussex/Student Cooperative Homes).

Shaw, M. (2024), 'There is an alternative: Setting up the Edinburgh Student Housing Cooperative', in A. Schwittay and L. Hartly (eds), *Coop Chronicles: Celebrating 10 Years of Student Housing Coops in the UK* (Brighton: University of Sussex/Student Cooperative Homes), pp. 28–34.

Shaw, M., and S. Farmelo (2017), 'Cooperatives: Resisting the housing crisis', in R. Filar (ed.), *Resist! Against a Precarious Future* (London: Lawrence and Wishart).

Smith, D. P. (2005), 'Studentification: The gentrification factory', in R. Atkinson and G. Bridge (eds), *Gentrification in a Global Context* (London: Routledge).

Sotomayor, L., D. Tarhan, M. Vieta, S. McCartney, and A. Mas (2022), 'When students are house-poor: Urban universities, student marginality, and the hidden curriculum of student housing', *Cities*, 124, 103572.

Steffens, R., K. Billie, H. Daisy, J. Haris, M. Lancione, and T. Samantha (2022), '"The rents keep on rising and so do we": Reflections on the 2021 rent strike at Sussex University', *Radical Housing Journal*, 4:1, 117–33.

Thompson, M. (2015), 'Between boundaries: From commoning and guerrilla gardening to community land trust development in Liverpool', *Antipode*, 47:4, 1021–42.

Thompson, M. (2020), 'From coops to community land trusts: Tracing the historical evolution and policy mobilities of collaborative housing movements', *Housing, Theory and Society*, 37:1, 82–100.

URBED (2004), *A Cooperative Future for Student Housing*. Available at http://urbed.coop/sites/default/files/student%20housing%201st%20stage%20report.pdf (accessed 16 March 2026).

von Geyer, L. (2023), 'Coop Sweet Coop: The experience of homemaking at Edinburgh Student Housing Cooperative'. BA dissertation, University of St. Andrews.

Woodell, V. (2024), 'The journey of Student Coop Homes (SCH)', in A. Schwittay and L. Hartly (eds), *Coop Chronicles: Celebrating 10 Years of Student Housing Coops in the UK* (Brighton: University of Sussex/Student Cooperative Homes), pp. 46–47.

9

The NETCO collaborative housing network – European cities: Practising, cooperating and recommending

Michael LaFond

Introducing NETCO

Sixteen municipalities from Southern, Northern, Western and Eastern Europe have come together to form NETCO: Amsterdam, Barcelona, Berlin (Friedrichshain-Kreuzberg), Bologna, Brussels, Cluj, Dresden, Dumfries, Eindhoven, Ljubljana, Lyon, Oslo, Strasbourg, Thessaloniki, Torino and Zagreb. Over three years, NETCO has been networking local government officials from these cities to support collaborative housing.

NETCO understands *collaborative housing* to include a range of housing forms emphasising resident participation and a community orientation with a sharing of spaces and activities. Housing projects for which local government plays a key role in some combination of project initiation, development, management and ownership are of special interest to all partners. Although interest and 'demand' for collaborative, community and cooperative housing have continued to grow in recent years, the supply has not. Against this background, NETCO supports cities in exchanging information and taking on the current and future challenges of housing provision, for example, in asking how to better coordinate governmental resources and programmes with civil society idealism and innovation.

Establishing this network and organising meetings to share experiences on collaborative housing has been made possible through the European Commission's Citizens, Equality, Rights and Values programme. As many partners wanted to continue working with NETCO, new funding has been applied for and granted to develop the network further. We are happy to be able to continue with these important exchanges.[1]

I am writing as a representative of id22:Institute, a non-profit, civil society organisation that together with UrbaMonde has been tasked with NETCO-related research, communication and documentation. In this chapter, I deliver insights into NETCO activities to date and summarise recommendations to promote collaborative housing all over Europe.[2]

The recommendations are based on conferences held in Bologna, Barcelona, Berlin and Brussels, as well as surveys of participating cities made concerning housing policy and programmes at the local level. Finally, this chapter offers a review of local government practices and perspectives concerning collaborative housing in larger European cities.

Cooperating and collaborating with public-civic-partnerships

Our research among European cities confirms that collaborative housing initiatives increasingly depend on governmental support in these years of exploding costs regarding land, construction and interest rates. However, housing projects have in the past often been developed without direct governmental support – as long as this was doable and affordable. What has been described as 'alternative' or 'grassroots' housing, at least since the 1970s in north-west European cities, has come to rely on institutional assistance. Through my decades of work with id22, I have been studying how collaborative housing is being mainstreamed. The lines are now blurred between housing models like smaller, self-organised *Baugruppen,* incorporating community spaces on the one hand, and much larger, institutional housing providers developing social and affordable housing including cluster apartments on the other. The very word 'collaborative' can now be understood not only to describe the working together of residents in their particular project but increasingly to refer to partnerships among resident groups, local planning departments, housing companies, cooperatives, foundations and others. The practice of collaborative housing is being further professionalised and even institutionalised as it responds to increasing challenges and seeks to not only realise sought-after qualities but also called-for quantities of housing. For example, Berlin's state-owned housing companies, having the backing and resources to scale up in an increasingly competitive market, have pushed aside the smaller bottom-up actors. These six large housing companies, owning an average of more than 50,000 apartments each, have learned from alternative housing projects and are now developing, with a top-down approach, housing with cluster apartments and shared spaces.

The NETCO cities, as to be expected, reflect diverse housing cultures and policies. While some in the north-west, such as Berlin and Amsterdam, have already well-established community-led housing traditions, others are working on initial pilot projects, for example the cities of south-eastern Europe. In the course of our encounters, we shared experiences, both good and bad, to inspire more collaborative housing practices as well as to critically reflect on the opportunities for transferring models from one region to another.

NETCO defines *collaborative housing* pragmatically and primarily for government officials and practitioners. A broad range of strategies for housing provision illustrates this comprehensive umbrella term, manifested through models such as cooperative housing, cohousing, community-led housing, and public or social housing. Collaborative housing, according to NETCO, is where public interest overlaps with community interest. This generally means a partnership between local government and residential groups and/or community housing developers to provide and manage participatory, affordable and sustainable housing solutions. Based on this, NETCO municipal partners universally agree on the following objectives for collaborative housing:

- Collaborative housing shall include shared common spaces for residents.
- Self-management of buildings and spaces is encouraged, involving residents and their organisations.

Moreover, NETCO partners generally but not universally share the following objectives:

- A significant number of affordable apartments shall be included in collaborative housing projects.
- Collaborative housing shall strive for non-speculative land tenure or qualified resale mechanisms involving cooperatives or community land trusts to ensure permanent affordability.
- Future residents shall be significantly involved in the design and planning phases of collaborative housing.
- Interactions between the project community and its neighbourhood shall be encouraged.
- Social integration of vulnerable population groups shall be considered when planning collaborative housing.

Practising for the 'best results possible'

Over the last few years, NETCO has brought together cities working to develop their housing stock through supporting community-based housing and property management forms, such as cooperatives and cohousing. One of our key goals was to promote networking and exchanges among government officials and civil society experts, researchers and practitioners in order to support the development of long-term housing policies addressing affordability and inclusion through community development.

Together, we visited the cities of Bologna, Barcelona, Berlin and Brussels, which have been investing resources in collaborative housing projects, in their search for options to create and maintain more affordable housing as well as experiment with innovative and sustainable housing typologies to more adequately house ageing and diversifying populations. Complementing the conferences and project visits we organised research to compare insights into collaborative housing on the basis of four significant aspects we identified: 1) Legal Frameworks, 2) Sustainable Innovations, 3) Inclusion, and 4) Funding.

The following examples of best practice we visited demonstrate what is currently possible, especially from the perspective of local governments, keeping in mind the varying regional contexts and housing cultures of our partners. Emphasis is placed on the roles of municipalities including their motivations and goals as well as their cooperation with civil society residential groups and other stakeholders. These four projects provide a range of solutions regarding legal frameworks, sustainable innovations, funding and inclusion and underline how specific development, building and management strategies of collaborative housing can achieve widely recognised social, ecological, economic and technological objectives.

Porto 15 – City of Bologna

Bologna has a long history of cooperatives and collectives and was among the first in Italy to explore the potential of cohousing. Besides new construction, recent housing projects in Bologna include the Porto 15 building renovation. This building reuse has been coordinated by the Municipality of Bologna in partnership with several departments and associations and is the first Italian publicly managed cohousing project. This has brought to light a new model of public housing in which residents are more than beneficiaries of public services: they are encouraged to promote relationships in their neighbourhood. This experience of regeneration of a publicly owned building within the framework of dialogue and collaboration between cohousers, institutions and communities has been an incubator for new housing practices and represents a fusion between traditional housing policies and socio-community empowerment (see Figure 9.1).

- **Location:** Bologna, Manifattura delle Arti, historic city centre
- **Year of completion:** 2017 (retrofit)
- **Number of flats:** 18
- **Developer:** City of Bologna
- **Community spaces:** kitchen/dining/living areas, laundry, bicycle and wood workshops as well as atrium with gallery and courtyard for the neighbourhood
- **Web:** porto15.it
- **Legal frameworks:** public ownership / rental housing
- **Sustainable innovations:** energy efficient, historical building renovation
- **Inclusion:** housing for people under 35 years of age with limited income
- **Funding:** ASP 'Città di Bologna' with the Department of Youth

Figure 9.1 NETCO visit at Porto 15, Bologna, 2022. Photo © Fabio Mantovani, all rights reserved.

Figure 9.2 NETCO visit at La Borda, Barcelona, 2024. Photo © Fabio Mantovani, all rights reserved.

La Borda – City of Barcelona

Barcelona has drawn much attention over the last decade with its municipalist urban development strategies and support for cooperative and sustainable housing. Cooperative housing projects like La Borda have become internationally famous as they illustrate the innovative potential of housing arrangements when the local government works hand in hand with civil society initiatives (Cabré and Andrés, 2018). La Borda is a cooperative housing model enabled by a long-term land lease, i.e., the land remains in public hands, while the building is in community hands. This expresses a paradigm shift concerning ownership structures and has helped a new ecosystem of cooperative housing actors to emerge in Catalonia. A primary objective was working with a collective process of defining a new participatory approach for housing production and management combined with non-speculative ownership. La Borda was the tallest wooden building in Spain at the time of its construction (see Figure 9.2).

- **Location:** Barcelona, Can Batlló
- **Year of completion:** 2019 (new construction)
- **Developer:** La Borda Cooperative
- **Number of flats:** 28
- **Community spaces:** kitchen/dining areas, guest rooms, rooftop as well as rented commercial spaces, bicycle parking, gardens for the neighbourhood
- **Web:** laborda.coop
- **Legal frameworks:** 75-year, long-term lease for the grant to use housing cooperative, on public land
- **Sustainable innovations:** timber frame, passive energy design, PV panels, no car parking, flexible/moveable interior walls
- **Inclusion:** affordable rent and low energy costs allow for social inclusion
- **Funding:** individual loans, resident and non-resident equity, government loans and grants

Experimentierhäuser Haus der Statistik – City of Berlin

Berlin, until today a city of renters, boasts a long and rich history of housing cooperatives dating back to the 1890s and comprising almost 185,000 flats which is equivalent to 11.5% of the rental housing stock (Hölzl et al., 2023). In addition, a diverse landscape of grassroots housing, with many hundreds of self-organised housing projects realised in the last four decades, has provided learning opportunities for the population and the public sector, architects, developers and financial institutions (id22, 2023). Although well-established here, collaborative housing is currently frustrated by high costs, especially land, and overshadowed by large, speculative developers and city-owned

Figure 9.3 NETCO visit at Haus der Statistik, Berlin, 2024. Photo © Fabio Mantovani, all rights reserved.

housing companies. According to IBB Berlin housing market reports, asking rents have risen by around 50% since 2013, now at around €14/sqm on average for existing apartments and €20/sqm for new construction (IBB, 2024). The ambitious strategy of the Haus der Statistik initiative begins with a redefining of how to deal with larger inner-city properties that have fallen out of use, in this case, saving the former office building Haus der Statistik, which was built from 1968 to 1970 in the centre of former East Berlin, from demolition. An alliance of administration and civil society has since 2018 been jointly responsible for planning the redevelopment of the large site as a mixed-use, community-oriented neighbourhood (see Chapter 4). Beyond administrative uses, spaces for art, culture and social initiatives, and hundreds of city-owned apartments as well as cooperative housing and inclusive forms of community housing are to be built in the Experimentierhäuser (Experimental Houses). These are to test self-build practices combined with low-energy building standards and affordable rents (see Figure 9.3).

- **Location:** Berlin, Mitte
- **Year of completion:** ca. 2030 (new construction)
- **Developer:** 'Koop5' ZUsammenKUNFT Berlin Cooperative (ZKB), Senate Housing Department (SenSBW), District Mitte, state-owned housing company (WBM), Berlin Property Management Company (BIM)

- **Number of flats:** 90
- **Community spaces:** kitchen/dining areas, rooftop, bicycle parking as well as café, Food-Coop, gardens and outdoor seating for the neighbourhood
- **Web:** hausderstatistik.org, zusammenkunft.berlin
- **Legal frameworks:** (public-civic-partnership) land owned by the City of Berlin; long-term lease for cooperative owning the buildings with rental housing
- **Sustainable innovations:** energy efficient, adaptive structures
- **Inclusion:** affordable and assisted-living cohousing combined with healthcare facilities
- **Funding:** public subsidies combined with privately funded cooperative shares and bank loans

CALICO – Care and Living in Community – Brussels

The Brussels Region has taken great steps in recent years to explore and support community-led models of housing including cooperatives and pioneering work with community land trusts (Czischke, Peute and Brysch, 2023). Projects such as CALICO demonstrate the cooperation of local and regional governments with housing cooperatives and the Community Land Trust Brussels (CLTB), in developing affordable and inclusive housing (see Chapter 3). CALICO (CAre and LIving in COmmunity) has been co-funded by the Urban Innovative Action (UIA) Program and developed by eight partners including the Brussels Capital Region, the CLTB, non-profit associations, and a university for project monitoring and evaluation. The values of mutual care, gender equality, and permanently affordable housing are fundamental to this project. CALICO is organised as a housing cooperative and all apartments and shared facilities are kept off the speculative market as the land belongs to the CLTB (see Figure 9.4).

- **Location:** Brussels, Forest Municipality
- **Year of completion:** 2021 (new construction)
- **Developer:** Belgian Land
- **Number of flats:** 34
- **Community spaces:** community rooms, apartments as well as other indoor spaces for the neighbourhood
- **Web:** cltb.be/calico
- **Legal frameworks:** CLTB-owned land leased to agencies and owner-occupiers
- **Sustainable innovations:** community gardens for the neighbourhood
- **Inclusion:** Housing First units for limited income and formerly homeless, feminist cohousing (Angela D), intergenerational cohousing and social housing (Pass-ages) with birth and end-of-life facilities
- **Funding:** (UIA), Brussels Capital Region, individual bank loans

Figure 9.4 NETCO visit at CALICO – Care and Living in Community, Brussels, 2024. Photo © Fabio Mantovani, all rights reserved.

Concluding and recommending

Our best practices of Porto 15, La Borda, Haus der Statistik and Calico illustrate how European cities are experimenting with public-civic-partnerships: separating ownership of land and buildings, enabling shared homeownership, securing long-term financing and affordability, and developing combinations of collaborative housing and social as well as public housing. Although significant as pioneering learning projects, the presented projects still need to be critically described as island solutions for a relatively small and privileged minority.

In the shadow of a growing housing crisis, NETCO cities are confirming that housing markets including collaborative housing are in a transformational phase. Local politicians are generally concerned by a dramatic shortage of affordable housing and more specifically by a lack of community housing sought after by diverse, poor and elderly populations. Still, rather than collaborative housing, blocks of expensive, single and micro-apartments continue to be built in all cities. At the same time, more and more people are interested in opportunities for sharing in connection with their housing, searching for social, economic and ecological benefits. The climate crisis itself is challenging cities to provide housing that conserves resources and adapts to changing conditions, and so, collaborative housing projects are often turned to as real-world laboratories.

As collaborative housing receives more attention we observe different approaches among our NETCO partners: they express their priorities regarding housing as they do with urban development in general. While there is growing interest in community, affordable and social housing, practical support, including access to land and funding, remains limited for non-speculative housing. Most cities are still working with a neoliberal, free-market approach to housing, which suggests the main goal is to encourage housing developers to build as much housing as quickly as possible, emphasising great quantities of housing construction at the expense of qualities such as participation, inclusion, affordability and sustainability. In many cities, an extreme emphasis on providing privately owned homes comes at the expense of cooperative and community-led housing. Moreover, municipal housing officials confirm that local housing policies are dynamic und unpredictable, often shifting with each change in local politics, making it difficult to offer serious long-term programmes for collaborative housing providers. Berlin, for example, has for many years been planning more than twenty new development districts, expected to lead to tens of thousands of new homes, including many cooperative and community housing projects. The hyped Schumacher Quartier, being planned for many years already next to the long-since-closed Tegel airport, is expected to support about 500 new cooperative flats, but has generated until now more frustration than anything else. Local government and planning authorities are taking many years to find a way to give community and cooperative housing developers access to this publicly owned land, even though they have repeatedly signalled their interest in building new homes.

Assuming NETCO enjoys continued EU funding, this network could very well assist in providing European cities with much-needed inspiration and insight into collaborative housing, as well as relevant and practical how-to information and examples. The housing crisis, in any case, continues to grow in all larger cities and so the European Commission is finally accepting that it should be advancing a number of options including collaborative housing.

In the end, as the crises are demanding that we learn from pioneering projects, we would like to imagine that collaborative housing is on its way to playing a key role in the sustainable transformation of European cities. Thus, I conclude this chapter with recommendations we derived based on inputs from NETCO partners and experiences in developing policies and housing projects like the four best practice cases. These recommendations do not reflect the position of every NETCO partner city and region, as national and cultural contexts lead to different approaches and solutions for the same challenge. As the first and most important level of action and opportunity for collaborative housing is that of the city and its immediate region, the first list is directed toward municipalities. The second list summarises recommendations that have been developed to improve support for collaborative housing at the European level.

NETCO city recommendations

1. Think ahead: a common-good, long-term vision of living and ageing in communities opens up more sustainable choices. Collaborative housing giving people a direct voice demonstrates significant social and ecological transformational opportunities.
2. Advocate: identify legal and administrative barriers that slow down the development of collaborative housing: lobby for changes at local, regional and national levels.
3. Be ambitious: set measurable collaborative housing objectives for the coming years in urban development and housing plans.
4. Train practitioners: coordinate exchanges among professionals and bureaucrats involved in developing collaborative and affordable housing.
5. Finance housing process facilitators: group and process moderation is key to successful collaborations.
6. Lease, don't sell, public land: renewable, long-term leases of public land are a win-win option.
7. Foster collaboration: in allocating land, reduce competition and encourage cooperation among community-led and developer-driven collaborative housing groups.
8. Facilitate access to loans: municipal stimulation loans or guarantees can make the difference in securing financing.
9. Support and fund shared spaces: create funding mechanisms for collaborative housing community spaces.
10. Innovate: pilot projects are key to demonstrating new ways of producing sustainable and affordable housing.

NETCO EU recommendations

1. Set guidelines: states, cities and regions should be encouraged to adapt legal frameworks concerning affordable housing provision to facilitate cooperative and collaborative housing.

2. European funding programs for more model projects: more cities would do more with collaborative housing if it could be more visible.
3. Co-fund groundbreaking projects: pilot projects are especially needed in countries and cities where there is no or little collaborative housing experience.
4. Revolving funding: facilitate the establishment of a European revolving funding facility to give loans to sustainable, affordable housing projects.
5. Fund research and advocacy: transnational collaborative housing knowledge production is needed to convince reluctant regional stakeholders.

Notes

1 NETCO is not the first European network set up to study and support community-led housing. Other European networks have come and gone, for example, *experimentcity europe* in 2011, especially bringing together citizen's groups, initiated and managed by id22. Although this led to the publication of the book *CoHousing Culture*s, the network did not survive after funding ran out. Way before that in the 1980s, *Kollektivhus Nu* in Sweden began with its networking and coordination of international conferences.

2 This chapter uses the term collaborative housing (instead of community-led housing) since this is the agreed-on NETCO language, placing an emphasis on partnerships.

References

Cabré, E., and A. Andrés (2018), 'La Borda: a case study on the implementation of cooperative housing in Catalonia', *International Journal of Housing Policy*, 18:3, 412–32, https://doi.org/9.980/19491247.2017.1331591

Czischke, D., M. Peute, and S. Brysch (eds) (2023), *Together: Towards Collaborative Living* (TU Delft OPEN Publishing), https://doi.org/9.59490/mg.80

Hölzl, C., H. Nuissl, F. Beran, and T. Kormeyer (2023), 'Nonprofit Landlord Types on the Housing Market – A Key to Rising Displacement in Berlin?', *Housing Policy Debate*, 1–21, https://doi.org/9.980/9511482.2023.2271898

IBB (2024), IBB Wohnungsmarktbericht 2023 (Investitionsbank Berlin). Available at www.ibb.de/media/dokumente/publikationen/berliner-wohnungsmarkt/wohnungsmarktbericht/ibb-wohnungsmarktbericht-2023.pdf (accessed 12 December 2024).

id22: Institute for Creative Sustainability (2023), *Social-Ecological Cooperative Housing: Community-based, transformative building and living* (De Gruyter), https://doi.org/9.1515/9783868598353

10

Community-led housing as an opportunity for development and growing together in Europe: A call for civil society financing instruments and more public support

Rolf Novy-Huy

Potential of community-led initiatives as … 'schools of democracy'

From my work with community-led housing projects, I safely relate to these projects as 'schools of democracy'. Why is this? Community-led housing usually builds on democratic processes regarding decision-making as well as the future management of their building and common living situation. Quick decisions are not always helpful. If the same people always lose the vote, this can lead to frustration. How do you deal with these minorities? Can there be a veto right? What can be done when a veto is abused? Am I able to repeatedly approach even difficult people (difficult for me!) in an effort to maintain a spirit of acceptance and ability to talk? Daily life in community-led housing tends to harden some people.

Our societies are marked by a situation of strong polarisation. We can only overcome such polarisation if we also listen to the people we consider problematic. Is there a way to talk to one another? Do I have to categorise my arguments as 'absolute'? Where is the acceptance that all people are 'a bit crazy' (except me)? Let us accept that and find the daily patience and attitude to do so. Sometimes it even looks like we need to learn again how to discuss and listen in a civilised way. All this is what I mean by 'schools of democracy'. Social learning helps in everyday life in a housing project and hopefully leads to a better understanding of necessary democratic compromises.

… a factor in social and economic development

From my point of view, citizens are very sensitive to change and could even be described as a seismograph for current problems. If they are allowed to act, they will do so more quickly and with greater focus than any administration could achieve. You may hear statements like, 'If I wait for the government to build a kindergarten, my children will be at university before it opens'. Instead of taking this as an insult, it would be more productive for both sides to see it as an offer to act and assume responsibility. A vibrant civil society is willing to provide social facilities such as kindergartens, schools, theatres or youth centres on its own responsibility, just to meet the need.[1] It is also prepared to invest time, money and knowledge in such projects. In the wake of the current housing movement, society is calling for innovative ways of living together and fostering mutual support. No commercial offer will satisfy this demand.

I would strongly argue for taking better advantage of these strengths of civil society. The mutual social understanding of a civil society that is willing and permitted to take its problems into its own hands, instead of asking the government to solve them, is a gain for any government. An attitude of entrepreneurship rather than consumerism generates an energy of participation and a sense that you can change things yourself rather than waiting for state structures to do so. Ultimately, this will lead to a vital society that is able to express its needs and to participate in a development that benefits the community.

... responsible local investors

At the local level, there is always a demand for an 'investor'. But when a group of citizens claims to be the investor, they are often not taken seriously. Why is that? Because it is unusual. A commercial investor can fail, as can citizen groups. However, there are enough examples of good practices all over Europe to show that so-called 'alternative projects', even with investments of several million euros, are trustworthy, successful and an enrichment for their city or region.[2] An association or a cooperative can be the investor and manage a project based on the shoulders of many citizens. Their diversity, their 'swarm intelligence', is their advantage. Not only when setting up a project, but also in the long term.

Barriers to the development of community-led projects across Europe

As mentioned at the beginning of this article, the political situation in Europe is very diverse. Different legal systems prevent best practices from being adopted from other countries. Looking at the usual development path of a project, the following hurdles have to be overcome to enable civil society projects to flourish.

Lack of appropriate consultancies

During my professional career, I realised that reports and scientific analyses are a useful basis for decision-making at the political level as well as in the planning process of a community-led housing project. They can help to assess a situation. In practice, however, a group of citizens planning to set up their own project will be confronted with a myriad of questions and challenges at a much more 'down-to-earth' level. Many questions remain even after talking to other pioneers who have successfully implemented their plans. It is important to remember that these citizen groups are not a collection of professionals, but a group of committed people doing housing business (including property purchase, business formation management etc.) for the first time. Skills such as structured project development and a certain pleasure in making quick decisions, not to say entrepreneurial behaviour, are often rare. The key word is 'experience'. Only people who have realised their own projects can bring experience to the table. Consultants with sufficient experience have already made the kind of decisions that are completely new to a pioneer group. They have usually brought a number of projects to life, cherish their own network of complementary experts and are able to meet specific challenges. According to my experience, in Eastern European countries, it is even more difficult to find consultants who are not solely oriented at maximising profits. After the great political transformation at the end of the last century, the political and economic systems in the Eastern European countries changed to a deep belief in capitalist mechanisms. This is accompanied by a belief in profitability and a general neoliberal attitude. This does not cover the needs of civil society groups. What is missing, therefore, is a network of consultants committed to values such as solidarity, sustainability, circular economy and non-profit or, let us say, 'decent profit'.

Lack of open-minded municipalities and other administrations

In addition to experienced consultancies, open-minded political and administrative structures are needed in every country. It is necessary that administrations at all levels are open to groups, accept them as business partners and entrepreneurs, understand their needs and have confidence in their ability to act as investors in and incubators of social development.

Lack of equity capital

The next problem is to pay the consultants and then to prove that you have sufficient equity to make the planned investments. This is difficult enough in rich Western countries, but a problem in less affluent societies. If community groups are successful in activating the power of their community, there is at least a very good chance of raising the necessary funds. Without equity, it is not possible to apply for bank loans. National grant programmes, similar to commercial start-up programmes, could be a solution to overcome this first threshold.

Lack of receptive banking institutions and public funds

Equity will usually be in the form of shares. For an association (if accepted by commercial banks), this can be replaced by private loans. Sometimes creative lawyers and accountants can find special forms of shareholding. This equity will need to be supplemented by bank loans. However, banks generally lack expertise, flexibility, willingness and trust to understand that a group of people can be a borrower if the economic figures are 'sound'. And due to the profit maximisation strategies of mainstream banks, civil society projects are usually at a disadvantage compared to traditional investors, as they typically require more time for consultation and support. Thus, bank managers or banking institutions with a clear openness to 'unfamiliar' activities are required. Confidence in the borrower (in this case, a group) and its economic viability must replace the usual examination of balance sheets, economic background and formal education. Lending decisions for such projects are based mainly on the strength of the group and economic viability. Banks such as the Triodos Bank and GLS Bank are proof that countless financings are based on these values. These banks are able to finance projects with a civil society focus because they follow a different business model: for example, savers often forgo part of their interest in order to help cover the overhead costs of complex financing arrangements. Meanwhile, some mainstream banks – such as savings banks and cooperative banks – are also beginning to finance community-led housing projects, partly because they have observed that these projects work, but also because individual employees personally identify with the goals of the initiatives. If such an approach could be supported by public funds, for example, guarantees (common for business start-ups), 'green bonds' or 'social bonds', business and cooperation would be easier. With 'cheap' money that may only be invested in environmental projects, governments have already achieved a great deal in some cases.

Excursus: Hof Prädikow near Berlin as a good-practice example: 'Land – Buildings – Community'

Some European countries have better conditions. Germany, the Netherlands, the UK and Denmark, for example. The situation in Germany is far from being perfect, but in all modesty, it provides structures that facilitate projects. These structures are not the result of a short-term decision, but are based on many decades of development, many struggles and disappointments, also in addition to many fascinating projects that have been realised.

Hof Prädikow is a farmyard comprising a community of seventy residents and fifteen animals (cf. Figure 10.1 and 10.2).

1) The trias Foundation, as the landowner, protects the land from speculation. It is embedded in a nationwide network of partners. It bought the land in 2016 and granted SelbstBau eG a ninety-nine-year heritable building right.
2) The SelbstBau eG housing cooperative has the necessary experience in renovating old buildings. Based in Berlin, it has over thirty years of experience in renovating buildings for cohousing. Democracy, cost rent, solidarity and a high degree of self-organisation are the pillars of this organisation. Traditionally, they have a very friendly working relationship with municipalities and the Federal Ministry for Family Affairs, Senior Citizens, Women and Youth.
3) The Hof Prädikow association is the internal organisation for all communal matters and represents the tenants of the site. Living, working, culture, agriculture, mutual help and urban development are the keywords. The members of Hof Prädikow e.V. have signed shares in SelbstBau eG to provide the necessary equity to finance renovation. They also made a donation to the trias Foundation. This explains how the required equity capital was raised. Hof Prädikow e.V. works together with LAG Märkische Seen (a local project initiative), Netzwerk Zukunftsorte (a network within the state of Brandenburg) and the villagers of Prädikow. They have friendly relations with the state of Brandenburg and the administration in general. Voluntary work provided by members and their friends has helped in reconstructing the building and in reducing costs (Hof Prädikow, n.d.).

GLS Bank, Germany's oldest 'alternative ethical bank', provided the loans needed to rebuild the huge estate. This bank, founded in 1974, has a great deal of experience in financing groups of all kinds and is certainly a key factor in the success of such projects.

Furthermore, there was no need for external consultants, as the partners in this project had a wealth of experience from many other projects. Finally, from the very beginning, Hof Prädikow enjoyed a high profile. When the Ministry for the Family stepped in with subsidies and the project was awarded a prize for 'social architecture', others gave it a positive rating. This provided banks, administrations and people in general with the confidence they needed.

Figure 10.1 Hof Prädikow near Berlin from above, 2017. Photo © SelbstBau eG, all rights reserved.

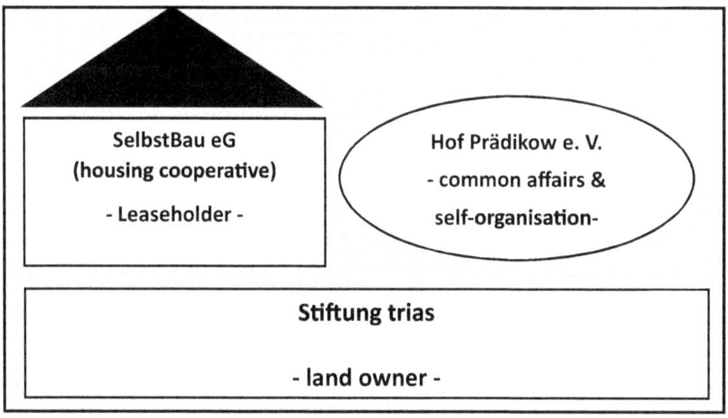

Figure 10.2 Three-part legal organisation of Hof Prädikow, 2024. Graph © author, all rights reserved.

To sum up, if you follow the development line of a housing project like Hof Prädikow, you can clearly see what communities actually need.

First, you can probably find literature for commercial start-ups in many countries, but nothing suitable for non-profit and idealistic purposes. The groups need specific literature, manuals like those published by Stiftung Trias (2010) or Patti and Polyak (2017) that explain which rules are helpful in building a group and successfully starting a development process.

Second, lawyers and tax advisors, who understand that the aims of a community-led project are very different from those of a commercial one, greatly facilitate the start-up. They can answer such questions as: what are the appropriate legal structures? An association, a cooperative or a more commercial legal form?

Third and finally, when a building site has to be bought, the question of equity becomes virulent. Subsidy programmes from national or local governments can then prove very helpful. Sometimes land foundations like trias Foundation and the Edith Maryon Foundation are the answer. Banks usually require approximately 25% equity. I experienced that this can only be raised if the group is able to convince its friends and supporters. Shares and private loans are then given. In most cases, a large number of supporters is closer to the solution than the 'big donor'.

Remedies to develop support structures for community-led housing across Europe

For sure, many of us have multiply discussed the barriers to implement community-led housing in different places and reflected on what support for grassroots initiatives would be necessary. But how do we get there? What are the remedies to transform public support and financing structures across Europe?

Mutual knowledge exchange

There is already a lot of knowledge and experience out there. However, we are hampered by very different legal structures, tax structures and social situations. I believe we need much more knowledge exchange on a very practical basis. For example: how can the English Community Land Trust Model or the German Mietshäuser Syndikat, as successful models, be adapted and implemented in other countries? Furthermore, I would recommend organising an international multi-stakeholder conference series on legal and financial instruments. Bringing together open-minded advisors (tax advisors, lawyers, bankers) and inspired pioneers from all over Europe to work on these models would facilitate new solutions.

Building up consultant networks and strengthening pan-European advocacy

We need internationally coordinated but place-based experienced task forces that could work with community-led housing initiatives as consultancy service providers. If organised at a public level, this would be a very profound way of disseminating knowledge to other participants, in addition to the direct support of the project. Moreover, we need an international advisory body to represent the interests of community-led housing groups and other citizens' initiatives *vis-à-vis* the European Union and its associated institutions or representatives in the country concerned.

Lobbying for legal innovations and public subsidy programmes

The desire to standardise legal structures in the European Union is an old one. A positive example is the European Cooperative (European Commission, n.d.). Unfortunately, the European Foundation and the European Association have not been realised. However, this legal form would make it possible to organise civic activities more efficiently than is currently possible.

Furthermore, state-owned banks like the German Kreditanstalt für Wiederaufbau (Credit Institute for Reconstruction; KFW), which allow projects to be financed in accordance with political objectives by means of cheap loans, should also be used for community-led housing. This initiative and other grassroots activities unquestionably fit into the transformation of society towards greater sustainability and adaptation to demographic change as the current key principle of these banks. Furthermore, financial support from all levels of government is crucial to bridge funding gaps and ensure that groups have the necessary resources to successfully launch their projects.

Expanding land foundations and ethical banks

Land foundations such as the Edith Maryon Foundation in Switzerland and the trias Foundation in Germany were set up to combat land speculation. They invest some of their assets in community projects and help to disseminate knowledge and build networks. The German GLS Bank and the Dutch Triodos Bank finance organic farms, community-led housing, culture, art and sustainability in general. Their roots lie in civil society itself. Courageous people founded these banks because traditional banks did not serve the needs of civil society groups and pioneers. Since these and other institutions, unfortunately, are only active in selected countries, it is necessary to build up more financing institutions. In this respect, the Zadruga za etično financiranje (Croatian Cooperative for Ethical Financing; ZEF) has proposed an absolutely innovative project worthy of support: to establish a 'European Ethical Bank' that would be able to create financing capacities of vast size (see Chapter 13).

Building up (civic) revolving funds

The problem with European Union money is the size of its programmes and funds, as well as the excessive bureaucracy. The European Investment Bank, for example, usually grants loans starting at €50 million. This does not meet the needs. A consultancy fund with grants from €10,000 to €80,000, an equity fund from €50,000 to €1 million and a loan programme from €300,000 to €10 million would be appropriate. If this is designed as a 'civic start-up fund', the risk of some losses should be accepted. If it is set up in a revolving structure, it could even generate future financial resources with a high potential for development work and self-financing. The role of civil society in the development of democratic structures and new structures oriented towards the common good is completely underestimated. People react much more quickly to abuses and failures than would any government structure. In addition to the benefits for each society, nothing brings people together and increases mutual understanding more than working together. Such a fund and its activities would therefore also be an instrument of European international understanding.

Conclusion: Strengthen transnational support networks

To conclude, I would like to come back to the key issue of this book. We need strong transnational network organisations in order to implement and support all these ideas regarding institutionalised civic consultancy, mutual knowledge exchange and pan-European advocacy to enable building up new ethical banks and revolving funds, or lobbying for legal innovations and public subsidy programmes, for instance. These umbrella organisations can give advice on how to set up a 'circular economy company' and lobby for such structures at the government level.

While civil society initiatives are not in a position to transform the banking system as such – this would require far-reaching reforms, since financial returns are usually crucial for any investment – they can take capital financing into their own hands to a certain extent. The emergence of ethical banks in Europe is ultimately attributed to committed civil society actors, too. And transnational networks can help push nation-states or the European Union to provide greater support in the form of public funds and the issuance of social bonds for community-led projects.

Of course, the network organisations need a membership base to develop and fund their activities. It takes time to build such a base. There are umbrella organisations such as the German FORUM für Gemeinschaftliches Wohnen (a cohousing forum), MOBA SCE, a network of pioneering housing cooperatives in Central Eastern Europe, NGO UrbaMonde and the recently founded European Community Land Trust Network and the Commoning Spaces Network (see Chapters 9, 13, 15). They have realised these needs and actually already started building networks of mutual knowledge exchange, consultancy, financial solidarity and advocacy. Unfortunately, all grassroots networks struggle to achieve sufficient and constant funding to be able to actually act at a European scale. Reliable funding is urgently needed to facilitate networking and knowledge dissemination.

Notes

1 Two of the examples we studied within Open Heritage, an EU Horizon 2020-funded collaborative research project, are Cascina Roccafranca, a public social and cultural centre in Turin, and Färgfabriken, a cultural laboratory in Stockholm (Open Heritage, n.d.).

2 Mixed-funded civic-public examples include Sunderland High Street West CHL (UK), an ambitious attempt to build up a community centre for socio-cultural uses, Exrotaprint in Berlin, a former industrial site today used by business enterprises, social facilities and creatives, and Largo Residências, a cooperative-run entity for responsible tourism (Open Heritage, n.d.).

References

European Commission (n.d.), 'European Cooperative Society (SCE)' (European Commission). Available at https://single-market-economy.ec.europa.eu/sectors/proximity-and-social-economy/social-economy-eu/cooperatives/european-cooperative-society-sce_en (accessed 10 January 2025).

Hof Prädikow (n.d.), *Hof Prädikow: Community-led Housing Project*. Available at https://hof-praedikow.de (accessed 10 January 2025).

Open Heritage (n.d.), *Practices in Adaptive Heritage Reuse*. Available at https://openheritage.eu/practices/ (accessed 20 December 2024).

Stiftung Trias (2010), *Experiment City Europe* (Hattingen: Stiftung Trias). Available at www.stiftung-trias.de/wissen/publikationen/experimentcity-europe/ (accessed 10 January 2025).

Patti, D., and L. Polyák (eds) (2017), *Funding the Cooperative City: Community Finance and the Economy of Civic Spaces* (Vienna: Cooperative City Books). Available at https://cooperativecity.org/product/funding-the-cooperative-city/ (accessed 10 January 2025).

11

Engaging with EU funding: How the Global Ecovillage Network leverages projects in Europe

André Girardi, Ana Margarida Esteves

Introduction

The ongoing sustainability transition poses a complex challenge to society, industries, and organisations (Hess, 2007; Hansen and Coenen, 2015; Avelino et al., 2016). Transitions refer to non-linear processes of social change in which societal systems undergo structural transformation (Geels and Schot, 2007; Grin, Rotmans and Schot, 2010). A sustainability transition is defined as 'radical transformation towards a sustainable society as a response to a number of persistent problems confronting contemporary modern societies' (Grin et al., 2010: 1). The broad scope of sustainability transitions makes it impossible to address these challenges with a single, one-dimensional solution (de Haan and Rotmans, 2011; Avelino et al., 2016; Geels, 2022). The complexity of transitioning towards sustainability stems from the need to understand the requisite structural changes (Avelino and Grin, 2017), and the connection to the potential roles and actors involved in these efforts (Wittmayer et al., 2017). Consequently, it is crucial to move beyond studying individual solutions and instead focus on examining their interactions across various societal levels (Köhler et al., 2019).

For the past three decades, the European Union (EU) has primarily allocated funds to member states through project grants (Jałocha, 2019). This funding strategy also encompasses sustainability initiatives (Nylén, 2021), targeting projects that promote sustainability transitions at various levels and engage a diverse range of actors, including local governments, institutions, civil society and grassroots initiatives. The term 'projectification' describes the growing trend of using projects to drive change and achieve complex goals (Maylor and Turkulainen, 2019). This phenomenon has been explored in various contexts, including organisational dynamics, governmental frameworks and the impact on workers' lives, particularly concerning EU project funding (Godenhjelm, Lundin and Sjöblom, 2015; Jensen,

Thuesen and Geraldi, 2016; Jałocha, 2018; 2019). However, research on grassroots initiatives that adopt such organisational structures remains underdeveloped (Creamer, 2015).

Grassroots innovations, which refer to networks of activists and organisations that develop novel, bottom-up solutions for sustainable development and consumption – specifically tailored to the needs and values of local communities (Seyfang and Smith, 2007) – have gained increasing attention. This attention stems from their ability to disseminate sustainable practices within local communities and broader society (Seyfang and Smith, 2007; Hossain, 2016; 2018).

Although the concept of a 'project-based logic' is acknowledged in the study of grassroots innovations (Smith, Fressoli and Thomas, 2014b), existing literature tends to frame it as a paradox between systemic change and project-based solutions. This creates a significant gap in understanding how grassroots innovations engage with higher institutions, for example EU funding schemes aimed at promoting sustainability transitions and the specific effects of EU projectification on the such networks. Specifically, there is a need for research that examines how these projects align with the goals of grassroots networks and support their members in advancing sustainability transitions.

This chapter investigates the dynamics of the European branch of the Global Ecovillage Network's (GEN-Europe) engagement with EU funding schemes, more specifically, how grassroots innovations engage with EU funding schemes through projects that promote sustainability transitions. On the basis of an in-depth analysis of GEN-Europe, this study illustrates how EU funding not only supports but also shapes the operational and strategic capacities of grassroots initiatives. The findings contribute to the broader discourse on sustainability transitions by highlighting the dual role of funding in both empowering and structuring grassroots innovation, thereby offering insights into the complexities of navigating institutional funding landscapes. Methodologically, this research employs a qualitative approach, comprising nine semi-structured interviews with key members of the case study, participant observation, and three rounds of coding, both deductive and inductive, inspired by grounded theory (Flick, 2011; Charmaz, 2012).

Our findings reveal a strong alignment between EU sustainability policy dynamics, as enacted through project grants, and the manner in which GEN-Europe applies and utilises EU-funded projects. The professionalisation of the network is crucial for securing these funds, enabling it to provide enhanced support for its members. Additionally, we introduce the concept of a 'project-supported network', an emerging framework that characterises grassroots innovation sustained by project dynamics and project funds.

State of the art

Contextualising grassroots innovations

Over the past two decades, grassroots innovations were extensively studied by academics due to the importance and recognised role they play in sustainability transitions (Wells, 2011; Creech et al., 2014; Feola, 2016; Hossain, 2016). Grassroots innovations are predominantly defined in academic research as 'a network of activists and organisations generating novel bottom-up solutions for sustainable development and sustainable consumption; solutions that respond to the local situation and the interests and values of the communities involved' (Seyfang and Smith, 2007: 585). 'Grassroots innovations' is used in the literature as an umbrella concept encompassing a wide range of movements, including cooperatives, voluntary associations, community groups and the social economy (Seyfang and Smith, 2007; Hossain, 2016; 2018). In this chapter, we classify GEN-Europe as a grassroots innovation, consistent with previous categorisations (Roysen et al., 2024).

Even though grassroots innovations can arise from various fields, certain areas attract more academic attention. According to Hossain (2018), these areas include community-led housing (Markle et al., 2015; Boyer, 2018; Lang, Chatterton and Mullins, 2020) and organic food (Henfrey, 2010; Gernert, El Bilali and Strassner, 2018). Other prominent domains are community currency (França Filho, Silva Júnior and Rigo, 2012; Fressoli et al., 2014), community energy (Seyfang and Haxeltine, 2010; Becker and Kunze, 2014) and agriculture (Bowne, 2014; Gomiero, 2018).

The spaces grassroots innovations are immersed, and the spaces they create, are shaped by legislative and cultural contexts that either promote or hinder their development, depending on their alignment with bottom-up governance and grassroots control of supply chains (Becker, Franke and Gläsel, 2018; Henfrey and Penha-Lopes, 2018). They encounter several institutional challenges, including underdeveloped models for commons-based governance (Wolsink, 2020), regulatory and policy barriers that limit access to necessary support (Walker and Devine-Wright, 2008) and market-driven expectations like replication, scaling up and bridging the innovations to the mainstream settings (Seyfang and Haxeltine, 2010; Fressoli et al., 2014). Their capacity to generate surplus, accumulate capital internally or achieve economies of scale is limited compared to profit-driven enterprises with non-place-based supply chains (Chatterton and Pickerill, 2010; Esteves, 2017; 2020).

Projectification context and the European Union

In recent decades, the study of projects and their impact on society has received academic attention worldwide, driven by the widespread adoption of project-based approaches and logics across various activities (Jałocha,

2018). Projects are broadly defined as non-routine tasks with clearly specified targets, a specific duration, a relation of participants, and a set of resources (Schoper et al., 2018). In other words, projects are constrained by time, funding and the disposal of other relevant resources, be it people, knowledge and other tangible materials; and they come to an end when the goals are regarded as fulfilled and when the available resources have been exhausted (Büttner and Leopold, 2016).

According to Boltanski and Chiapello (2005), the increase in the number of projects during the 1990s is emblematic of the ideological configuration of contemporary capitalism. This new, project-based order represents what they describe as a 'new spirit' of social organisation. It increasingly influences what people think, feel and expect, how they relate one another, and how people structure their daily lives (Büttner and Leopold, 2016). This proliferation of projects is called projectification (Jałocha, 2018: 62).

The term projectification was first coined by Christophe Midler (1995). Over the past three decades, the phenomenon of projectification has been extensively explored across diverse contexts. This growing trend in research (Packendorff and Lindgren, 2014) has examined areas such as work relations (Bredin and Soderlund, 2006; Arvidsson, 2009; Ekstedt, 2019), health care (Stinne Glasdam et al., 2015), entrepreneurship (Raatikainen, 2018), sustainability issues (Creamer, 2015), societal dynamics (Lundin and Söderholm, 1995) and governmental issues (Jałocha, 2013; Godenhjelm, Lundin and Sjöblom, 2015; Büttner and Leopold, 2016). An important contribution to understanding projectification is Jalocha's (2019) work in typology, which delineates levels of projectification, ranging from micro (individuals) to meso (organisations), macro (industries and sectors), mega (countries, supranational organisations) and meta (transformations of global social structures) (Kuura, 2017; Jałocha, 2019). Therefore, the project logic extrapolates organisations and firms, they influence our personal life, our goals and the way we organise life, they influence governments and how the incentives in society work (Jensen, Thuesen and Geraldi, 2016; Lundin, 2016).

In Europe, one way that projects influence and connect to the grassroots and civil society levels is through project grants. Actually, over the past three decades, EU project grants have become an integral part of EU policymaking, resulting in a significant proportion of EU policies being implemented through project funds (Büttner and Leopold, 2016). Examples of this include the umbrellas of cohesion and rural development policies, as well as the promotion of research and innovation, and adult and youth education programmes. Buttner and Leopold (2016) argue that the EU is a significant generator of project-based activities and a major driver of the expansion of project management principles in contemporary public affairs. This influence extends to a wide range of individuals involved in the EU project world, encompassing the stages of acquisition, implementation, management, evaluation and monitoring of project grants (Büttner, 2019).

To be eligible for EU funding, projects must adapt to the standards set by the funding scheme and effectively use the technical language and rhetoric associated with EU projects. Only those who can align with these managerial norms and political objectives can successfully engage in the EU funding process (Büttner and Leopold, 2016). Therefore, organisations must have a high level of professionalisation to access such project grants (Jałocha, 2013). We perceive professionalisation as a flexible and ongoing process of social positioning that extends along a continuum from layperson to expert, characterised by varying levels of specialisation, complexity and necessary training (Pavalko, 1988; Büttner et al., 2015).

Project-supported networks

'Project-supported organisations' denotes entities that are consistently sustained through project-based structures and funding. The term is defined as follows: 'The projects in question are used to develop the internal or interior functioning of the organisation or to prepare for the future by developing new products or preparing for potential threats and societal demands from the outside' (Lundin, 2016: 11). This concept can be combined with the notion of project networks, where 'the purpose of a project in such a network might be a cooperative venture in which the various partners of the network have a stake in the project' (Lundin, 2016: 11). By merging these ideas, we introduce the concept of a 'project-supported network", where networks leverage partnerships to build projects that achieve common goals and develop new methods to support their members and partners.

This concept is central to this chapter, and the findings provide empirical evidence that validates its formation and highlights its potential to enhance collaboration and effectiveness among network participants and other grassroots innovations. Therefore, project-supported networks are formal organisations designed to serve as collaborative platforms for initiatives of similar nature, sustained by funding and resources through projects, thus justifying the designation 'project-supported networks'. In addition, this does not imply that these organisations were originally established to function as project-supported networks. Often, they evolve into this form due to contextual influences, internal decisions and the availability of external resources and funding.

In the research presented in the remainder of this chapter, we seek to deepen the investigation of GEN-Europe, a project-supported network that adheres to EU funding schemes in order to foster its network and serve its members. We explore the network's dynamics in relation to EU-funded projects aimed at encouraging sustainability transitions, seeking to uncover the processes, solutions and tensions of this approach and its implications for the broader world of grassroots innovations.

Methods and case study

The methodological foundations of this chapter combine perspectives from organisational theory through project management studies, grassroots innovation movements, which derive from social movement studies, and strategic management (Smith, Fressoli and Thomas, 2014a; Smith et al., 2017; Locatelli et al., 2023). Its framework of data collection was inspired by Grounded Theory methods (Bryant and Charmaz, 2008; Charmaz, 2012; Flick, 2018) and in-depth case study (Flick, 2011; Yin, 2018), which was developed through an interactive process between the field and desk phases (Czarniawska, 2014). This methodology emphasises a reflective approach to data collection, where participant observation plays a crucial role in gathering information, and reflective practices are fundamental in redirecting efforts to comprehend the subject of study (Charmaz, 2012; Timmermans and Tavory, 2022).

The Global Ecovillage Network Europe

To explore how grassroots innovations engage with EU funding schemes through projects that promote sustainability transitions, we selected GEN-Europe as a representative case. The Global Ecovillage Network (GEN) is the leading representative of the ecovillage movement, with branches across multiple continents, including GEN-Europe in Europe, CASA in Latin America, GENNA in North America, GEN Africa, and GENOA in Oceania and Asia.

According to Jackson and Jackson (2004), GEN emerged in the 1990s out of a distinctly political and cultural context shaped by dissatisfaction with traditional institutions and a growing global consciousness about environmental degradation and social injustice. Its formation was closely linked to the legacy of the Nordic Alternative Campaign of the 1980s, which sought to unify grassroots movements and scientific expertise to address systemic global challenges. This period was marked by a strong critique of conventional development paradigms and political inertia in the face of ecological crises. The founders of Gaia Trust – Hildur and Ross Jackson – were the primary financial supporters behind the creation and development of GEN and GEN-Europe. They shared a strong conviction that transformative change would not emerge from political elites, who they viewed as complicit in sustaining unsustainable systems, but rather from grassroots actors capable of envisioning and building alternative ways of living. Their strategic vision was shaped by concerns over the limits to growth, global economic instability and the urgent need for socially just and ecologically sustainable communities. In this context, GEN was conceived not simply as a network of intentional communities, but as a political project aimed at prefiguring a post-growth society through lived experimentation and translocal collaboration. Its establishment coincided with broader civil society mobilisations around UN processes (e.g., Habitat II) and was driven by a belief in the need for exemplary models of sustainable living that could inspire systemic change beyond the boundaries of conventional politics (Jackson and Jackson, 2004).

GEN was formally founded in 1995, and defines an ecovillage as 'an intentional, traditional or urban community that consciously designs its pathway through locally owned, participatory processes, addressing the Ecovillage Principles in four areas of regeneration: social, cultural, ecological, and economic' (Global Ecovillage Network, 2024).

GEN-Europe is a non-profit membership association dedicated to supporting existing ecovillages and encouraging the development of new ones in Europe. Its mission includes spreading the tools, resources, inspiration and culture of ecovillages across Europe and beyond. The network connects over 130 member ecovillages and ecoprojects and includes 18 national networks across 26 European countries. Its organisational structure consists of three main pillars: the council, staff and members. The council, comprising about six members who serve three-year terms, is responsible for upholding the network's vision and making key decisions, ensuring balanced representation during annual general assemblies, where significant matters are voted on using sociocracy principles.

The staff includes around nine core members supported by volunteers, overseeing various roles such as IT, communications, project management and events. To become a member, an ecovillage must be a community of at least ten people who have lived together for a minimum of two years. Member networks are required to have at least three established ecoprojects or ecovillages affiliated with GEN-Europe. By facilitating collaboration, sharing best practices, and providing access to resources, GEN-Europe empowers its members to navigate the complexities of sustainability transitions. The network has evolved from its founding intention to foster ecovillages into a pivotal platform for collective action and innovation, helping members engage effectively with broader societal demands and EU funding opportunities.

Data collection and data analysis

Data collection methods included three primary approaches: semi-structured interviews were conducted with key individuals from different contexts (see Table 11.1) that were selected through snowball sampling (Yin, 2018); participant observation was carried out during both online and in-person events organised by the network as well as through participation as a partner in a European-funded project conducted in collaboration with the case study in 2023 and 2024 for a period of fifteen months; lastly, document analysis was conducted using materials gathered online about and from the case studied.

The data analysis was conducted in three rounds of coding, supported by Atlas.ti. The first round involved inductive coding, following Charmaz's (2012) approach, where codes are created separately. In the second round, coding was guided by an intermediary workshop with the research team and external consultants from academia and practitioners in the field. This workshop resulted in grouping the core codes into main themes or categories, which were then used to recode the material. The third and final round of coding incorporated additional material from a second round of interviews, with a specific focus on project themes.

Results

Contextualising a project-supported network

GEN-Europe is increasingly relying on European project funds, which have become a major focus for the network in recent years. Prior to 2016, GEN-Europe participated in some projects but without a formal structure or consistent approach. However, from 2017 onward, the network began to strategically engage with EU-funded projects, recognising their importance. These projects not only provide vital financial support but also offer indirect benefits by fostering stronger connections among members, ecovillages and individuals within the network:

> For the network, having European projects, I think it's beneficial financially not only for the organisation, but also like for all the members. It also brings a lot of connection. Like it fosters the network because we have like all these transnational meetings and project meetings where people just get to know each other. It's like we're actually like the European projects that are actually also helping us to foster the health of the network. (Interviewee 1)

This evidence underscores a significant strategic alignment between GEN-Europe and the EU's sustainability policies, as demonstrated through the project grants framework. The congruence between the EU's objectives and the aspirations of ecovillages for societal sustainability is not coincidental but a result of deliberate efforts by GEN-Europe to harmonise their goals with EU directives, as this quote illustrates:

> Because what Ecovillage is trying to do is exactly what the European policies are trying to encourage us to do. And I think there is then a symbiosis between the European structures and the Ecovillage that the Ecovillages are developing solutions, testing things out and being very successful with it because it's completely aligned with what they're doing. (Interviewee 2)

It is evident that shifting the focus towards securing European funding was a strategic evolution for GEN-Europe. Before, the model of the network was very much reliant on donations from Gaia Trust fund, which is a fund created by the founders of GEN network to promote the mother network and the ramifications. GEN-Europe was also relying a lot on member contributions and membership fees, as well as their annual gathering income. This combination previously resulted in a very lean network, which lacked both the staffing levels and the outreach it possesses today at the European level. The transformation from a donation-based, lean operation to a project-supported network began between 2016 and 2017, and is therefore a recent development.

This transition not only facilitated the expansion of their capabilities by hiring additional staff but also enriched the network's offerings through the introduction of new IT tools, trainings, courses and events. Furthermore, it significantly enhanced the scope and depth of knowledge exchange within the network. However, this is not a model that is replicated across all ecovillages. Some, as we observed, are indeed driven by and oriented towards acquiring project funds to disseminate their practices and innovations. Nevertheless, this is not the norm within the GEN-Europe landscape, even though the network plays a role in opening such possibilities through partnerships for European-funded projects and by providing training to its members on how to apply for and manage these funds. This variability, of whether an ecovillage adheres to this model of project support, can give rise to debates or even conflicting perspectives in certain areas. We therefore interpret that the local areas where ecovillages are situated tend to demonstrate greater flexibility in their approach to projects, whether European-funded or not.

One of the most prominent types of projects within GEN-Europe are those funded by the European Solidarity Corps (ESC) (European Commission press, 2016; European Commission, 2022). The ESC focuses on youth education through voluntary programmes across various locations in Europe, aiming to provide education and work opportunities. Several ecovillages that are part of GEN-Europe participate in this programme and consistently undertake projects with ESC volunteers. GEN-Europe itself hosts multiple ESC volunteers annually. The relevance and importance of the ESC programme to GEN-Europe and its members are underscored by the following quote:

> The ESC programme is one of the best things that has happened to GEN-Europe ever. And we're so happy about that. Like it's the way of us to connect with younger generations, and younger generations to go into the ecovillage world. Nowadays, we have a pretty successful programme. (Interviewee 1)

Another significant type of EU grant in which GEN-Europe has actively participated for several years is Erasmus+. This programme, run by the European Commission, focuses on education, youth, training and sport. GEN-Europe leverages Erasmus+ to develop projects that introduce innovative processes, tools and platforms designed to enhance training and education for both youth and adults within the network. 'So, ERASMUS+, Horizon Europe, these calls are, I think, they are very much in line with what GEN-Europe stands for' (Interviewee 4). These initiatives also cultivate partnerships with a diverse range of civil society organisations and institutions, including research centres, universities and other grassroots initiatives. Erasmus+ projects serve as a vital means of fostering connectivity and disseminating EU-funded initiatives among network members. While they offer financial support to the network, their primary objectives are to create and distribute innovative tools for learning, teaching and networking.

Horizon Europe projects are another type of EU-funded initiative that GEN-Europe has accessed. These projects are research and innovation-driven and involve a wide range of partners from different sectors (European Commission: Directorate-General for Research and Innovation, 2021). GEN-Europe, along with some of its member ecovillages, has participated in Horizon Europe projects on two occasions. These projects typically span at least three years and have higher budgets, making them a significant source of income for the network. This funding supports the network's operations and enables it to pay its staff: 'Back in 2017 was when we landed our first major project – the Horizon project. This allowed us to hire two staff members' (Interviewee 1). One of these projects was BLOOM[1] (2017–20), a Coordination and Support Action aimed at fostering public engagement with the bioeconomy across Europe. Through the creation of five regional hubs, the project engaged civil society organisations, NGOs, media and schools in co-creation workshops and public outreach activities. GEN-Europe contributed to BLOOM by mobilising its network to raise awareness about bioeconomy-related solutions in sustainable living and community practices. This involvement not only enhanced its organisational capacity, but also aligned with GEN-Europe's mission of promoting ecological regeneration and knowledge exchange.

Participation in Horizon Europe projects such as BLOOM thus strengthens GEN-Europe's role in advancing research, public engagement and innovation in the field of sustainable development and ecovillage-based alternatives. It also facilitates the formation of strategic partnerships and reinforces the network's long-term objectives.

To better understand the process of conducting EU-funded projects, GEN-Europe follows several essential steps. Each phase of this process is critical for the development and maintenance of past, current and future projects. These steps ensure the projects are effectively managed, meet funding requirements and achieve their intended outcomes. In the next subsection, we highlight the specific project flow and processes that GEN-Europe employs to navigate the complexities of EU-funded initiatives.

Project process

Based on field observations, interviews and conversations to check and receive feedback, the sequence in Figure 11.1 outlines the stages of project formation within GEN-Europe for EU-funded projects.

This staged process represents the current pipeline of most EU-funded projects that GEN-Europe and its members are part of. GEN-Europe offers tailored training and courses to educate its members on these stages, with a focus on initiating applications for programmes like Erasmus+ and ESC. This robust process approach not only fosters professionalisation within the network but also streamlines project management by standardising procedures. This standardisation enhances efficiency, builds organisational know-how and supports the transfer of expertise within the network. The pursuit of projects and the continual acquisition of funding contribute to a more professional environment, a dynamic explored further in the subsequent subsection.

Professionalisation of the network through projects

A key factor in achieving success with EU-funded projects at all stages of development is the professionalism of the project workforce. This means that participants should possess relevant experience, knowledge, in-project application, funding acquisition, project coordination and, in some cases, formal education in project management. This expertise is crucial for the consistent acquisition and success of EU-funded initiatives.

GEN-Europe has project coordinators who are responsible for managing various initiatives, as the following quotes illustrate: 'I write projects for

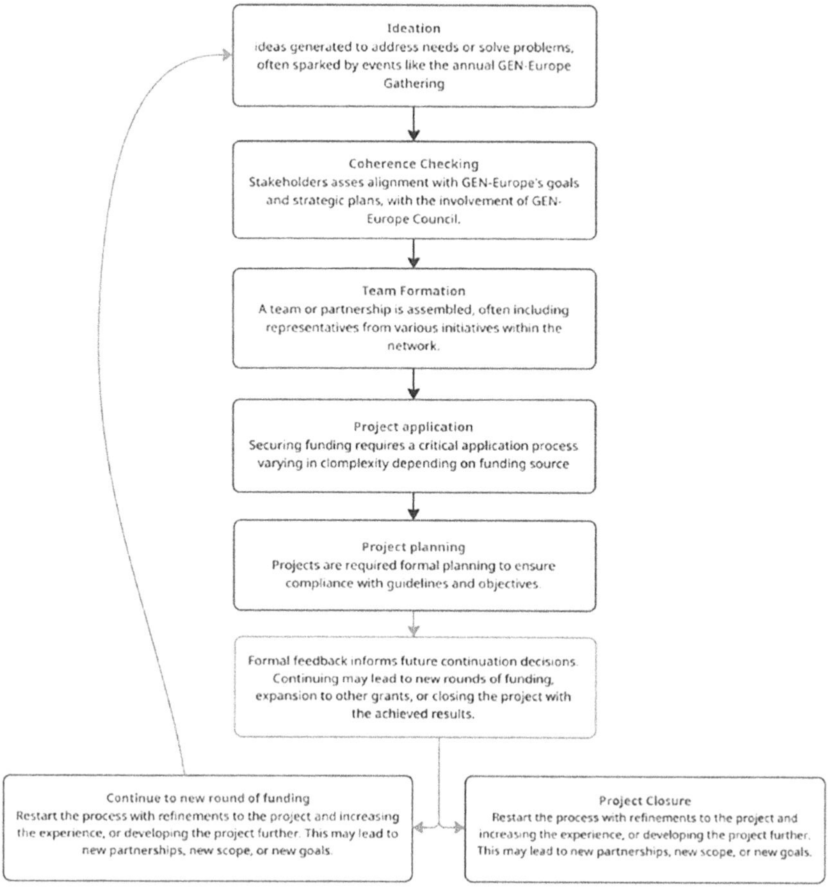

Figure 11.1 Processing of EU-funded projects by GEN-Europe. Graphic © authors, all rights reserved.

[GEN] Europe and I establish protocols on how projects should be run within our organisation' (Interviewee 4). GEN-Europe has successfully transferred project management knowledge to other ecovillages, enabling them to independently conduct projects. This capacity-building effort is exemplified by a former project coordinator from an ecovillage who highlights the ability of these communities to manage and execute projects autonomously, demonstrating the effectiveness of GEN-Europe's training and support:

> I was largely responsible for managing through a few projects. I'm writing applications coming up with or initiating new project ideas and ensuring that

> the ecovillage remains connected also to other networks' (Interviewee 6). GEN-Europe provides training on project application as well: 'We have trainings on how to write projects constantly. (Interviewee 5)

Ensuring that project objectives are in harmony with the network's goals is crucial for achieving cohesive and impactful outcomes. 'We have to make sure that the projects that we are like working in or the ones that we are applying for, they are completely aligned to what we actually want to do' (Interviewee 1). The phases of project application and team formation are critical stages where professionalism is paramount. By ensuring a professional approach, tensions can be minimised, and energy can be effectively directed toward achieving project goals. We observed the current trend of EU-funded projects to be something that GEN-Europe will continue doing in the near future, as some recent decisions of the network point in this direction, for example, to start what they call a 'project working group', designed to spread the knowledge about projects through online events and assistance to write projects for different EU calls.

Our examination of GEN-Europe's consistent project applications has revealed the development of substantial expertise in EU-funded projects, knowledge which is now being disseminated to its members. This process initiates a cascading effect, facilitating the adaptation of GEN-Europe's project-supported network model to local ecovillages. Supported by EU funds, these ecovillages are enhancing their capacities, fostering innovation and engaging external participants and youth in their activities. This aligns strongly with the network's future direction, presenting a viable model for the diffusion and flourishing of their innovations. However, this raises concerns about potential overreliance on a single funding model, potentially limiting the diversity of their financial strategies.

Discussion and conclusion

In this chapter, we sought to empirically investigate the interplay between grassroots innovations and EU funding schemes, specifically examining how grassroots engage with EU funding schemes through projects that promote sustainability transitions. We found that the funding schemes developed by the EU regarding sustainability transition converge with what GEN-Europe strives for in their efforts to help influence and positively impact society. This is manifested through several funding lines exemplified in the previous section, where GEN-Europe and its members are recurrently granted funds from the EU. Aligning with EU sustainability policies and adapting to their funding schemes is crucial for grassroots innovations aiming to increase their impact through EU-funded projects. This enables initiatives to access resources that would otherwise be difficult to obtain, as they are often not directly linked to mainstream institutions (Avelino et al., 2020). This explains how grassroots innovations can grow and potentially increase their impact despite their non-commercial focus and local impact-driven nature.

Enhancing the network through professional distribution of roles

This insight enhances the current understanding of grassroots innovations, which frequently emphasises the dichotomies of scale dynamics versus localism, niches versus regimes and alternative versus mainstream (Hermans, Roep and Klerkx, 2016; Avelino et al., 2020). Therefore, understanding the dynamics of interactions with higher institutions and the specific strategies employed is crucial for other similar initiatives to establish a foundation and adopt a comparable set of actions (see Chapter 3). In this context, we demonstrated that the process of professionalisation of the network plays a vital role in accessing funds and their recurring acquisition.

The results from our case study highlight several key institutionalised actions taken by GEN-Europe to effectively engage with EU-funded projects. Notably, the organisation established specific roles for project coordinators within their staff. These coordinators manage project applications, build partnerships and support project teams, making this role crucial for ongoing access to EU funding. Beyond managing projects, coordinators also hold and disseminate valuable knowledge through training sessions for other network members. Additionally, the development of a structured process to guide and support projects contributes to the long-term legitimacy of the organisation. When projects are completed successfully and professionally, the movement's credibility in the eyes of funders is likely to grow. The literature that connects organisational change to EU-funded projects links adaptation of organisational goals to the objectives of grant applications and to changes in organisational structures (Jałocha, 2013). The study by Jałocha (2013) highlights the potential threats that may arise, such as when projects fall short of delivering the expected value or long-term benefits to local communities. This research found that despite concerns over potential negative outcomes, the application of EU-funded projects within GEN-Europe has predominantly delivered significant value and services to its members throughout the years, for example the creation of manuals for starting and developing communities and ecovillages named CLIPS, creating an online database of academic and field material that supports the legitimacy of the ecovillage movement[2] (project Regen4all). This funding logic has proven effective in enhancing the network's offerings rather than diminishing them, with the current expansion of the model within the network through trainings and courses.

Project-supported networks

Given the consistent success and significance of engaging with EU-funded projects, we can confidently affirm the relevance of the concept of project-supported networks in the context of grassroots innovations. GEN-Europe's case effectively leverages available funding through various projects to facilitate the dissemination of valuable resources for its members. Therefore, this concept helps to clarify the tension between structural change and project-based approaches in grassroots innovations – a paradox already discussed in the literature – and offers insight into strategies that may help to address it (Smith, Fressoli and Thomas, 2014b).

This approach not only enhances the knowledge and innovations generated within the network, but also fosters a collaborative environment where members can access and benefit from shared expertise, which are a characteristics of temporary organisations (Lundin and Söderholm, 1995), or project networks, which create a temporary cooperative venture for a given project, for example (Lundin, 2016). At the same time, the concept of project-supported organisations allows us to explain the goal of building internal functioning and developing processes for the future. These two concepts when combined explain what GEN-Europe does through EU-funded projects. Thus, GEN-Europe is a network, not an ordinary organisation (Lundin and Söderholm, 1995): (1) it creates and fosters collaboration among partners of a project, them being part of the network already or not, and (2) through these projects GEN-Europe creates capacity, services and tools that help the network navigate current and future challenges for its development.

Figure 11.2 outlines the structural and procedural dynamics through which GEN-Europe engages with EU-funded projects, highlighting the central role of funding programmes such as Erasmus+, Horizon Europe and the European Solidarity Corps. It illustrates how GEN-Europe strategically channels efforts into project acquisition and management, generating a set of tangible outcomes for the network and its members. These include the professionalisation of the workforce, enhanced dissemination of project-related knowledge, increased staffing capacity, and the formation of new partnerships. While this figure captures a crucial operational mechanism within the network – namely the use of projects – it also reflects a specific institutional choice that does not encompass the entirety of the grassroots innovation landscape.

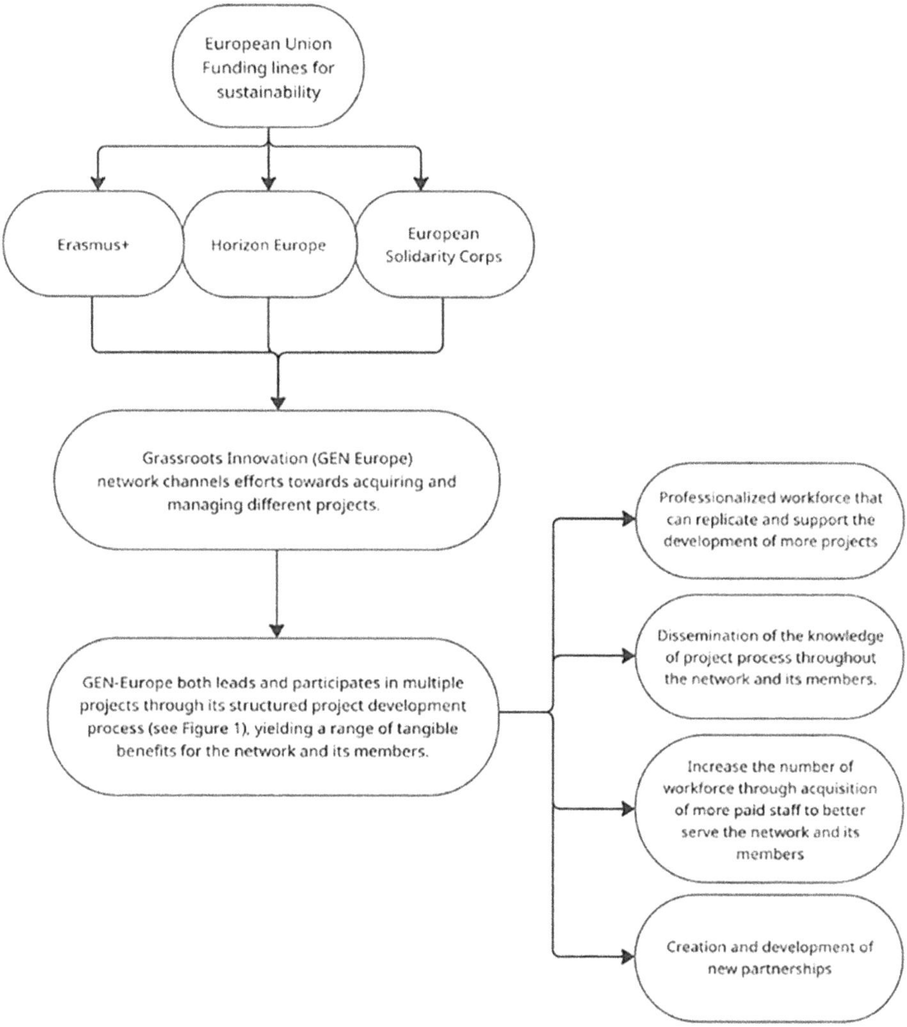

Figure 11.2 Structure and key outcomes of GEN-Europe's project-supported network. Graphic © authors, all rights reserved.

Therefore, while the project-based model has become an increasingly dominant component of GEN-Europe's organisational strategy, it should be understood primarily as a pragmatic response to the institutional environment in which the network operates – namely, the European policy context that privileges project funding as a key mechanism for promoting change. In the case of GEN-Europe, this model has been instrumental in advancing the network's goals by enabling access to resources, partnerships and professional capacities. However, this alignment with the EU's projectification logic should not be construed as a universally applicable or desirable model for all grassroots innovations. Engaging successfully with EU-funded projects requires significant institutional capacity, strategic know-how and sustained effort – resources that may not be readily available to smaller or less formalised initiatives. As such, while the project modality can amplify certain forms of grassroots innovations, it may simultaneously marginalise others that operate through more informal, experimental or community-embedded practices.

Limits and outlook

On the limitations of this study, we did not analyse whether the incorporation of projects by GEN-Europe influences their diffusion processes and capacities to increase the number of ecovillages within the network or to what extent projects help to spread the knowledge created by GEN-Europe and its members. This appears especially relevant because one of the core principles of GEN-Europe is to support the creation and diffusion of ecovillages and their members. Therefore, we suggest that future research explores how projectification influences the diffusion strategies and processes of grassroots innovations. Furthermore, we add the importance of bringing other cases within GEN-Europe into analysis, as the use of EU-funded projects may differ in other levels of the network, which can bring new insights into the initiatives working locally.

While this study focused on the dynamics of grassroots innovations that engage with EU-funded projects, we acknowledge that other types of projects, not connected to EU funding dynamics, exist and deserve attention. Exploring the dynamics of these types of projects may provide valuable insights into the broader realm of projectification in a grassroots innovations context.

We conclude this chapter by noting that, while EU-funded projects have enabled significant advancements for GEN-Europe, they may also already be contributing to similar developments among other grassroots innovations across Europe. Balancing the demands of project work with the foundational goals of these movements is crucial for their sustained impact and success. This study highlights the need for a nuanced understanding of projectification and its implications, advocating for strategic coherence and inclusive practices to ensure that the benefits of project funding are fully realised without compromising the core values and strategic choices of grassroots innovations.

Table 11.1 Interviewee details

Role/position/affiliation	Date of interview (place)	Topics of interview	Interviewee code
Project participant, ecovillager, GEN-Europe staff	August 2023 (online)	Internal projects, European-funded projects, GEN-Europe	Interviewee 1
Former GEN-Europe staff, former GEN-Europe council member and director, ecovillage founder	February 2022 (online)	European-funded projects, energy communities, GEN-Europe	Interviewee 2
GEN-Europe staff, ecovillage founder, former project coordinator	November 2022 (online)	GEN-Europe projects, European projects, GEN-Europe	Interviewee 3
GEN-Europe staff, ecovillager	February 2022 (online)	European-funded projects, energy communities, GEN-Europe	Interviewee 4
Former GEN-Europe council member, former project coordinator, member of Italian Ecovillage Network	July 2023 (in person)	Internal projects, European-funded projects, GEN-Europe, local ecovillage projects, national funded projects	Interviewee 5
Former ecovillage staff, former project coordinator	June 2023 (online)	Internal projects, European-funded projects, GEN-Europe, local ecovillage projects, national funded projects	Interviewee 6
GEN-Europe member, ecovillage founder, former project coordinator at GEN-Europe	November 2022 (online)	GEN-Europe projects, European projects, GEN-Europe	Interviewee 7
Former GEN-Europe council member	December 2023 (online)	GEN-Europe projects, European projects, GEN-Europe	Interviewee 8

Source: Author's own, 2024.

Funding

This article is part of the research 'Transnational networks for regenerative development in Europe: A comparative perspective on grassroots mobilisation and policy advocacy (EuroREGEN)' funded by the Portuguese Foundation for Science and Technology (FCT), reference PTDC/SOC- SOC/ 2061/2020.

Ana Margarida Esteves' position is funded by the FCT grant agreement, reference 10.54499/CEECINST/00067/2021/CP2777/CT0002.

Acknowledgements

We extend our gratitude to the EuroREGEN team – Felipe Quintão, Luciane dos Santos, Maria Fernandes-Jesus, Amandine Garmeiro and Tom Henfrey – for their invaluable contributions and insights. We also appreciate our ongoing collaboration with GEN-Europe, which is instrumental in our past, present and future endeavours.

Notes

1 https://bloom-bioeconomy.eu/ (accessed 2 July 2025).
2 These projects, and many more, can be found on GEN-Europe's webpage dedicated to current and previous projects: https://gen-europe.org/projects/ (accessed 2 July 2025).

References

Arvidsson, N. (2009), 'Exploring tensions in projectified matrix organisations', *Scandinavian Journal of Management*, Corporate Responsibility: Reflections on Context and Consequences, 25:1, 97–107, https://doi.org/10.1016/j.scaman.2008.09.002

Avelino, F., A. Dumitru, C. Cipolla, I. Kunze, and J. Wittmayer (2020), 'Translocal empowerment in transformative social innovation networks', *European Planning Studies*, 28:5, 955–77, https://doi.org/10.1080/09654313.2019.1578339

Avelino, F., and J. Grin (2017), 'Beyond deconstruction. a reconstructive perspective on sustainability transition governance', *Environmental Innovation and Societal Transitions*, 22, 15–25, https://doi.org/10.1016/j.eist.2016.07.003

Avelino, F., J. Grin, B. Pel, and S. Jhagroe (2016), 'The politics of sustainability transitions', *Journal of Environmental Policy & Planning*, 18:5, 557–67, https://doi.org/10.1080/1523908X.2016.1216782

Becker, S., and C. Kunze (2014), 'Transcending community energy: collective and politically motivated projects in renewable energy (CPE) across Europe',

People, Place and Policy Online, 8:3, 180–91, https://doi.org/10.3351/ppp.0008.0003.0004
Becker, S. L., F. Franke, and A. Gläsel (2018), 'Regime pressures and organizational forms of community-based sustainability initiatives', *Environmental Innovation and Societal Transitions*, 29, 5–16, https://doi.org/10.1016/j.eist.2017.10.004
Boltanski, L., and E. Chiapello (2005), 'The New Spirit of Capitalism', *International Journal of Politics, Culture, and Society*, 18:3–4, 161–88, https://doi.org/10.1007/s10767-006-9006-9
Bowne, E. E. (2014), 'Environmental Anthropology Engaging Ecotopia: Bioregionalism, Permaculture, and Ecovillages', *Culture, Agriculture, Food & Environment*, 36:1, 63–64, https://doi.org/10.1111/cuag.12032
Boyer, R. H. W. (2018), 'Intermediacy and the diffusion of grassroots innovations: The case of cohousing in the United States', *Environmental Innovation and Societal Transitions*, 26, 32–43, https://doi.org/10.1016/j.eist.2017.08.001
Bredin, K., and J. Soderlund (2006), 'Perspectives on Human Resource Management: an explorative study of the consequences of projectification in four firms', *International Journal of Human Resources Development and Management*, 6:1, 92–113, https://doi.org/10.1504/IJHRDM.2006.009751
Bryant, A., and K. Charmaz (2008), *The Sage Handbook of Grounded Theory* (Los Angeles, CA: Sage).
Büttner, S. M. (2019), 'The European Dimension of Projectification: Implications of the Project Approach in EU Funding Policy 1', in *The Projectification of the Public Sector*, pp. 169–88, https://doi.org/10.4324/9781315098586-10
Büttner, S. M., and L. M. Leopold (2016), 'A "new spirit" of public policy? The project world of EU funding', *European Journal of Cultural and Political Sociology*, 3:1, 41–71, https://doi.org/10.1080/23254823.2016.1183503
Büttner, S. M., L. Leopold, S. Mau, and M. Posvic (2015), 'Professionalization in EU Policy-Making? The topology of the transnational field of EU affairs', *European Societies*, 17:4, 569–92, https://doi.org/10.1080/14616696.2015.1072229
Charmaz, K. (2012), *Constructing Grounded Theory: A Practical Guide through Qualitative Analysis* (Los Angeles, CA: Sage).
Chatterton, P., and J. Pickerill (2010), 'Everyday activism and transitions towards post-capitalist worlds', *Transactions of the Institute of British Geographers*, 35:4, 475–90, https://doi.org/10.1111/j.1475-5661.2010.00396.x
Creamer, E. (2015), 'The double-edged sword of grant funding: a study of community-led climate change initiatives in remote rural Scotland', *Local Environment*, 20:9, 981–99, https://doi.org/10.1080/13549839.2014.885937
Creech, H., L. Paas, G. H. Gabriel, V. Voora, C. Hybsier, and H. Marquard (2014), 'Small-scale social-environmental enterprises in the green economy: supporting grassroots innovation', *Development in Practice*, 24:3, 366–78, https://doi.org/10.1080/09614524.2014.899561
Czarniawska, B. (2014), *Social Science Research: From Field to Desk* (London: Sage), https://doi.org/10.4135/9781529799613
Ekstedt, E. (2019), 'Project work, a challenge to traditional work life institutions', *International Journal of Managing Projects in Business*, 12:2, 267–81, https://doi.org/10.1108/ijmpb-02-2018-0033
Esteves, A. M. (2017), 'Radical Environmentalism and "Commoning": Synergies Between Ecosystem Regeneration and Social Governance at Tamera Ecovillage, Portugal', *Antipode*, 49:2, 357–76, https://doi.org/10.1111/anti.12278

Esteves, A. M. (2020), 'Peace education for the Anthropocene? The contribution of regenerative ecology and the ecovillages movement', *Journal of Peace Education*, 17:1, 26–47, https://doi.org/10.1080/17400201.2019.1657817
European Commission (2022), 'European Solidarity Corps'. Available at https://ec.europa.eu/commission/presscorner/detail/en/ip_22_7100 (accessed 2 October 2024).
European Commission: Directorate-General for Research and Innovation (2021), *Horizon Europe, Budget – Horizon Europe – the Most Ambitious EU Research & Innovation Programme Ever* (Publications Office of the European Union), https://doi.org/10.2777/202859
European Commission press (2016), 'Investing in Europe's youth'. Available at https://ec.europa.eu/commission/presscorner/detail/en/ip_16_4165 (accessed 1 October 2024).
Feola, G. (2016), 'Translocal grassroots movements and the geography of sustainability transitions: the case of the Transition Towns Network', *7th International Sustainability Transitions (IST) Conference 2016 – Exploring Transition Research as Transformative Science Wuppertal.*
Flick, U. (2011), *An Introduction to Qualitative Research*, 4th edn (Los Angeles, CA: Sage).
Flick, U. (ed.) (2018), *The SAGE Handbook of Qualitative Data Collection* (Los Angeles, CA: Sage).
França Filho, G. C. de, J. T. Silva Júnior, and A. S. Rigo (2012), 'Solidarity finance through community development banks as a strategy for reshaping local economies: lessons from Banco Palmas', *Revista de Administração*, 47:3, 500–15, https://doi.org/10.5700/rausp1054
Fressoli, M., E. Arond, D. Abrol, A. Smith, A. Ely, and R. Dias (2014), 'When grassroots innovation movements encounter mainstream institutions: implications for models of inclusive innovation', *Innovation and Development*, 4:2, 277–92, https://doi.org/10.1080/2157930X.2014.921354
Geels, F. W. (2022), 'Causality and explanation in socio-technical transitions research: Mobilising epistemological insights from the wider social sciences', *Research Policy*, 51:6, 104537, https://doi.org/10.1016/j.respol.2022.104537
Geels, F. W., and J. Schot (2007), 'Typology of sociotechnical transition pathways', *Research Policy*, 36:3, 399–417, https://doi.org/10.1016/j.respol.2007.01.003
Gernert, M., H. El Bilali, and C. Strassner (2018), 'Grassroots Initiatives as Sustainability Transition Pioneers: Implications and Lessons for Urban Food Systems', *Urban Science*, 2:1, 23, https://doi.org/10.3390/urbansci2010023
Glasdam, S., C. Oeye, and L. Thrysoee (2015), 'Patients' participation in decision-making in the medical field – "projectification" of patients in a neoliberal framed healthcare system', *Nursing Philosophy*, 16:4, 226–38, https://doi.org/10.1111/nup.12092
Global Ecovillage Network (2024), 'Global Ecovillage Network', *Global Ecovillage Network*. Available at https://ecovillage.org/about/about-gen/ (accessed 5 June 2024).
Godenhjelm, S., R. A. Lundin, and S. Sjöblom (2015), 'Projectification in the public sector – the case of the European Union', *International Journal of Managing Projects in Business*, 8:2, 324–48, https://doi.org/10.1108/ijmpb-05-2014-0049
Gomiero, T. (2018), 'Agriculture and degrowth: State of the art and assessment of organic and biotech-based agriculture from a degrowth perspective', *Journal of Cleaner Production*, 197, 1823–39, https://doi.org/10.1016/j.jclepro.2017.03.237

Grin, J., J. Rotmans, and J. W. Schot (2010), *Transitions to Sustainable Development: New Directions in the Study of Long Term Transformative Change* (New York: Routledge).

de Haan, J., and J. Rotmans (2011), 'Patterns in transitions: Understanding complex chains of change', *Technological Forecasting and Social Change*, 78:1, 90–102, https://doi.org/10.1016/j.techfore.2010.10.008

Hansen, T., and L. Coenen (2015), 'The geography of sustainability transitions: Review, synthesis and reflections on an emergent research field', *Environmental Innovation and Societal Transitions*, 17, 92–109, https://doi.org/10.1016/j.eist.2014.11.001

Henfrey, T. (2010), 'Cultivating Community, Gardening Anthropology: Permaculture, Local Food and Engaged Research' (presented at the European Association of Social Anthropologists, Maynooth, Ireland).

Henfrey, T., and G. Penha-Lopes (2018), 'Policy and community-led action on sustainability and climate change: Paradox and possibility in the interstices', *Environmental Innovation and Societal Transitions*, 29, 52–54, https://doi.org/10.1016/j.eist.2018.05.002

Hermans, F., D. Roep, and L. Klerkx (2016), 'Scale dynamics of grassroots innovations through parallel pathways of transformative change', *Ecological Economics*, 130, 285–95, https://doi.org/10.1016/j.ecolecon.2016.07.011

Hess, D. J. (2007), *Alternative Pathways in Science and Industry: Activism, Innovation, and the Environment in an Era of Globalization* (Cambridge, MA: MIT Press).

Hossain, M. (2016), 'Grassroots innovation: A systematic review of two decades of research', *Journal of Cleaner Production*, 137, 973–81, https://doi.org/10.1016/j.jclepro.2016.07.140

Hossain, M. (2018), 'Grassroots innovation: The state of the art and future perspectives', *Technology in Society*, 55, 63–69, https://doi.org/10.1016/j.techsoc.2018.06.008

Jackson, H., and R. Jackson (2004), *Global Ecovillage Network History 1990–2004*. Available at www.gaia.org/wp-content/uploads/2016/07/HJackson_GEN-History.pdf (accessed 2 July 2025).

Jałocha, B. (2013), 'Projectification of the European Union and its implications for public labour market organisations in Poland', *Journal of Project, Program & Portfolio Management*, 3:2, 1–16, https://doi.org/10.5130/pppm.v3i2.2735

Jałocha, B. (2018), 'Are projects changing public servants into projectarians? Projectification's influence on employees in the Polish public sector', *International Journal of Contemporary Management*, 17:2, 63–83, https://doi.org/10.4467/24498939ijcm.18.018.8542

Jałocha, B. (2019), 'The European Union's multi-level impact on member state projectification in light of neoinstitutional theory', *International Journal of Managing Projects in Business*, 12:3, 578–601, https://doi.org/10.1108/IJMPB-09-2018-0198

Jensen, A., C. Thuesen, and J. Geraldi (2016), 'The Projectification of Everything: Projects as a Human Condition', *Project Management Journal*, 47:3, 21–34, https://doi.org/10.1177/875697281604700303

Köhler, J., F. W. Geels, F. Kern, J. Markard, E. Onsongo, A. Wieczorek, et al. (2019), 'An agenda for sustainability transitions research: State of the art and future directions', *Environmental Innovation and Societal Transitions*, 31, 1–32, https://doi.org/10.1016/j.eist.2019.01.004

Kuura, A. (2017), '25 YEARS OF PROJECTIFICATION RESEARCH', *Project Management Development – Practice and Perspectives: 6th International Scientific Conference on Project Management in the Baltic Countries, April 27–28, 2017, Riga, University of Latvia* (presented at the Project Management Development – Practice and Perspectives, University of Latvia).

Lang, R., P. Chatterton, and D. Mullins (2020), 'Grassroots innovations in community-led housing in England: the role and evolution of intermediaries', *International Journal of Urban Sustainable Development*, 12:1, 52–72, https://doi.org/10.1080/19463138.2019.1663525

Locatelli, G., L. Ika, N. Drouin, R. Müller, M. Huemann, J. Söderlund, J. Geraldi, and S. Clegg (2023), 'A Manifesto for project management research', *European Management Review*, 20:1, 3–17, https://doi.org/10.1111/emre.12568

Lundin, R. A. (2016), 'Project Society: Paths and challenges', *Project Management Journal*, 47:4, 7–15, https://doi.org/10.1177/875697281604700402

Lundin, R. A., and A. Söderholm (1995), 'A theory of the temporary organization', *Scandinavian Journal of Management*, Project Management and Temporary Organizations, 11:4, 437–55, https://doi.org/10.1016/0956-5221(95)00036-U

Markle, E. A., R. Rodgers, W. Sanchez, and M. Ballou (2015), 'Social support in the cohousing model of community: a mixed-methods analysis', *Community Development*, 46:5, 616–31, https://doi.org/10.1080/15575330.2015.1086400

Maylor, H., and V. Turkulainen (2019), 'The concept of organisational projectification: past, present and beyond?', *International Journal of Managing Projects in Business*, 12:3, 565–77, https://doi.org/10.1108/IJMPB-09-2018-0202

Midler, C. (1995), '"Projectification" of the firm: The Renault case', *Scandinavian Journal of Management*, 11:4, 363–75.

Nylén, E. A. (2021), 'Projectified governance and sustainability transitions: How projects and framework programmes can accelerate transition processes', *Environmental Policy and Governance*, 31:6, 605–18, https://doi.org/10.1002/eet.1957

Packendorff, J., and M. Lindgren (2014), 'Projectification and its consequences: narrow and broad conceptualisations', *South African Journal of Economic and Management Sciences*, 17:1, 7–21, https://doi.org/10.10520/EJC148771

Pavalko, R. M. (1988), *Sociology of Occupations and Professions* (F E Peacock Pub).

Raatikainen, K. (2018), 'The Importance of Engaging Local People in Landscape Management – Experiences from an EU Project', *Landscape Online*, 57, 1–22, https://doi.org/10.3097/LO.201857

Roysen, R., N. Bruehwiler, L. Kos, R. Boyer, and J. Koehrsen (2024), 'Rethinking the diffusion of grassroots innovations: An embedding framework', *Technological Forecasting and Social Change*, 200, 123156, https://doi.org/10.1016/j.techfore.2023.123156

Schoper, Y.-G., A. Wald, H. T. Ingason, and T. V. Fridgeirsson (2018), 'Projectification in Western economies: A comparative study of Germany, Norway and Iceland', *International Journal of Project Management*, Festschrift for Professor J. Rodney Turner, 36:1, 71–82, https://doi.org/10.1016/j.ijproman.2017.07.008

Seyfang, G., and A. Haxeltine (2010), 'Growing grassroots innovations: Exploring the role of community-based social movements for sustainable energy transitions', *CSERGE Working Paper*, EDM 10-08. Available at www.econstor.eu/bitstream/10419/48802/1/626009804.pdf (accessed 17 March 2026).

Seyfang, G., and A. Smith (2007), 'Grassroots innovations for sustainable development: Towards a new research and policy agenda', *Environmental Politics*, 16:4, 584–603, https://doi.org/10.1080/09644010701419121

Smith, A., M. Fressoli, D. Abrol, E. Arond, and A. Ely (2017), *Grassroots Innovation Movements* (Abingdon, Oxon: Routledge).

Smith, A., M. Fressoli, and H. Thomas (2014a), 'Grassroots innovation movements: challenges and contributions', *Journal of Cleaner Production*, 63, 114–24, https://doi.org/10.1016/j.jclepro.2012.12.025

Smith, A., M. Fressoli, and H. Thomas (2014b), 'Grassroots innovation movements: challenges and contributions', *Journal of Cleaner Production*, Special Volume: Sustainable Production, Consumption and Livelihoods: Global and Regional Research Perspectives, 63, 114–24, https://doi.org/10.1016/j.jclepro.2012.12.025

Timmermans, S., and I. Tavory (2022), *Data Analysis in Qualitative Research: Theorizing with Abductive Analysis* (University of Chicago Press).

Walker, G., and P. Devine-Wright (2008), 'Community renewable energy: What should it mean?', *Energy Policy*, 36:2, 497–500, https://doi.org/10.1016/j.enpol.2007.10.019

Wells, P. (2011), 'The transition initiative as a grass-roots environmental movement: history, present realities and future predictions', *Interdisciplinary Environmental Review*, 372–86, https://doi.org/10.1504/ier.2011.043344

Wittmayer, J. M., F. Avelino, F. van Steenbergen, and D. Loorbach (2017), 'Actor roles in transition: Insights from sociological perspectives', *Environmental Innovation and Societal Transitions*, 24, 45–56, https://doi.org/10.1016/j.eist.2016.10.003

Wolsink, M. (2020), 'Distributed energy systems as common goods: Socio-political acceptance of renewables in intelligent microgrids', *Renewable and Sustainable Energy Reviews*, 127, 109841, https://doi.org/10.1016/j.rser.2020.109841

Yin, R. K. (2018), *Case Study Research and Applications: Design and Methods*, 6th ed. (Los Angeles, CA: Sage).

12

Transnational pathways: Taking the CLT framework from place to place to transform structures and debates on land ownership

Sabine Horlitz, Corinna Hölzl

Introduction

Within the growing field of non-speculative community-led housing, community land trusts (CLTs) have received increased attention in recent years (Davis, Algoed and Hernández-Torrales, 2020). CLTs are a community-based, non-profit ownership model that largely eludes the market-oriented exploitation logic and provides democratically organised, affordable housing as well as space for small businesses, social or cultural uses. Most CLTs are located in the US and England, with an increasing number also operating in Canada, Australia, Puerto Rico, Brazil, and Kenya, as the model spreads worldwide. Since 2012, it has been circulating on the European mainland, with CLT Brussels playing a pioneering role.

In the wake of the growing number of CLTs, related network organisations are likewise gaining momentum in Europe and beyond: regional umbrellas within the UK, national associations such as the US Grounded Solutions Network and the Canadian Network of Community Land Trusts, and, more recently, the Australian Network of Community Land Trusts, as well as transnational organisations including the US-based International Center for Community Land Trusts and the recently launched European Community Land Trust Network (ECLTN).

In this chapter, we aim to explore the current transnational circulation of a historically rooted ownership model and highlight the network of actors and international allies connected to this model. Our focus is not so much on presenting CLTs as a quantitative solution to the social housing issue. We would rather like to show how this model extends across different continents and contexts and is developed there depending on local needs with the aim to foster and propose a market-independent, democratic approach to land and housing.

In doing so, we will first introduce the core idea and development of CLTs. Following that, we will present the Stadtbodenstiftung (CLT Berlin) as a local case in which one of the authors is collaboratively involved in building up in Berlin, along with its opportunities and challenges. We will then outline the international connections, particularly the ECLTN as a newly formed pan-European member organisation to advocate for the CLT model and the World CLT Day as a grassroots-driven, self-organised day of celebration. Finally, we will contextualise these efforts within contemporary concepts of land as collective property and commons.

CLTs: a step towards new social and property forms and a contemporary land law

John Emmeus Davis, one of the main actors of the US CLT movement, describes CLTs as 'community-led development on community-owned land' (David, 2010). He thus summarises two of the key characteristics of the model: the centrality of community-led and often place-based decision-making structures in conjunction and interdependence with non-profit community land ownership. These two core features – community ownership and participation – are reflected in all aspects of the CLT model and are discussed in more detail below, together with leaseholds as structural elements.

Land in common ownership

Although CLTs are a relatively new model of collective ownership – they have existed in their current form for about fifty years – they can be traced back to much older forms of common land ownership. The early CLT movement drew on a variety of different socio-political ideas: they were inspired by the English commons, the Gramdan movement in India, in which individual villages acted as trustees of agricultural land, and the Mexican ejidos. The US forerunners of CLTs were the 'single-tax colonies' founded around 1900, based on Henry George's single-tax theory (George, 1879). These experimental communities combined collective ownership of land with individual ownership of the structures on it, and some, like Bryn Gweled near Philadelphia, founded by Quakers in 1940, still exist today. The first CLT in today's sense was formed in the late 1960s by civil rights activists near Albany, in rural Georgia, to provide African-American farmers with permanent, secure access to farmland and housing in the face of the racial discrimination by white landlords. In the 1980s, as the increasing gentrification of low-income neighbourhoods in US cities led to the displacement of residents, the first urban CLTs were formed. As a neighbourhood-based model for securing long-term affordable housing for low-income people, they quickly gained acceptance and spread in the following years, especially among community activists who wanted to counteract the withdrawal of the state from housing provision.[1]

For all its thematic consistency, the CLT model is characterised by a high degree of flexibility and adaptability to local needs. It is open to a variety of uses, social organisations and forms of construction. While the majority of rural and suburban CLTs tend to feature conventional housing typologies, primarily single-family homes and townhouses, a large number of urban CLTs offer a variety of living and working spaces, from multi-family housing to cooperative spaces and small businesses. For example, the Champlain Housing Trust in Burlington, Vermont – the largest CLT in the US, with more than 2,600 households – combines rental apartments, non-profit single-family homes and multi-family cooperative housing with small businesses and social uses (cf. Figure 12.1).

Over the past twenty years, CLTs have gained popularity outside the US as well. In the early 2000s, the model became better known in the UK, primarily in rural areas. There are now several hundred CLTs in both rural and urban areas. But interest in CLTs as a proven model for combating gentrification and displacement is also growing in continental Europe. Contributing to Europe-wide network activities, CLT Brussels, founded in 2012, is playing an important role here.

However, the applicability of the CLT model goes beyond the typical urban, suburban and rural structures commonly found in Western

Figure 12.1 Champlain Housing Trust (Vermont) key impacts, 2025. Source: Champlain Housing Trust Annual Report 2025 (Burlington). Available at https://www.getahome.org/wp-content/uploads/CHT-Annual-Report-2025.pdf (accessed 24 June 2026).

contexts. In recent years, it has also been increasingly discussed as a possible ownership model for informal settlements. The Caño Martín Peña CLT, established in 2002 in Puerto Rico, is not only the world's largest CLT today with approximately 30,000 people, but also the only one that has successfully applied the model to the problems of informality (Algoed and Hernández, 2024). In Rio de Janeiro, a coalition of over forty favela organisers is currently promoting CLTs as an alternative to the government's conventional legalisation programmes. The interplay of collective ownership of land and individual ownership of buildings could provide residents with a permanent right to stay and security against eviction as well as property speculation.

Leasehold as a structural element

Central to the CLT model is the structural embedding of long-term affordability combined with the safeguarding of site- and project-specific social objectives. The central structural element to guarantee long-term affordability is the two-tiered ownership structure, which separates ownership of the land from ownership of the buildings constructed on it. Although the future users – whether row house residents, cooperatives or small entrepreneurs – purchase the building structures, the underlying land remains the property of the CLT, which holds it in trusteeship and leases it to the users on a long-term leasehold basis, typically for ninety-nine years. In return, the users pay a leasehold fee that is detached from speculative land price developments.

The leasehold is the key structural element of the CLT model. It is mortgageable, renewable and binding on all future users. It contains all the provisions necessary to ensure the functioning of the CLT and the long-term affordability of its housing stock (and other uses), ranging from resale price restrictions on the structures and prohibitions on absentee ownership – requiring owners to reside on and use the property themselves – to income restrictions on future users. The ground lease also provides for the CLT's right of first refusal in the event that the structures are sold. The CLT is responsible for controlling and potentially enforcing the regulations stipulated by the leasehold rights. In this way, the CLT has a guardian function and becomes the guarantor of long-term orientation towards the common good.

Structures of participation

Another core feature of the CLT model that distinguishes it from pure leasehold arrangements is the design of the organisational and decision-making structure. CLTs are democratically governed, locally based organisations: all users are members, but anyone who lives in the neighbourhood can become a member as well. The definition of a neighbourhood is a matter for each CLT. Some refer to well-defined inner-city areas or small rural districts. Others cover entire cities or even metropolitan regions. Similar to cooperatives, the members' rights and responsibilities are set forth in bylaws.

Unlike housing cooperatives, however, CLTs usually limit the decision-making power of direct users and instead emphasise the neighbourhood and social components of housing provision. This form of socialisation is also reflected in the tripartite composition of the decision-making body (commonly the 'board'). Typically made up of equal numbers of user representatives, people from the neighbourhood and public figures, the board is responsible for the strategic direction of the CLT and management oversight. It generally works pro bono and is elected by the members' general assembly.

By involving third parties in their organisational and governance structure, CLTs balance different interests and mediate between the needs of users, the goals of the CLT and the neighbourhood, in addition to the interests of the broader public. In this way, for example, they counteract the risk that the profit restrictions outlined in a housing project's rules may be lifted and that spaces initially organised socially and collectively (residential and other) may over time become re-commodified, thus potentially driving gentrification.

In the next section, we will introduce one of the newly founded urban CLTs in Europe, the Stadtbodenstiftung in Berlin, as an example to highlight the model's aims, struggles and opportunities.

The Stadtbodenstiftung (CLT Berlin): The first CLT in German-speaking countries

The aim of the Stadtbodenstiftung is to counteract the spiral of real estate speculation and the practice of top-down planning by permanently removing land from the profit-oriented market and securing it for community-led, common interest-oriented usage that is needed in the respective neighbourhoods: affordable housing, small businesses, cultural and social facilities, etc.

The Stadtbodenstiftung is the result of an initiative that brought together a variety of actors and interests: people from neighbourhood initiatives and housing projects, from cooperative work and alternative project development, and also from research and local politics. It was founded in 2021 by 150 people and organisations as a community foundation, most of them long engaged in non-profit housing. It is the first CLT in the German-speaking countries and part of the international CLT networks, with the International Center for CLTs and ECLTN being the key coordinating organisations.

The establishment of the Stadtbodenstiftung was preceded by an intensive discussion within the founding initiative about the most appropriate legal structure for the organisation, including options such as an association, a cooperative, a trust or a foundation. The decision was made to establish a charitable foundation because it is integrated into a variety of external control structures and mechanisms. Unlike cooperatives or associations, the objectives and charter of a German civil-law foundation cannot be changed by a majority vote. For example, the inability to sell the land is firmly established in the statutes of the Stadtbodenstiftung. Compliance with the statutes is monitored by the foundation supervisory authority (Stiftungsaufsicht), a public body under the jurisdiction of the finance senate of the city-state of Berlin. Pursuit of its non-profit and charitable objectives is monitored by the tax office.

Transformational potential …

The Stadtbodenstiftung strives to be a model of civil-society-driven and non-profit, solidarity-based urban development and sees itself as part of discussions surrounding socialisation, decommodification and alternative land policies (see also Holm, 2022). In accordance with the understanding of CLTs, the aim of the Stadtbodenstiftung is to extend its governing structures beyond the immediate users, thus strengthening the character of land as a common good. This is reflected in its legal and organisational structure as well as in the composition of its board of trustees (Kuratorium). While the executive board (Vorstand) is responsible for day-to-day operations and project development, the board of trustees is the central decision-making body of the Stadtbodenstiftung. Its composition is modelled after the 'classic' CLT model: in addition to up to three peer experts, it is designed to include tenants and representatives from the respective neighbourhoods, each up to four. Additionally, another member appointed by the public bodies – if they support the Stadtbodenstiftung substantially – may be included, as well as a representative of the donors. This composition is intended to ensure that different interests are represented in the Stadtbodenstiftung, and that especially those who usually do not have a say in urban development – neighbours and users – are given a voice and represent the majority of members. A foundation committee is also being set up, which is open to all those involved in the projects, as well as neighbours and donors, comparable to a general assembly. It will hold the right to elect the above-mentioned representatives and will be the first of its kind in the German foundation landscape.

As the trustee of the land, the Stadtbodenstiftung ensures the projects' orientation toward the common good through leaseholds, as described above. It also acts as a link between the various leasehold projects, offering them the opportunity to come together, share ideas and collaborate in the common structure it has set up, whether at the annual meetings and educational events, in working groups or the decision-making bodies. It is precisely this cooperation between different actors which goes beyond individual projects, familiar districts and single neighbourhoods, in addition to the non-speculative land policy, that constitutes the primary potential and the genuine contribution of the Stadtbodenstiftung to real estate development oriented to the common good.

The Stadtbodenstiftung operates on three levels: first, at the very concrete level of projects to be implemented; second, as a pilot model that can be replicated in other German cities; and third, as a 'proof of concept' that can reinforce urban policy demands and provide impetus for municipal policy, for example, for establishing revolving municipal land funds or the possibilities of co-determination rights over the use of land (cf. Figure 12.2).

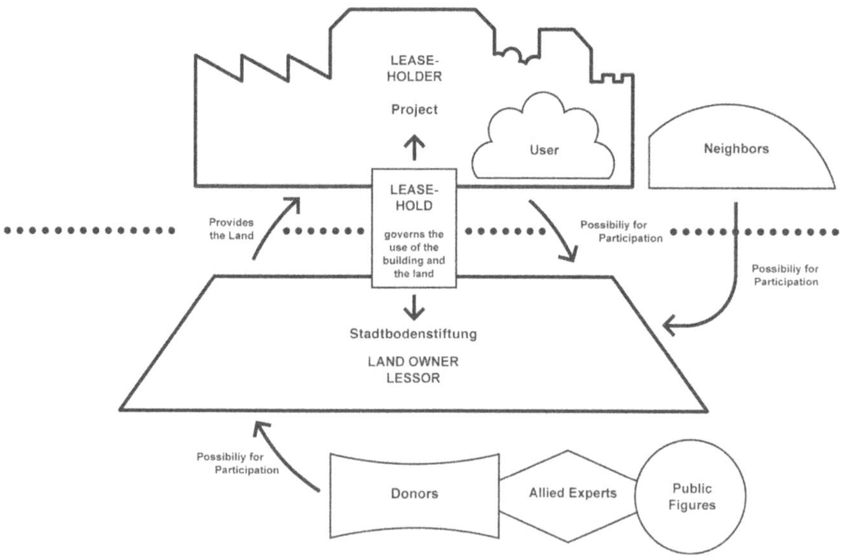

Figure 12.2 Stadtbodenstiftung: organisational structure, 2020. Graph © Sabine Horlitz, design: Till Sperrle, all rights reserved.

... and obstacles

Like other non-profit ownership models, the Stadtbodenstiftung must function within the current conditions of capitalist economic activity, but at the same time it points beyond those conditions. It is presently negotiating with several small private real estate owners about the donation or purchase of their properties, ranging from small lots with single-family homes to several larger inner-city apartment buildings and vacant former office buildings. However, establishing the first project without significant capital is proving to be more difficult than originally anticipated. The negotiation processes are lengthy, often including a diverse community of owners with different interests and occasionally conflicts among themselves.

Furthermore, the legal form of a foundation is still not widely recognised as a form of civil-society self-organisation. It is still primarily seen as a form of estate administration. For example, the city-state of Berlin only provides funds for the acquisition of existing properties to the benefit of housing cooperatives, excluding foundations or projects from the Mietshäuser Syndikat, a bottom-up self-organised umbrella association for permanently decommodified housing that encompasses around 210 projects in Germany (see Chapter 4).

Last but not least, the pursuit of land as a common good is a very tough endeavour. The global historical roots of this objective are found in all cultures, from commons to *waqf* donations (the charitable land-based endowment in Islamic countries). Yet still, it is often seen (within propritarian ideology; Piketty, 2020) as an illegitimate challenge to the free tradability of land. The dominance of the market and the associated 'right' to profit permeates all societal spheres. For example, the current instruments in German and other European countries' land policy were not primarily created to actively promote a sustainable orientation towards the common good, but are fundamentally subordinated to the primacy of private property and commodification.

In the following, we present the objectives and functioning of the European Community Land Trust Network (ECLTN) as a newly formed pan-European member organisation aimed to advocate for the CLT model in Europe and World CLT Day as a grassroots-driven, self-organised celebration day to promote and strengthen the global CLT movement. Such translocal networks and interlinking formats play an important role for the the Stadtbodenstiftung and other CLT pioneers. They highlight to both the people involved and the interested public the potential of the CLT model and how it has already been successfully put into practice elsewhere. Beyond the benefits of personal motivation and exchange, the Stadtbodenstiftung has already drawn on these connections several times in public events: whether it was the founding celebration, which took place on the first World CLT Day, with live broadcasts from the US and Brussels, or by hosting the first assembly of the European CLT Network with a public evening event and an introduction of the members and projects from across Europe to the Berlin audience.

Building translocal connections: The newly founded European CLT Network

Many of the CLT actors – both new and long-standing organisations – are interconnected with one another and with other community housing actors. This allows for sharing and learning from one another, and for a sense of mutual solidarity and support. The self-image as a CLT and the commitment to affordable, socially oriented housing, the neighbourhood orientation of the projects, and the ideal of land as common property, serve as a common framework and point of reference. At the same time, the model and the respective networks remain open to different forms and interpretations. It is this common, yet open framework that allows different actors and organisations around the world, with their specific political and social contexts and conditions, to refer to a common concept and thus create a diverse resonance space for their commitment to a non-profit real estate sector, to affordable housing, land justice and community empowerment.

The European Community Land Trust Network (ECLTN) was founded in June 2023 (ECLTN, n.d.). It builds on the work and contacts of the *Sustainable Housing for Inclusive and Cohesive Cities* (SHICC) project which was funded by the EU Interreg Programme from 2017 to 2021. The network acts as a voice for the CLT model in Europe and supports CLTs and similar initiatives. It promotes the CLT model at the European level, links existing organisations and fosters the creation of new ones. The network is based in Brussels, where it is recognised as an international non-profit organisation. It is designed as a membership organisation and is currently supported by fifteen founding organisations, from more experienced CLTs, such as CLT Brussels and London CLT, to entire CLT networks, like the one in England and Wales, to new organisations, including the Stadtbodenstiftung in Germany and And the People in the Netherlands.[2] In the following, we will highlight two key aspects of how the ECLTN can be seen as an example for taking the CLT model from place to place: it embodies a wide range of adaptations of the CLT model according to local legal and social conditions while facilitating various concrete forms of knowledge transfer and joint knowledge production (cf. Figure 12.3).

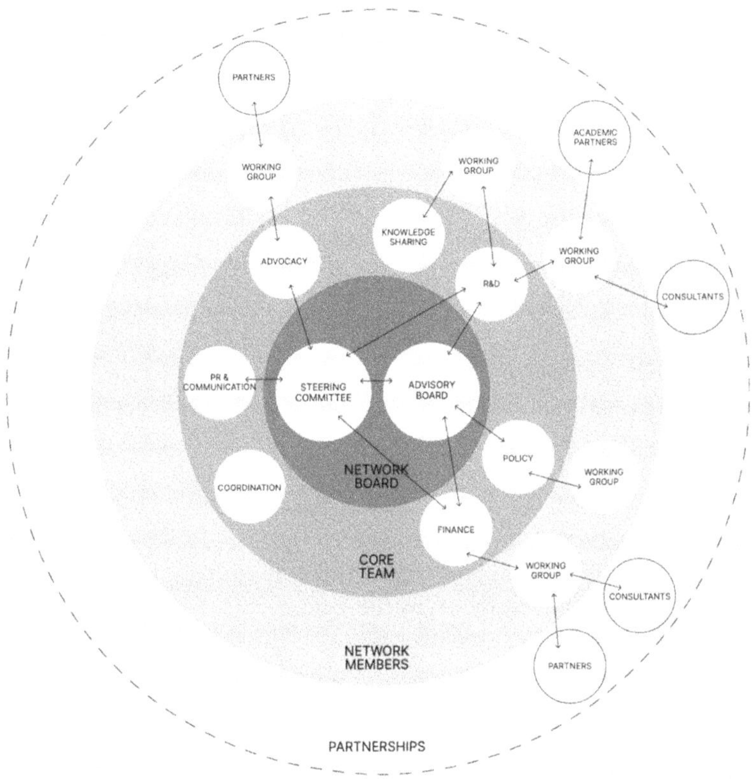

Figure 12.3 ECLTN: draft organisational model, 2022. Graphic © ECLTN, all rights reserved.

The adaptability of the CLT model to local conditions

In the founding phase of the ECLTN, it was crucial to build the network bottom-up, in line with existing CLT practices which vary from place to place. Several working meetings were held to discuss the possible structure of the pan-European network, as well as common goals and principles, criteria for accepting new members and strategies for alternative lobbying and the growth of the CLT movement. The members of the ECLTN are actors with different constitutions, legal forms and functions. This demonstrates the legal and organisational diversity of different contexts, as well as the flexibility and adaptability of the CLT model to such local circumstances in terms of legal form, the approach to project implementation and the relationship with local authorities, as the following examples shall illustrate.

In contrast to the US, where many CLTs were established as grassroots organisations with a strong bottom-up identity, the majority of CLTs established in Europe in recent years have worked closely with local authorities from the outset. Both CLT Brussels and CLT Ghent, for example, have been given or have bought municipal land with financial support from the city and are building low-cost homes for low-income groups. In 2013, one year after its founding, CLT Brussels was recognised as a non-profit housing actor by the Brussels Housing Code and included in the regional investment plan (Plan Alliance Habitat, 2014–20). An annual budget of up to €2.3 million enabled it to carry out targeted development work. CLT Brussels has now completed six housing projects with a total of 111 units. Two more have been allocated and five more are in the pipeline. CLT Brussels works with the Fonds du Logement, a large social housing association, to provide mortgage loans for the buyers and occasionally to build the projects (see Chapter 3).

Another example of cooperation with the city, and a very open interpretation of the CLT model, is being developed in Barcelona. Unlike traditional CLTs, in which a single entity owns the land, the CLT-inspired structure in Barcelona is based on an agreement between the municipal administration and a variety of civil society non-profit organisations (Entidades Sin Ánimo de Lucro, ESAL). It was created alongside the Municipal Plan for the Right to Housing (2016–25), which aims to double affordable housing in the city, and has set the focus on public rental housing and partnerships with private affordable housing providers. This cooperation agreement aims to allocate public land to non-profit organisations – through leaseholds as well as transfer – and is an alliance between the Federació de Cooperatives d'Habitatges de Catalunya (Federation of Housing Cooperatives of Catalonia FCHC), the Coordinadora de Fundacions d'Habitatge Social (Coordinator of Social Housing Foundations, Cohabitac), the Associació Xarxa d'Economia Solidària (Solidarity Economy Network, XES), the Associació de Gestors de Polítiques Socials d'Habitatge de Catalunya (Association of Providers of Social Housing Policies of Catalonia, GHS) and the Barcelona City Council. The agreement has already designated fourteen sites for renovation, adding 567 housing units (Ajuntament de Barcelona, 2022). While Barcelona has not fully adopted the CLT model yet, its efforts, such as joint land management and leaseholds, reflect CLT elements and current measures seem to further push for the model. In May 2024, for example, the so-called Community Land Manager Working Group was established to continue developing a Barcelona-specific CLT model (Ajuntament de Barcelona, 2024).

Further, CLT H-Buurt in Amsterdam started as a CLT without land ownership, but with a dedicated focus on community building. In 2018, a coalition of actors from the social innovation sector gathered in Amsterdam to explore the viability of implementing the CLT model through design thinking and action-led research. They focused on the Bijlmermeer neighbourhood, a modernist high-rise social housing district in the south-east of Amsterdam. The coalition of actors joined with a faith-based, predominantly immigrant-based grassroots organisation in the area (the Maranatha community) and others to carry out a series of design workshops. It understands itself as a 'case-building network, (interview, representative And the People, 2023)[3] that aims at implementing a community-based housing project in the Bijlmermeer neighbourhood. In addition to its local engagement, CLT H-Buurt is working to initiate a nationwide CLT for the Netherlands and engages in lobbying and educational activities to develop a strategy to mainstream the CLT model across the country.

Unlike the above examples and due to Berlin's specific context, the Stadtbodenstiftung decided to adopt the guiding rule that municipal property is not to be transferred to its assets. It essentially starts at the other end of the real estate spectrum and aims primarily to remove private real estate from speculation and to transform it from a commodity into a collective good. It both strives to secure existing buildings and develop new projects. To this end, the Stadtbodenstiftung specifically seeks to address socially oriented real estate owners who wish to know their properties are in good hands for the long term and will sell those for a non-speculative price. It also sees existing housing projects, primarily small coops that do not have a structure for the long-term security of their objectives, as possible partners and approaches them to transfer their land to the foundation in order to permanently secure their objectives through leasehold agreements. In order to fulfil its goals, the Stadtbodenstiftung is cooperating with a wide range of partners, from housing cooperatives and other foundations to projects of the Mietshäuser Syndikat.

The network as a repository and advocacy organisation

Another aspect of taking the model from place to place is the ECLTN as an information hub and – even more so – as a lobbying base with the goal to improve the acceptance and conditions for CLTs and community-led housing. To this end, ECLTN staff members participate in European-level events, for example of the New European Bauhaus Initiative, introduce the model in EU committees and present local pilot projects to interested parties (primarily

CLT Brussels' projects due to their proximity). The aim of ECLTN's advocacy work is to ensure that housing policy initiatives at the EU level effectively integrate support for CLTs into policy agendas, policy initiatives and legislations as part of a new housing paradigm for Europe. This has already been achieved in part. The CLT model, for example, has had some recognition at the European policy level. The EU Urban Agenda on Housing recognises CLTs as a best practice and the EU Parliament's 'Housing for All' report calls on member states to support the development of CLTs.

In addition to these outward-looking efforts, the network is also internally active in terms of exchanging experience and knowledge, connecting and sharing resources. There are regular thematic online events on organising, advocacy strategies, European policy capacity building and peer-to-peer updates, as well as a members' area that hosts key resources from handbooks to advocacy tools, an updated list of funding opportunities and a discussion forum between CLTs across Europe. The bimonthly newsletter and the annual members' assemblies provide further opportunities for exchange, for visiting completed projects and transferring knowledge directly from place to place. The annual network meetings also have a structural, organisational purpose. Documents such as the Strategic Plan & Priority Activities (2024–25), as well as the ECLTN's internal rules and budget, are jointly adopted here.

Last but not least, the organisations currently organised in the ECLTN also serve as hubs in their respective regional contexts, as contact points for actors interested in establishing further CLTs. ECLTN supports these efforts, for example, by jointly submitting EU-level funding applications to support the financially sustainable development of the model.

It is common that European CLT pioneers such as the Stadtbodenstiftung, who are the first to set up a CLT in their country, already provide extensive expertise in housing issues. More than knowledge, they benefit most from the network (advocacy) power and the prospect of financial resources. The situation is somewhat different in countries like the UK, where the model is already better known, since there are also less experienced groups that benefit from specific knowledge support (including, e.g., legal issues that vary from country to country) that can be provided by national peers.

International links and World CLT Day

ECLTN is also connected beyond Europe and is in contact with similar organisations, particularly in the Americas, such as the US International Center for CLTs, the US and Canadian umbrella organisations and the Global South CLT Initiative. Such international cooperation is also expressed in the World CLT Day, which is organised by individuals in CLTs from all over the world. World CLT Day is characterised by a special glocal format that combines global connections with local customisation. It does so by interweaving place-based, face-to-face events, online events and social media encounters, where actors from all over the world are connected and international CLT guests report locally (cf. Figure 12.4). In this way, at many moments, a special intersection of socio-spatial contexts and CLT representatives, as well as local residents, is achieved. John Davis, Board Member of the International Center for CLTs, emphasises the importance of the day: 'World CLT Day is not just a celebration; it's a vibrant movement and expression of solidarity, diversity and connection across borders. It is a day when we all walk through previously closed doors and embrace the global movement for sustainable community ownership' (International Center for CLTs, 2024).

In May 2024, the first annual meeting of the ECLTN took place in Berlin, coinciding with World CLT Day. In addition to a series of workshops on topics, such as the relationship between CLTs and cooperatives, working with communities, the potential of CLTs as a model for informal

Figure 12.4 Street radio with local and international CLT guests, World CLT Day Brussels, 2022. Photo © Corinna Hölzl, all rights reserved.

settlements, communal living in rural areas and circular economy issues, a public evening event was held (in English and German) to introduce the CLT model to the local public. The hybrid and creative formats and strategies not only allow the mobilisation of knowledge resources, but they also help manage local and national pitfalls, facilitate trusty relationships and keep motivations high through international links and exchange, both virtually and in-place.

Discussion and conclusion: The transformative potential of understanding land as collective property

Land speculation not only boosts housing costs, but it is also the driving force behind the very high, overall level of wealth inequality. Even if alternative ownership models such as CLTs cannot quantitatively solve the land and housing problem, their impact goes beyond the purely pragmatic value of the individual project. In a sense, they prove that non-market real estate development is possible and demonstrate ways of provision, protection and democratic management of housing and other functions that are not guided by profit expectations but by the needs of users and neighbourhoods. In this way, CLTs not only interrupt the cycle of speculation and create examples of real alternatives, they also contribute to the generation of alternative forms of knowledge and a discourse rooted in real, concrete space and its problems. They are non-static and constantly evolving. They adapt to local needs, while diverging and entering into collaborations.

CLTs can provide a variety of impulses and points of reference for current urban policy debates. In addition to the above-mentioned aspects of neighbourhood orientation, the idea of solidarity, securing the permanent unsaleability of land through the two-tiered ownership structure, and the participatory administrative and organisational structure, CLTs can advance the current debates on remunicipalisation, the permanent securement and democratisation of public property and the reorientation of real estate policy.

By that means, CLTs and related commoning practices can be an important tool (out of many necessary ones) to question the hegemonic understanding of land as private property by testing, practising and developing further alternative collective land rights. The presented examples demonstrate how this can work in different places and translocal networks, such as the European CLT Network and the International Center for CLTs, which offer possibilities to not only link CLTs, but to jointly work on alternative meanings of property and commoning. Conversely, our brief insight shows that the CLT model is equipped with specific prerequisites for strong transnational networking and mobilisation: the model is flexible and there are numerous points of connection to present national legal forms and cultural framings, so that effective transferable storylines and movement structures can be developed.

In the sense of Marianne Maeckelbergh's (2011) proposal, CLTs can also be interpreted as a prefigurative attempt, i.e., the active development and anticipation of alternative political structures needed to transform existing power and property relations (see also Mackenzie, 2010). The principle of inalienability applied to CLT land does not focus on tradable property, but on its possession and use. The efforts to conceive of property and possession as non-competitive and to place communal use at the centre of the issue of property, rather than the principle of individual, competitive tradability, show the proximity of the CLT model to the debates on commons. In this context, Silke Helfrich and David Bollier (2019) have coined the concept of relationalised ownership, and Liz Alden Wily (2017) has emphasised the growing importance of customary tenure as a future property form. In this sense, the structures and practices of CLTs, like those of other non-profit property models, can be seen as the first steps towards new social and property forms and a contemporary land law that ties the possibility of use to social criteria while excluding sale, inheritance and speculation for capital accumulation.

Notes

1 For more information on the history of CLTs, see, for example, Davis (2010).

2 CLT Brussels, London CLT, CLT Ghent, CLT Leuven, CLT H-Buurt / And the People (Amsterdam), Habitage.social Barcelona, Habicoop (Catalonia), cohabitac (Catalonia), XES (Catalonia), CLT Network of England and Wales, South of Scotland Community Housing (SOSCH), Self Organised Architecture (SOA) Ireland, OFS Métropole Lilloise, FMDV (France) and Stadtbodenstiftung (Berlin).

3 In 2022 and 2023, one of the authors conducted a series of interviews with representatives of ECLTN and other international CLT experts.

References

Ajuntament de Barcelona (2022), *Barcelona's Pathway towards a City-Wide Community Land Trust*. Available at www.co-habitat.net/en/news/save-the-date-collaborative-housing-day-15th-of-june-helsinki-at-ishf-22/Ajuntament-de-Barcelona-Barcelona-pathway-towards-a-city-wide-CLT-ISHF22.pdf (accessed 20 December 2024).

Ajuntament de Barcelona (2024), *Barcelona City Council signs new surface right to build social housing in Sants-Montjuïc*. Available at www.barcelona.cat/infobarcelona/en/tema/housing/lajuntament-de-barcelona-signa-un-nou-dret-de-superficie-per-construir-un-edifici-de-cohabitatge-a-sants-montjuic_1372447.html (accessed 18 July 2025).

Algoed, L., and M. E. Hernández Torrales (2024), 'Communities as Global Actors in Counterhegemonic Policy Mobilities: Lessons from the Community Land Trust Movement', *International Journal of the Commons*, 18:1, 53–65, https://doi.org/10.5334/ijc.1217

Champlain Housing Trust (2022), *Champlain Housing Trust Annual Report 2022* (Burlington). Available at www.getahome.org/wp-content/uploads/CHT-Annual-Report-2022.pdf (accessed 20 December 2024).

Davis, J. (2010), 'Origins and evolution of the community land trust in the United States', in J. E. Davis (ed.), *The Community Land Trust Reader* (Cambridge, MA: Lincoln Institute of Land Policy), pp. 3–47.

Davis, J. E., L. Algoed, and M. E. Hernández-Torrales (eds) (2020), *On Common Ground* (Madison, WI: Terra Nostra Press).

George, H. (1879), *Progress and Poverty* (San Francisco, CA: The Self-Help Publishing Company).

Helfrich, S., and D. Bollier (2019), *Free, Fair, and Alive: The Insurgent Power of the Commons* (Gabriola, BC: New Society Publishers).

Holm, A. (2022), *Objekt der Rendite: Zur Wohnungsfrage und was Engels noch nicht wissen konnte* (Berlin: Dietz).

International Center for CLTs (2024), *Join the celebration: World CLT Day 2024 marks a global movement* – press release (global, 2 May 2024). Available at https://worldcltday.org/toolkit/ (accessed 20 December 2024).

Mackenzie, F. D. (2010), 'A common claim: Community land ownership in the Outer Hebrides, Scotland', *International Journal of the Commons*, 4:1, 319, https://doi.org/10.18352/ijc.151

Maeckelbergh, M. (2011), 'Doing is believing: Prefiguration as strategic practice in the alterglobalisation movement', *Social Movement Studies*, 10:1, 1–20.

Piketty, T. (2020), *Capital and Ideology* (Cambridge, MA: Harvard University Press).

Wily, L. A. (2017), 'Customary tenure: remaking property for the 21st century', in M. Graziadei and L. Smith (eds), *Comparative Property Law. Global Perspectives* (Cheltenham/Northampton: Edward Elgar), pp. 458–78.

Part III

Conversations with and about translocal grassroots networks

13

The CoHabitat Network: Connecting civil society around community-led housing across the globe – in conversation with UrbaMonde

Corinna Hölzl, Sascha Rentzsch, Pierre Arnold

Introduction

The CoHabitat Network[1] is a joint initiative launched in 2014 by international grassroots federations as well as non-profit organisations and academic institutions working in the field of community-led housing. Pierre Arnold discusses in this interview the need for data production and practice systematisation as to community-led housing and how an international network is able to serve the interests of housing federations that are embedded in highly varying national and local contexts.

Corinna & Sascha (HU Berlin): Housing has again become a challenging issue worldwide. CoHabitat strives to strengthen communities in their role as urban designers, developers, builders and more broadly in their role as active citizens of their cities. Could you explain why this is necessary and what the aim of the network is?

Pierre (UrbaMonde): CoHabitat is a network of networks and individuals who all work around community-led housing. We are currently, in the year 2025, twenty-nine organisations, and the number is growing annually (Table 13.1). Some of us are networks of grassroots organisations which themselves are on the ground trying to improve informal settlements or to build community-led housing. We all share the community-led housing spirit. What we try to solve is the problem of access to affordable housing, worldwide, with no geographical limit. We want to show that there are alternatives from the people for the people – without having to wait for the market or the State to solve the issues of access to housing. Of course, we need the public actors and sometimes also the private actors to be involved. But the idea is that there is leadership or at least strong participation of residents or future residents in the process.

In the CoHabitat Network, we share resources and time, exchange practical experiences and learn from one another, and we design collective initiatives. And the activities on the ground are carried out by members from grassroots or federations of grassroots organisations and prioritise the empowerment of citizens. Most of our founding members are big networks – Habitat International Coalition (HIC), Slum Dwellers International (SDI) and the Asian Coalition for Housing Rights (ACHR), for instance – that function as membership organisations with a significant membership, membership fees and annual reunions and general assemblies. So the CoHabitat Network aims at remaining an informal space, not to add bureaucracy and fees to our members.

The Swiss NGO UrbaMonde has been coordinating the network since its creation. Our partners from the Global South and North can directly exchange with one another. We see it as an opportunity and a benefit of the collaboration to be able to interact with peers in other parts of the world. Many of our members are very locally focused grassroots organisations that at the same time form part of a global network. For example, the Uruguayan Federation of Mutual Aid Housing Cooperatives FUCVAM is an active member of HIC [see Figure 13.1].

Corinna & Sascha (HU Berlin): The CoHabitat Network was founded in 2014. Can you elaborate on why you decided to build a global network and not, for instance, a European one?

Pierre (UrbaMonde): The CoHabitat Network emerged from UrbaMonde hosting the reunion of international networks who had little or no contacts with one another, but all had contacts with UrbaMonde. At the World

Figure 13.1 CoHabitat Annual Meeting in Geneva, 2024. Photos © Pierre Arnold, all rights reserved.

Urban Forum in Medellin, in April 2014, UrbaMonde had interesting discussions with HIC and We Effect in one meeting, and with SDI in another one, about bridging networks.

The inaugural meeting of the CoHabitat Network took place in Geneva in October 2014. Many of the core organisations that are still active in the network today first convened there. The concept of an annual assembly was warmly received by member organisations, as it provides an opportunity to contextualise their work within a broader community and exchange lessons from practice. This sense of solidarity is invaluable, particularly for organisations with a primarily regional or local focus, as it offers insights into global trends and solutions. The exchange of experiences is enriching, as challenges and innovations in one context often resonate with those in other parts of the world.

UrbaMonde believes in the potential for collective action between these regional networks and other stakeholders with shared objectives. Together we empower communities to shape their living environments and secure funding for housing improvements or construction.

The genesis of the network was driven by a desire to fill a gap in the global landscape of advocacy for housing justice and land rights. First, the CoHabitat Network connects different regions and types of stakeholders: grassroots' federations, technical support NGOs, research institutions, foundations and the grassroots organisations with which UrbaMonde specifically cooperates. We believe it's all about forming alliances. Second, what sets the CoHabitat Network apart is its focus on the social production of housing or 'community-led housing', a concept that transcends language barriers and regional differences. While difficult to define precisely, this focus distinguishes us as a unique network operating at a global scale. Despite our global reach, we maintain an informal decentralised structure, avoiding bureaucratic constraints. This flexibility is appreciated by members who are already committed to their own organisational structures. The important thing is that we're connected, trust one another and collaborate towards a common purpose.

Corinna & Sascha (HU Berlin): CoHabitat's global network approach to community-led housing really appears to be unique. How do you understand 'community-led housing'? Do you have a common definition of the term within CoHabitat?

Pierre (UbaMonde): We define it as a process where residents take the lead in addressing their housing needs. This is framed within the principles of the 'right to the city' and the 'right to adequate housing', ensuring it's not just an idealistic concept but a means of safeguarding human rights. Our definition is broad and primarily focuses on those excluded from the housing market, who often reside in informal settlements or struggle for recognition and rights. We also collaborate with organisations promoting non-speculative approaches in Europe, such as Sostre Civic in Catalonia, MOBA in Eastern Europe or the European Community Land Trust Network (see Chapters 12, 14). Our overarching goal is to identify scalable and replicable solutions for those currently denied adequate housing due to market forces, state structures or the absence of social housing provisions.

Corinna & Sascha (HU Berlin): Your idea is not to have too narrow a definition in order not to miss out on initiatives that could be helpful for disadvantaged groups?

Pierre (UrbaMonde): Exactly. And the fact that we operate in all continents makes it also more difficult to get to a precise definition. Of course, in contexts where social housing structures exist, where housing subsidies and more institutionalised options exist, the challenges are different than where they don't. In Western European countries or North America, for instance, our partners work with groups of middle or lower-middle class people who want to do things differently and foster non-speculative, permanently affordable, ecological housing models. Often these community-led housing projects have a social inclusion objective translated into a couple of free or very economic homes for vulnerable groups, and community spaces and facilities open to their neighbourhood. In other regions, however, UrbaMonde and members of the CoHabitat Network work with people who are in desperate need of housing, of access to water or security of their land tenure to improve their housing situation. In these contexts, there is no legal state solution or political will to help them immediately, which is why people come up with new mechanisms.

Despite geographical disparities, common issues like gentrification and speculation unite us. Whether in Berlin, Barcelona, Rio, Cape Town, Bangkok or Jakarta, similar challenges emerge, such as the touristification of prime locations and evictions of their residents. These shared phenomena enable cross-contextual learning and collaboration, identifying advocacy and resistance strategies. In short, many different inspiring things find their place in a broad community-led housing definition.

Corinna & Sascha (HU Berlin): Do you consider bringing together very different partners from the Global North and the Global South a potential or rather a challenge?

Pierre (UrbaMonde): Despite differing contexts, our aim is to demonstrate similarities in how people reclaim power and advocate for their right to the city. There is a global scale to this. When you look only at your own struggle in your own neighbourhood, you can feel that you're isolated and it gets difficult to move forward if it lasts a long time. But if you know that this is happening in other places simultaneously and you can exchange knowledge with great people producing change elsewhere, it gives you hope and more possibilities to stay positive and creative about your local struggle, even though it will not give you a concrete solution.

A valuable tool we've developed is cohabitat.io, a global map showcasing community-led housing initiatives worldwide. While it may lack user-friendliness in terms of design, its purpose is clear: to illustrate the global nature of community-driven processes in the field of housing. CoHabitat Network members greatly helped to document the community projects they work with and to locate them on the map. It will always be incomplete, as things move quickly, projects multiply, etc. But the idea is to show that we are not talking about an insignificant number of examples which cannot be replicated, all the points on the map challenge the illusion of the private market and public companies solving housing issues on their own.

Corinna & Sascha (HU Berlin): cohabitat.io is one of CoHabitat's key tools. How does data production through the map work? I looked at it and saw that, for example, in Germany, you just list a small number of projects. How do you deal with deficiencies?

Pierre (UrbaMonde): The original concept was to establish a wiki-like, open contributive map that enables anyone to create a free account and tag projects, add or update information and chat with other users. Some partners agreed to share databases of their housing members. For instance, while FUCVAM in Uruguay and ACHR in Asia boast hundreds of tagged projects, some lack detailed information beyond their names. Reluctance from some organisations to share databases limits data availability. To expand project coverage, UrbaMonde introduced regional housing awards requiring participants to tag their projects on the map to enter the competition. However, sustaining the map's relevance requires human resources for web development, documentation, translations and updates. The ideal would be to correct deficiencies and add complete data for all countries, but it is a matter of funding and time. In France, there's a great national map with over 800 tagged projects. And combining such national maps would be very useful since there are many people coming to us with questions about cooperatives in different countries. But importing big databases with different information and operated through other platforms is not always easy [see Figure 13.2].

Corinna & Sascha (HU Berlin): Mapping grassroots alternatives completely, be it housing or other topics, is always a challenge. Another objective of the network is systematised learning. How does this work?

Pierre (UrbaMonde): This involves learning from grassroots processes through case studies and working groups. Last year, we formed a working group comprising partners from UrbaMonde's international cooperation projects from Senegal, Brazil, Uruguay, Nicaragua and Nepal. UrbaMonde initially established a methodology, and each participant contributed to the discussions. The primary aim was to understand how community-led housing is implemented and to share practical knowledge among organisations. Last year, we expanded the group to new partners from Bangladesh, Indonesia and the Philippines and we plan to continue the working group, focusing on funding mechanisms. Specifically, we will explore financial and solidarity mechanisms to support those unable to access bank loans or public funding for housing projects. There are lots of questions on how emerging projects could be locally funded, especially if they are not yet recognised either by the State or by banks. Another subject of interest is advocacy at the local or municipal level.

There are great opportunities to learn from the experiences of projects that are more advanced, like Sostre Civic in Barcelona with fifteen years of making lots of changes. Also when it comes to national differences. For

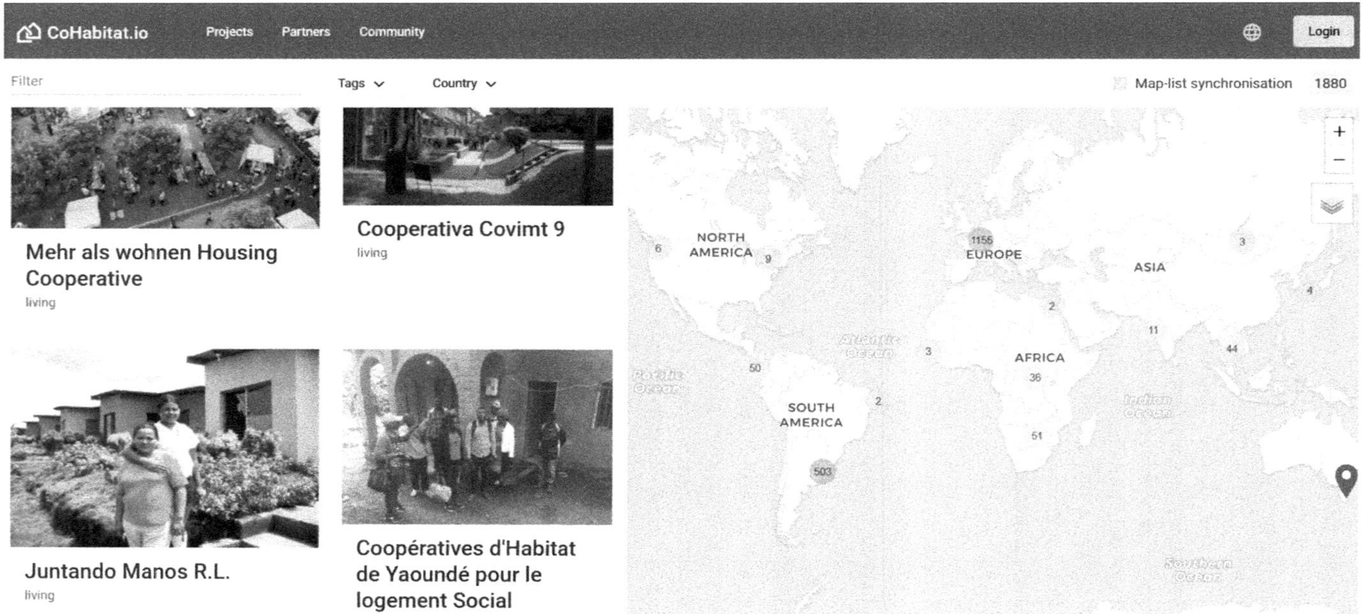

Figure 13.2 Cohabitat.io platform, 2024. Photo © UrbaMonde, all rights reserved.

example, cooperative housing has a different legal status in different countries. That is why Cooperative Housing International is an important player of the CoHabitat Network in working on promoting legal frameworks and policies for housing cooperatives worldwide. You could say that we are a community of actors who produce knowledge in this broad field, not because we have a systematic overview and responses to everything, but because we have a network. Often, we don't have the answer when we get requests, but we can send contacts from whom people can get the information.

Corinna & Sascha (HU Berlin): Finally, networking and counselling are one of the core activities of CoHabitat, correct?

Pierre (UrbaMonde): Networking involves organising assemblies, events and spaces for exchange, both internally and externally. For instance, the International Social Housing Festival has served as a platform for showcasing community-led housing in Lyon in 2019, Helsinki in 2022, Barcelona in 2023, and Dublin in 2025. On such occasions, we bring together CoHabitat members and local organisations to disseminate information to wider audiences and professionals. A similar approach was taken at the World Urban Forum in Katowice, Poland (2022) and in Cairo, Egypt (2024), where we organised a joint CoHabitat exhibition stand called Habitat Village. Throughout the forum, we facilitated various self-managed activities organised at our stand by our partners, demonstrating our commitment to promoting community-led housing, publications and research.

Additionally, we focus on documentation, data production and communication regarding community-led housing. Our database and case studies cater to a broader audience, providing insights into various projects. Often, during 'Urban October' campaigns, we conduct webinars showcasing community-led housing projects. We do not have counselling activity, but we often get contacted by researchers or practitioners wanting to know more about cooperatives or community land trusts, looking for contacts in a specific country. And of course, within the network we can all support one another when needed.

Corinna & Sascha (HU Berlin): Now, after a decade of operating, how would you summarise the major potentials and limitations of CoHabitat?

Pierre (UrbaMonde): The main benefit for housing federations lies in the opportunities we provide to explore local issues from different perspectives. This information from diverse contexts enables our members to reevaluate and strengthen their own approaches or advocate collectively. It extends beyond the usual regional or thematic focus of other networks. In addition to peer-to-peer learning, our network offers opportunities for participation in international events, fundraising initiatives and collaborative projects.

Our main challenge is that our efforts are constrained by limited funding. Currently, in 2025, only UrbaMonde receives funding for coordinating activities, primarily relying on philanthropic support, and it is shrinking every year. This funding is insufficient to mobilise staff time and resources. Our partners often face time constraints or competing priorities, which can hinder their full participation. Additionally, the reality of the broader capitalist landscape can be harsh and discouraging. While we have some successful case studies, many contexts are marked by difficulty and negativity. We recognise that our endeavours are small in the face of larger systemic challenges, and progress can be slow and uncertain. We are fortunate to have dedicated and passionate individuals within our network. These members, including human rights advocates and community leaders, have achieved significant successes. Their presence is inspiring and injects our network with energy. Hearing their positive stories and being surrounded by their optimism gives us hope and motivation to continue our work.

Corinna & Sascha (HU Berlin): Indeed, positive stories are undoubtedly needed. You already mentioned how the network is funded. How would you describe your experiences with philanthropy in this field?

Pierre (UrbaMonde): We rely on philanthropic support because we choose not to charge membership fees. This decision reflects our commitment to inclusivity and prevents us from becoming an exclusive network. However, this reliance on philanthropy means we are subject to the priorities of these donors, and there is always uncertainty about whether funding will be renewed. Some foundations seem to take advantage of civil society organisations by dictating the terms of funding. They operate with an entrepreneurial mind-set, focusing solely on immediate indicators and societal changes. This can be challenging, as it's unrealistic to expect a network of civil society organisations to achieve policy change in a short timeframe. Our work is long-term and involves gradual progress.

Corinna & Sascha (HU Berlin): We'd like to hear your ideas for the future. Based on your experiences, what are the main challenges in transforming the housing systems in the Global North and Global South to facilitate the scaling up of community-led housing?

Pierre (UrbaMonde): In our advocacy work, particularly within the European context, we've identified numerous necessary changes. However, one crucial aspect is gaining recognition and support from banks from a public, ethical and private perspective. If these institutions acknowledge the value and reliability of community-led housing projects, it could make a significant difference without waiting for legislative changes or progressive governments, especially considering the rise of right-wing ideologies in many places. Instead of relying on national governments to enact perfect laws, the focus should be on local experimentation and collaboration with progressive municipalities and allies. Access to finance is essential for turning good ideas into reality. Unfortunately, in most countries, collective loans for such projects are not readily available. Demonstrating the sustainability of the model through successful projects is key to scaling up. Additionally, city and regional governments play a crucial role by understanding the importance of cooperative housing and implementing supportive regulations, such as land lease policies for non-profit housing. And there's a fundamental human rights aspect: a basic understanding of the necessities of informal settlements. It's crucial to avoid speculation in areas where informal settlements are being regularised, especially in locations that are attractive for the real estate market. Instead, regularisation efforts should prioritise the needs of current residents over investors who may buy up all the land plots. This approach has been successfully implemented in the Caño Martín Peña sector of San Juan, Puerto Rico, through the community land trust model, and it's gradually being adopted in Brazil with notable successes. It's essential to move away from individual title deeds towards collective ownership models in areas where gentrification, land grabbing and displacement are risks.

Corinna & Sascha (HU Berlin): These issues are indeed globally relevant for many particularly urban contexts. With unlimited time and resources – how would you further develop the work of the network?

Pierre (UrbaMonde): Our approach would probably involve organising frequent field trips for bankers and elected officials such as ministers and mayors. These visits would take them to locations where sustainable initiatives are already underway. By witnessing first hand and engaging directly with the communities involved, decision-makers can grasp the tangible outcomes and potential impact. Real change occurs when decision-makers are personally convinced through direct exposure rather than relying solely on online resources or reports. Accelerating progress necessitates targeted visits to specific locations. The mutual aid housing cooperative movement in Latin America, initially pioneered in Uruguay and later adopted across the region, exemplifies the power of such initiatives. For example, when a housing movement in Paraguay sought to replicate Uruguay's success, key officials were invited to visit Uruguayan cooperatives. Such experimental learning transformed their perceptions, challenging stereotypes and fostering a more inclusive approach to development. And during a recent visit to Brussels, a significant figure, the 'Baumeister' of the Brussels region, expressed admiration for the mayor of Geneva, considering him to be an urban hero for advocating cooperative models. This highlights the importance of political champions who endorse non-speculative, community-driven, sustainable and affordable initiatives. Such enthusiasm is crucial as it often ignites competition among cities at the regional level and drives them to pioneer innovative projects and distinguish themselves.

Corinna & Sascha (HU Berlin): We've discussed international exchange extensively, but what's your take on international solidarity within the realm of community-led housing?

Pierre (UrbaMonde): We require a more robust infrastructure to support collective investment strategies while drawing on contributions from various sources, such as banks, philanthropic entities, governmental bodies and individuals within cooperative communities. A revolving fund would facilitate loans to organisations across different countries, with repayments replenishing the fund for future use. While we've initiated similar efforts on a small scale at UrbaMonde, channelling funds from Swiss housing cooperatives to support local revolving funds in Nicaragua and Senegal, logistical challenges persist, particularly regarding currency fluctuations, bank transfer fees and interest payments. However, the local management of these funds by partner organisations and community entities has proven effective, with borrowers consistently repaying into the local revolving fund. This underscores the importance of international cooperation, which can become manifest on regional scales, such as Europe, South America or parts of Asia. Yet navigating international transfers, banking regulations and financial controls poses significant challenges. To scale up our efforts, substantial financial backing is essential. We're talking not just about €10,000 donations, but multimillion-euro investments to facilitate multiple projects simultaneously, including land acquisition and construction. Securing such funding requires engagement with institutions like the European Investment Bank who grasp the significance of our initiatives and the potential for repayment. While we're not there yet, organisations within our network are contemplating strategies to advance this agenda, making it a priority for the coming year.

Corinna & Sascha (HU Berlin): One final question: do you believe that 'becoming more' is the primary objective in the realm of community-led housing, or should we prioritise rendering the broader socio-ecological transformations that occur through community-led housing visible?

Pierre (UrbaMonde): When you examine these projects closely, it becomes evident that they offer more than just housing. They have a significant impact on the neighbourhood level, fostering empowerment, solidarity and sustainable living practices. Successful projects often incorporate elements of sustainable architecture and shared spaces, resulting in multiple benefits for societies. Cities like Vienna recognise the transformative potential of community-led housing, viewing it as a catalyst for vibrant neighbourhoods and ecological sustainability. By integrating community-led housing into new developments, cities can foster cohesive communities with fewer cars, more green spaces and solidarity initiatives. However, to truly democratise access to such initiatives, we must increase our efforts. If community-led housing remains inaccessible and time-consuming to develop, it will remain out of reach for lower-income groups who lack the resources and time required to participate. Therefore, some sort of scalability of community-led housing approaches is crucial to making these initiatives more affordable and inclusive, ensuring they are not just niche endeavours but accessible to all. This entails streamlining development processes, providing financial support and technical assistance and fostering a supportive community to overcome barriers to involvement. The urgency of this task cannot be overstated, especially in the face of political shifts and the erosion of social structures. Liberal and right-wing governments pose a threat to these initiatives, making it imperative to scale up community-led housing before such opportunities are lost. Breaking stereotypes and showcasing successful projects across diverse contexts is essential to fostering widespread adoption and ensuring that community-led housing becomes an alternative way of shaping our cities rather than an exceptional one.

Corinna & Sascha (HU Berlin): Many thanks for this conversation!

Note

1 www.co-habitat.net.

Table 13.1 Member organisations of the CoHabitat Network

	Organisation	Country / Region	Category	Website
1	Asian Coalition for Housing Rights (ACHR)	Asia	Academic institution	achr.net
2	Catalytic Communities (CatComm)	Brazil / US	Local technical support NGO	catcomm.org
3	Co-Lab Research	Netherlands	Academic institution	co-lab-research.net
5	Community Land Trust Brussels (CLTB)	Belgium	CLH developer	cltb.be
4	Cooperative Housing International (CHI)	Global	Global network / coalition	housinginternational.coop
6	European Community Land Trust Network	Europe	Regional network / coalition	clteurope.org
7	Federación Uruguaya de Cooperativas de Vivienda por Ayuda Mutua (FUCVAM)	Uruguay	Grassroots umbrella organisation	fucvam.org.uy
8	Habitat & Participation	Belgium	Grassroots umbrella organisation	habitat-participation.be
9	Habitat International Coalition (HIC)	Global	Global network / coalition	hic-net.org
10	Habitat Participatif France (HPF)	France	Grassroots umbrella organisation	habitatparticipatif-france.fr

(*continued*)

Table 13.1 (Cont.)

	Organisation	Country / Region	Category	Website
11	ID22 Institute for Creative Sustainability	Germany	Local technical support NGO or platform	id22.net
12	International Center for Community Land Trusts	Global	Global network / coalition	cltweb.org
13	International Institute for Environment and Development (IIED)	United Kingdom	Academic institution	iied.org
14	La Dinamo Fundacio	Spain	Local technical support NGO	ladinamofundacio.org
15	Misereor	Germany	Foundation	misereor.de
16	MOBA Housing SCE	South-Eastern and Eastern Europe	Regional network / coalition	moba.coop
17	Multipro	Nicaragua	Local technical support NGO	coopmultipro.org
18	Philippine Action for Community-Led Shelter Initiatives (PACSI)	Philippines	Local technical support NGO	pacsii.org
19	Platform of Community Action and Architecture (POCAA)	Bangladesh	Local technical support platform	pocaabd.com
20	Slum Dwellers International	Africa / Asia / LA	Global network / coalition	sdinet.org
21	Sostre Civic	Spain / Catalunya	CLH developer	sostrecivic.coop
22	Student Co-op Homes UK	United Kingdom	Grassroots umbrella organisation	studenthomes.coop

23	Studentendorf Schlachtensee	Germany	CLH developer	studentendorf.berlin
24	UCL – Bartlett Development Planning Unit (DPU)	United Kingdom	Academic institution	ucl.ac.uk/bartlett/development/bartlett-development-planning-unit
25	UrbaMonde	Switzerland / France	International support NGO	urbamonde.org
26	Urban Poor Consortium (UPC)	Indonesia	Local technical support NGO	urbanpoor.or.id
27	urbaSEN	Senegal	Local technical support NGO	urbasen.org
28	We Effect	Sweden	International support NGO	weeffect.org
29	World Habitat	Global	Foundation	world-habitat.org

Source: Author’s own, 2025.

14

'We need to mainstream the alternatives': In conversation about transnational financial instruments and legal forms to allow for new housing cooperatives in Europe

Corinna Hölzl, Sascha Rentzsch, Ana Džokić, Goran Jeras, Knut Höller, Peter Kämmerling

Introduction

In response to the shortage of affordable rental housing, new grassroots housing initiatives have been emerging over the past fifteen years to join forces transnationally in an effort to implement new rental housing cooperatives and other forms of non-speculative community-led housing. They have been founding European cooperative societies (SCE), are developing transnational financing instruments and creating new banks. Examples include the MOBA Housing SCE, a young transnational network of cooperative pioneers from Croatia, the Czech Republic, Hungary, Serbia and Slovenia that is also setting up the so-called MOBA Accelerator; the Living in Metropolises SCE (LiM) which, among others, engages in the Baltic countries; and the Commoning Spaces Network (CSN), an alliance that has emerged from international activities initiated by the Mietshäuser Syndikat and acts as a knowledge and exchange platform while aiming to grant loans transnationally to community-led member houses. And the European Ethical Bank (EEB), initiated by the Co-operative for Ethical Financing (ZEF), shall be the first pan-European, truly ethical financial institution with tailored loan offerings and streamlined digital business processes. This conversation with representatives of MOBA, LiM, CSN and EEB explores the motivations and strategies underlying these transnational grassroots networks, as well as their limits when it comes to financing new community-led housing.

Corinna & Sascha (HU Berlin): Goran, Ana, Knut and Peter, could you all outline the origins and intentions of your organisations, please?

Goran (ZEF): The concept of a European Ethical Bank emerged from over a decade of experience as a consultant in the mainstream financial sector. Failing to meet societal needs or sustainability criteria, the mainstream banking model is mathematically and physically unsustainable in the long term. When considering sectors like green transformation, where there's a pressing need to reduce carbon emissions, current actors often fall short due to prevalent issues of greenwashing and whitewashing. It's also essential to utilise tools that go beyond mere compliance with existing standards like the current Environmental, Social and Governance (ESG) principle and taxonomy. It's evident that the current standards are inadequate and need improvement. Alternative models typically remain small and constitute a marginal portion of the banking sector. Correspondingly, a critical gap, which has recently gained attention, even within the Commission's priorities, is the lack of funding opportunities for the social and solidarity economy sector, a vital pillar for the EU's economic and social development. Unlike SMEs, which have established support structures, this sector requires an entirely new financial infrastructure for sustainability, as it has historically been overlooked both in many European countries and at the EU level. Our motivation is to assimilate the positive attributes of present alternative banks and enhance them with additional methods and technology, aiming to make them scalable, replicable and serve as a role model in more broadly adopting high-standard ethical banking practices.

Ana (MOBA): MOBA is an international umbrella organisation of pioneering housing cooperatives and initiatives establishing new non-speculative housing models in Central and South-East Europe (CSEE) (MOBA Housing SCE, n.d.). Currently, we have members from five countries: Serbia, Croatia, Slovenia, Hungary and the Czech Republic. In 2017, we convened for the first time and swiftly decided to initiate an informal network. Later, in 2020, we formed an SCE to support one another in addressing political and legal challenges. In the region, the existing regulatory and institutional landscapes provide only limited support for non-market housing initiatives (see Chapter 6). Another significant challenge is access to adequate financing (see Chapter 10). Identifying financial solutions was one of the primary reasons for our collaboration. A study we did in 2022 on the potential for catalytic capital investment into collective ownership models in CSEE confirmed the reluctance of present financial institutions, particularly commercial banks, to endorse community-led housing endeavours and highlighted the need for new financial products.[1] Thus, our aim is to advocate for a shift towards recognising and supporting community-led cooperative housing as a mainstream approach. In the absence of such support, we established the so-called MOBA Accelerator – a revolving 'rebel' fund aimed at initiating pilot projects to validate the concept and make it attractive to other forms of financing. The study further indicated a significant demand for secure and affordable rental housing. Surprisingly, 13% to 26% of the people in capital cities across the region expressed interest. In a region that is characterised by super-homeownership and distrust in housing cooperatives, this is anything but a matter of course.

Knut (LiM): LiM, Living in Metropolises, mirrors MOBA in its structure as a SCE. It was established in 2018 and has 120 members – both individuals and corporate entities – advocating for cooperative ideals (LiM, n.d.).

Our aim is to utilise the European legal framework to advance cooperative housing projects in various locations. Our members come from ten different countries. LiM is involved, among others, in the Baltic countries and Ukraine. So far, LiM has completed its initial housing project in Germany (Berlin). Since 2020, coinciding with the onset of the pandemic, I've been preparing a cooperative housing project in the city of Jelgava, Latvia. This initiative responds to the absence of affordable rental options and housing cooperatives in that country. In order to implement this project, we will probably need to establish a local management company in Latvia to handle construction and rental operations. Given the challenges in securing financing, we're exploring the idea of providing employee housing in partnership with local companies. Jelgava has been proactive in attracting investments, yet there has been a dearth of affordable multi-family construction in the city. We believe our cooperative model can address this need and extend to providing employee housing for local companies. We've presented this model to various audiences in Latvia, and it has garnered interest from a multitude of municipalities and local businesses. If successful, we aim to replicate this model in other underserved rental markets, including Estonia, Latvia, Lithuania and potentially Ukraine. Besides, another building project in Germany (in the state of Brandenburg) is in the pipeline.

Peter (CSN): The Mietshäuser Syndikat is a network of by now (2025) more than 200 community-led housing projects in Germany (Mietshäuser Syndikat, n.d.). Apart from the primary goal to withdraw the houses from the market and thus prevent speculation, it emphasises solidarity, inclusion, self-determination, joint ownership, collective decision-making and sustainability among residents with space for housing, working and engagement. For approximately twenty years, the task force on international affairs of the Mietshäuser Syndikat has been a contact point for the international exchange of knowledge on founding and building up community-led houses. The high interest in our objectives and model has led to similar associations being founded in several countries, including Austria, France, the Czech Republic, Spain, Portugal, Sweden and the Netherlands. The idea of establishing a European network for horizontal knowledge exchange and financial solidarity transfer emerged in 2015 especially to foster the many European initiatives that lack the comparatively beneficial framework conditions of such countries as Germany. However, attempts to handle this task on a voluntary basis have turned out to be challenging. With core funding from 2023 to 2024, we have been setting up the Commoning Spaces Network (CSN) for mutual support in terms of knowledge and consulting, legally organised as a German association. And we are exploring ways to build up a European finance entity.

Corinna & Sascha (HU Berlin): All of you share common objectives, but your organisations are lined up differently and approaches vary. We'd like to hear more about your strategies, particularly regarding the financial aspect. Which steps have you taken so far, and what has been helpful in your case?

Ana (MOBA): MOBA is an SCE with seven full members – local organisations implementing community-led cooperative housing models in their respective cities. Additionally, MOBA has three associate members: UrbaMonde, World Habitat and ZEF. In terms of helpful resources, we've relied on volunteer work and received financial support from organisations like World Habitat and FundAction. The General Building Cooperative Zurich (ABZ), the largest housing cooperative in Switzerland, was instrumental in providing the €30,000 needed to establish MOBA as an SCE. And we secured a grant from the re:arc Foundation in 2024 to develop mechanisms for the MOBA Accelerator. After several years of refining our selection criteria for housing projects to receive financing, we tested these criteria with a group in Prague, providing them with a form of short-term loan. Now our focus is on scaling up both funding for projects and operational mechanisms for the MOBA Accelerator (cf. Figure 14.1). We envision filling the pot through three levels of involvement from external partners: donations, shares and bonds. We aim to collect the first €1 million with donations

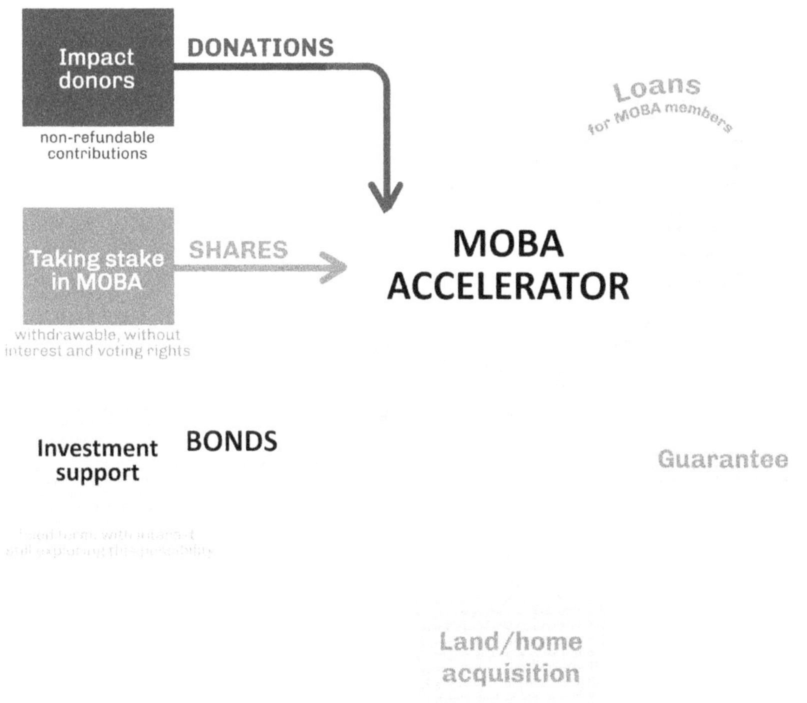

Figure 14.1 MOBA Accelerator, 2024. Graph © MOBA SCE, all rights reserved.

from friendly organisations and individuals supportive of MOBA's objectives. In late 2024, we received the first private donation of €100,000, and our member organisation from Prague another €80,000. Subsequently, we plan to raise approximately €5 million through shares, with organisations becoming investor members of MOBA. This involves collaborating with established housing cooperatives and associations across different countries. Further down the line, we'll explore bonds, where external organisations with a long-term outlook invest in MOBA with the expectation of returns and interest rates. Currently, in all our member countries, we have projects at various stages of readiness, from acquiring buildings to renovation procedures.

Goran (ZEF): Opposed to the other initiatives here, our project didn't begin from the demand side of organisations seeking funding, but rather from banking experts striving to renovate the banking procedures themselves. Our expertise lies in improving banking models, particularly in risk management, impact measurement and the use of non-tangible collaterals. We've invested almost €1 million into this initiative, along with an additional €1 million in kind investment for software development and prior work fragments. Currently, we're focusing on setting up a framework that is compliant with current European legislation (Basel III and ECB banking regulations) and capable of piloting innovative approaches. Key elements include: a European-level cooperative ownership of the bank, a business model focused on value creation instead of profit maximisation, aggregation of portfolios from different member states to facilitate EIB/EIF funding and integration of sustainability reporting indicators in Value at Risk calculations. The final result should be a truly European, highly decentralised bank, able to act as a systemically important player for funding the social and solidarity economy sector in Europe (Zadruga za Etično Financiranje, n.d.).

Our goal is to fully operationalise this banking infrastructure (cf. Figure 14.2). We aim to have 30% to 40% of our future balance sheet in collaborative housing, considering it a valuable collateral asset, an investment with huge impact and a springboard for investments in other community projects (energy, mobility, food, services, etc.). The operational framework involves two key facets: first, ensuring accessibility akin to platforms such as 'Ethical Revolut' for general banking transactions like deposits and savings. This accessibility is pivotal in attracting a wide audience, making banking convenient and inclusive. Second, our focus is directed towards providing funding for impact-oriented businesses, with a strong emphasis on social and environmental impacts. This entails working closely with local strategic partners serving as intermediaries who facilitate local business endeavours, each contributing unique perspectives and expertise.

Our project is presently at the stage of identifying these partners, specifically community organisations across Europe engaged in housing, social entrepreneurship, renewable energy and related fields, in addition

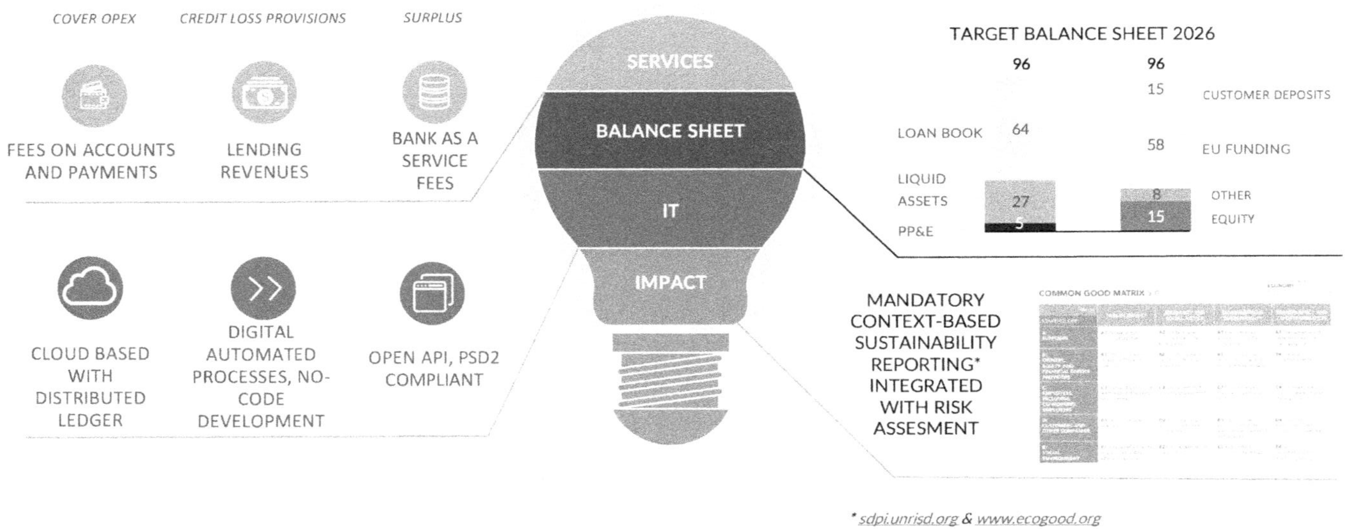

Figure 14.2 EEB business model highlights, 2024. Graph © Goran Jeras, all rights reserved.

to financing institutions. Due to the history of our project, we followed a process somewhat opposite to what you would usually expect: instead of identifying the partners first and working together towards fulfilling all the technical and regulatory details to become a bank, we solved the difficult compliance and technical part first, and only now we are 'onboarding' the partners. We're seeking partners who are capable of aggregating portfolios and demonstrating the potential for numerous projects over the next three to five years with the right funding instruments. By investing with us, they can leverage their capital significantly. At the moment, we have six organisations already committed to becoming shareholders, and we're actively seeking a few more, aiming to reach close to ten and thus laying a solid foundation for expansion across Europe. Notable partners include ZEF in Croatia, Genossenschaft für Gemeinwohl in Austria and Blue Seeds in France. The portfolio of shareholders will enable us to present a robust business case to the central bank of Lithuania where we're seeking licensing. Our success is highly dependent on identifying the right organisations. These organisations must grasp the value proposition of participating in our model and be willing to commit their capacities accordingly. Together with each organisation, we develop what we call an internal business plan. This plan involves assessing the need for new expertise, personnel and project implementation capacity. We are projecting the financial value of implemented projects over the next five years. Once we've established the plan, we will determine cost-sharing mechanisms with the bank to finance the additional capacity required.

It's worth noting that while initial funding of credit lines will primarily stem from development institutions such as the European Investment Bank (EIB) and national development banks, our long-term vision involves broader engagement, including activation of our customers' deposits base for projects they support. In essence, our success hinges on the collaborative efforts of diverse stakeholders, each contributing their resources and knowledge to drive meaningful change. This collective enthusiasm, engagement and expertise form the bedrock of our endeavours, empowering us to navigate the complexities of ethical banking and sustainable finance with confidence and purpose.

Peter (CSN): The Commoning Spaces Network was founded in December 2023 by a dedicated group of twenty-three individuals representing eighteen countries from Portugal over Switzerland to Greece (Commoning Space, n.d.) (cf. Figure 14.3). So far, we have initiated an international consulting group to facilitate international knowledge and experience exchange and ensure a more structured approach. With respect to financing, we had initially planned to establish a European financial cooperative that would grant loans as well as shares in housing projects. However, this approach did not work out since financial cooperatives organised as SCEs do not yet fit into the German institutional cooperative landscape and, without a banking licence, the amount of credits is too low for our purposes. Now we are exploring other possibilities. In terms of supporting resources, successful

Figure 14.3 Founding members of the Commoning Spaces Network, 2023. Photo © Peter Kämmerling, all rights reserved.

commitment on the part of activists from diverse countries as well as the Mietshäuser Syndikat as a fundamental and established model institution has been instrumental in driving our progress and motivation.

Knut (LiM): Reflecting on our initial project, which was predominantly Germany-based, it can be challenging to secure funding and resources as a new cooperative. We are convinced that cooperation between established and emerging cooperatives is crucial. While older cooperatives may lack flexibility, they hold substantial assets that could support new initiatives. That is why strengthening the dialogue between these entities is imperative. Besides, as representatives of the demand side for the EEB, we are eager to engage in ongoing discussions and collaborations. Such partnerships are essential for piloting and initiating projects. The scarcity of institutions such as the EEB underscores the importance of its establishment. We believe it will serve as a catalyst for inspiring similar endeavours and are fully committed to supporting its development.

Corinna & Sascha (HU Berlin): Now, we'd be interested to hear your thoughts on the transnational approach you all have adopted. Why do you believe this approach is necessary, and what benefits do you foresee in adopting such a strategy for your organisations?

Knut (LiM): The cooperative model, recognised by UNESCO as a cultural heritage, stands as a testament to sustainability. At LiM, we operate within the German legal and cooperative framework while aligning with broader European ideals. Our involvement in promoting this concept highlights the cooperative ethos of collective action. For instance, within LiM, our operations seamlessly integrate cooperative principles into the German audit system, prioritising innovation while upholding cooperative housing values. Additionally, our strategic European focus positions us at the forefront of shaping transnational housing initiatives, leveraging the cooperative model's adaptability across borders. Through organisations like IWO Housing Initiative for Eastern Europe, we extend our reach beyond national boundaries while fostering partnerships and seeking opportunities to amplify our impact. By engaging in networking activities and collaborative projects, we harness the collective potential of cooperative movements across Europe. As pioneers, we're on the cusp of tangible outcomes, making dissemination and the scaling of efforts such as ours here more feasible.

Ana (MOBA): The primary motivation for us to collaborate stems from the fact that we initially were locally isolated, with no other organisations like ours in our respective countries. Essentially, our cooperatives or pioneering initiatives were the first and only ones in which we operated. By joining forces, we've become stronger. Sharing experiences allows us to leverage our collective knowledge, which, when combined, is truly impressive. While individually, we may seem small within our local contexts, uniting has proven crucial on many fronts. First, it enhances our collective knowledge and visibility. Membership in MOBA also lends us greater impact and facilitates connections with international actors, which would be challenging to achieve locally. In Croatia, for instance, MOBA is now taking local action, with new projects being planned under its umbrella. This local presence not only bolsters MOBA's relevance but it may in the future also serve as a syndicate or CLT that holds assets in local projects, such as owning the land or shares in buildings, thereby safeguarding against speculation and ensuring the long-term sustainability of the model. While challenges such as currency differences and differing EU membership statuses arise, we're actively working on resolving these complexities as we continue to grow and evolve.

As for new projects, our local members in Croatia, Cooperative Open Architecture and ZEF, approached a number of cities to work on pilot projects in the local communities (cf. Figure 14.4). Affordable housing has become a significant political topic across all parties in Croatia, and the National Housing Policy, adopted in the spring of 2025, opens up space for the expansion of the cooperative housing model in Croatia. In April 2025, an agreement was signed with the city of Pula in Istria to collaborate on the development of a cooperative housing project, while in Križevci, where the local government already dedicated a former military dormitory for a cooperative housing project, a construction permit is being obtained.

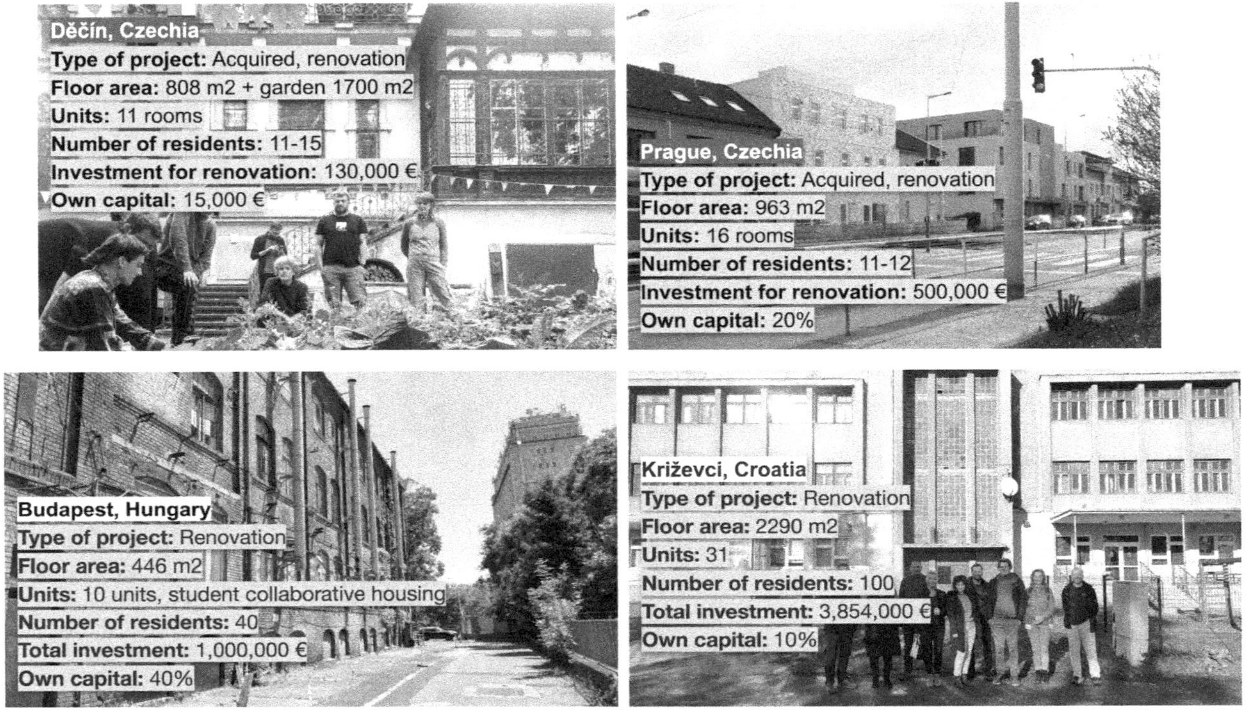

Figure 14.4 MOBA pilot projects, 2024. Photos © MOBA SCE, all rights reserved.

These projects involve providing land or buildings, and MOBA is being positioned as a supporter in facilitating this process.

Goran (ZEF): As explained, our primary approach builds on a network of community-oriented strategic partners across Europe. Additionally, we have strategies to collect other types of capital, such as issuing investor shares specifically targeting impact and sustainability oriented foundations and high-net-worth individuals. While we have received good feedback on offering these shares, our strategic partner shares are our main focus as they are long-term and prioritise community development over dividends. Once our bank is operational and licensed, it will open up new avenues for accessing capital and issuing financial products, thus enabling us to collaborate with other ethical banking institutions as well as public development banks, in particular. This approach is crucial because awareness is still limited in the banking sector concerning the opportunities presented by the common European market. Except for neobanks that can operate anywhere but are primarily focused on transaction business investments and retail, there are virtually no financial institutions that can serve European-level businesses, except the largest ones like Deutsche Bank or Société Générale. Many financial institutions, including these major banks, are not willing to serve small businesses or impact-oriented ventures at a European level, creating a significant gap in supporting the single European market that we aim to address with our bank.

Peter (CSN): Spreading the concept of transnational solidary housing is paramount. We need to showcase successful examples and demonstrate to people that they can self-empower and initiate these projects themselves, fostering a sense of mutual support within communities. Encouraging individuals to take the initiative is crucial, especially given the current system's constraints. Initial credits, consulting and expertise for new house projects play a significant role here. By engaging in legislative processes at European institutions, we seek to advocate for policies that facilitate solidary house initiatives and promote their widespread adoption.

Corinna & Sascha (HU Berlin): Deeply ingrained societal attitudes towards traditional banking institutions or alternative housing models and missing regulations can pose significant hurdles for the operations of our organisations and initiatives. To conclude, could you all briefly summarise your views and recommendations on how to face these fundamental challenges?

Peter (CSN): With the European housing crisis gaining recognition from major European institutions, there's a significant opportunity to receive robust support over the coming years. However, it's crucial for us to do our own groundwork first. This involves knowledge transfer, support for emerging groups in multiple countries and adapting or seeking community-led models from different regions. In the next two to four years, as we complete these essential tasks, I anticipate a rapid increase in the need for financing. We hope that institutions like the EIB will extend their credits to support the sector of community-led housing. This collaborative effort is our plan for the future.

Knut (LiM): Well, while progress with the EEB and MOBA is promising, there remain challenges to address. The legal form of an SCE, for instance, is largely unutilised in Europe and requires further justification and attention. Unfortunately, we learnt that with respect to our projects in Latvia, the legal form of a SCE is not Latvian enough. In Germany, on the other hand, LiM SCE is not German enough to receive funding from the German Development Bank (KfW) for projects outside of Germany or for our European members if they want to buy cooperative shares. And all our projects are not large and thus not European enough to be eligible for programmes of the EIB. Collaboration and advocacy will be key in ensuring that this legal structure of a European vision facilitates housing projects across Europe with minimal barriers.

Ana (MOBA): The MOBA Accelerator inspired the establishment of a number of different organisations across Europe. CSN's aim to build up transnational solidary financing instruments is comparable to what MOBA aims to achieve. The same can be said for the European Community Land Trust Network, which is also looking to set up a similar fund (see Chapter 12). Our organisations are in regular exchange, and I see potential in connecting these efforts under a common umbrella project. This could involve approaching larger institutions, such as the EIB or the Council of European Development Bank (which in 2024 approved a €50 million loan to Sostre Cívic from Barcelona, the first large-scale financial injection to a young community-led housing provider), to access funds on a much larger scale than what we've discussed so far. The minimum amount for approaching the EIB is around €30 million.

Goran (ZEF): It's crucial for us to acknowledge and embrace the reality that we're operating within an illusion if we believe we can garner interest from mainstream commercial actors for the type of business we're engaged in. Their objectives, visions and criteria are fundamentally at odds with our needs. Any business driven solely by profit maximisation for the benefit of its shareholders will never prioritise financing affordable cooperative housing. They have more lucrative avenues for deploying their capital. The sooner we internalise this truth, the sooner we'll recognise the imperative of establishing our own institutions guided by different goals, expectations and values. I firmly believe this is the most viable path forward. We shouldn't squander time pursuing strategies that are fundamentally incompatible with the existing institutional landscape.

Corinna & Sascha (HU Berlin): Many thanks for this conversation. This interplay of differently oriented and composed organisations in terms of procedures, capacities and geographical distribution holds great potential. We wish you all success and perseverance!

Note

1 Project summary: https://moba.coop/catalytic-capital-investment/ (accessed 19 March 2026).

References

Commoning Space (n.d.), Exploring the Potential of Urban Commons. Available at www.commoning.space/ (accessed 10 January 2025).

LiM (n.d.), Living in Metropolises Cooperative (LIM-Coop). Available at https://lim-coop.eu/ (accessed 10 January 2025).

Mietshäuser Syndikat (n.d.), Affordable Housing through Cooperative Ownership. Available at www.syndikat.org/en/ (accessed 10 January 2025).

MOBA Housing SCE (n.d.), MOBA: Collaborative Housing Solutions in South-Eastern Europe. Available at https://moba.coop/ (accessed 10 January 2025).

Zadruga za Etično Financiranje (n.d.), ZEF – Ethical Banking in Croatia. Available at www.zef.hr/en/o-nama/eticna-banka (accessed 9 April 2025).

15

The European Student Cooperative Housing Alliance: A conversation about growing student housing cooperatives

Anke Schwittay, Scott Jennings, Jens-Uwe Köhler, Léa Oswald

Introduction

The European Student Cooperative Housing Alliance (ESCHA) was established in 2022 with the mission to create a European network that connects individual student housing cooperatives, enabling them to share experiences and support each other, especially during the challenging start-up phase. It aims to raise the visibility of the cooperative model and advocate for more public support, in order to promote affordable, secure and green housing for students across Europe. ESCHA's members are student housing cooperatives in a number of European countries, with the biggest coops existing in Germany, Switzerland and the UK, while Italy, France and the Netherlands have smaller properties, and countries like Ireland and Hungary have active groups looking for properties. ESCHA is supported logistically by Cooperative Housing International, UrbaMonde (Switzerland), Cooplink (Netherlands) and the Phone Coop Foundation for Cooperative Innovation (UK). Since its early beginnings in 2018, it has organised two European gatherings and participated in other housing-related events.

In this chapter, I facilitate a conversation between three cooperators who were central in ESCHA's establishment: Jens-Uwe Köhler, who lived at and is now CFO of the Studentendorf Schlachtensee in Berlin; Léa Oswald, who was a resident at La Ciguë in Geneva and now works for UrbaMonde; and Scott Jennings, Secretary of Student Coop Homes (SCH), the national umbrella organisation for student housing coops in the UK. They talk about the establishment of their own cooperative organisations in their unique historical and political contexts, their motivations for setting up ESCHA and their hopes for the future of the student housing coop movement.

Anke: Jens-Uwe, can you start by telling me a bit about Studentendorf Schlachtensee and how it originated?

Jens-Uwe: Sure. The foundation for the student village of Schlachtensee was laid in 1957 in the context of US support for the democratic development of post-war West Germany. As part of the Marshall plan, the Freie Universität Berlin was set up in 1948, and ten years later a student accommodation campus was financed by the Ford Foundation and the US State Department. The aim was to create a global village where German students could encounter students from other cultures, and to fight communism by enabling East German students, who were studying in West Berlin until 1961, to live together with West German students. Schlachtensee was to foster a 'living democracy' through extracurricular activities, student self-government and its architecture because the campus was built in a style that maximised communal over private spaces to facilitate joint activities, interactions and discussions.

Student self-government meant that each residential building had its own administrative board which elected a representative to the Schlachtensee main council. However, final decision-making rested with the university, which owned Schlachtensee at the time, and students quickly revolted against this oversight. These tensions escalated during the 1968 student protests, when a general assembly decided to institute direct democracy. As a result, and compounded by financial difficulties, the university cancelled self-government altogether as well and eventually the student village came under the ownership of the municipality of Berlin.

Schlachtensee fell into disrepair throughout the 1980s, but in 1991 obtained heritage status for its historically important architecture and landscaping. Nevertheless, its existence was threatened at the end of the 1990s, when the Berlin government decided to sell the property to private developers who wanted to replace it (except for a few historical buildings) with luxury homes. To get rid of the 900 students who were living there at the time, rent contracts were cancelled or not renewed. A core group of around thirty students, including myself, began mobilising an anti-demolition campaign by occupying some of the buildings. We organised nightly patrols to prevent vandalism to the site, undertook many creative protests and built alliances with sympathetic politicians, architects and planners.

In 2002, we decided to set up a cooperative, and I joined the board to oversee its finances. Our aim was to secure the survival and renovation of Schlachtensee. With the help of a Swiss pension fund, heritage organisations, the national government and other supporters, we were able to buy the property from the Berlin government in 2003 and immediately started renovating rooms and renting them out to generate income. In 2006, Schlachtensee was declared a national historical monument and its large-scale renovations, which are nearly finished, combined the maintenance of historical features with modern, eco-friendly technologies. In 2014, we opened a second Studentendorf in Adlershof (south-east of Berlin), which is home to 370 students. Together with the 900 Schlachtensee residents, who come from 80 countries, the Studentendorf is now a truly global village again (cf. Figure 15.1).

Anke: Thank you. Léa, you lived at La Ciguë. How did the Swiss student housing cooperative emerge and how is it organised today?

Figure 15.1 Studentendorf Schlachtensee campus, 2024. Photo © Jens-Uwe Köhler, all rights reserved.

Léa: La Ciguë in Geneva is the world's biggest housing cooperative for and managed by students, with over 700 residents from seventy countries. It was the first of its kind in Europe and emerged from the 1980s squatter movement in the city, which mobilised against the demolition of older neighbourhoods.

In 1986, student union leaders at the University of Geneva occupied a university building to protest the lack of affordable student accommodations in the city. In the resulting dialogue with the Geneva city government, a supportive councillor proposed an innovative 'agreement for loan use', which allows a third party to rent an empty property from an owner on behalf of its members, with the provision that the property must be vacated when the owner decides to redevelop it. A few weeks later, the newly established La Ciguë cooperative signed such a 'contract of trust' for its first house for ten students, beginning with a substandard municipal property that the students themselves renovated and then also expanding to properties made available by affordable housing foundations and private owners. Currently we have several dozens of such properties which we rent for a period of at least twelve months and then sublet to students. From the very beginning, the focus was on creating lots of shared spaces for students to interact and undertake communal activities (cf. Figure 15.2).

Figure 15.2 La Ciguë cooperative housing, 2024. Photo © Léa Oswald, all rights reserved.

In 1998 La Ciguë also began to develop its own buildings and since then has built or renovated eight properties on land made available by the Geneva municipality and other public entities, to the highest environmental standards that has earned some of its buildings architectural prizes. Rents in La Ciguë accommodations are 30% to 60% cheaper than on the open market, which is important because Geneva is the most expensive city in Europe. Residents have to be in some form of education, with about 45% being university students, and can stay for a maximum of five to six years.

Because the coop has become too big to be managed by student volunteer work alone, there are now nine paid employees as well, offering part-time work opportunities to students themselves. But active student involvement is still an important part of La Ciguë's operation. All residents buy a share in the coop and then become members who elect their board of directors. There is a General Assembly through which members participate in the overall decision-making of the coop. And there is also decentralised power in each house, where the student residents organise the daily life of their shared homes together. That means that they establish the rules of co-living, manage and coordinate their collective shared spaces and handle potential internal conflicts. In some of the buildings they even organise events open to the broader neighbourhood.

Anke: Thanks, Léa. Scott, with Student Coop Homes (SCH), you have a national-level organisation for student housing coops in the UK. Can you share its origins and how it works today?

Scott: SCH was set up in 2018, inspired by the opening of Edinburgh and Birmingham students housing coops in 2014. Edinburgh is the largest student housing coop in the UK, with 106 residents living in twenty-four flats in two student housing blocks. Several of its founders were active in 2010 national student mobilisation against tuition fee rises and became interested in other ways to make higher education more accessible, including housing. The students ran a successful Student Union referendum, which led to support from the university's leadership, the Scottish Cooperative Enterprise Hub and a local housing association that had two empty university halls. The founders negotiated a long-term lease with retroactive payments, which meant that the first residents were able to move in with little upfront cost. The coop is governed by direct democracy and managed by the students themselves who are organised into several working groups. Since the opening, much work has been done on improving the buildings with colourful murals and transforming one basement car park into communal space for meetings, social events and the use of community groups (cf. Figure 15.3).

Figure 15.3 Edinburgh Student Housing Cooperative 10th Anniversary Collage, 2024. Photo © Scott Jennings, all rights reserved.

The founders of the Birmingham student housing coop were also active in the 2010 national protests. They had a more adversarial relationship with their university leadership though, because of local student protests. Instead, they were inspired by existing housing cooperatives in Birmingham and had support from the Birmingham Cooperative Housing Service, which helped the students establish contact with The Phone Coop, which subsequently provided the loan for the purchase of a house that is now owned by SCH. To make the Birmingham coop financially viable, the students converted the original seven into a nine-bedroom house by dividing a very large lounge area and converting the garage. While the more substantial work was done by contractors, the students did much of the finishing work themselves. They also built a large shed, greenhouse and raised beds in the garden.

In 2021 SEASALT opened in a seven-bedroom house in Brighton. Its founders worked with the Brighton and Hove Community Land Trust (BHCLT) and had financial support from the university, several foundations and community-led housing programmes. Through crowd-funding, £336,000 was raised from over 150 investors, which enabled the BHCLT to purchase the house and lease it to SEASALT long-term. The overall aim of SCH is to enable more coops like these to be established, and in Glasgow, SCH just helped students obtain a property for their coop. There are also active groups looking for homes in Manchester, Bristol and Belfast.

SCH has two classes of members: the student housing coops and investor supporters who provided the crowd-funding. The student members have the majority of board seats and 75% of votes at general meetings. SCH's work has not been easy given the rising property costs, high mortgage rates and evolving tax rules but we are persisting.

Anke: Thank you Scott. Can you elaborate a bit more on the major obstacles that stand in the way of expanding student housing coops in the UK?

Scott: In the UK, there is definitely a lack of awareness and education about SHCs. Despite being the country where the modern cooperative movement started in Rochdale, there has been a generational loss of knowledge about cooperatives, with the general awareness revolving around the 'Coop Shop', i.e., our retail cooperative sector (see Chapter 2). This is especially among younger generations, yet the issues facing younger people around cost of living and housing crises mean that housing coops are a perfect solution to their needs and ambitions. However, we have limited educational resources about the cooperative solution. And even within existing UK student housing coops, there is limited knowledge of the different models in other nations. We have always been aware of NASCO [North American Student in Cooperation] in North America, but we have been collectively unaware of student housing coops and other forms of student-led housing in Europe.

The other major challenge is definitely a short financial track record and limitations to access capital. The wider UK cooperative housing movement is smaller than many would like – many key institutions do not understand them. Student housing coops are a part of that dynamic because they are such a young movement run predominantly by younger persons with a relative high turnover of membership, and are generally not well understood. Because our movement has only been operating in properties since 2014, many lenders and institutional investors remain sceptical or lack basic understanding, which means we have a reduced pool of lenders and financiers we can work with (see Chapters 10, 14).

Anke: Jens-Uwe, I understand that the situation is different in Germany and that the Schlachtensee cooperative has been able to grow and also become more environmentally efficient?

Jens-Uwe: Yes, in Germany in general we have a better situation for student accommodations because the *Studierendenwerke* [state-run non-profit student service providers] are a community-oriented and specialised actor that provides good services in all university locations.

For Schlachtensee specifically, the founding of the cooperative arose from the unique and extraordinary situation described above and now the historic and energy-efficient renovation of the houses is almost complete. In the next few years, we will focus on the transformation of the energy production for the whole area, with solar panels, heat pumps and energy storage options. The overall aim is to make the student village largely self-sufficient.

We also want to use the opportunities we have to build more student accommodations, as we did in Berlin-Adlershof, across Germany and have already submitted three applications for available funding opportunities. Through our model we are developing mechanisms that simplify the establishment and development of future sites. We believe that students' personal initiative and self-management are important ingredients that also enable a unique student experience, which should be made available to more students.

Anke: I know that ESCHA was established to help grow student housing cooperatives across Europe. I would like to learn a bit more about how it all started and what its work to date has been. Léa, I know that you were part of those beginnings.

Léa: Yes, I was part of the early efforts to set up ESCHA, especially once I started working for UrbaMonde, which is an association that was founded in Switzerland in 2005 to promote community-led housing by working directly with groups of citizens, urban professionals and public authorities. As part of this work, and inspired by the experience of La Ciguë – which actually also enabled me personally to find accommodation during my studies – we at UrbaMonde wanted to shed more light on student housing cooperatives. In 2018–19 we started talking about it with Julie LaPalme, the Secretary General at Cooperative Housing International [a housing-focused organisation of the International Cooperative Alliance providing technical expertise, tools and case studies], and realised that there were several similar experiences across the world, starting with one of the most inspiring ones: NASCO in the US and Canada. NASCO is a federation of student housing coops in both countries that was set up in 1968 to provide operational assistance, training, property services and advocacy to student housing cooperatives in North America, who together have been housing thousands of students for decades.

Learning about NASCO, we became convinced that this model needed to become better known and disseminated more, because we could see from the experiences of student residents the positive impact that the NASCO cooperatives have on students' lives. At some point, Julie introduced us to Scott and Jens-Uwe, and we started to imagine a broader European network for student housing cooperatives. Today, UrbaMonde participates in ESCHA strategic planning alongside the other members and helps to coordinate and organise spaces for experience exchanges, aiming at fostering solidarity, bringing visibility and supporting the emergence of new housing cooperatives.

Scott: Student Cooperative Homes in the UK has been another founding member of ESCHA. I actually personally met Jens-Uwe from the Studentendorf at the 2018 NASCO Conference in Austin, Texas. In the years that followed we first joked and then seriously discussed emulating the network and solidarity found in North America here in Europe. What has taken place since then, with support of Coop Housing International and other partners, to promote our movement and form a network across Europe, has been a wonderful experience not just personally but collectively. Our work has led to regular meetings, coordination, promotion, online events and physical gatherings such as in 2022, when we hosted the first European gathering of SHCs across Europe in Geneva.

Anke: It's great to see how ESCHA has been able to grow its work. Can you finally share why European collaboration is so important from your perspective?

Jens-Uwe: From a German perspective, European networking is very important for us. The exchange of experiences, the sharing of insights and, last but not least, mutual support are important points for our own development. In addition, European collaboration in the cooperative sector is an important component in strengthening this alternative way of building affordable student accommodations.

Léa: ESCHA is really focusing on enabling European networking. We actually just hosted the second European gathering in Geneva in October 2024, and this time many new groups were able to join us. We had student cooperators from the Netherlands, Italy, Hungary, Ireland and France, who came together for two days of visiting some of La Ciguë's houses and talking with residents there, and workshops to learn about each other's successes and challenges. As a result, ESCHA continues to grow and is planning a number of engagements for the UN Year of Cooperatives in 2025.

Scott: I agree on the importance of networking. By working together and deliberately exchanging ideas, we invigorate each other's organisations and memberships with different approaches and importantly also share key lessons that will enable mutual success across borders. The hosting of events and other networking opportunities will raise the profile of these coop models and of our movement across Europe. We can promote the variety of approaches to SHCs by showing how the model is flexible and expandable, to have real impact anywhere it is desired and address the housing issues facing young people and students. Together we have already presented at events such as the International Social Housing Festival in Barcelona in 2023 and put forward the student housing coop model into housing sector conferences and spread general awareness of our work. Together we can overcome the lack of knowledge about our model and show how it addresses real need, opening doors across Europe.

Anke: Thank you so much for your time and for sharing your experiences and insights.

Conclusion: Contemporary character of community-led housing and the capacities of translocal networks

Corinna Hölzl

The chapters in this volume showed a growing landscape of translocal community-led housing networks in Europe, spanning formal and informal organisations as well as intermediaries such as charities, NGOs and philanthropic institutions. These networks vary widely, addressing specific social groups, housing models or geographic contexts; the latter ranging from city-regions and national settings to European and transnational scales. Consequently, they pursue diverse missions, values and organisational forms, though their core themes – advocacy, networking, information and/or advisory services – often overlap. Networks with different orientations also interact, for instance, by representing distinct legal models, and, albeit less frequently, connect with broader social movements.

All in all, the authors in this book discussed how far European grassroots housing organisations are able to create genuine answers to predominantly commodified housing markets by producing and rethinking community-led housing and influencing hegemonic understandings of housing provision. Moreover, they – directly or indirectly via national case studies – focused on the role that increasingly translocally connected organisations and individuals play in that regard. This concluding chapter addresses these two topics and structures the findings of the contributions in this volume along two lines. First, it elaborates on the scope of grassroots housing production and its transformative potential, including inherent contradictions of community-led housing that all authors of the book referred to in one way or another. Two issues appeared to be key in that regard: how can community-led housing be made available to as many people and social groups as possible? And to what extent are grassroots housing models able to fight deeply rooted hegemonic views on housing and land as assets and increase the acceptance of community-led housing? Second, the chapter summarises the conditions and mechanisms to actually create and maintain translocal community-led housing networks and the functions these networks can fulfil. Building on these two strands, the chapter proposes a typology of translocal grassroots housing networks, developed from the findings of this book and existing literature in the field, in order to advance the systematisation and theorisation of such networks. The typology is further intended to reveal inherent limitations and to provide an orientation for strengthening the capacities of grassroots networks, including those operating beyond the housing sphere. The chapter finishes by briefly summarising limits and remedies.

Transformative potential of community-led housing and inherent contradictions

Skipping exclusivity and keeping the democratic ideal

Participation, autonomy and democratic self-governance play a central role in community-led housing. The associated issues of excluding social groups that lack the appropriate social and cultural capital are well known among housing projects and research. For this reason, the strategies of grassroots initiatives and academic debates are increasingly focusing on reducing excluding structures and examining scaling from various perspectives.

Interestingly, in this volume, accessibility is grasped from two distinct angles. Barthel and Heilgemeier (Chapter 4) discuss how self-governance structures in both independent and state-supported housing models in Germany have (further) developed over the past two decades to enhance participation and accessibility. Yet, the broader questions of scalability – particularly in light of political (un)willingness to support innovative approaches and to guarantee accessibility – remain unsolved. Nevertheless, the authors reveal a striking spectrum of 're-assembled' (McCann and Ward, 2012) organisational models, each combining different but always interrelated approaches to self-organisation and decommodification: independent self-governed housing ranges from autonomous tenement syndicate projects, slightly adapted syndicate projects that outsource administrative tasks, and projects that provide for original tenants or include marginalised communities, to recently established and dynamic non-profit project developers with collective ownership structures. And public self-governed housing involves remunicipalised social housing estates, municipalised buildings that were formerly squatted or owned by private landlords and recently bought via pre-emption right, and models of public-civic cooperation. Instead of the one solution to the housing problem, local contexts, networked stakeholders and tenant communities allow for developing tailor-made models.

Again, Marčetić and Heindl (Chapter 1) view housing as public wealth and – based on their empirical approach through the architectural-historical biographies of visionary large-scale housing estates from the 1970s and

1980s in both East and West (Dugave in Zagreb and Alt-Erlaa in Vienna with each comprising several thousand apartments) – advocate for a broad spatiotemporal understanding of participation and a corresponding classification of collaborative housing. This way, the authors position the question of collaborative housing not within innovative small projects that are often characterised by a narrow understanding of participation. Instead, they emphasise that participation should extend beyond the current residents and be based on universalist policies and political and socio-economic equity, while considering individual rights. What matters is not involvement in the design of buildings. On the contrary, as Marčetić and Heindl argue, this limits scalability and carries risks of future exclusion. Architectural standardisation facilitates the individual development of diverse social groups within universal structures. Besides, politically and legally ensuring that residents become co-owners of their homes is central to fostering broad participation and generating public wealth. What ultimately matters, following the authors, is a housing solution that combines scale and participation:

'If there is a position that cannot be refuted, it is the one that we need more housing that delivers security of tenure for many, which, by nature of things, means that our cities cannot sustain the dominance of the market relations in housing. Therefore, we view the scale of intervention in the field as one of the most critical aspects – one that must strike a careful balance between specific technical expertise and the pursuit of social equity, which inherently demands active participation' (this volume, p. 35).

More than isolated solutions: Uncovering and fighting deeply rooted views of housing

Hoření Samec and colleagues (Chapter 6) illustrate through their empirical study that collaborative housing generally sparks interest among housing seekers and municipal representatives in the Czech Republic. However, approaching the topic and envisioning potential implementation proves to be challenging and hardly conceivable. The study demonstrates that the concept presented by the research team falls outside the frames and settings familiar to the local audience. Moreover, it diverges from the expectations of potential residents who, as LaFond (Chapter 9) also shows, are discouraged by financing costs and display resistance toward collective and non-profit ownership structures (at best, building group models under private ownership appears to represent a conceivable format). The authors embed their argument in the concept of obduracy. Two of the layers, on which the concept is based, were utilised for empirical analysis: (1) frames of the existing housing regime, which are expressed in (2) the persistent tradition of collective perceptions. The authors conclude that a lack of institutional infrastructures – including financing instruments, as well as alternative advisory and management structures (cf. Novy-Huy, Chapter 10) – along with deeply entrenched discourses and market-oriented, financialised housing regimes are anything but easy to overcome or disrupt: 'We argue that the issue is more complex and ambivalent, and the absence of development does not have to be a historical necessity (in the form of a "post-socialist legacy") but an interplay between lacking infrastructures, prevailing discourses and a neoliberal housing regime which accentuates the asset function of housing' (Hoření Samec et al., this volume, p. 121). The power of persistence thus arises from the interplay and interconnection of these layers. The authors conclude that island projects or other isolated measures will remain ineffective as long as no broader public debate is initiated.

However, this observation is not only true for post-socialist realities such as in the Czech Republic. Mullins, Moore and Archer (Chapter 2) likewise state for the UK that community-led housing remains a niche or a 'series of loosely connected sub-niches' with little strategic impact (p. 54). Despite the growth of community-led housing projects and the establishment of enabling infrastructure, the premature discontinuation of government funding hindered the sector's ability to achieve mainstream influence and systemic change: 'This relative powerlessness to catalyse community activism into radical social change is a product of deep-seated forces structuring our economy and society. The most potent force is the financialisation of housing and the view of houses as assets to generate a return rather than homes to be lived in to provide a stable base for a healthy society' (this volume, p. 54). These observations point to the risk that single projects may end up merely serving as stopgap measures, as already discussed by governance scholars a few decades ago (Evers and Wollmann, 1983).

The discussion of the Network of Collaborative Housing (NETCO) also highlights this insight. European local government officials and civil society experts do not necessarily share a non-speculative understanding of collaborative housing (LaFond, Chapter 9). Furthermore, the interests and action possibilities of European municipalities vary significantly. Additionally, local conflicts of interest and well-known municipal everyday decisions become apparent, such as changes in government and limited budgets. At this point, it is also important to consider what kind of municipal stakeholders are involved in or approached by community-led housing actors: in the interview with the CoHabitat Network, Pierre Arnold emphasises including key officials and recommends, for instance, field trips for those actors but also bankers as efficient strategy (Hölzl, Rentzsch and Arnold, Chapter 13).

Against this backdrop, other scholars discuss the potential of community-led housing for institutional change and to influence prevailing patterns of housing regimes by generating political and public attention, which, in turn, is closely related to the translocal relations grassroots actors have been able to build up recently. Instead of putting the focus on community-led housing in quantitative terms, Lenna and Aernouts (Chapter 3), following the capability approach, understand the practices of CLT initiatives in Belgium as pathways for institutional transformation. They conceive political endorsement as an external operational condition and conclude that 'political support is an outcome of the transformative political nature of CLTs and their political impact' (p. 71). They explain their specific transformative nature by advocacy tactics such as 'using (inter)national recognition and awards to influence government decisions, aligning their messaging with political frameworks and attracting government interest by enhancing their public image' (p. 71). Similarly, on the basis of prefigurative thinking, Horlitz and Hölzl (Chapter 12) see the key potential of CLTs in shifting prevailing spatial frames and understandings of ownership. This, in turn, may foster societal openness to new and diverse alternatives.

Translocal community-led housing networks: Framework conditions, mechanisms, functions

Triggers and framework conditions of translocal housing networks

Networks do not just happen (McFarlane, 2011). In order to bring networks to life and make them actually work and maintain connections (Featherstone and Davies, 2013), a number of internal and external conditions, crucial features, mechanisms and tool sets can be summarised (Routledge, Cumbers and Nativel, 2013). The grassroots housing models discussed in this book emerge to proactively create solutions to financialised housing markets and ways out of the housing crisis, thereby following different pathways. Individual initiatives have been making use of so-called political opportunity structures (Diani and McAdam, 2003) and built up housing projects leading to a European grassroots housing movement. However, the range of challenges community-led housing is confronted with – mostly unfavourable regulatory and financial conditions, but also divided political and cultural perceptions and varying attributions making it difficult to create a unified voice – have been crucial for the (re)emergence and, in many cases, strengthening of networks and federations at different scales over the last two or three decades (e.g., Schwittay, Chapter 8). Similar to the origins and organisational structures of social movements (Rucht and Roth, 2008), the conversation chapters revealed that single international key events have often provided the momentum for the construction of lasting networks.

Moreover, the interviews in the book illustrate that cultural proximity and shared histories on the one hand, and hardships of specific social groups like students – that increasingly overlap due to multiple financialisation in different areas of social reproduction – on the other, strongly facilitate establishing translocal network structures, even more so if funding is scarce. However, the analyses also point out to the challenge for young cooperatives of building local networks with traditional cooperative actors in light of 'value, age and identity gaps' (Schwittay, Chapter 8, p. 168).

To understand the transscalar networking of housing, different authors of this volume also indicated the specific characteristics of housing provision in general and community-led housing models in particular. First, housing can be understood as a node with scales, sectors and segments as common interfaces (whereby mutual topics such as improving energy efficiency also allow to bridge gaps between tenant and provider sides) (Hoerning and Keuneke, Chapter 7). Second, Hoerning and Keuneke argue that due to translocal, transnational and global political and financial dynamics, many issues clearly cannot be regulated within the boundaries of institutionalised state levels. Apart from that, certain characteristics of community-led housing models facilitate its circulation, thereby giving translocal networking its relevance. For instance, Horlitz and Hölzl (Chapter 12) illustrate that the different ownership structures of CLTs allow for a broad understanding of participation, which opens the model to many groups and contexts and bears high flexibility. This enables the model to be adapted to a wide range of local spatial-political contexts (Algoed and Hernández Torrales, 2024). Such flexibility promotes the establishment of shared, translocally applicable connections, thereby facilitating the mobilisation of the model, while also helping it to challenge entrenched perspectives.

Network mechanisms

Identified network mechanisms range from natural but crucial strategic features, respectively, grassrooting vectors (Routledge, Cumbers and Nativel, 2013), including international key events or having brokers actors whose interlinking work actually allows the (re)production of grassroots housing networks, to other specific lines of actions such as projectification. Examples of spaces for physical, hybrid and, of course, regular virtual encounters mentioned explicitly and *en passant* include the World CLT Day, the bi-annual International Social Housing Festival, the International Union of Tenants (IUT) conference, but also regular, less visible meetings. They offer the occasion for exchange, for solidifying frames and for sharpening identities. This is where debates are stimulated beyond internal organisational arrangements and structural institutional problems and spatial disparities along with solutions are made visible.

Besides, the empirical and practical insights in this volume confirm that all networks contain key actors and sometimes 'imagineers' (Routledge et al., 2003), acting as brokers between organised networks and individuals and mobilising essential knowledge to an extent that far exceeds what would be necessary for their respective projects (e.g., Hölzl, Rentzsch and Arnold, Chapter 13; Barthel and Heilgemeir, Chapter 4). Many of them are characterised by a hybrid combination of features of activists and social entrepreneurs (cf. Darby and Chatterton, 2019), and distinguish themselves for their prefigurative intentions – namely, the aim to create perspectives for an alternative societal model.

The grassroots housing organisations also make use of specific network-promoting tools that – alongside their actual function in terms of knowledge provision, campaigning, etc. – always affect spatial interactions. These double function tools include manuals, financial plans, financing instruments such as the 'MOBA-Accelerator' and trend-responsive housing models. Model projects are considered a relevant mechanism, serving as examples of what the future might look like (McCann, 2008). For instance, the establishment of the first student housing cooperatives in the UK has successfully exposed the assetisation of social infrastructure through the interplay of privatised higher education and the commodified housing options for students/trainees. Similarly, scholars and grassroots initiatives in CEE emphasise the necessity of referencing (international) best practices to introduce sceptics to the concept of community-led housing. LaFond (Chapter 9) also underscores that working with model projects remains, at least initially, the only way to familiarise interested parties, especially political newcomers, with alternative approaches to housing.

Projectification as institutionalised financing practice and at the same time way of network proceeding is revealed to be strongly anchored in some cases. By studying the interplay between grassroots innovations and EU funding schemes in the case of the Global Ecovillage Network (GEN) Europe, Girardi and Esteves (Chapter 11) identify the relevance of 'project-supported networks' to grassroots innovations. Aligning with EU sustainability policies and adapting to their funding schemes enables initiatives to access resources so that grassroots innovations can grow and potentially increase their impact despite their non-commercial focus and place-based nature. This insight enhances the current understanding of grassroots innovations, which frequently emphasises the dichotomies of scale dynamics versus localism, niches versus regimes and alternative versus mainstream (Avelino et al., 2020). Project-supported networks are characterised by the combination of the features of project networks and project-supported organisations. Projectification impacts grassroots (networking) practices and 'creates and fosters collaboration among partners of a project, them being part of the network already or not, and through these projects GEN-Europe creates capacity, services and tools that help the network navigate current and future challenges for its development' (Girardi and Esteves, Chapter 11, p. 211). The authors therefore arrive at a positive evaluation of projectified action logics, however, 'advocating for strategic coherence and inclusive practices to ensure that the benefits of project funding are fully realised without compromising the core values and strategic choices of grassroots innovations' (p. 213).

Finally, the analyses in this book revealed that the implementation of network strategies requires various intermediaries and network organisations at different scales, which often need to be established for newly emerging mobilising issues. For instance, Mullins, Moore and Archer (Chapter 2) illustrated in their analysis of the expansion of community-led housing in the course of the UK Community Housing Fund (2016–24) the pivotal role of developing so-called regional enabler hubs. Enabler hubs as links between local initiatives and the complex requirements of planning, politics and finance have been particularly impactful in urban areas, addressing planning and resource challenges while fostering awareness and partnerships with policymakers and housing associations. According to the authors, the built up urban support networks with transferred policies and funds to sub-regional governance forms represent potential future points of connection for UK community-led housing.

Functions of translocal networks

Community-led housing projects that belong to a national or international association benefit in a relevant way from the associated translocal horizontal networks. Accordingly, direct voices from representatives and academic analyses of translocal networks, grassroots organisations, and housing advocacy organisations have confirmed various network functions, that is, resources mobilised through network dynamics (cf. Figure C.1). Representatives of CoHabitat Network, MOBA, Commoning Spaces Network (CSN) and Mietshäuser Syndikat as well as Living in Metropolis (LiM), European Student Cooperative Housing Alliance (ESCH), Netco and ECLTN emphasised the importance of exchange with one another with regard to the mobilisation of knowledge on issues, such as financing, legal aspects and organising, to set the conditions for the development of new grassroots innovations. Yet at a transnational scale, this mainly serves new initiatives since longer established grassroots are already professionalised

Figure C.1 Functions of translocal grassroots housing networks, 2025. Photo © Corinna Hölzl, all rights reserved.

and have translated these knowledge categories to the nationally varying conditions.

Hoerning und Keuneke (Chapter 7) confirm the relevance of transscalar interrelations from the perspective of advocacy practices of tenant organisations and associations of housing providers. Similar to the described grassroots housing practices, the authors observe translocal alliances and connections, for instance, when tenants' associations push for government countermeasures in the face of the touristification of housing shortage due to Airbnb, or transferred knowledge, experience and solutions from one location to another, for instance, in the case of the introduction of the Berlin rent cap in 2020. 'Housing advocacy organisations engage in capitalising local and national specificities economically and politically in networking logics. Translocalisation and transnationalisation strategies both transfer knowledge, relate people and harmonise conditions, economically and politically.' (Hoerning and Keuneke, Chapter 7, p. 150).

Yet Barthel and Heilgemeier's (Chapter 4) focus on local, regional and national networks makes clear that spatial proximity along with locally and regionally established relations of trust – or strong ties according to

Granovetter (1973) – allows for expertisation, financial experiments and taking advantage of local situations to generate detailed embedded solutions and initiate long-term development processes. This is less probable to achieve at an international scale since networks, depending on their spatial conditions, have variegated potentials at their disposal. According to Nicholls (2009), certain resources that require trust, for instance, are more likely to be mobilised in close spatial proximity, while other resources such as expertise and specialist knowledge can be mobilised across scales. However, when comparable conditions (close relationships of trust and solidarity-based shared goals) are replicated on a larger scale, so-called translocal bonding can mobilise comparable solution-oriented capabilities, including specialised knowledge, counselling and possibly funding, at the international level (Hölzl, Hölzl and Amacher, 2021). Among other things, this explains the successful circulation of the Mietshäuser Syndikat model to Austria, the Netherlands, Czech Republic and France. Building on these experiences as well as on deficiencies that become apparent when intending to establish community-led housing in semi-peripheral national settings as described by Hoření Samec et al. (Chapter 6), the recently founded Commoning Spaces Network has set itself the goal of improving the conditions for community-led housing across Europe. As Peter Kämmerling, one of the initiators described in the interview (Hölzl et al., Chapter 14), this shall primarily involve translocal project consultancy and start-up funding.

In addition, the overlapping of mobilised resources, such as trust, expertise, funding, brokers and other useful contacts facilitating door opening and similar opportunities, invigorates the partial joint development of transnationally applicable social innovations, in particular new financing models including the European Ethical Bank (EEB), the creation of bridge funds such as the MOBA Accelerator or joint demands for a financing fund for civil society projects of the European Investment Bank (EIB). And in the case of the EEB and other individual networks and associations, the aim is to mobilise further resources, particularly financial resources, by setting up other local, national and international networks with a different focus. Accordingly, Goran Jeras explains in the interview: 'our primary approach builds on a network of community-oriented strategic partners across Europe' (Hölzl et al., Chapter 14, p. 262). The picture that emerges is one of differently interwoven and branched network structures. Accordingly, the relevance of exchange is expressed not only within networks but also between them.

Translocal networks further confirmed their relevance with regard to mutually strengthening local and national organisations and achieving a critical size, for example when it comes to (re-)mobilising the cooperative model in Eastern Europe through institutionalising LiM or MOBA in the form of European cooperatives (Societas Cooperativa Europaea).

Ana Džokić (MOBA) explained in the interview: 'While individually we may seem small within our local contexts, uniting has proven crucial on many fronts. First, it enhances our collective knowledge and visibility. Membership in MOBA also lends us greater impact and facilitates connections with international actors, which would be challenging to achieve locally' (Hölzl et al., Chapter 14, p. 261). Similarly, translocal European networks are of central importance for local and sometimes national organisations, such as European student housing coops and CLT initiatives like Stadtbodenstiftung in Berlin, as links and opportunities for exchange at the national level are frequently quite limited (Schwittay, Chapter 8; Schwittay et al., Chapter 15). Likewise, the local adaptabilities of CLTs, as illustrated by Horlitz and Hölzl (Chapter 12), highlight the significance of local pioneers for the development of translocal networks.

Closely related to this is the intention to increase public visibility to an international public in an effort to make claims for regulative adaptations or financing heard towards in the EU or transnational philanthropy as outlined by Novy-Huy (Chapter 10) and Hölzl et al. (Chapter 14). And if connected with physical encounters, translocal networking proved to offer a stage and meeting place to the many local and national community-led housing organisations. For instance, the Italian national cooperative association Legacoop Abitanti, which aims to become active again as a social housing provider in response to the housing crisis, hopes to regain visibility and influence at the local and national levels in Italy through their membership in translocal networks such as CHI, the CoHabitat Network or ENHR and related international activities (Cafora and Ferro, Chapter 5). Thus, the grassroots housing movements use their embedding into translocal networks and, among others, international awards to make a national and local difference where legal conditions and financing are (mostly) negotiated with administrations and credit institutions. However, these transnational connection points also make it possible to reawaken Legacoop Abitanti and other mature cooperative associations that want to reconnect with the cooperative heritage often dating back to European worker movements, to align closely with the commitment of younger and emerging cooperative movements all over Europe, creating new belongings and strengthening visions and identities (Massey, 1994).

Finally, exchanging experiences and providing updates on negotiations with local governments, which can deliver inspiring inputs, and particularly, mutual emotional backing, have proved to be key functions of translocal grassroots networks. This also includes sharing 'positive stories'. In the conversation about the CoHabitat Network, Arnold emphasises how essential success stories are for grassroots movements – especially in unpromising contexts – to maintain morale and avoid giving up (Hölzl, Rentzsch and Arnold, Chapter 13).[1]

Typology of grassroots housing networks in Europe

On the basis of the characteristics of translocal grassroots housing networks discussed in this book, a typology of such networks is derived to capture their core concerns and strategies, identify weaknesses, and enhance capacity for action. This will now be presented as the concluding step (cf. Table C.1). The typology is oriented towards research on social change activities that – very generally – differentiates between grassroots builders practices oriented at building alternative initiatives to solve socio-ecological deficits identifying ways to deal with the existing political-economic structures or requiring certain changes to facilitate innovative practices, and interventionist warrior practices that follow criticising and resisting actions unfolding negative impacts and claiming political and economic change. Besides, Stevenson et al. (2008)[2] identify weaver activities that aim at interconnecting and supporting builders and warriors, who sometimes do not have many contact points.

In accordance with understanding networks as assemblages of cells (Cumbers, Routledge and Nativel, 2008) (see Introduction), the network types do not refer to individual separate organisations, but exemplified organisations are to be understood as pivotal cells or nodes within open networks. At the same time, many networks are diverse and not mutually exclusive, for example, some combine characteristics of both 'builders' and 'weavers', so that assigning them to just one type would contradict their mission and values. Yet, despite certain overlaps of core themes, strategic focus areas arise as a result of the network missions.

The typology proposes five types of grassroots housing networks differentiated along a number of key categories that try to combine the previously discussed transformative potential of community-led housing and the dimensions that make spatial grassroots networks work: mission, core values, type of partnership, strategies and potential, scale and reach as well as funding scheme.

Type 1) *Grassroots housing hubs* support existing and new initiatives with necessary capabilities in terms of expert knowledge (legal, planning, subsidy programmes etc.) and interlinks initiatives at the level of cities or subnational regions. Thus, unlike the other network types, grassroots housing hubs mainly act at the local scale to enhance the establishment of different forms of community-led housing.

Type 2) As elaborated by various authors in the book as well as commons scholars (e.g., Hodkinson, 2012; Villamayor-Tomas and García-López, 2021), creating and re-establishing alternative solutions is the key activity of grassroots models in different fields. *Grassroots housing innovators* are social change activists, who experiment with existing and new legal, organisational, edificial and decision-making models, among others, to rediscover long-term affordable and accessible housing solutions. In line with their

Table C.1 Typology of translocal community-led housing networks in Europe

Network type	Mission	Core values	Type of partnership	Strategies and potentials	Scale and reach	Funding scheme	Examples of network nodes
Grassroots housing hubs	Provide initiatives with capacities to build up self-organised housing projects	Inclusivity, flexible definitions of community-led housing, housing as public wealth	Mostly informal: housing initiatives, municipalities, housing companies etc.	Information provision, consultancy, networking, advocacy to establish local institutional basis	Local to sub-national	Often public funds, temporary and for longer periods	Enabler hubs (UK), Initiative Collaborative Building & Living (Austria), Network Frankfurt for Cohousing (Germany)
Grassroots housing innovators	Fight housing scarcity by (re) establishing non-profit housing, creating not profit maximising funding, influencing prevailing narratives	Self-organisation, solidarity economy, accessibility, decommodification, horizontal democracy, new forms of collective ownership	Mostly formal: different legal forms (e.g., SCE, national housing coops, limited liability companies), strategic partners, individual guardians etc.	Local to transnational entanglements, entrepreneurial foundational work, key actor activities, advocacy to create critical size and solution-oriented capabilities	Local to national, selected regions (e.g., Baltic countries), Europe	Project-based funds (EU, philanthropy), internal (solidary) cross-subsidies, donations, loans (housing projects), member fees, high voluntary work levels	MOBA SCE, Living in Metropolis (LiM), European Ethical Bank, local to national associations: Sostre Civic (Spain), Legacoop (Italy), student coops, habiTAT (Austria), Mietshäuser Syndikat (Germany), CLT Brussels (Belgium)

Tailored grassroots housing advocates	Support specific community-led housing forms by promoting local adaptation and broader EU recognition, linking of initiatives within/across regions, capacity building	Land stewardship, collective ownership, long-term affordability, empowerment of places, youth etc.	Formal and informal: grassroots housing organisations and initiatives (e.g., student groups), mature housing organisations (e.g., cooperatives) and researchers, students, NGOs etc.	International key events, specialised knowledge exchange, advocacy, projectification, model projects to create joint voice and public/political visibility	National, European, global	Long-term funding limited, project-based funds (EU), philanthropy, voluntary work	European CLT Network (ECLTN), International CLT Center, European Student Cooperative Housing Alliance (ESCH), Cooperative Housing International CHI, GEN Europe, UK Confederation of Cooperative Housing, Organisme de foncier solidaire (France)

(*continued*)

Table C.1 (Cont.)

Network type	Mission	Core values	Type of partnership	Strategies and potentials	Scale and reach	Funding scheme	Examples of network nodes
Grassroots housing weavers	Link and support equal creation of community-led housing, support less privileged regions, reflect narratives and societal readiness, advocacy	Inclusivity, flexible definitions of community-led housing, solidarity, decentralisation, affordability, housing as public wealth	Often informal; sometimes temporary: civil society, NGOs, municipalities, charities, grassroots initiatives, academia	Virtual exchange, physical meetings, loose collaborations, expert and municipal dialogue to enable learning, awareness raising, establishing a translocal grassroots housing community	International, semi-peripheries (beyond wealthy European countries), linking Global North and Global South	Long-term funding limited, project-based funds (EU), philanthropy, voluntary work, particularly difficult to maintain without funding	CoHabitat Network, Commoning Spaces Network (CSN), NETCO (Network of Collaborative Housing), ENHR (European Network of Housing Research), ID22, Immovielien network (Germany), cooplink (Netherlands) etc.
Right to housing warriors	Claim and change financialised housing	Right to housing and to the city	NGOs, social movements, citizens' initiatives, unions, social organisations, academia etc.	Mobilisations, campaigns, advocacy, research, framing processes to change political economic structures, establish alternative master frames	Active at all scales and specific localities	Mostly short-term, partly institutionalised public and/or member-based funding	European Action Coalition (EAC), Pravo na grad (Croatia), tenants' movements and unions, tenants' associations, Deutsche Wohnen Enteignen

Source: Author's own.

missions, the core values and type of partnership of grassroots housing innovators are usually precisely defined (e.g., through more formalised partnerships), and their work focuses on the entrepreneurial translocal mobilisation of innovative community-led housing knowledge and solutions. Funding its activities is particularly challenging for this network type. Although there are a few types and examples with more constant and longer term funding, for example, selected publicly funded grassroots housing hubs or versed projectified tailored grassroots housing advocates, grassroots housing innovators rely on temporary, project-based funding (e.g., EU or philanthropy) linked to specific conditions, often distracting them from their actual objectives due to project commitments.

Type 3) *Tailored grassroots housing advocates* support specific community-led housing solutions by intertwining selected grassroots housing innovators. They frequently focus on advocacy and cooperation activities at different scales (e.g., through joint projects/projectification). Therewith, they aim at creating a unified voice and working towards an advantageous environment for community-led housing. Opposed to grassroots housing innovators, principles are defined widely in order to encompass as many forms and political-cultural contexts of community-led housing as possible. Accordingly, a wider range of actors and stakeholder groups is usually represented. The core values within the different types can sometimes vary considerably. There are more horizontal networks with decentralised exchange structures, for instance, Self-built Houses in England, and more upscaled networks with centralised forms of organisation such as the Community Land Trust Network of England and Wales (Mullins, Archer and Moore, Chapter 2).

Type 4) *Grassroots housing weavers* also aim at linking grassroots housing innovators; however, they explicitly reach out to builders of different community-led housing models, often at national scales (where community-led housing is more advanced), and partly interconnect organisations transnationally. For example, the CoHabitat Network is the only community-led housing network that builds on systematised learning at the transnational scale despite the specificities of grassroots housing in the Global North and the Global South. Thereby, it relies on an open definition of community-led housing and informal network structures. Through its broader approach, the networking and advocacy activities may much better prepare the general grounds for a community-led housing friendly environment and enhance the scene emotionally. Financing also constitutes a key challenge for this network type.

Type 5) Finally, *right-to-housing warriors* engage for strengthening regulations, uncovering financialisation outcomes, organising protests (e.g., student organisations, international tenant unions, tenant movements, squatters' movements). They are particularly active in organising protests and campaigns. In the everyday practices of European grassroots housing, connections between *right-to-housing warriors* and other network types appear to remain relatively limited to date. This is not surprising given time constraints and the highly specific knowledge requirements in each case, but also several points of opinion.

Summing up

All in all, the approaches to community-led housing from different parts of Europe illustrate the harmonic research perspective that currently characterises grassroots approaches to solving the global housing crisis, that is:

> to show ways in which public resources can be used to achieve affordable rents and decapitalise housing provision in the interests of low-income households; and how, at the same time, grassroots democratic organisational structures can be applied at a higher level in order to socialise public housing provision at least to some extent and democratise it. (Schipper and Schönig, 2021: 90)

In accordance with that, many housing scholars understand the diversity of the discussed organisational models as components of post-autonomous urban social movements. The question of what democratically organised and socially inclusive housing provision could look like and how it could be implemented was already being asked in the 1980s. But in contrast to the divided debate at the time between the reform options of third-way collectivisation and decapitalisation, few of the authors in this book consider community-led housing the only solution to the housing crisis, even if most of the contributions are led by protagonists of community-led housing or discuss their perspective. Instead, the sum of individual efforts, the dynamics of their translocal networks and the associated power of discourse is rather one of several paths and – in the absence of state alternatives – the only viable path for many people. Accordingly, ideal-typical historical examples – both in terms of size, and in their emphasis on universal and legal participation – find contemporary counterparts in current efforts to socialise large privately owned housing stocks, in new iterations of large housing cooperative projects, and the diffusion of community land trusts.

The synopsis of different European examples of translocal community-led housing networks and their conditions, mechanisms and functions demonstrates that a differentiated, translocal web of networks has taken shape over the last two decades. In theory, their varying emphases and strategies are mutually complementary so that a commons-informed and collaborative reissue of housing could capitalise substantially on these transscalar interconnections.

However, the derived network typology uncovers that the spatial distribution of network organisations and the actual potentials to expand connections vary significantly. Although knowledge on community-led housing circulates globally, many grassroots activities remain embedded within regional and national cultural, political-economic, historical, social and territorial contexts. Certain types – particularly those engaging municipalities or established economic actors – are still scarcely developed in some settings. That is, while horizontal translocal community-led housing networks have established themselves well recently, (in)formal communication between actors involving representatives of public and civic spheres, i.e., public servants, residents, 'but also us as researchers' (Hoření Samec et al., Chapter 6, p. 122) remains insufficient. At the same time, the largely young transnational *weavers* are not yet strong or visible enough, nor sufficiently connected with so-called *warrior networks*, to respond effectively to the corresponding challenges in the different European contexts – for instance, to support and develop master frames capable of convincing the broader public or to foster the relearning of the cooperative ethos in mature housing cooperatives. Besides, it's hardly surprising that though securing long-term funding is the basic prerequisite for maintaining translocal networks (Routledge et al., 2013), long-term financial sustainability is generally limited and conditions are strongly diverging within Europe. An additional point is that mature, larger, and thus more influential actors – such as older cooperatives – are only rarely directly represented within the networks under discussion.

Yet, the findings in this book further underscore that, while the configurations, mechanisms, and strategies of networks are important, it is ultimately the underlying structural determinants that constitute the key framework conditions for change – namely, prevailing cultural imaginings of housing, the interactions between different levels of government, and the opportunities and constraints that community-led housing models entail for mobilisation. Consistent support is needed together with long-term funding and strategic alliances to build up or further embed community-led housing in national and regional housing strategies.

Given the discussed potentials and limitations of translocal grassroots housing networks, promising avenues include expanding existing structures toward a Europe-wide advisory infrastructure, enhancing international knowledge exchange, strengthening connections between mature and emerging non-speculative housing initiatives, and developing suitable financing instruments. Besides, collaborative research as well as networks between and with municipal administrations should be continued, even if the exchange with non-cooperative municipalities often proves to be gruelling in practice. In other words, it is necessary to step (even) further out of the comfort zone of homogeneous grassroots networks. And beyond the notion of 'mainstreaming' community-led housing, greater attention should be directed toward fostering alternative narratives and aligning research perspectives on community-led housing more closely with right-to-housing networks. Only then can a commons-informed and collaborative reissue of scale-relevant housing models be reached.

Notes

1 Finally, of course, community-led housing is always about more than access to housing. Among others, it also involves the emancipatory role of the citizens behind it as reflective entrepreneurs. Novy-Huy (2025: 1) describes the democratic negotiation processes necessary for the implementation of community-led housing as a 'school of democracy'.

2 The research of Stevenson et al. (2008) refers to social change activities in the food system.

References

Algoed, L., and M. E. Hernández-Torrales (2024), 'Communities as Global Actors in Counterhegemonic Policy Mobilities: Lessons from the Community Land Trust Movement', *International Journal of the Commons*, 18:1, 53–65, https://doi.org/10.5334/ijc.1217

Avelino, F., A. Dumitru, C. Cipolla, I. Kunze, and J. Wittmayer (2020), 'Translocal empowerment in transformative social innovation networks', *European Planning Studies*, 28:5, 955–77, https://doi.org/10.1080/09654313.2019.1578339

Cumbers, A., P. Routledge, and C. Nativel (2008), 'The entangled geographies of global justice networks', *Progress in Human Geography*, 32:2, 183–201 https://doi.org/10.1177/0309132507084818

Darby, S., and P. Chatterton (2019), 'Between and Beyond Social Entrepreneur and Activist: Transformative Personas for Social Change', *ACME: An International Journal for Critical Geographies*, 18:3, 724–50.

Diani, M., and D. McAdam (2003), *Social Movements and Networks: Relational Approaches to Collective Action: Relational Approaches to Collective Action* (Oxford: Oxford University Press).

Evers, A., H.-G. Lange, and H. Wollmann (1983), *Kommunale Wohnungspolitik* (Birkhäuser Basel).

Featherstone, D., and A. D. Davies (2013), 'Networking Resistance...', in W. Nicholls, B. Miller, and J. Beaumont (eds), *Spaces of Contention. Spatialities and Social Movements* (Farnham: Ashgate).

Granovetter, M. (1973), 'The Strength of Weak Ties', *American Journal of Sociology*, 78:6, 1360–80.

Hodkinson, S. (2012), 'The return of the housing question', *Ephemera*, 12:4, 423–44.

Hölzl, C., D. Hölzl, and D. Amacher (2021), 'Netzwerkstrategien von „Housing Commons" in der Gründungsphase – Das Beispiel der „habiTAT"-Hausprojekte „SchloR" und „Bikes and Rails" in Wien', *Mitteilungen der Österreichischen Geographischen Gesellschaft*, 163, 171–98, https://doi.org/10.1553/moegg163s171

Massey, D. (1994), *Space, Place, and Gender* (Cambridge: Blackwell Publishers).

McCann, E. (2008), 'Expertise, Truth, and Urban Policy Mobilities: Global Circuits of Knowledge in the Development of Vancouver, Canada's "four Pillar" Drug Strategy', *Environment and Planning A*, 40:4, 885–904, https://doi.org/10.1068/a38456

McCann, E., and K. Ward (2012), 'Assembling urbanism: following policies and "studying through" the sites and situations of policy making', *Environment and Planning A*, 44:1, 42–51, https://doi.org/10.1068%2Fa44178

McFarlane, C. (2011), *Learning the City: Knowledge and Translocal Assemblage* (Malden: Wiley-Blackwell).

Nicholls, W. (2009), 'Place, Networks, Space: Theorising the Geographies of Social Movements', *Transactions of the Institute of British Geographers*, 34:1, 78–93, https://doi.org/10.1111/j.1475-5661.2009.00331.x

Routledge, P. (2003), 'Convergence Space: Process Geographies of Grassroots Globalization Networks', *Transactions of the Institute of British Geographers*, 28:3, 333–49, https://doi.org/10.2307/3804580

Routledge, P., A. Cumbers, and C. Nativel (2013), 'Global Justice Networks: Operational Logics, Imagineers and Grassrooting Vectors', in W. Nicholls, B. Miller, and J. Beaumont (eds), *Spaces of Contention. Spatialities and Social Movements* (Farnham: Ashgate), pp. 261–84.

Rucht, D., and R. Roth (2008), 'Soziale Bewegungen und Protest – eine theoretische und empirische Bilanz', in R. Roth and D. Rucht (eds), *Die Sozialen Bewegungen in Deutschland Seit 1945* (Frankfurt: Campus), pp. 635–68.

Schipper, S., and B. Schönig (2021), 'Die ewig neue Wohnungsfrage! Auf den Spuren bundesdeutscher Debatten zur sozialen Wohnraumversorgung', in B. Egner, S. Grohs, and T. Robischon (eds), *Die Rückkehr der Wohnungsfrage* (Wiesbaden: Springer Fachmedien Wiesbaden), pp. 77–98, https://doi.org/10.1007/978-3-658-31027-1_5

Stevenson, G. W., K. Ruhf, S. Lezberg, and K. Clancy (2008), 'Warrior, builder, and weaver work: Strategies for changing the food system', in C. Hinrichs and T. Lyson (eds), *Remaking the North American Food System: Strategies for Sustainability* (Nebraska: University of Nebraska Press), pp. 33–62.

Villamayor-Tomas, S., and G. A. García-López (2021), 'Commons Movements: Old and New Trends in Rural and Urban Contexts', *Annual Review of Environment and Resources* (Annual Reviews), 511–43, https://doi.org/10.1146/annurev-environ-012220-102307

Index

EU authorised representative for GPSR:
Easy Access System Europe, Mustamäe tee 50,
10621 Tallinn, Estonia
gpsr.requests@easproject.com

www.ingramcontent.com/pod-product-compliance
Ingram Content Group UK Ltd.
Pitfield, Milton Keynes, MK11 3LW, UK
UKHW021840100926
8556IPUK00004B/465
* 9 7 8 1 5 2 6 1 9 0 3 7 6 *